Praise for Dean Smith

"What's more impressive to me about Dean than his record is how good he is as a teacher of basketball. I've always said he's a better teacher of basketball than anyone else. I couldn't begin to teach players the things Dean has taught them. Also, I've admired him because there's more to him than just wins."

—JOHN WOODEN

"Dean is one of the most organized and brilliant minds that I've ever met in basketball. He shared ideas and thoughts and philosophies with me that people just don't share with others, and I will always be grateful and respect him for that. He did me a tremendous favor. One of the greatest gifts you can share with somebody is the knowledge that you have."

—JOHN THOMPSON

"Coming out of high school, I had all the ability in the world, but I didn't know the game. Coach taught me the game: when to apply speed, how to use your quickness, when to use that first step, or how to apply certain skills in certain situations. I gained all that knowledge so that when I got to the pros, it was just a matter of applying the information. Dean Smith gave me the knowledge to score 37 points a game and that's something people don't understand."

—MICHAEL JORDAN

"Michael has had the most media hype I've ever seen in professional basketball, and I was around Dr. J for three years. He has handled it all extremely well. It is a tremendous tribute to the way Dean Smith, who is one of the greatest coaches of all time, handled this guy. You can see his training. We are very fortunate that he has had that coaching background."

—KEVIN LOUGHERY, former coach of the Chicago Bulls,
who coached the Bulls when Jordan came
into the league in 1984–85

"I can't think of a more deserving coach to break that record than Dean Smith. He's done so much for the game of basketball—I think it's terrific. He's a credit to the profession. He's not only a role model for the state of North Carolina, he's known throughout the world."

—BIGHOUSE GAINES,
former coach at Winston-Salem State

"He has a basketball program; he doesn't have a team. And when you have a program, you're concerned about the kids' entire lives, their entire existence . . . and what they're going to do after they leave you and what kind of effect you can have on them as they mature. I think that's his greatest strength. I've always felt that he's the best there is on the court, but he's even better off the court in what he gives to those people who come in contact with him."

—ROY WILLIAMS, coach at the University of Kansas

"North Carolina had a great reputation when he took over, but he took that and built on it. In order to stay on top, you've got to change, innovate, and develop, and he's done that. He was ahead of his time. He was far ahead of everyone else in the use of personnel. We have to change rules because of Dean."

—NORM STEWART, former coach
at the University of Missouri

"Every day in practice we mention his name because things are named after him. Fastbreak, they run this, transition offense—that's Carolina this or that. When you start having things named after you, you've done something. It's an incredible thing. . . . A twenty-game winner for twenty-five years and you still can't beat the guy."

—BILL CARMODY, former coach
at Princeton University, now at Northwestern University

"I think the more you mature in this business, the more you appreciate two things: longevity and excellence. To put both of them together in one package, as Dean has, is incredible. He has created the IBM of college basketball. It's mind-boggling, what he has done."

—PAT KENNEDY, coach
at DePaul University

"I don't think any of the lettermen can really express the family atmosphere that he's built, the tradition that he's built of loyalty and camaraderie. It's a fraternity that's very much admired by basketball people everywhere. We get a lot of abuse because of our loyalty to one another, but we love being a part of it. The meaning of tradition doesn't exist in sports anymore. It's fading, from the Yankees to the Steelers to the Dodgers. The great tradition in pro basketball is fading because of free agency and college basketball because of guys leaving to go pro. North Carolina still remains very, very special. The loyalty is unprecedented. The man behind it all is Coach Smith."

—GEORGE KARL, head coach
of the Milwaukee Bucks

ABOUT THE AUTHORS

DEAN SMITH was born in Emporia, Kansas, in 1931. He became head basketball coach of the University of North Carolina at age thirty, and in his thirty-six years in that position, he established ACC and national coaching records that may never be broken. His UNC teams had a record of 879–254, a winning percentage of .776. The 879 victories are the most by any coach in college basketball history. His Carolina teams also won or shared a record seventeen ACC regular-season titles and won a record thirteen ACC tournament championships. Smith was head coach of the 1976 U.S. Olympic basketball team, which won the gold medal. A special panel assembled by ABC and ESPN named him one of the seven greatest coaches of the twentieth century in any sport.

JOHN KILGO is an award-winning newspaper columnist in North Carolina who has known Dean Smith for three decades. He hosted Smith's television show for fourteen years and his call-in radio show for twenty-one years. Kilgo lives in Davidson, North Carolina.

SALLY JENKINS is the author of *Men Will Be Boys,* the coauthor with Lance Armstrong of the *New York Times* bestseller *It's Not About the Bike,* and the coauthor of Pat Summitt's first book, *Reach for the Summit.* A veteran sports reporter whose work has been nominated for the Pulitzer Prize, she has worked for *The Washington Post, Sports Illustrated,* and *Women's Sports and Fitness.*

ALSO BY DEAN SMITH

Basketball: Multiple Offense and Defense

A COACH'S LIFE

A COACH'S LIFE

DEAN SMITH

with John Kilgo and Sally Jenkins

RANDOM HOUSE TRADE PAPERBACKS · NEW YORK

All rights reserved under International and Pan-American
Copyright Conventions. Published in the United States by
Random House Trade Paperbacks, a division of Random House, Inc.,
New York, and simultaneously in Canada by Random House
of Canada Limited, Toronto.

RANDOM HOUSE TRADE PAPERBACKS and colophon are trademarks of Random House, Inc.

This work was originally published in hardcover and in slightly different form by
Random House, Inc., in 1999.

Library of Congress Cataloging-in-Publication Data
Smith, Dean.
    A coach's life / Dean Smith
  with John Kilgo and Sally Jenkins.
      p.   cm.
    Includes index.
    ISBN 0-375-75880-1 (trade paper)
    1. Smith, Dean, 1931–   . 2. Basketball coaches—United States—
Biography.   3. North Carolina Tar Heels (Basketball team)   I. Kilgo, John.
II. Jenkins, Sally.   III. Title.
GV884.S54 A33   2002
796.323'092—dc21   2001048537
[B]

Random House website address: www.atrandom.com

9 8 7 6 5 4 3 2

First Trade Paperback Edition

Title page photograph © Bob Donnan

To my family, past, present, and future; to all of the players I coached at the Air Force Academy and at North Carolina; and to all of my assistant coaches and members of the basketball office staff, who made coming to work each day an enjoyable experience

Acknowledgments

Wanda Chappell, who was senior vice president and deputy publisher for Random House, and I met for lunch in New York in the summer of 1998. A charming woman, she was also an undergraduate and law school graduate of the University of North Carolina, as well as a knowledgeable UNC basketball fan. I had said from the moment I retired from coaching in the fall of 1997 that I would not write a book, even though several leading publishing houses were encouraging me to do so. Wanda had persuasive reasons why I should. I discussed it further with trusted friends, who agreed. Shortly afterwards, I signed with Random House to undertake this project. Wanda offered inspiration and encouragement as we began the book. Tragically, she died on December 23, 1998, when the apartment building in which she lived caught fire. Without her advice and help, there would not have been a book.

John Kilgo, a longtime friend and writer from Charlotte, was another who helped convince me that there should be a historical record of what the players on these thirty-six North Carolina basketball teams accomplished. Over a period of fourteen months, we spent many hours talking about those Carolina teams and the people who made them so noteworthy. John's work and advice were invaluable, and if this book accomplishes its mission of presenting an accurate account of Carolina basketball from 1961 through 1997, he deserves much of the credit. John came to understand that when he'd deliver material for this book, I would check it, then recheck it, take a few days off, and then review it again, all in the name of accuracy. I apologize to him now for being so meticulous, but I did want this to be an *accurate* account of this period.

After Wanda's death, Sally Jenkins, a writer based in New York, was asked to join the team to do some of the work that Wanda had planned to do. Sally is a talented young woman who did a superb job, even though she probably found it difficult at times to think like a sixty-eight-year-old man.

Before Wanda's death, she had the wisdom to assign Scott Moyers to the role of senior editor of this book. Scott put out many brushfires and kept us moving toward our eventual destination. I'm sure there were days, however, when he doubted that we would ever meet a deadline. He is a brilliant editor who has a gift of stringing words together in a way that makes them read more rhythmically. In coaching we call people like Scott team players, who make those around them better. Scott pointed out to me on numerous occasions that John and Sally worked together harmoniously and well. This was a team project.

During those times when Scott was dealing with other matters, we found a helping hand, as well as a good friend and adviser, in the person of Kate Niedzwiecki, an assistant editor at Random House.

Special thanks to my wife, Linnea, for reading the manuscript and offering her probing, intelligent, and candid advice.

My sister, Joan Ewing, not only gave good advice, but was also a valuable and reliable resource in recollecting our days growing up in Kansas. Joan called on these Emporia people to help her: Greg Jordan, Keith Hughey, Orval Nelson, Sue Brown Schafer, and Lee Hoskins.

My current pastor at Binkley Baptist Church in Chapel Hill, Jim Pike, and my former pastor, Bob Seymour, helped me organize my beliefs, which doesn't necessarily mean they agree with them.

Linda Woods and Ruth Kirkendall, members of the basketball office staff at Carolina, made telephone calls, arranged interviews between John and me, typed transcripts, and somehow kept up with many pieces of paper that were easily lost in a growing pile of notes and commentary. Angela Lee and Kay Thomas of the office staff were also a big help.

Rick Brewer, associate athletics director for sports information and communications at North Carolina, read the manuscript and checked it for accuracy. Steve Kirschner, UNC's director of media relations for men's basketball and football, did a good job of poring over old records. And

Sherry Brooks, Bert Woodard, and Craig Distl, of the *Carolina Blue* newspaper staff, were also good fact finders and able critics.

I received valuable advice from the Faculty Fellows, a group of University of North Carolina professors. They were also writing books in the winter and spring of 1999, and in our Tuesday-afternoon meetings they were generous in their advice and criticism for this rookie author. My thanks to Professors Mark Evan Bonds, Charles Capper, Stanley Chojnacki, Sylvia Hoffert, Michael Hunt, George Lensing, Mark McCombs, James Peacock, Kenneth Reckford, Alan Shapiro, Mark Taylor, Thomas Tweed, Ruel W. Tyson, Jr., and Peter Filene.

Contents

Introduction:
The Carolina Family

I t's not just the great ones I remember. I remember each of them, and not just as ballplayers. I remember the easy laughers and the ones who were more serious. I remember those players who became doctors and lawyers and ministers, the corporate soldiers and the nonconformists who did me the favor of conforming for the good of the team. I remember those who wanted to coach and those who wanted no part of it.

I remember the ones who didn't play much but nevertheless helped our teams in countless ways, as well as those who went on to win individual honors, and those fifty-two who played in the NBA and ABA. I remember each of these. You see, this was about championships, and we were lucky enough to win our share. But what I enjoyed most were the pursuit of the championships and the journeys each team traveled together—coaches and players—in quest of the dream. It was about the thousands of small, unselfish acts, the sacrifices on the part of the players that result in team building. When it all comes together, as it often did with our North Carolina teams, it was beautiful to see.

Basketball, more than any other sport, is a team game. That's one reason I love it so. One man can't do it by himself, not in our sport. I taught a physical education class at the Air Force Academy in the late 1950s, part of my assignment in serving as assistant coach to head basketball coach Bob

Spear, a brilliant man about whom you will hear much in this book. One day during summer tryouts in phys ed, a first-year cadet just didn't get it. The thought of passing the ball and sharing it with his teammates never entered his mind. I must say that he shot only when he had the ball. Finally, I pulled his four teammates off the court.

"Okay, play them by yourself," I said.

He gave me a quizzical look. "Who takes the ball out of bounds, sir?" he asked.

"Good," I said. "Now you've learned that you need two, anyway."

I feel the same way about this book. It should not be strictly about me, or my wife and children, and it isn't. I won't kid you: This was hard work. But it was fun too, in that it gave me a chance to review all of my thirty-six teams as North Carolina's head coach, which brought back one warm memory after another. It was never my goal to write an autobiography, that's for sure. Friends convinced me that there should be an accurate historical record of this period of North Carolina basketball, and after months of saying no, I agreed. Quite frankly, I never thought I would write another book. Along with Bob Spear, I wrote one in the late 1970s: *Basketball: Multiple Offense and Defense*. That project took me roughly eight years to complete. Each spring I would write the publisher to say that I wouldn't be able to devote the time to finish the book that particular year. Finally, he wrote back: "Dean, either complete the book, or we'll just publish all your letters to us saying why you didn't have time to finish it."

This isn't a real autobiography. Frankly, I don't think I've done enough to qualify for an autobiography anyway. This is a memoir. The distinction is important. An autobiography is the life story of an individual, whereas a memoir is an impressionistic account of events and people written from one's memory and personal knowledge. That is what I'm interested in writing.

Not long ago I was talking to Michael Jordan regarding biographies. I asked him if he had read any of David Halberstam's biography of him. Michael said he had read about twenty pages and stopped. He added, "It makes me feel like I'm reading my obituary—he is saying so many nice things. But I'll probably read it in fifteen years." I told him the latest biography of me had several mistakes, and I would read it this summer. My "obituaries" came with retirement. Writers across the country were extremely nice to me. Of course, there is a vast difference between the celebrity status of Michael and me!

The hardest thing about writing a book like this is deciding what to put in and what to leave out. That was particularly hard for me because I had thirty-six teams at North Carolina. Each team and each player is important to me. I wanted to include *all* of the games they played, because all of them were special. But our North Carolina teams played 1,133 games plus thirty-seven exhibitions with me as coach, and to include them all would result in a work containing more volumes than an encyclopedia.

Of course, without my players there would be no need for this book. They are the stars. They are the real story. I never had any trouble understanding that, thank goodness. The name of each of them is printed in the book's appendix, and a picture of each team also appears. These players have enriched my life so much that at first I wanted to entitle this book *Just Call Me Lucky!* Lucky for having coached them. Lucky for having coached at the University of North Carolina. Lucky to have selected great people as assistants and staff, to live in Chapel Hill, and to have been a part of Binkley Church.

When my college coach, Dr. Phog Allen, was asked if he considered a certain group of players one of his best, he would reply: "Wait twenty years from now for me to judge the success of these players." Obviously he was judging each player by what he did with his life after basketball. Using that standard, our players are successful!

While we've gone to great pains to be as accurate as possible in recalling conversations, times, dates, and events, there still will be names of friends who are left out, people who have helped me and to whom I'm indebted. All of those have my genuine gratitude.

You'll read in a later chapter about some of the people who influenced my coaching career. Those people did indeed teach me, and I will always be grateful to them. However, the people who influenced my basketball most were the men who served as my assistant coaches. I spent more time with them than I did with my own family, as do most basketball coaches. That's the way this profession is. I spent hundreds and hundreds of hours with my assistants looking at tapes, talking about how best to use our personnel, scouting opponents, and plotting our recruiting strategy.

They are so important to what we accomplished at North Carolina that I insist on saying a few words about them now. Other head coaches, as well as corporate leaders who depend on trusted lieutenants, will know why.

Ken Rosemond: Frank McGuire brought Ken to our staff from the University of South Carolina to coach our freshmen and assist with the varsity prior to the 1959–60 season, at a salary of $4,000 a year. Ken had played for Frank at North Carolina and was a reserve on the 1957 NCAA championship team. When I was named head coach upon Frank's departure to coach in the NBA prior to the 1961–62 season, I retained Ken as my only assistant coach. He was a tireless recruiter who remained on my staff until he became head coach at Georgia after our 1965 season.

Ken returned to Chapel Hill to enter private business after his coaching career ended at Georgia. His business was extremely successful. I always provided him with two season tickets to our home games. He requested tickets at the end of the court. I later learned that he liked to sit there so he could yell at the officials.

I took Ken with us on our trip to Hawaii in December 1992 to play in the Rainbow Classic. He had fought cancer for two years and died five days after North Carolina won the national championship in 1993.

Betsy Terrell: When I became head coach, the university had funds for two assistant coaches, or one assistant coach and one secretary, so having Betsy as our administrative assistant was like having another coach in the office. She was sensational at her job, and with Ken and me on the road recruiting and scouting, she dealt with our players, ran the office, typed all the correspondence, answered the telephones, and generally did the work of three or four people.

When Ken left for Georgia, I received permission to hire two assistants as well as keep Betsy. A head coach absolutely can't afford to make a mistake in hiring his assistants. I never did. The men I hired for those positions were talented, loyal, worked hard, and contributed greatly to the success of our program. My policy was to rotate the assistants each year so they could get a full view of coaching basketball, from both offense and defense. We have stations in practice for fundamentals, and I made sure the coaches rotated among them. However, if one coach had a special gift that set him apart, I made sure we took advantage of it. For instance, Phil Ford was one of the best point guards ever to play basketball, and I would have been dumb not to have him work with our guards on an individual basis. I also kept one coach in charge of the shooting station. It's the same premise as having one golf teacher. Too many voices would serve to confuse the student instead of assisting him or her to build a more efficient golf swing. It was my belief that players would become confused if they heard too many people telling them how to shoot. I wanted one voice doing the shooting instructions, although as head coach, I made suggestions.

John Lotz: John's brother, Danny, had played for Coach McGuire at Carolina, and was captain of our 1959 UNC team the first year I was assistant to Frank in Chapel Hill. I knew John through Danny, and when we had openings on our staff prior to the 1965–66 season, John was high on my list to interview. He was coaching basketball at Berner High School in Massapequa,

New York. He is a brilliant public speaker, and right before interviewing him for a position on our staff I heard him speak to a Fellowship of Christian Athletes conference, at which he did an amazing job.

John became a great recruiter. He enjoyed being on the road and meeting people. He was an excellent judge of talent, with a gift for finding good prospects who weren't highly recruited. He could certainly coach and teach, but I kept him on the road more at his request. He was a great shooter in his own right, providing a great example, so I left him in charge of our shooting station the entire time he was on the staff. He could also motivate. When we divided our squad into two teams in the preseason to have our Blue-White scrimmage before a full house, John would begin motivating the players on his team three days before the game. And this was for a scrimmage! And he was successful.

John was a meticulous dresser who enjoyed nice clothes. When he went out, everything was neat and in place. Before his marriage to Vicki Joyner, his bachelor apartment and his office contradicted his sartorial elegance. With papers and books and tapes and letters scattered all over the floor, scraps of paper posted to the wall, you really had to tread carefully in his office. I am hardly one to talk, however. In that way, John and I are very much alike.

John remained on our staff until after our 1973 season, when he became head coach at the University of Florida, where he was chosen Southeastern Conference Coach of the Year. He is now assistant athletics director at Carolina.

Larry Brown: You'll meet Larry several times in the ensuing pages. He came as my assistant the same year John Lotz did, after being our captain on Carolina's 1963 team. He coached the freshman team and assisted with the varsity in his two years on the staff. He left to fulfill his dream to play professional basketball. As you will see, Larry has charisma, great talent, and a wonderful sense of humor. His Kansas team won a national championship in 1988, and he took another Kansas team and UCLA to the Final Four as head coach, winning a National Coach of the Year one time. He is now head coach of the Philadelphia 76ers in the NBA. Most of his NBA teams have made the play-offs in his seventeen seasons as a professional coach.

Bill Guthridge: He replaced Larry on our staff prior to the 1967–68 season. He coached our freshmen and assisted with the varsity. He also brought a sense of organization to our staff, which we needed badly. He certainly relieved me of many of those organizational duties, for which I will always be grateful. Bill is also a great judge of high school talent and seldom was he ever wrong on a prospect. Bill turned down many chances to become a head coach to remain at North Carolina, where he was happy. When I retired from coaching prior to the 1998 season, Bill was named North Carolina's head coach. He and his staff are doing a tremendous job, so good, in fact, that Bill was voted National Coach of the Year after the 1998 season.

Eddie Fogler: When John Lotz left for Florida in 1973, I moved Eddie up from graduate assistant to full-time assistant coach. What a good move that was! Eddie was a cocaptain of our 1970 team. He was grad assistant one year and assistant coach for fourteen seasons. One would be hard-pressed to find any weaknesses in Eddie's coaching résumé. He is a tireless, persistent worker in recruiting, while a patient teacher of the game. He was National Coach of the Year at Vanderbilt in 1993 and at South Carolina in 1997. He coached our jayvee team beginning with the 1972–73 season. For a period of time, Eddie wasn't sure he wanted to be a head coach in college basketball. He thought he might take a similar job in high school or go into business. But Wichita State persuaded him to become its head coach in 1986, and he was named Missouri Valley Coach of the Year. He has been head coach at three universities, and has done a fabulous job at each stop.

Eddie had his hands full coaching our jayvees, assisting with the varsity, and being on the road with extensive recruiting responsibilities. He needed help so we hired a young high school coach who had worked our camp.

Roy Williams: Roy graduated from Carolina in 1972 and came to our staff from Owens High School, located in the mountains near Asheville, North Carolina, to serve as varsity assistant and to coach our jayvees. We helped his wife, Wanda, secure a job teaching high school English, and Roy supplemented his income selling team calendars and getting up at the crack of dawn Sunday mornings to drive tapes of our television show to distant points in North Carolina. Eddie took Roy on the road recruiting with him that first year and actually taught him much about that part of the job. When Eddie went to Wichita State in 1986, Roy was in charge of recruiting. Roy is an excellent teacher and sincere recruiter, and players respect him. He was on our staff for a total of ten years before succeeding Larry Brown as head coach at Kansas, where his program has been one of the most successful in the country. He also has been National Coach of the Year twice!

Dick Harp: You'll meet him when I talk about the men who influenced my coaching. He was my assistant coach when I played at the University of Kansas in the early 1950s. I was also his assistant with the Kansas freshman team following my graduation from college. He was head coach at Kansas with Wilt Chamberlain when Kansas lost to North Carolina for the 1957 national championship. When Eddie Fogler left us to go to Wichita State in

1986, Dick came on as administrative assistant. He had retired as executive vice president of the Fellowship of Christian Athletes when I invited him back to coaching basketball after a long period away from the game. He was sixty-eight years old. He stayed on our staff for three years, retired again, and subsequently moved back to Lawrence.

Phil Ford: I had Phil in mind for a long time. He demonstrated as a player what an outstanding mind he has, as well as a charismatic personality in communicating with young people. As a former National Player of the Year, NBA Rookie of the Year, and NBA all-star, he's a person student-athletes should certainly want to listen to and learn from. When Roy Williams left after the 1988 season to go to Kansas, we hired Phil. Hugh McColl, now the CEO of Bank of America and a Carolina alumnus, had helped Phil with a position at NationsBank along with other former players. He surely didn't want to lose Phil but understood. Phil has been called to interview for several head-coaching positions but has elected to remain on Bill Guthridge's Carolina staff for now. Phil continues to enjoy coaching the jayvee team also.

Randy Wiel: A former player on our team, graduating in 1979 before playing on the Dutch national team, Randy coached our jayvees and assisted with the varsity before becoming head coach at UNC-Asheville. He was outstanding in building the UNC-A program from scratch before accepting another challenge as head coach at Middle Tennessee State, where he has made remarkable progress. He taught physical education here while earning his master's degree. He speaks seven languages fluently and is a classical guitarist. He is a great young coach from whom I predict much will be heard in the years ahead. Randy was on our staff for eight years.

Dave Hanners: When Randy left, Dave Hanners—who had been grad assistant in 1977 after playing on the 1976 team—was brought in as coach. He was coaching under Les Robinson at East Tennessee State and helped Les do a terrific job there, recruiting and coaching. Dave assisted with the varsity and now under Coach Guthridge has become a great recruiter. He is a keen judge of talent. And he has an excellent feel for the X's and O's.

John Lacey and Marc Davis: The best in the business at their work as athletic trainers, they had the respect of our players and coaches. I was fortunate to have them, and they and their wives remain special friends.

Dr. Joe DeWalt and Dr. Tim Taft: Our players and coaches had complete faith and confidence in these two men, who were our team doctors. Both have been personal friends in addition to being colleagues. Joe died in 1994. Tim, who is a gifted orthopedic surgeon, frequently takes care of our former players who still come back to him for treatment, including some of our NBA players.

Harley Dartt and Ben Cook: Harley became our first basketball strength coach in 1986. He set up the program, and when he left, he was succeeded by Ben Cook, who also did a tremendous job.

Sarge Keller and Ken Crowder: The two best equipment managers a coach could ever have.

Pat Sullivan: He played on three of our teams that reached the Final Four, and was a key member of the 1993 national champions. He was video director on my last Carolina team, and when I retired, Coach Guthridge made him his third assistant. Pat is going to be a great head coach one day.

Linda Woods: She came to our staff in 1978 when Betsy Terrell wanted to go part-time, and has been here since. Linda was my administrative assistant when I retired in 1997 and serves in the same role now for Coach Guthridge. Giving Linda an assignment was sort of like putting the ball in Phil Ford's hands and going to Four Corners—nothing but good things were going to happen.

Linda is ably assisted by Kay Thomas, who joined our staff in 1975; and by Angela Lee, who came in 1982 after earning her law degree from UNC. She is the daughter of State Senator Howard and Lillian Lee, who are close personal friends since 1965. I have known Angela since she was twelve years old. Ruth Kirkendall came to help us in the fall of 1987. There is no such thing as "office hours" for a basketball staff. The good ones stay until the work is done, which is what this staff always did.

John Thompson: John has done one of the all-time great coaching jobs at Georgetown. He was one of my two assistants on the 1976 Olympic team. Although I worked directly with him for only six weeks, he has had a great influence on me, which will be discussed.

One of the greatest pleasures involved in doing this book was totally unexpected. I was invited to join an elite group of eleven professors chosen to be given the 1999 spring semester off to write a book. They were described as "Faculty Fellows" by the Institute of Arts and Humanities. We met every Tuesday for three and a half hours in a small room in West House Hall on the university campus. It was a great experience for me to be with professors of such different disciplines and hear them discuss their books. When Evan Bonds, a music professor at Carolina, said he was writing a textbook, *A History of Western Music,* I learned it was about Beethoven, Bach, and the works of Western civilization, not about Willie Nelson and Garth Brooks!

Fortunately, I had three genuine basketball fans in this group, which put me at ease. Alan Shapiro, an English professor as well as a nationally honored poet, still plays pickup games in Woollen Gym on campus and cheers for his beloved Boston Celtics. Tom Tweed, a professor of religion, is a former high school basketball coach in Florida. Dr. Mark Taylor, a visiting professor from Williams College, studied at Carolina in 1981 and likes Carolina basketball. He has written at least twenty-five books and is the world's foremost scholar on Danish philosopher Søren Kierkegaard. He even has a patent on the doodling done in Kierkegaard's own handwriting.

Each Tuesday one of the professors would present his or her book, and the group would discuss it. Quite candidly, I might add. George Lensing, an English professor, was writing *The Four Seasons in the Poetry of Wallace Stevens*. A fellow member of the group, Jim Peacock, an anthropology professor, said he wanted to know the inside of Stevens. "Tell me what time he got up, what time he went to bed, whether or not he got along with his wife, what kind of life he led."

In that spirit, let's get this over with quickly:

I go to bed past midnight but still manage to get seven or eight hours' sleep a night. I'm also fortunate to go to sleep quickly, and generally sleep peacefully through the night even after tough losses. I have a desk that is stacked so high that if you covered it with a sheet, a stranger might think it concealed a corpse. I have an enormous amount of "stuff" in my office that clutters the floor and peeks out of book racks. When a visitor comes in, I have to clean out a chair so he'll have a place to sit. My successor at Carolina, Bill Guthridge, is so neat he could organize a bowl of chop suey. When he passes my office, he can only shrug and look amazed. Maybe that's why we were such a good team for more than thirty years. They say opposites attract. Eddie Fogler and Roy Williams also were highly organized and into clean desks.

Our office staff has a standing rule: They don't hand me anything important without having a copy of it for themselves. That's so they can find it when I inevitably misplace the original. I'm not one to save photographs, either—even important photographs—so when I searched for pictures of old friends I wanted to include in this book, I couldn't find many of them. My friends know me and will understand.

I'm also completely disorganized in handling money. I have hundreds of gasoline, hotel, and food receipts stuffed in airline ticket folders tucked away in cases in my attic. I'm sure some of them date back thirty years. I might one day get around to filling out expense reports. It helped that the university finally arranged for me to have a credit card to use with hotels and restaurants back in 1980. Fortunately, in 1980 I met Bill Miller, a Charlotte accountant and big Carolina basketball fan. He came to my rescue in making some kind of sense out of my financial picture. Had it not been for Bill, I might have had to coach until I was a hundred. He can't have time for many clients since he handles finances for those assistants I named before, in addition to me. Since the Arkansas game in February 1984, he has seen 555 consecutive Carolina basketball games at home and on the road through the 1999 season. He doesn't plan to interrupt the streak soon.

I'm a big tipper. Some say it might be a sign of low self-esteem and an attempt to buy popularity. I don't think so. When walking through a New York hotel lobby with Frank McGuire in the late 1950s (when a dollar was really worth something), a bellhop called out: "Hello, Coach McGuire!" Frank smiled and tipped him two dollars, and then told me: "If they remember my name, they get two dollars; if they don't, they get a dollar." Money has never been important to me. My family was split on the issue. Dad had a carefree attitude about it, which was passed along to me. Mom watched money carefully. Before ordering in a restaurant, she would ask the waiter: "Is salad or dessert included with the price of the meal?" I was never tempted to change jobs because of money, never felt an urgent need to have a big bank account.

I had a summer basketball camp for thirty-five years at Carolina. Thousands and thousands of young men attended. I would like to have a campers' reunion one day, but it would be too large, too many campers. Up until the last fifteen years, I checked each young man in on Sunday and knew his name by the time he departed on Friday afternoon. My long-term recall is still strong, but I'm not quite as good with names as I was then. I was once asked to name my happiest time of the year. That was easy—it was the last day of camp. Nobody drowned in the pool, no one was run over by a car, nobody got sick from the food. Not all of coaching big-time college basketball is glamorous.

Still, I can't think of anything I would have rather done. We were teaching young people the fundamentals and beauty of the game and creating new Carolina fans along the way, although most of them were already loyal to UNC before coming to camp here.

My priorities over the years should have been God, family, coaching. Undoubtedly, I messed that up at times along the way. Mine really is a story of good luck. My mind I owe to my genes, and along life's journey I've received help from many, many people. I'm not superhuman. I try to be honest about my mistakes and admit them. I can't tell you all the dumb things I've done but will try to tell some in this book, which won't hurt anyone now.

As a coach, I remember all the losses. Why? Because they were mine. I told our players from day one, and I meant it: "If you do what we ask you to do, the victories will belong to you, and the losses to me." I sincerely believe that when we lost, it was my fault.

Good coaching means teaching your players how to play individually and then unselfishly as a team. If players do that and play hard in the process, then losing should not be so debilitating, although I know it's much easier to say that than to live it. One year I recall trying to get the National Association of Basketball Coaches board of directors to give their coaching award to Bob Spear at Air Force. A coach who does much better than expected with little talent to work with should be honored and appreciated. Bob Spear did a remarkable job in coaching Air Force to more wins than losses over his long career. Air Force was not expected to win often in Division 1 basketball, so Bob's record was remarkable.

To be sure, I was lucky (there's that word again) to coach basketball for thirty-six years at the University of North Carolina. It's a great university in the perfect college town, and it attracted student-athletes who were a pleasure to teach. So many words and phrases are overworked these days that they become hackneyed and trite. Knowing that, I still believe that what we had with our basketball program at Carolina was a real family. King Rice, class of '91, didn't play with Michael Jordan, class of '85. But when King called for play-off tickets to a Bulls game, Michael not only got him two good seats, but after the game took him and his wife to his restaurant for dinner. It's that "Carolina family" so many talk about.

This is what Jeff Lebo, class of '89 and now head coach at Tennessee Tech, told a newspaper reporter recently: "It's an amazing group of guys. It's a fraternity. I might not know a guy who played for Coach Smith in 1976, but I know if I needed help and picked up the phone and called that guy, he'd be there for me. That's what a lot of people don't understand. The group would run to help anybody."

George Karl, the successful coach of the Milwaukee Bucks and Carolina class of '73, was recently quoted: "There is definitely a University of North Carolina fraternity in the [NBA]. We get a lot of ribbing from the other players and colleges, but we're pretty loyal. Everybody knows we love the blue. The meaning of tradition doesn't exist in sports anymore. It's fading, from the Yankees to the Steelers to the Dodgers. The great tradition in pro basketball is fading because of free agency and college basketball because of guys leaving to go pro. North Carolina still remains very, very special. The loyalty is unprecedented."

Our players develop a feeling for their teammates that is unique. They are in each other's wedding parties. When Henrik Rödl was married, George Lynch was his best man. Henrik is white, George is black. Henrik is from Germany, George from Virginia. They have a bond from their days as Carolina basketball players. They are friends for a lifetime. Eric Montross, who is white, had teammates Derrick Phelps and Brian Reese, both black, in his wedding. Eric plays in the NBA; Derrick and Brian play in Europe. Worlds apart, but they stay in touch. It's hard to tell you exactly how that makes their old college coach feel.

That's what I'm interested in, the complete picture. I've witnessed some significant cultural shifts, from the civil rights movement to the burgeoning of collegiate basketball as a commercial enterprise worth billions, and one can't do that without deciding there is more to life than strictly Carolina basketball. Oliver Wendell Holmes said: "As life is action and passion, so a man must participate in the action and passion of his times, at peril of being judged not to have lived." All I did was participate in my times—and many basketball games.

Like most people who reach this stage in their life, I look back and see some things left undone. I'm talking about the persistence of things such as social injustice, racial bias, and the continuing struggle to keep college athletics in proper perspective.

In a way, I wish we hadn't kept score, but of course that would have killed the interest.

When you keep score, you lose sight of the larger purpose of the game, and the process of separating people begins. A single point's difference between two teams in forty minutes of intense basketball can earn some the label of "losers." You would think that rational people would not react that way, but our society is so concerned with the "number one" syndrome that often there is nothing left for others who competed with integrity and gave their all, but came up short on the scoreboard. What happened to honoring people for doing their best?

Although our game is imperfect, I firmly believe there is value in exploring the athletic heart on the championship level. I think I was meant for college basketball. I love the college atmosphere, the studious pace of life, the sense of intellectual hunger in the air. I loved practice, the teaching, and seeing the possibilities of each team.

You get a new team *every* year in college basketball. The seasons come and go, but with each new year there is an excitement to coach that year's team. I wanted to coach them. I wanted to see what would become of them. I wanted to see how our best performance would stack up against the best the game had to offer. That's my competitive side coming out.

Let's face it: College coaches have to win to keep their jobs. We hear all the time in college basketball: "We want to graduate our players, run a clean program, care for our athletes." I've known many coaches who did that admirably and still lost their jobs. Their shortcoming? They didn't win enough to suit somebody. One of the striking things about my profession is that not many coaches retire on their own timetable. Most of us are not that lucky. I was. Again, thanks go to my players. I do remember all of them.

A COACH'S LIFE

A Kansas Childhood

I'm a Kansan, even though I've lived most of my adult life in North Carolina. I speak like a Kansan, in a flat Midwest voice free of any accent. I'm not quick to say aloud what's on my mind. I say what I think—just not everything I think—and some would say that, too, is speaking like a Kansan.

In Kansas the sky seems somehow bigger. Driving through, it feels like the longest state in the union, and it's a fact that the sun rises thirty minutes later on the western border than it does on the eastern. Lines of dark limestone hills crested by mustard-colored tall rippling grasses seem to go on forever, and so do the blacktop roads that roll up and over the hills. The monotony is broken every few miles by midwestern towns, each one much like the last. Among them is a place called Emporia, a university town of low-slung brick buildings, tree-lined streets of Victorian houses with inviting front porches, and a railroad track. That's where I spent the first fifteen years of my life, before moving to the capital of Kansas, Topeka.

The austere landscape of Kansas, its hills and prairies, belie its tempestuous history and even more tempestuous—some would say biblical—weather, which brings the state more than its share of twisters, blizzards, hailstorms, prairie fires, and locusts. I was never blown to Oz as a child, but I may have come close.

Once upon a time, as they say, a family named Smith settled in Kansas, and unlike some of their neighbors, managed not to become farmers. (Ninety-six percent of the land in the state of Kansas is devoted to farming, but farmers actually make up a small percentage of the people who live there.) I'm the son of schoolteachers.

My mother, Vesta Edwards, taught at all levels, from elementary school reading to college psychology courses. She was also our church's organist. My father, Alfred Smith, was a teacher and coach of the football, basketball, and track teams at Emporia High, as well as a church deacon. Teaching and coaching was all I ever thought about as a profession because it struck me that in addition to being very good people, my parents were also deeply happy ones. It seems fitting to me that Emporia is now the home of the National Teachers Hall of Fame.

I grew up in a small stucco bungalow that was built by my parents with the help of my mother's father, a cement mason who also poured the foundation for one of the local Baptist churches. The house cost $3,500 when they put it up in 1936, which was actually a substantial price in those days. By way of comparison, you could wander down to Gould's Cafe and buy a chicken dinner with salad, three vegetables, and a roll for 35 cents. You got a choice of iced tea or coffee and dessert too. My parents were so happy in Emporia that when my father was offered the head football coaching job at Wichita North High School, one of the largest schools in the state, he turned it down because he and my mother didn't want to leave.

Five of us lived in the two-bedroom house, which had just a single bath with hardwood floors and a second-floor sleeping porch, which became my room. My sister, Joan, was born the year before the stock market crash in 1928, and I was born in 1931, and between us and my Grandmother Edwards, who moved in with us when she was seventy-two, the house was pretty crowded. That was what you did in those days: You took care of your grandparents. It wasn't unusual for three generations to live in one small house.

Emporia was a town of only about fourteen thousand, but it had prosperity and a cultural life unusual for a place of that size because we had two colleges, Kansas State Teachers College (later Emporia State) on the east side of town, and a Presbyterian university called the College of Emporia on the west side of town. Also, the legendary newspaper editor William Allen White was building a national reputation with his *Emporia Gazette,* and became a friend of my father's, who was a pallbearer at his funeral. All of this

Paul Terry, the first black to play for Emporia High School, is pictured in this team photo at the bottom right. My father, who coached the 1934 Emporia team to the state championship, is pictured just below the trophy to the left of the picture of the high school.

My father's 1936 track team at Emporia. He is standing in the back row at the far right. Two of the team (Smith and Holt) ended up at North Carolina College in Durham (now North Carolina Central University).

With my sister, Joan, in the mid-1930s on the steps of the First Baptist Church in Emporia.

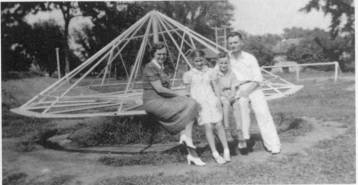

Joan and I with our parents in 1937, in Garnett, Kansas, where we were visiting my father's parents.

My mother, Vesta Smith, my sister, Joan, and me in 1939.

The Emporia Junior High basketball team in my ninth-grade year. I'm number 00 in the middle of the back row, and Dad, who coached me for the first time that year, is in the back row, far right. My friend Shad Woodruff, who died of polio the following summer, is number 11 in the back row.

A partial view of our beautiful school, Topeka High School.

The Topeka house in which we lived during my senior year in high school. My room was upstairs behind the double windows.

My 1949 Topeka High School yearbook senior picture.

Just prior to our Kansas team taking the court to beat St. John's for the 1952 national championship in Seattle, we get last-minute instructions from our head coach, the legendary Doc Allen. I'm in the middle, next to one of our big men, B. H. Born.

I sank a free throw late in the game to help us beat rival Kansas State on the road. Al Kelley and I celebrate a happy moment for Kansas basketball.

Dad visits with University of Kansas players in the hotel lobby on the day of the 1953 NCAA championship game between Kansas and Indiana. From the left are Kansas players Dean Kelley, me, Gil Reich, and Al Kelley. We lost the game that night by one point.

At the fortieth reunion of my Kansas class of 1953. From left to right, my close friends Henry Alberg, Galen Fiss (a great linebacker for the Cleveland Browns), Jack Rodgers (co-founder of the Starbucks coffeehouses), Mark Rivard, roommate Charlie Hoag, and Bob Mayer.

Landsberg, Germany, 1955. At left, in the background, Ron Johnson shakes hands with coach Adolph Rupp, while I greet the legendary Bob Cousy. Rupp and Cousy, along with Red Auerbach, were there to put on a memorable basketball clinic for members of the Army and Air Force in Europe.

My former boss at the Air Force Academy, Bob Spear, visited me in Chapel Hill for one of our games in the early 1990s. Bob did a remarkable job in his tenure as head basketball coach of the Air Force Academy.

Our Air Force Academy team picture from the 1957–58 season, my last year serving as an assistant basketball coach to Bob Spear. Coach Spear is at the far left of the front row, and I'm in the second row, directly behind him. Next to me is longtime trainer at the academy Jim Conboy, a special friend and person. That basketball team accomplished some amazing things; three became Air Force generals!

With Frank McGuire during my second season in Chapel Hill as his assistant coach.

Jack LaRocca and Danny Patrissy were two of Coach McGuire's best friends, and they became my special friends too. (Have you ever seen such dapper dressers?)

Our extremely talented 1960 North Carolina team. This was my second season at Carolina as assistant to Coach McGuire.

© Dan Crawford

It looks as if I'm trying to calm things down in this 1963 photo taken during one of our games in tiny Woollen Gym. Notice how well dressed the students in the stands were. Those young men in coats and neckties behind our bench were members of our freshman team.

Betsy Terrell, who was my first administrative assistant when I was Carolina's head coach, shows me some correspondence.

Ken Rosemond, my first assistant coach at North Carolina, and I visit with freshman star Larry Miller as Carmichael Auditorium is being constructed behind us, fall 1964. Larry went on to have a great career for us at Carolina. Sadly, Ken Rosemond died of cancer in 1993, shortly after we won the national championship.

Some people say my first two name recruits at Carolina were Bob Lewis (left) and Larry Miller. The press called them the L&M Boys. They certainly thrilled their head coach with their play.

Larry Brown and I are carried off the court after winning the ACC championship over Duke in 1967. My other assistant, John Lotz, was lost in the celebration somewhere. It was our third win over Duke that year. This team was the first of three straight to win the ACC and advance to the NCAA Final Four.

It was certainly a special time for me when our great players from the 1967–69 teams returned to Chapel Hill for their thirtieth reunion. Those teams accomplished the amazing feat of winning three straight ACC regular-season championships, three ACC tournament championships, and three NCAA East Regional championships. The cumulative record of those three teams was an astounding 81–15, against very tough schedules.

I'm flanked at the end of our bench by assistant coaches John Lotz (left) and Bill Guthridge. Members of this 1969 ACC champion team are, from left: Bill Bunting, Jim Delany, Rusty Clark, Lee Dedmon, and Charles Scott. That team finished 27–5.

A golf outing at gorgeous Grandfather Mountain with some of my all-time favorite people. Pictured from left are Dr. Chris Fordham, who became chancellor of our university; the late Dr. Earl Somers, one of the dearest friends I ever had; Bill Guthridge, the 1998 National Coach of the Year; Doug Moe, one of the greatest players at North Carolina and later a superb NBA coach; Simon Terrell, whose wife, Betsy, helped run our basketball office for two decades; Larry Brown, my former player and assistant coach, who is now one of the best coaches in the world; and me.

It was an emotional and exciting moment for me and assistant coaches John Thompson and Bill Guthridge as we stood off to the side and saw our U.S. basketball team awarded the gold medal for returning the Olympic championship to the United States in the 1976 Games in Montreal. Carolina players Phil Ford, Mitch Kupchak, Walter Davis, and Tommy LaGarde were members of the U.S. team.

Courtesy of Ted Oldenburg

John Thompson and I direct some traffic in the championship game of the 1976 Olympics. Mitch Kupchak is number 18.

Our U.S. Olympic team poses for the team picture outside Olympic Village just before we began play in the Games.

Taking a break from a golf outing at Grandfather Mountain in 1976 to sign some drawings for my good friend Hugh Morton.

Coaching in the old East-West college all-star game, this one held in Tulsa, Oklahoma, April 1976. Each head coach had the right to appoint his assistant coach for the game, and I chose my father, who sits with me on the bench. He was seventy-eight at the time.

Linnea and I on our wedding day, May 21, 1976, in Ojai, California. A special day for me!

A big occasion: my parents' fiftieth wedding anniversary in Topeka in 1976. Seated from the left are daughter Sharon Kepley, my parents, and my niece Elizabeth Ewing. Standing from the left are my son, Scott, daughter Sandy, me, Linnea, my sister, Joan Ewing, her husband, Jim, and my niece Sarah Ewing.

In front of the Old Well, one of the most famous landmarks on Carolina's campus, with three of my children (all three of whom graduated from UNC), in the spring of 1977. Behind me, daughter Sandy, who was a Carolina junior at the time, son Scott, who was a freshman, and daughter Sharon, who was a senior.

On the deck in the back of our house in Chapel Hill, in 1979, Linnea holds daughter Kristen, who really does look like a doll. My son, Scott, is on the right, and our three golden retrievers joined us.

Our coaches at work. From left, Bill Guthridge, me, Eddie Fogler, and Roy Williams. I don't think that any head coach ever had better assistant coaches on his staff than I did over my career.

By the looks of this picture, you might think we lost the 1982 NCAA championship game to Georgetown. Exhausted, I'm waiting for our postgame press conference to begin. Our Sports Information Director, Rick Brewer, is standing, while James Worthy is saying a prayer and Jimmy Black is in deep thought.

John Thompson and I in the rear of the New Orleans Superdome shortly after our two teams played a great game for the 1982 national championship. John is one of my best friends, and I will always marvel at the brilliant job he did throughout his years as Georgetown's head coach. He'll go down as one of the all-time greats.

inspired someone to get a rather exalted view of the place and to name it "The Athens of Kansas." Emporia was the third largest feeding station for cattle and sheep in the nation at the time, and the Santa Fe railroad ran right through town.

The main avenue in town was Commercial, an old-fashioned main street anchored on one end by the campus of Emporia State and on the other end by a public park with a baseball diamond and bleachers, where we played American Legion baseball—and where I fractured my leg sliding into second base when I was fifteen. Also on Commercial, halfway between Fifth and Sixth Streets, was the Red X Pharmacy, a department store called Newman's, and three different movie theaters: the Granada, the Strand, and the Lyric. There was a barber shop where my father and I got haircuts every Saturday night, and a sporting goods store called Hassingers, where my father bought most of the uniforms and equipment for his teams. I purchased a baseball glove for a dollar and paid in installments, 10 cents a week.

Looking back on it, my mother was uncommonly strong opinioned and well educated for a woman of her place and time. At first glance she appeared quiet, perhaps, and she usually had the look of someone about to offer you a piece of apple pie. When you looked closer you saw a woman who radiated intellectual energy; her eyes were piercing and suggested that she didn't tolerate nonsense. My mother was meticulous, highly organized, punctual, and relentlessly frugal (the opposite of me, with the exception of punctual). She handled all the household finances like a drill sergeant, to my frustration. She earned her master's degree from Emporia State in educational psychology in 1946, the same year Joan graduated from high school, and she was an educator in the true sense of the word. She had one uncompromising rule: I had to read a book a week. I tried to satisfy her with sports books and stumbled onto a series by a writer named John R. Tunis, who wrote *The Kid, The Kid Comes Back,* and *All American,* now regarded as classics.

When we were small, my mother gave up teaching for a few years in order to be home for us in the afternoons, but she always worked. She was the church organist, and while I was in grade school, she was director of the weekday Bible schools for Emporia. For a salary of $75 a year she would line up the Bible teachers and choose the curriculum.

Later, when I was in the ninth grade, she became superintendent of schools for Lyon County. The gentleman who had occupied the position resigned before his term was up, and it's an indication of the regard in which my mother was held that she was chosen to complete his unexpired term.

After serving eighteen months she had a chance to run for the job and win it in an election, but she said she wasn't the type to run for political office, so she went back to what she was best at, which was educating.

My father matched my mother's strong personality, although he also seemed unassuming. He was measured, slow to anger, soft-spoken, and easy to smile, but he was also implacable. He had a way of persuading people to do what he wanted them to. When he and my mother were in their eighties and disagreed over whether to move to North Carolina—my mother didn't want to leave Kansas—I predicted to my sister, Joan, "He'll win. It may take a while, but he'll win." And he did; they moved to Springmoor Retirement facility in Raleigh. I have my father's hooked nose, sharp chin, and straight line of a mouth. I think I got a lot more too. My father once said, "His mother taught him organization and to work hard; I gave him athletic desire and atmosphere." I hope so.

My father was the first real coach I ever knew, and I'm sure I was shaped by him in ways I'm not even conscious of. He taught hygiene and physical education, and in the afternoons he coached football, basketball, baseball, and track. He became head coach for Emporia High in the year I was born, 1931, and the job came with certain pressures. In those days perhaps even more than now the entire town was involved with whether the high school team won or lost. Emporia High was a relatively small school of about six hundred students at any given time, and we had to compete against much larger schools from the big cities like Topeka and Wichita, in which we took a certain pride. The atmosphere was a lot like the one depicted in the film *Hoosiers*—gymnasiums packed with crowds caught up in the fever pitch of regional rivalries. It was a different game then; the one-handed jump shot hadn't been invented yet, players didn't rise above the rim, and practically everybody used the underhanded scoop shot at the free-throw line.

During basketball season I spent most afternoons in the gym and went on every road trip. My father had three different classrooms and four different teams to keep abreast of. I was the kind of kid who was always on the sidelines, pestering the older players and trying to shoot the ball on one end of the court while they practiced on the other end, until finally somebody would run me off. I memorized all of the jersey numerals of more than thirty guys on the football team, and on the team car trips the players would quiz me and make sure I could match up names to the numbers.

"Thirty-four?" they'd holler.

"Jack Snow!" I'd shout back.

Some of my father's former players are still around, although most of them are in their eighties. They remember Alfred Smith as calm and in control on the bench, and his players seemed to exude the same attitude on the court. But he was a quietly staunch disciplinarian too, and one who wasn't afraid to do what he believed in. He made no big deal about his principles, no outward show, but his players understood very well that he would follow through on enforcing them—there was no doubt about that.

Certainly he was determined to take a stand when he thought it mattered. In 1934, for example, he decided that the integration of Emporia High's basketball team mattered. The 1934 Emporia High team coached by my father won the state championship, which was a major upset in and of itself, but more significant was that the roster listed a young man named Paul Terry, who was black. My father had a problem with the state coaches' association because of it.

Some people have given me kind but undue praise for integrating North Carolina's basketball team in the early 1960s. My father was the family's true reformer, however. In 1934 he chose to play a black teenager, the son of a janitor who swept the floors at the local bank, whom he had known as a junior high school student. What gave him the independence of mind to come to his beliefs and the courage to act on them? I can't fully answer the question because I was only three at the time, and I don't remember the involved discussions that must have taken place on the subject in our house. But I do know how we were raised.

My father said, "Value each human being." And we did. We were taught to believe in the "human family" from day one, and other than that there wasn't much talk about it. Racial justice wasn't preached around the house, but there was a fundamental understanding that you treated each person with dignity.

It's hard to evoke just how strange and unreasoning the old barriers of race were. There was only one junior high school and one high school in town, so all of Emporia's children were educated together regardless of color. But that often ended when you stepped outside of the classroom. We didn't have any black members at our Baptist church, and we were told by my parents that was wrong. In the summers we did play recreation-league softball with a relatively diverse population of Mexican and black kids, and I remember my parents speaking to us about that and insisting they be treated fairly and like any other children. My parents were determined that we see every person as valuable, unique, and particular—and equal before our Creator.

There is no intent here to single out Kansas for its segregative atmosphere. It was supposed to be a "northern" state, and many Kansans had a condescending attitude toward the South and its handling of racial issues. But prejudice was everywhere, and still is.

In 1934, Paul Terry entered the tenth grade at Emporia High. My father had known Paul throughout his time at Lowther Junior High School, because he taught Paul physical education from the seventh through ninth grade. When Paul got to Emporia High, my father suggested that if he wanted to try out for the varsity, he'd be welcome. Paul wasn't trying to break any barriers; he just loved the game. "What did I know about making a statement?" Paul said years later. "I just liked sports."

As soon as word got around that Paul had joined the team, some people in town started getting upset. I'm told that my father received calls from the town school board asking him what he thought he was doing, and the superintendent of the Eastern Kansas Athletic Conference also raised objections. But my father was firm about it: Paul was a member of the team. He was a guard, a sixth man who came off the bench.

Paul's own father almost forbade him to play because he knew what it would mean for his son to be on that team. Charles Terry was a janitor at the Emporia bank, his mother, Rossae, was a homemaker, and they knew much better than Paul and probably even my father what the potential repercussions were. But Paul wanted to play so badly, Charles finally relented. "Afterwards I learned the situation Coach [Smith] was in," Paul told a newspaper interviewer a few years ago. "Young people don't think of things like that, but I understand now that he put his job on the line by having me on his basketball team. My being on the team meant there was going to be one white boy who didn't make it."

For the most part, the white kids and Paul got along easily enough; I don't think my father would have permitted anything else. But nobody save for Paul can know what he was really feeling on the bench, or on road trips, or on the court when the opposing crowds and players spat epithets at him. "It was rather hostile at times," he said. "I took some verbal abuse from fans and other players."

Some moments had to be searing for him. He can remember riding along on car trips with all of the boys laughing and horsing around, and then someone would say an ugly word, something boys raised in an all-white culture were used to tossing off, but a word that, one can hope, made them all cringe with Paul sitting among them. "We'd be riding along," he says. "I'd be the only black one in there, and another player would slip and make a racially derogatory remark. As soon as he would slip, it would get deathly silent in there."

One day my father received a Western Union telegram. It was sent by the principal of a school in Chanute, Kansas, that Emporia was scheduled to play in an upcoming game. "Leave the Negro boy at home," the telegram said, "Or don't come."

My father had no intention of leaving Paul behind. They packed up, went to Chanute, and walked out onto the floor. They went ahead and played, and nobody made much of a comment to my father. In fact, Paul has fond memories of that game because Chanute was a tough rival and starred a player named Ralph Miller, who would go on to be a celebrated athlete at the University of Kansas, an All-American in football and basketball in 1940, and still later a renowned basketball coach who won a Big Ten championship at Iowa, and had great NCAA teams at Oregon State.

When the team traveled, my father would seek restaurants willing to serve them, but Paul remembers that more often than not they were refused service. My father would get up from the table along with the rest of the team, and they would all walk out. They'd drive around looking for a place where they could eat together, but they would usually have to settle for leaving Paul in the car with a sandwich while they ate. Sometimes he ate back in the kitchen.

Things like that made Charles Terry want to take Paul off the team, but Paul insisted that he wanted to finish out the season. "It meant so much to me to be on that team," he says. Then Emporia made it into the state tournament. Unfortunately, nobody had much of a choice in what happened next. The state tournament officials wouldn't allow Emporia to enter the tournament if Paul played. For years everybody has assumed that Paul played, because he was listed on the roster, but the truth is that he was left home—and was devastated. He never got another chance to compete at the top level again.

After single-handedly integrating high school sports in Kansas, Paul went on to father eight children, all of them college educated. He went to Kansas State Teachers College at Emporia after high school, graduating in 1938, and throughout his undergraduate years there he played on all-black intramural teams; he never bothered to tell the athletic department that he was a high school state champion. After graduation he went into the dry-cleaning business and he and his wife, Odessa, raised their eight children, of whom five received graduate degrees, one a doctorate. Remarkably, three of them played Division 1 basketball.

A few years ago things came full circle with the Smiths and the Terrys. Paul's son, John Terry, played for the University of California–Berkeley, and in 1974 he came with his team to Chapel Hill to meet ours. Before the game I sought him out and told him I wanted to meet him. We said hello and shook hands and chatted for a moment. I told him I was aware of who his father was and that I wished I'd known him better. As I stood on the sideline and watched John Terry jog onto the court so self-assuredly, it was a moment worth reflecting on.

Still later, in 1982, I went back to Emporia for the first time in many years. I was teaching a clinic to high school coaches in Wichita, which gave me a chance to stop by Emporia and see some of my old best friends, like Gene Bloxom, whose father had been an assistant to my dad and succeeded him as Emporia High's basketball coach. Gene and I saw another old friend, Larry Collins, and we strolled around town in a mood to revisit old landmarks. I asked if Paul Terry still lived in the same house. Gene said he did. We called him to see if we might stop by. He was home, and we sat in the living room and reminisced about some of those events of 1934. But Paul was really more interested in talking about his eight children, of whom he was so proud. It was clear he considered them his real accomplishment. He is eighty-one now and still lives in Emporia.

Martin and Charles Terry played basketball for Arkansas, and Martin at one time held five Razorback school records. John and Martin are now in sales, and Charles is an assistant coach at Drury College in Springfield, Missouri. Norman is head of the graphics department at a Wichita high school; Beverly works in personnel for a firm in California; Barbara has a Ph.D. and is a teacher; Russell works for the Kansas City school district; and Nadine is a social worker in Emporia. Back in 1991 Paul's wife, Odessa, passed away. On the day of the funeral, his children each picked a day of the week to call their father. Every day, one of them does.

Paul Terry was just the first black to play for my father. From 1935 to 1937 a young man named Chick Taylor joined the Emporia basketball and football teams. Every year my parents would host dinners for the mothers of the boys on the team. Everybody came over for a family-style dinner and sat around in the living room. Mrs. Taylor was very quiet. My mother made a point of seating my sister, Joan, next to her, which typified the way the issue was handled in our house. "We want to be nice to all the mothers," my mother said, "but we want to make a special effort to make Mrs. Taylor feel at home."

In the years afterwards, the Paul Terry and Chick Taylor stories had lasting reverberations for me. When I arrived at North Carolina, I was amazed to come across a number of black athletes who had played for my father at Emporia, and who had found their way to the Carolina area of all places. Richard Mack, a great track star at Emporia, was the longtime basketball coach at Southern University, where a building is named for him. After being coached by Dad, he was a great athlete at North Carolina Central University. Another was Larry Stevens, who was athletic director at North Carolina College (now North Carolina Central University). A few of Dad's track squad at Emporia were also athletes at N.C. Central University. The best was Lee Smith, who was also a football star there.

It began to dawn on me that the subject of racial injustice went far beyond Emporia, Kansas.

Emporia in the 1930s and 1940s wasn't exempt from the politics and realities of the day. If you grew up in Kansas in the 1940s, you thought it was the center of the United States, and geographically it quite literally was. It also seemed that anybody of real importance came from there. Amelia Earhart was from there, and Walter Chrysler, and of course, Dwight D. Eisenhower, who was born in Abilene, Kansas.

As a whole the state was Republican, and then there was my father, who made all other Republicans look soft. I vividly remember the 1940 election because all my parents could talk about was Wendell Willkie and Franklin Delano Roosevelt. They were so obsessed with Willkie that I got sick of hearing about him. One weekend we drove to the Ozarks for a weekend vacation with our good friends the Penningtons—Frank Pennington was in auto supply, drove a big Hudson, and was as die-hard a Republican as my father—and the whole way they kept talking about Willkie this and Willkie that. I was just a frustrated nine-year-old trapped in the backseat, and finally I couldn't take it anymore. I burst out and said, "I hope Roosevelt wins!" That set off a horrified reaction in the car.

In those barely post-Depression years, it wasn't unusual for people to work two jobs. Because my father was a school employee, he was only paid for nine months out of the year. In the summers, he supplemented his income by painting buildings for the school system along with some other teachers. I worked too from the time I was in junior high. When I was twelve, I got a job at Emporia State mopping floors for 25 cents an hour, two hours a day. Later, I spent a couple of summers digging ditches for the city for 75 cents an hour.

My father knew how to demand a lot of his players and yet befriend them too. He was strict with his players, but kind, and it seemed as if they were always coming by the house to talk to him. Looking back on it, his values were pretty simple; I learned from him that you didn't need a whole lot of rules, just a few important ones that you were willing to stick to no matter what.

After the Paul Terry episode, anyone who still doubted that my father would do what he thought was right learned differently the day in 1942 when he left most of his first string at home for a game. Emporia was about to play what seemed to us an important game against Plainview, a big school from Wichita. There was a dance planned for the night before the game, and my dad set a curfew and promised that anyone who wasn't home and in bed by the appointed hour wouldn't play against Plainview. Adolescent boys being what they are, several of them ignored him and went to the dance anyway. Maybe they figured they were too important to be disciplined. Well, they stayed out too late, and the next morning he asked them what time they had gotten in. Times being what they were, the players actually admitted it.

My father suspended all four starters who had gone to the dance, and the thing about it is that he never yelled. He simply announced that they would be staying home. "You knew what time you were supposed to be in," he said quietly. "You'll miss the game."

It was not a popular decision, to say the least. The players were important to Joan and me. "What's the big deal?" Joan wanted to know. I rode in cars with them to games and sat in their laps and kept their secrets, and I never squealed when one of them smoked. But my father stood on principle and refused to change his mind. The next day, Emporia High sent a team of reserves onto the floor—and somehow managed to beat Plainview by a point. It think it was the most animated I ever saw my father over a game.

It reinforced his long-held view that the only way to win consistently in basketball is to play as a team, a view that suffused my upbringing and my own philosophy of the game. That win over Plainview convinced him, and later me, that teams could overcome the loss of key players for a game or two, as long as the available players dedicated themselves to achieving a common goal. It took sacrifice, unselfishness, and discipline. Sometimes adversity brings a team closer together and forges a bond, a team chemistry, that is hard to beat. Young people can do marvelous things when responding to a formidable challenge.

I'll give you another example of the kind of coach my father was. I would be credited years later with inventing the practice of having a scorer point to the passer to thank him for the assist. But the germ of that idea came from watching my father coach and listening to his dinner-table conversation. "Passers should get more credit," my father said.

I was always picking up things from him. He could see I was interested in X's and O's, even at a very young age. When I was ten or twelve, I remember drawing up my first football play, something involving the double wing. My father studied it appreciatively, and then he gently pointed out that I had forgotten to block somebody.

At first I thought I wanted to be a football coach, but I probably would have been fired years ago. I had the kind of football mind that thought it was a good idea to fake into the line and throw the pass on fourth and inches on the opponents' 40-yard line. I was a quarterback in football, and in those days quarterbacks called their own plays. I was a guard in basketball, which meant I got to call the plays there too, and I was a catcher in baseball, which meant I got to call the pitches. A pattern was developing: I liked to be in control.

I was taught as a boy to never, ever brag about myself. My father suggested, "The more you brag, the less you must have to brag about." Someone genuinely secure in himself and his abilities had no need to brag, he said. It simply wasn't done in our family, and on the one or two occasions I tried it, I was sharply ridiculed for it. One afternoon when I was in the eighth grade, I came home with my picture in the school paper as the Man of the Week and showed it off proudly to my sister. Joan just stared at me coolly. "You are about the most conceited little kid I've ever known," she said. She was right, and it did help me to reassess my abilities.

I never heard profanity in our home. My father would not allow me to take a summer job as a caddy at the Emporia Country Club, because he knew I'd be around a kind of language he didn't want me to pick up. I believe to this day that profanity isn't necessary to express anger. I don't want to give the impression that it made me better than anyone else, and it doesn't bother me when other people use it, but I never permitted swearing when our players were on the floor in games or practice. A transgression meant the team had to run sprints. A few years ago Phil Ford, Carolina's great player from 1974 to 1978 and my longtime assistant, said about me, "He never swears. But he has the ability to speak to you in such a way that sometimes you wish he would." That pleased me to no end.

Tobacco and liquor were forbidden in our household as well. That didn't make us uncommon; Kansas was old Prohibition territory. I did start smoking regularly after I left college, and quickly became a heavy smoker. When I was growing up everyone in the movies was smoking. Also Dad told me not to smoke, which made it more attractive. Nicotine was extremely addictive, of course, and I succumbed to it and was a pretty poor example for a number of years. I was finally able to quit smoking in October 1988, and it was one of the best things I ever did.

I suppose you'd call my father a disciplinarian, but the truth is he knew how to get young men, including his son, to behave themselves and to compete hard without having to resort to harsh measures. Take the issue of dinner dishes. Many nights after dinner we would go into the basement and play a game of Ping-Pong. The loser would have to go up and help my mother with the dinner dishes. With the stakes so high, you can imagine how heated the competition was. I made some of the greatest comebacks of my career in that basement. I'd be trailing badly, but the thought of doing dishes would make me frantic. My father would urge me on. "Never give up," he'd say. Somehow I would rally and tie the game. After I'd won, he'd cheerfully tromp back up the stairs and stand at the sink with my mother, his hands in soapy water. We played so often that when I was thirteen, I became the YMCA state champion for my age.

Years later my father told a Carolina sportswriter that it was all by design, that he let me back into those games on purpose to teach me the virtue of never quitting. I find it difficult to accept that he *let* me win. I really believed I mounted those magnificent comebacks on my own. But the more I think about it, there may be something to what he said.

The war came, and in 1941 it seemed as though every great athlete in Emporia—every boy I hero-worshipped—suddenly wore a military uniform instead of a basketball or football jersey and left to ride trains and troopships. We wouldn't see many of them for years, and some we would never see again.

During the war, my parents planted two victory gardens in empty lots directly across the street. People were encouraged to grow as much of their own food as possible during the war as part of the conservation effort, and those victory gardens were a small way of showing patriotism and support for the men and women in the service. We grew everything you could think of: all kinds of vegetables, beans, cabbages, potatoes, carrots, peas. We even grew grapes in our backyard. We cared for those gardens constantly, until I swore I wasn't going to be a farmer or even have a garden when I grew up. It was too much work. "We have to do what we can for the boys overseas," my mother said. "Everyone has to sacrifice."

In the last couple of years, World War II has been rediscovered in books and films as the great American drama of the twentieth century, and while

I'm glad, it's also important to remember that the war wasn't all cinematic heroism. People of all economic levels served side by side, and to my mind, never has there been a greater team effort than that of the American people in World War II. Even the schools would have paper drives collecting old newspapers.

Most servicemen were quite ordinary young men who served in the infantry or Army Air Corps without renown. A Kansas farm boy named Walt Ehlers won a Congressional Medal of Honor at Normandy, and another Kansan named Robert Dole fought with the Tenth Mountain Division in the Italian Alps. Today at the American Legion building in downtown Emporia there is a glass-covered wall that lists the names of the 150 or so young men from the Emporia High School classes of 1937, 1938, and 1939 who served their country; many of them were regular infantrymen. Almost a third of them died overseas. My father had to watch his players march away to those kinds of odds.

Gradually, some of the young men we knew in the service began to come home on furlough. They seemed older and more mature, even though it had only been a few months. Invariably, they all came to visit my father. They would sit on the front porch talking with him about war news and what they had been through. They respected my father because he was the disciplinarian who had gotten them through tough times before, and who had taught them how to endure hardships.

One afternoon in the summer of 1943, Jack Snow showed up on our front doorstep. Jack had won honors playing end on the football team and center on the basketball team for my father in the late '30s, and he had gone on to Emporia State. He had a memorable head of red hair. After Pearl Harbor he joined the Army Air Corps and was stationed in California, and he came home on furlough that summer as a second lieutenant, a bombardier. My father was pleased to see Jack standing in the doorway in his lieutenant's uniform. They sat in the living room talking quietly for a long time.

Just a few weeks later, we got the news that Jack was dead. He had been fatally wounded in action on July 6, 1943, in the Alaskan area. The Aleutian Islands off the western tip of Alaska were the scene of some crucial fighting in the Pacific in 1942 and 1943, and Jack must have been killed in a bombing run.

There were others. Jack McCoy, Jr., Emporia High class of '42 and a star athlete, was one of my personal idols and lived just two blocks away from us. He was a second lieutenant in the Air Corps. He was killed in the air over the Philippines, June 20, 1945.

I still get letters from some of the men who survived the war, like Fred Griffiths, Emporia High class of '37, who writes me regularly from San Diego and who has even visited Chapel Hill for ball games. That should tell you how strongly they felt about my father and what an impact he had on them, and I think their respect for him was what made me become a coach. I don't know of any other relationship that compares to that between a coach and a player, which has its own peculiar emotional sphere, separate even from the parental one. The sharing of work toward a common goal, the mutual shouldering of emotions that go with winning and the disappointments of losing can't be found in any other walk of life. I understand completely now why those men wanted to see Alfred Smith when they returned from the war, and why they chose to talk to him.

The war brought perspective to all of us. Games suddenly didn't seem as important as they once had. My father's fourteen-year career as Emporia's coach was coming to an end. In 1946 he traveled to Wichita to train for a job with the Veterans Administration, and a year later we would move to Topeka so he could go to work for the V.A. aiding the GIs who were coming home. They needed a place to go where they could learn what benefits they were entitled to, and get the help and information that would be vital to them in assimilating back into civilian society.

But first he wanted to coach me for a season. I had never played for him as a schoolboy athlete, but he decided to return to Lowther Junior High for my ninth-grade season so that we could spend it together. I was at the height of my game in the ninth grade. I wouldn't get much better, even in college. I could often make twenty-four of twenty-five free throws, and everybody told me that if I worked at it, I'd make a pretty good prospect. (But when I got to the University of Kansas, I couldn't even make twenty out of twenty-five in practice.)

Baseball was my first love. In a small town like Emporia during the war there wasn't much to do in the summertime except play American Legion baseball, so that's what I did. By the summer between my eight- and ninth-grade years, I was five foot ten and what you'd call an early bloomer. I wouldn't grow any more; I probably measure five nine now. But back then I qualified as a prodigy, and I became the youngest kid to make the local American Legion team. I genuinely thought my future was on the diamond.

You couldn't be an athlete in the 1940s and not revere the game, given the men who were playing it. I was captivated by the Brooklyn Dodgers, with Jackie Robinson at second, Pee Wee Reese at shortstop, Gil Hodges at first, Duke Snider in center, Carl Furillo in right, and Roy Campanella at catcher.

We probably felt about the major leagues the way most kids feel about the NBA today. Our family would drive over to see the Kansas City Blues, a Triple A farm team of the Yankees, and I knew every member of the team by number, including shortstop Phil Rizzuto, second baseman Gerry Priddy, Johnny Sturm at first, and Vince DiMaggio in the outfield.

In 1945, my father interviewed for a job with the American Red Cross in St. Louis, and he took me with him so I could see the Cardinals at Sportsman's Park. It was a major expedition for a boy from Emporia, and for my father too. We took the train to Union Station, and then my father hailed a cab and asked the driver to take us to the Hotel Claridge. It was a long cab ride, lasting at least fifteen or twenty minutes, the meter clicking steadily. Finally, we pulled up in front of the hotel. When we got to our room, my dad pulled back the curtains to show me a view of the city—and there was Union Station, visible beneath us! Still, I got to see the Cardinals in a double-header, so the trip wasn't a total fiasco.

I hung a baseball from a rope attached to the ceiling in our basement, and I would go down in the evenings and on rainy days to take my cuts. I was a switch-hitter, maybe a little better from the left side. Before we had Legion ball I spent the summer playing baseball in the empty lot down the street, catching without a mask. The kid who pitched to me most often throughout my childhood was a neighbor, an all-state pitcher named Dick Hiskey. In 1947, Dick graduated from Emporia, and I moved to Topeka. We wouldn't see each other again until 1958, when I arrived in Chapel Hill as a young assistant coach only to find that the university had just hired a new chemistry professor named Dick Hiskey. It's hard to calculate the long odds of two kids from Emporia, sandlot battery mates, winding up in Chapel Hill together. In 1980 he became the university's faculty chairman of athletics while heading up the chemistry department.

I was so wrapped up in baseball that I even snuck out of church once to play a game. It was no small transgression for me, and certainly not for my parents. My father did not believe in playing games at all on Sundays. Instead, we spent four hours of the day in church. First there was Sunday school, followed by the regular morning service, and in the evenings we went back again for a second service plus youth group. Not a single weekday went by without prayer either. Every evening before dinner we held a short devotional period.

On this particular Sunday, my American Legion team was supposed to travel to Abilene for a game, and the coach announced the bus would be boarding at 11:45 A.M.—right in the middle of services. I was determined to go on the trip, but my father was adamant. "I don't want you playing baseball on Sundays," he said. It was probably the only time in my life that I totally disobeyed him—well, not counting the time in ninth grade I told him I wouldn't play ball unless I could have the car keys. During the service I snuck out the door of the church, walked to the departure point for the bus trip, and hopped on with the team, bound for Abilene.

Back in Emporia, it was a traumatic day for the rest of the Smith family. My parents were deeply upset. A neighbor named Mr. Hubbard made matters worse, from what I heard later. Mr. Hubbard was an elderly local gentleman, and every Sunday different members of the church took on the chore of driving him to and from services. This Sunday it was our turn, unfortunately. In the car after services ended, Mr. Hubbard railed at my father for what I had done. "I cannot believe you would allow your son to play baseball on a Sunday," he said. My father ignored the remark. He had just had a radio installed in his car, and perhaps as a way of telling Mr. Hubbard to mind his business, he turned a ball game on the radio and started listening to it.

Mr. Hubbard was scandalized. "It's just as wrong for you to listen to a ball game as it is for Dean to play in one," he said.

We won the game, but on the trip back I began to wonder whether it had been worth it. The closer we got to Emporia, the more I dreaded facing my father. I was scared to death of the scene I expected to have with him.

Maybe my father was put off by Mr. Hubbard's narrow-mindedness, or maybe his temper cooled over the course of the day. Either way, I was surprised by the welcome I got when I arrived home. There seemed to be no end to my father's patience. Instead of letting me have it, he sat me down and we talked, and at the end of the conversation he struck a deal with me. Under no circumstances was I ever to skip out of church again, he said. But I could play baseball on Sundays as long as it didn't directly interfere with church activities. When there was a conflict, I had to choose the church.

Not long afterwards, a larger event in our lives reminded me that there were more serious matters than the outcome of a baseball game. One of my friends in those years was a boy named Shad Woodruff, a housepainter's son who was just about the best athlete in town. He was the leading dash man on our ninth-grade track team, a top scorer on the basketball team, our baseball center fielder, and my favorite receiver on the football field. He was popular too, an open-natured young man who was impossible to dislike, and his entire family was the same way. His mother, whom we called Boots, was warm and sincere, and kids naturally gravitated to her house.

On the July 4 weekend of the summer of 1945, Shad and I played in an American Legion baseball doubleheader. Afterwards he said he didn't feel too good and decided to go home. By the time he got there, he was so ill he had to be taken to the hospital. The diagnosis was bulbar polio. I hurried to the hospital and stood outside his room, but nobody would let me in to see him, because polio was thought to be so contagious. It was before the Salk vaccine, and polio was epidemic. A lot of communities had quarantines in effect, and we heard stories of kids being confined to their homes and back-yards for whole summers. But I never expected it to visit Emporia like this. Shad and I had shared the same water bucket on the Fourth.

I stood vigil outside Shad's room for most of the day and into the night. Four days later he died. It shattered all of us. Despite the realities of the war, it was the first time I had lost someone truly close to me, my own age, and I struggled to understand it. I found it so impossible to grasp that I spent days leafing through clippings and pictures of Shad. Finally, I took a pair of scissors and began to trim the newspaper clippings into neat squares and paste them into a book. I cut and pasted until I had created an entire album of Shad. I carried the album over to the Woodruffs' and gave the book to Shad's parents. We stayed in touch for the rest of their lives, until they died fifteen or so years ago.

To me, that period was very much about loss. Jack Snow and Shad Woodruff seemed part of the same ungraspable sorrow. One day they were vivid presences in our lives, and the next, they were photographs in an album. I think anyone who grew up during World War II, in that era of victory gardens and polio epidemics and young soldiers poised on the doorstep, must remember their childhoods as bittersweet.

In comparison, ball games offered simplicity. They had a beginning, a middle, and an end. The final score told me everything I needed to know.

My father didn't have to push me into sports; I loved them all. I played any game that involved a ball. By far the tougher job for him was to make sure I had a balanced existence, some notion that there was a life of the mind too—and he was clever at it. When I was in junior high he turned school into a competition by offering to pay me $100 if I got higher marks than Joan did. In three years of junior high school she had gotten just one B. Back then $100 was a princely sum, and the bribe worked so well that I made straight A's. I saved every report card and logged every grade. My father paid me off without a murmur.

In 1947, after my father had spent a year in Wichita training for his post with the Veterans Administration, we moved to Topeka so he could start work there. Joan stayed behind to go to Emporia State University, while I transferred to Topeka High School for my junior year. I was apprehensive about the move, which represented a huge leap for me, and I felt lonesome without Joan, who had become my best friend and confidante as a teenager. But it was probably good for me to widen my horizons. Emporia High had about six hundred students, but Topeka High had twenty-seven hundred, and the building was so sprawling that I actually got lost in it on my first day of school. More than one hundred young men came to football tryouts, and they all seemed big and fast to me. Luckily, two of the starting seniors at Topeka High that year, Ray Ulsh and Paul Fink—who later became principal of the school—took me under their wing. They introduced me around, took me to eat lunch, and made the transition from Emporia to Topeka a lot easier.

I threw myself into the arena where I felt most comfortable: the athletic department. I was a three-sport athlete: a second baseman in baseball, a guard in basketball, and an alternate at starting quarterback on the football team. Topeka was one of the real schoolboy football powers, annually finishing among the top five teams in the state. I called my own plays as the quarterback, and I still loved gambling, fake punts, and surprising plays.

No sooner did I think I was a big deal at Topeka High than I had a setback that reminded me that perhaps it wouldn't be wise to count on a career as a big-time athlete. One night we went to Wichita's Lawrence Stadium for a critical football game before thousands of fans against Wichita North, an archrival ranked number one in the state. With thirty seconds left the score was 7–7. I faded back to pass and looked downfield for Adrian King, a great end who I hoped would catch the game-winning touchdown. I threw the ball, and Wichita North intercepted it and returned it the length of the field for a touchdown. Final score: Wichita North, 14; Topeka, 7. They finished first in the state, and we finished third. Coach D. L. "Heavy" Erwin eventually forgave me for that.

The next year Topeka's football coach was a gentleman named Bob Briggs, who had played football at Kansas State. I was anxious to learn from him, which he must have sensed because he had a way of making me feel valuable even when I made a mistake, and he involved me in the smallest decisions. He taught me that allowing a player to have a voice isn't a bad thing, a policy I borrowed from him later. After calling a play, he would often look at me and say, "What do you think?" He taught me to call one play to set up the second play.

Like any teenager, my biggest worry in moving to Topeka was whether I would ever make new friends. But when basketball season came around I met three other seniors: Bill Bunten, a future member of the state legislature and chairman of the Ways and Means Committee; Charlie Crawford, who would become a Big Seven tennis champion at Kansas University; and Delbert Schuster, who would become an Air Force colonel. With Ulsh and Fink, we all knocked around town together, going to teen centers and dances. Topeka was a thriving industrialized railroad capital full of things to do, and through which five high school boys could cut a wide swath. We liked to listen to Stan Kenton and Count Basie, who came to the Meadow Acres nightclub, where we held our Topeka High formals. My folks and I couldn't believe there would be four formals between Christmas and New Year's. What a social life for our basketball team!

Bill Bunten and I were teammates on Topeka High's basketball team that finished third in the state, and to this day Bill loves to parade around a newspaper headline that says, "Bunten Man of the Hour, Smith on Time Too." There were always four or six of us crowded into Bunten's Buick Roadmaster every night. Yet another friend at Topeka High was a young woman by the name of Nancy Landon Kassebaum (Baker), who dated my friend Charlie Fisk, and who was in Miss Stewart's geometry class with me. Nancy went on to become a Republican senator from Kansas. She was a caring person, and I agreed with her on most issues, even though I'm a Democrat.

In baseball season, I met a cutup type of guy named Bud Roberts, and we became good friends. Bud was a junior like me and a young man who could both worry and smooth over a parent effortlessly, and my mother absolutely adored him. Bud even called her by her first name. When we stayed out late, Bud would show up at the house the next morning and say, "Gosh, I feel so good today, Vesta. I was in bed by ten o'clock last night. By the way, what time did Dean get in?"

Bud could do no wrong with my mother. The summer between my junior and senior years we took a family trip to Greenlake, Wisconsin, for the American Baptist Assembly, and Bud came along with us. I drove part of the way, my mother complaining the entire time about how fast I was going. "Be careful, slow down, you're going too fast," she'd say. Then Bud would take the wheel, and my mother wouldn't say a word. "Now Vesta," Bud would say, "I'll take care of the driving. You just settle back down there and get some rest. Maybe you'd like to fall asleep."

I wasn't a very highly recruited athlete coming out of Topeka High, and I was probably considered more of a football and baseball prospect than I was basketball. The kinds of schools that were interested in me were Emporia State and an American Baptist school called Ottawa. But the school I had my heart set on was the University of Kansas, which I had followed my whole life. When I was three years old, my father went off to Lawrence to complete his master's degree and sent me a postcard from there with a picture of the football stadium on the front. He wrote, "I hope to see you running down the field here one day." He showed me the card about ten years later.

My best bet for college aid wasn't an athletic scholarship but an academic one. I was in a special class of thirteen students at Topeka High that had an extraordinary academic record; there were twelve A's made in the class and one B, mine. *The New York Times* did a story on us, and many of us went on to Ivy League schools. Another in the class was Walter Menninger, who went to Stanford and then became CEO of the famed Menninger Clinic and Foundation. Columbia actually sent a representative to recruit some of us. Columbia asked for my transcript and the rep tried to sell me on their excellent School of Education, but I didn't want to go that far from home.

Kansas wrote me some letters, but didn't offer me a scholarship. I went to Kansas State on a recruiting visit at the invitation of an assistant coach named Tex Winter, the now-legendary L.A. Lakers assistant. Back then he was an aide to Kansas State's head coach, Jack Gardner, and he entertained me for an afternoon in Manhattan. We played some basketball (tryouts were legal then), and then Tex took me to the swimming pool, where he showed off his diving skills, doing half gainers. I found out later he had been a world-class pole vaulter at the University of Southern California. At the end of the day Tex said he could work out an academic scholarship for me and get me a job selling football programs to make some extra money if I wanted to come to school there. Before committing, though, I wanted to find out what the situation was at Kansas.

I was so determined to go to school in Lawrence that I ended up calling them. I heard through my friend Harold Lowe, a Topeka High basketball teammate who had gone on to Kansas, that assistant coach Dick Harp thought I was a decent basketball prospect. I called Dick and asked him if I could visit. I was afraid to call the head coach, the legendary Phog Allen, even though I had met him a handful of times, thanks to my father. I told Dick what Kansas State had offered me, and he said University of Kansas could do the same: give me an academic scholarship based on my strong transcript, and allow me to sell football programs on the side. I jumped at the chance.

2

Leaving Home

I spent my first year at the University of Kansas playing on the freshman football and basketball teams and working to make extra money. In those days freshmen did not compete nor did they have a freshman baseball team. They were ineligible for varsity games, which meant we spent most of our time studying and practicing fundamentals, and to this day I firmly believe it was an excellent policy, one that ought to be revived. Freshmen would be much better off if they spent a year getting on firm ground academically and learning the principles of their sport.

You could make great pay selling football programs, at least $40 for each home game, sometimes as much as $50. Dick Harp also got me a job in the towel room, which was easy work and allowed a lot of time for studying; I could read and hand out towels without even looking up. I didn't stay in that job long because I got the Coke-machine rights at the Phi Gamma Delta fraternity, which meant I earned profits from the soda sales. But it was also a dangerous position to hold because it was considered my fault when the machine malfunctioned. Among my fraternity brothers were some great athletes such as John Amberg, who later played football for the New York Giants, Charlie Hoag, a football All-American, and Bill Hougland, who with Hoag was a member of the 1952 Olympic basketball team, and who carried the American flag in the 1956 Olympics in Melbourne. Jim Potts was the top pole vaulter at KU, and Jack Rodgers was a quarterback for Kansas, who in 1988 would be among the four founders of a little coffeehouse company called Starbucks. (Jack asked me to invest, but I reasoned to myself, *It'll never fly.*) The president of the fraternity was Gil Reich, a transfer from West Point and a *Look* magazine football All-American. My roommates were Hoag, Potts, and Bill Bunten from Topeka, with whom I played a lot of one on one in our spare time.

My football career was short lived. I was third out of six quarterbacks on the freshman depth chart, and I also played a little safety. My gridiron days were typified by one Monday scrimmage when I tried to be a tough guy. Forrest Griffiths, the star fullback on our Kansas team that had been to the Orange Bowl, broke loose on a trap play. I chose to stop him—all five foot ten and 155 pounds of me—and I hit him as hard as I could. He knocked me cold. The next thing I heard was the sound of head coach J. V. Sikes yelling. "Get this ———— guy off the field," Sikes said. "We have work to do."

After the season I went to Sikes and asked him what my chances were of ever playing. Sikes was a nice man off the field, and he leveled with me. "As I see it, Dean, you're going to be sixth, at best, on the depth chart for spring practice. But Doctor Allen tells me that if you work hard and improve, you have a chance to be a second-string guard in basketball. So for your sake, maybe you should concentrate on that." I listened to his advice and gave up football.

I went on to have a far more acceptable basketball career than I had a right to expect under Forrest C. "Phog" Allen. I wasn't always conscious of it at the time, but in Allen and his invaluable assistant Dick Harp, I had met two of the most interesting basketball authorities the game has ever known. It was impossible to play for those men and not learn something. Moreover, I got to play for them during a heyday when Kansas won the 1952 national championship and missed repeating in 1953 by just 2 points. Harp was a slender, distinguished man with a fiercely loyal nature, a quiet style, but an astute mind. Allen was more garrulous and peculiar, with a habit of coaching in homilies. He'd say things like, "You've got to win in your own backyard if you want to feel strong." Or, "Dean, you can't stop at every dog that barks or you'll never get the mail delivered."

It was typical of Allen that he discovered osteopathy before anyone really knew what it was. He got his degree in osteopathy in 1912 because he felt that he would be ahead of other coaches if he knew how to prevent injuries and how to heal the ones that did occur. Osteopathy is a system of medical practice based on a theory that disease is chiefly due to a loss of structural integrity that can be restored by bone and muscle manipulation. He liked to be called "Doc," but I had such respect for him that I couldn't quite say it. I usually swallowed the word or whispered it. Finally, I decided on a compromise and called him "Doctor Allen."

Doc Allen must have had a gift for osteopathy, because he gained a national reputation in the field and was always working with athletes from other sports who came to see him. He carried his massage table everywhere and would try to get people to lie down on it so he could adjust their sacroiliacs. He thought an adjustment to the sacroiliac would cure just about anything. Yankee Johnny Mize came to Doc to rehab a shoulder injury, Joe Page came, as did Mickey Mantle, before he was so well known. I'll never forget when I glimpsed Mantle running around the basketball court one day. I was astounded by him: He had the build of a fullback but real quickness, the kind of speed you had to see in person to believe.

Undergraduates are a skeptical bunch, so Doc Allen's players didn't know quite what to make of his medical practice, and we even made fun of it. But he cured some of us of that early on. One day a professor came to the gym doubled over and in so much pain he could barely walk. Doc Allen worked on him for a while. The professor walked out of there ramrod straight, as if nothing were wrong. We players figured it was a put-on—that he was a friend of Doc's and it was prearranged—but now I'm certain Doc actually helped him.

Not everybody believed in osteopathy the way Doc Allen did. A few years later, when I went to Chapel Hill to interview for my first job there as an assistant to Frank McGuire, Frank told me a funny story. He spent some time with Doc Allen right after Kansas won the 1952 championship. Doc and Frank were on a college all-star tour with the Harlem Globetrotters, and they were roommates.

"How you doing?" Doc Allen said to Frank.

"Gosh, Doc," Frank said. "I have this awful headache."

"Take off your pants," Doc said.

Frank backed up and said, "Whoa! For a headache? Don't you come close to me!"

Doc was charismatic, flamboyant, and opinionated, with a penchant for wearing brightly colored clothes and a love for being on center stage. But he was also conservative, a staunch Kansas Republican, and a longtime Sunday-school teacher in his Methodist church. He lived in a small house all of his life, and I think he was quite happy with it. He was nearing the end of his career when I played for him, and as he got older, he could be absentminded. But he had loyal assistant Dick Harp to keep him on track.

We had just beaten Creighton, 65–47, in Omaha on December 10, 1951, when we stopped at a restaurant for a postgame meal. After we ate and boarded the bus, Doc sat in his seat studying the bill closely. He was as frugal with the university's money as he was with his own. "This isn't right," he said, and got off the bus. He marched back in to question the manager. After a while, Doc came back out of the restaurant, but instead of getting on our bus, he took a wrong turn and got on a city bus. The players roared with laughter. But Harp leaped out of his seat and told us to be quiet. He sent a manager to rescue Doc from the city bus, and turned to the rest of us. "If any of you utter one word, if I hear one laugh or even a murmur, you'll answer to me tomorrow," he said. That was typical of Dick's loyalty.

When it came to basketball Doc Allen was extremely creative, and he was a spellbinding motivator. As a player, I wasn't always sure what Doc was getting at, but I learned not to question him. Early in that 1952 season we were playing in an exhibition game when Doc said, "I want to see the four-man weave against the zone." I went over to Dick Harp and said, "Dick, we can't weave against the zone."

"Shut up, Smith, and do what Doc said!"

Doc just wanted movement because he thought we were standing around too much. Even if I didn't always follow his thinking, from then on I knew there was an ulterior motive to what he asked of us.

Doc believed players shouldn't get tired. His players knew that if they asked to sit on the bench for a rest they might never get back in the game. Also, he believed in fundamentals to the point that we would work on just pivoting for ten and fifteen minutes at a time. A typical practice would last three hours, or longer if we didn't get done what he wanted, but we were the soundest team around in our fundamentals.

Another of Doc's pet theories was that the basket should be raised to a height of twelve feet instead of ten feet. He even had four goals in our gym set at twelve feet. He thought it would be a better game with the basket at twelve feet, because he believed it would make big men less dominant and force them to develop into better all-around players. I disagreed with him on that one; I felt that raising the baskets would actually emphasize the big man, since more shots would be missed, and rebounding would be even more important.

Our 1952 Kansas team went 28–3 and won the national championship with me coming off the bench sparingly. I was simply one of eleven lettermen on an eighteen-man team. That team employed a great innovation: a pressure man-to-man defense that absolutely smothered opponents by overplaying. The idea was to cut off the passing lanes and make it hard to complete even the simplest pass. This was unheard of at the time, really the first instance of man pressure as we now know it. The closest thing to it was Henry Iba's 20 Defense at Oklahoma State, which was a half-court man-to-man pressure defense, but the Kansas defense was a far more extreme version.

The Kansas defense had a lasting influence on the game. In the summer of 1953 Phil Woolpert, the great coach from the University of San Francisco, came to study it with Dick Harp. His USF teams went on to win NCAA championships in 1955 and 1956, although that might have had something to do with the presence of a great shot blocker underneath the basket named Bill Russell and a pressuring guard named K. C. Jones. The defense stood the test of time, too. This is how innovative it truly was: Almost exactly forty years later in the 1991 Final Four, I couldn't help noticing that all four teams—Carolina, Duke, Las Vegas, and Kansas—used schemes that stemmed from that first Kansas pressure defense.

We won fifteen straight games after Doc Allen implemented the defense. We beat Texas Christian University, 68–64, in the first round of the national tournament, and then knocked off St. Louis and Santa Clara in order to reach the championship game in Seattle, where we defeated a St. John's team coached by my future boss, Frank McGuire, 80–63. I played just sparingly, about three minutes against Santa Clara, and I got onto the floor for the last twenty-nine seconds of the title game.

That year of 1952 was also an Olympic cycle, and in those days the NCAA champion entered the trials as a team, so we all went to New York for tryouts. We had a couple of big nights out, touring the Latin Quarter and the Copacabana, where Doc Allen worried about how much everything cost. Usually Doc pored over every dinner check, and he had been known to argue with the waiter if he thought the bill was too high. But on this trip Dick Harp convinced him to pick up the tab for us to go to the shows and clubs. "I didn't know how to spend money until I came to New York and Dick showed me how," Doc joked.

Kansas ultimately sent seven players to the Olympics in Helsinki, and I was briefly named as an alternate before I got bumped. The Kansas board of regents was so thrilled with our season that it began fund-raising for the three alternates to go to Helsinki (which was legal in those days). They raised enough money to send our first two alternates, B. H. Born and Larry Davenport, but were just shy of the $1,500 needed to send me. As a consolation they gave me the leftover cash, which was about $300. I decided to put my expense money toward a car instead, since I was about to be a college senior and had never owned one. I had my eye on a 1940 Chevy, but I was still $100 short, so my sister, Joan, kicked in the rest from her own hard-earned money, which was like her. But since I had never had a car, I didn't know about things like upkeep. During my senior year we took a road trip to Stillwater to play Oklahoma State, and while we were away there was a hard freeze. I had neglected to put any antifreeze in the car, and it was ruined.

Kansas came within 2 points of repeating as national champions in 1953, despite the fact that we were an inexperienced young team picked to finish no better than the middle of our conference. We had lost a great All-American and Olympian, Clyde Lovellette, to graduation as well as three other starters, including the player who would go on to captain the 1956 Olympic team, Bill Hougland. Charlie Hoag, a returning Olympian, saw his brilliant athletic career end because of a knee he'd injured in football, so I was just one of two returning seniors. I was cast in a sixth-man role. But we had some great competitors who were ready to step up, such as Gil Reich, Harold Patterson, and Al Kelley, who played on the 1960 Olympic team for coach Pete Newell.

Captain Dean Kelley, the other senior on the team, and I began to think we knew more than the coaches. Our starting center was the six-ten B. H. Born, and behind him was a six-six talent from Pittsburg, Kansas, by the name of Eldon Nicholson, who had better passing and shooting skills. Early in the season Dean and I went to Dick Harp and told him straight out we thought Nicholson should be playing more than Born.

"Would you mind letting us coach the team?" Dick snapped.

Born ended up an All-American and the MVP of the Final Four in 1953, which shows just how much we knew. Nicholson failed to receive much playing time. Kansas fooled everybody, winning the Big Seven conference title and finishing third in the polls, and we got all the way to the championship game again before we suffered a disappointing loss to Indiana, 69–68.

As my career wore on, I still harbored faint hopes of being able to play a sport professionally. My best chance, I felt, was in baseball. I was named starting catcher for Kansas in my sophomore year, and caught our top pitcher, Carl Sandefur. I told myself that players got discovered and signed to big league contracts all the time.

My roommate for road games was Galen Fiss, the son of a wheat farmer from Johnson, Kansas. Galen was our second-string catcher, with a great arm to second base, and he was also a tremendous football player, a fullback and linebacker. We were on a trip at Iowa State one afternoon when there was a knock on our hotel room door. I opened it. The gentleman at the door introduced himself as a scout for the Cleveland Indians.

I felt a slow flush of excitement. He was for real. It was happening.

Then he spoke. "I'd like to talk to Fiss," he said.

What a letdown! The scout wanted to talk to our second-string catcher. But Galen wouldn't be second string for long. He alternated with me as a starter in my junior year, and he would go on to do far more substantial things as an athlete than I would have. Drafted by the Cleveland Browns, he chose to play baseball for the Indians instead. He was hitting over .300 in the minors when he suffered a terrible beaning that left him with impaired vision. He gave up baseball, went back to football, and captained the Cleveland Browns defense for a number of years.

By the time I was ready to graduate from Kansas my only remaining ambition was to become a high school teacher and coach, unless the ADA Oilers would sign me for amateur basketball. My father told me to make sure I came out of college accredited to teach high school math, because, as he reasoned, "It's harder for schools to find math teachers than it is for them to find physical education teachers."

Doc Allen wanted me to be a doctor. His son, Bob, was a doctor, and he thought medicine would be a good calling for me too. "Don't go into coaching," Doc would say. "Too many ups and downs. Too much heartache."

But I was my parents' son.

3

Becoming a Coach

I studied mathematics, so I can say with some authority that the odds of my becoming anything other than a coach were nonexistent. When you deal in odds and probability you deal in options. The fact is, coaching was what I really wanted to do, whether it be football, basketball, or baseball.

The first real coaching I did was during my junior year at Kansas, when Doc Allen asked me to teach our offenses and defenses to the football players who, having finished their season, joined the basketball squad late. I thought he must consider me fairly insignificant to send me off to the side for thirty minutes each practice, tutoring other players. Still, Dick Harp told me, it would save him and Doc time, and give me practical coaching experience.

While I was in college the Korean War erupted. At the end of my freshman year in 1950, most of KU's football and basketball players had signed up for Air Force ROTC on the advice of our coaches, who told us it would keep us out of the draft. But it also meant we would face two years of active duty at the completion of our senior years. Still, it was sound advice. Bud Laughlin, Kansas's starting fullback and a fraternity brother, took a gamble and didn't sign up for ROTC, and he was indeed drafted. Bud was a highly recruited player from Kansas City, Missouri, and Kansas alums were so upset at losing him to the army that that they accused Missouri loyalists of pulling strings to get him drafted.

I graduated in the spring of 1953, a two-year service commitment ahead of me with the rank of second lieutenant. We had our basic training in the summer before our senior year. Those of us in ROTC were told we weren't likely to be called to active duty before the spring of '54, so I had to support myself until then. Doc Allen offered me two opportunities: I could take a job teaching math and coaching in Haven, Kansas, at $6,000 a year, or I could stay at the university as an assistant to Dick Harp in coaching the freshman team and assist Doc and Dick with varsity practices, without pay. I didn't think twice about the money; I just wanted to coach. Doc called the Lawrence Paper Company and secured a position for me in the accounting department, where I worked from 8 A.M. to 2 P.M. before reporting to the gym.

But I still felt more like a player than a coach. When I was offered a chance to play semipro basketball for the National Gypsum Company in Parsons, Kansas, at Christmastime of 1953, I jumped at the chance. I worked a desk job in quality control, but my real job was to play for their AAU team at a very good salary. I was hoping to eventually play for a team being organized by a Kansas graduate named Bud Adams, who was putting together a franchise called the ADA Oilers. Adams later owned another franchise, the NFL Houston Oilers.

My Air Force orders came through in April 1954. I was assigned briefly to Lackland Air Force Base in San Antonio and then Scott Air Force Base outside of St. Louis for school in communications. During this period I wed Ann Cleavinger, a fellow Kansas student whom I had met on graduation night, introduced by her twin brother, Hal. Ann was an intern in occupational therapy in Topeka in the summer of 1953, and we dated throughout the year and married before I was sent overseas in 1954. She was artistic, industrious, and frank. She was gifted as an occupational therapist and years later, the doctors with whom she worked talked her into coming out of retirement twice.

I shipped out to Germany in late September. I handled the cruise across the Atlantic well enough until I was ordered below to check on some enlisted airmen, most of whom were sick and throwing up. I was miserable from then on. When I arrived in Germany in the fall of 1954, I announced that I would never travel by water again. Ann had stayed behind for her last rotation at the Mayo Clinic in Minneapolis, but she joined me in December.

My tour of Germany lasted just over a year and I spent much of that time on the basketball court, thanks to General Blair Garland. When Garland wasn't dealing with weightier matters he was a passionate college basketball fan, and it was no accident that most of the young officers he assigned to Andrews Air Force Base near Washington, D.C., were renowned ballplayers. There were Cliff Hagen, Frank Ramsey, C. M. Newton, and Lou Tsioropoulous of Kentucky; Dean Kelley and Bob Kenney of Kansas; and Dick Knostman and Bob Rousey of Kansas State. The Andrews team dominated armed forces competitions, which persuaded Garland that the Air Force should have a team in Europe too. He thought it would boost Air Force morale on the continent.

The team was based at Fürstenfeldbruck AFB near Munich, and I was assigned to it along with two players from Bradley University who had played for an NCAA championship, Dick Estergard and Ron Johnson, as well as Mac Cramer, who had played at the Naval Academy. Our coach was a captain and former World War II bombardier named Jack Schwall. We won the USAF championship in Europe, but in the midst of the tournament in Wiesbaden my daughter, Sharon Ann, was born. We had a day off between games, so I hitched a ride on a C-47 back to base so I could be with Ann. She had Sharon in the middle of the night, and as soon as I knew everything was all right I flew back to the tournament that next morning and played on no sleep. I played one of my best games, and we qualified for the Worldwide Air Force Championships in Orlando, where we lost to, you guessed it, the Andrews Air Force Base team stocked by General Garland!

In our second season most of the guys were transferred to Bitburg with the entire AACS wing, but I stayed since I had orders to return to the States before Christmas. I became player-coach of the new squad, which was made up mostly of a great group of enlisted men. We went 11–1 before I was shipped back home. On my leaving, the team gave me an engraved Rolex watch, which touched me and which I still treasure.

To show you what a devotee of the game Garland was, in the summer of '55 he arranged for basketball legends Red Auerbach, Bob Cousy, and Adolph Rupp to come to Lanscaster, Germany, to put on a clinic for Army and Air Force personnel. I was assigned the job of finding players to serve as demonstrators. One of the guys we brought in was a young Army private from Brooklyn named Sid Cohen, who showed a lot of ability. Three years later in August before I arrived at North Carolina as an assistant to Frank McGuire, Frank told me he was in the midst of recruiting a New Yorker named Sid Cohen. "I know all about him," I said. But it turned out we were late getting to Cohen. Another coach already had him wrapped up: Adolph Rupp.

During the clinic in Germany I played some one on one with Cousy, and he took me inside and hurt me with that hook shot of his. Afterwards, I went to the Officers Club to say hello to General Garland and thank him for assigning me to Fürstenfeldbruck and for making my time in the service so pleasant. Garland, Rupp, and the base colonel were seated at the head table having lunch when I arrived, still in my sweats. "Hello, General, I'm Dean Smith and I want to thank you for all you've done," I said. Garland seemed pleased to see me, even out of uniform, and asked the colonel to move down a table to make room for me. When I saw Coach Rupp again in 1960, he was still talking about how General Blair Garland moved a base colonel so I could sit down in my sweats and have lunch with him. Rupp came to speak at a North Carolina banquet and told the story. "I wonder about the priorities of the Air Force," Rupp said, to laughs.

One of the more interesting fliers stationed in Europe at that time was Major Bob Spear, who had piloted a B-54 in the Berlin airlift of 1948. Spear was not only a decorated pilot, he was also a nationally ranked tennis player and an outstanding basketball coach who had coached at the Naval Academy as assistant to Ben Carnevale. Later, in retirement, he pursued his second love and became a painter of some note. But then he was coaching an Air Force team in Châteauroux, France, and when our Fürstenfeldbruck team traveled to France to play his squad, he invited me to his house to talk about the 1953 Kansas team and our pressure defense. We hit it off and became instant friends.

On that visit, Bob told me he was going back to the States to become head coach at the new Air Force Academy. When we ran into each other again not long after the USAFE tournament in Wiesbaden, Bob asked me to consider being his assistant. I told him I was planning to go back to the University of Kansas as a second assistant after my tour of duty was up in April 1956. But I told him I would consider it if he could work through the Air Force bureaucracy. That summer I heard from personnel that if I signed an "indefinite" commitment guaranteeing the service a minimum of one more year, I would be assigned to the Air Force Academy. I called up Bob and said if he was sure the orders would come through, then I would love to be his assistant.

In December 1955 my family and I left Germany and took up residence at the temporary academy headquarters at Lowry Air Force Base in Denver. I was one of a number of first lieutenants at the new academy, many of them West Point graduates, brought in to train the first class of cadets. It was a wonderful social situation and pleasant tour of duty, thanks to Bob's wife, Dottie, one of the best hostesses I ever met. The athletic department was staffed with many athletes who had joined the ROTC, such as former NFL star and TV commentator Tom Brookshier, with whom we played a lot of bridge. One part of the job was easy: We never had to worry about curfew for our players. That was well taken care of.

While we were at Lowry, daughter Sandra JoDean was born in September 1956 and son Scott Edwards Smith was born in June 1958. Most evenings I'd eat dinner, help Ann put the children to bed, and then go over to Bob Spear's house to watch film for hours, trying to learn my new job. Many nights our whole family would dine in the backyard of the Spears' house on Grape Street in Denver.

The worst few days of my life up to that point came in August 1956. One day our daughter Sharon, who was sixteen months old, became ill. Ann and I took her to the Lowry pediatrician, who told us she had a mild touch of pneumonia and advised us to take her home and put a vaporizer in her room to help her breathing. At about five o'clock the next morning we were awakened by the sound of Sharon gasping for breath, her chest rattling badly. Every intake of breath seemed to rack her entire body.

Panicked, we called the doctor. He listened as we described her breathing, and he told us to rush her to Fitzsimmons Army Hospital. We wrapped Sharon up and hurried her out to the car, and as I turned the ignition, I glanced at the gas gauge. The needle was on empty.

I was raised with a great deal of faith, but I also knew that it doesn't work to pray for gasoline on an empty tank. Fitzsimmons was at least three miles from us. Ann was nine months pregnant with our second child. She could deliver any day, or any moment. I didn't want to frighten her any more than she was already frightened.

I looked at Sharon, heaving in Ann's arms, and realized that she was losing color. I had no choice. I stepped on the accelerator and held it there and drove upwards of 70 mph through the city streets to the hospital. Somehow, we had enough gas to make it.

Sharon was turning blue as we pulled up to the emergency entrance of Fitzsimmons Hospital. A nurse was waiting outside, and she grabbed Sharon out of my arms and rushed her through the doors. Inside, doctors performed an emergency tracheotomy.

It was touch and go; we weren't certain she would make it. Ann and I alternated at her bedside around the clock. It was a devastating time for both of us. I felt there was no way I could go on without my child. Absolutely no way.

Sharon's illness was a turning point for me. I knew that I had been altered. Throughout college, and then my tour in the Air Force, I didn't really take family or personal devotional time seriously in the way I had growing up. I hadn't prayed very much, either. I went to the Air Force chapel every other week or so. But during the four days that Sharon was in the hospital I began to read the Bible again and I prayed. I prayed for Sharon, and I prayed for her doctors.

After three days Sharon was off the critical list, but she still had some tough days ahead, and fortunately my parents had arrived to help out. Then Ann went into labor. (A favorite writer of mine, Catherine Marshall, once wrote that "Out of the pit of life comes creativity." I believe that, just as I believe that in order to have light, you need dark.) On September 4, 1956, while Sharon was still in the hospital recovering, our second child, Sandra JoDean Smith, was born. As it happened, Ann, Sharon, and Sandy all left the hospital on the same day with help from Grandpa Smith.

Basketball at the Air Force Academy was an exercise in making the absolute most out of less. First of all, the school had a size limit of six foot four. Any bigger and pilots wouldn't fit in the cockpits of the basic trainers. The cadets had to pass a flight physical and score a minimum of 2400 on the four parts of the old SATs to even be considered for admission. And since the academy was brand new, every single one of our players was a true freshman.

The elements against us were overwhelming. But Bob Spear learned at the Naval Academy to figure out ways to beat teams who had better players. There were ways to go about it—and sometimes you had to invent new ways of playing. Bob was a patient teacher who exuded tremendous confidence to the cadets, and I can't think of anyone who would have done a better job in that environment, not even the greats of the era such as Adolph Rupp, Doc Allen, or anyone else I knew of. He made me feel a part of the decision-making process, allowing me to implement ideas such as the Shuffle offense and some of the KU defensive principles. My confidence as a coach grew tremendously because of my experience with him. Because the job is almost impossible in basketball, as opposed to some other Olympic-type sports, he will probably go down as the only basketball coach with a consistent winning record there.

The cadets had virtually no free time because of their heavy course loads and military requirements. They rose at dawn to march and then went to class, and it was remarkable that they had an ounce of energy left for basketball practice, so by necessity our workouts were brief and crisp. We had to learn a severe form of time management since we were under strict orders not to keep them longer than two hours at practice. That included their shower time as well.

No one attends a service academy if his ultimate goal is the NBA. Basketball as a priority was way down the list for most cadets. Still, they gave all they had in each practice and game, and I loved working with them. The young men who played for us were committed to fly for three years after graduating, and shortly the commitment would be lengthened to five years. You had to respect their work ethic; they were bright and attentive and devoted. This is just how bright they were: The Academy produced thirty-one Rhodes scholars in the next thirty-eight years.

We played our first varsity schedule in the 1956–57 season, won eleven games and lost ten, and we considered that a triumph, given our restrictions. There was something deeply gratifying in watching the cadets' improvement, and in the masterful job Spear did teaching them how to compensate for their competitive disadvantages.

There was great camaraderie among the athletic department staff at the academy. We were all lieutenants and captains working in the same building, and we became great friends. What's more, we all recruited together as representatives of our university, not just for our individual sports. The academy saw us as goodwill ambassadors who were supposed to introduce the new "West Point of the Air." The first football coach hired by Colonel Bob Whitlow was Buck Shaw from the San Francisco 49ers, who had beat out an assistant with the New York Giants named Vince Lombardi. Shaw was succeeded by the brilliant Ben Martin, who brought in a fellow named Pepper Rodgers as one of his offensive assistants. Pepper was unapologetically cocky, always bragging about something, and could back it up, particularly when it came to his tennis game and football coaching. The rest of the coaches on both staffs knew something Pepper didn't: that Bob Spear had been a nationally ranked tennis player at DePauw University in Indiana. We would go behind Pepper's back and try to persuade Bob to play him. Bob said he didn't want to embarrass Pepper, but finally we talked him into it. As soon as Bob agreed, we raced over and began taunting Pepper.

"You think you're so good in tennis, but Bob Spear could beat you six-love," we said.

Pepper smirked and said, "Jack Kramer couldn't beat me six-love."

All of the coaches gathered to watch the long-awaited match, with Bob still protesting, "I don't want to embarrass Pepper." We had to talk him into it all over again. But he played, and in grand fashion won by the predicted 6–love. All of us got a huge kick out of it on the sidelines. But Pepper—cocky as always—acted as if nothing at all happened.

"Next set," he snapped. "Your serve."

The only person that day who actually felt sorry for Pepper was Jim Conboy, the athletic trainer and physical therapist for the academy. Jim was that type of man, a deeply compassionate and warm human being whose gracious personality kept Bob Spear and me from getting technical fouls on the bench. Jim was a common thread who bound together each of the cadet classes, forty of them altogether, until he died suddenly in October 1998. His funeral had to be one of the largest ever at the academy chapel.

Air Force was becoming a team to be reckoned with. In 1957–58, our second varsity season, we went 17–6. Once again, we had a team with no seniors and a severe height restriction: Our starters stood six one, six one, six feet, six four, and six four. Our leading scorer was Bob Beckel, who was an honorable mention All-American. In 1984, the National Association of Basketball Coaches chose a twenty-fifth anniversary team of players who went on to achieve significant things after their college years, and Beckel was one of them. He was a member of the Air Force Thunderbirds and had achieved the rank of lieutenant general before retiring to be president of New Mexico Military Institute.

No matter how many games we won, we were never allowed to forget that we were still in the Air Force. Spear and I always wore civilian clothes on the bench. In that second season we went to Creighton in Omaha, where a future NBA coach named Bill Fitch was a young assistant. The trip to Omaha meant more than the average road game for the cadets because Omaha was home to the Strategic Air Command under General Curtis LeMay.

We lost to Creighton, and in front of LeMay too, who had come to the game to root us on. When we got back to the academy, Spear got a call from the superintendent. LeMay wanted to know why we weren't in uniform for the game. We were just relieved he didn't ask why we lost.

Innovation is a funny thing. Often it's not as much a matter of sweeping change or a bolt of enlightenment as it is of small increments and contributions from a variety of people. Often it grows out of desperation or tough circumstances. A perfect example was the way Spear and I developed strategies at Air Force to compensate for the height and practice restrictions.

Our defense grew out of something that I saw happen on that 1953 Kansas team when we were runner-up for a national championship. One of our key players was a six-foot-one guard named Al Kelley who had a peculiar habit on defense. Whenever the ball handler would dribble toward Al, Al would leave his man to run and surprise the dribbler, attempting to steal the ball. Al got criticized by Doc Allen for going off on his own agenda, but it lent us an element of surprise—even if it sometimes surprised his own team as much as the opponent. I always thought it was an effective element of our defense, and when I became an assistant coach at the Air Force it came back to me.

Spear and I racked our brains trying to think up ways to neutralize the Air Force size disadvantage; we had to find a way to disguise our weaknesses and cause problems for the opponent. One afternoon I mentioned the Al Kelley technique to Bob. Bob was excited by the idea, and we implemented a form of it. We ended up using it after made foul shots and in catch-up situations.

A few years later, when I became head coach at North Carolina, I returned to the concept yet again and expanded on it, turning it into a full-fledged defense and not just a special situation. We called it the Run and Jump (really it should be called the Run and Surprise), and used it consistently for the next fourteen years. In my fifteenth season it underwent yet another permutation when I asked the original defender to stay on the dribbler, and create a double-team out of our normal man-to-man pressure. It became known as our Scramble defense. And that's how creativity happens—it grows out of something as unconscious as a nineteen-year-old's instinct to attack in 1953.

I learned another lesson in innovation from Clair Bee, or "Mister Bee," as everyone called him, the legendary coach from Long Island University. Clair was a beloved member of the collegiate coaching ranks until a gambling scandal hit college basketball (and some LIU and CCNY players among others) in 1951, causing his school to deemphasize the sport. Clair was so crushed by the scandal that he left the collegiate game, his real love, to become a coach, general manager, and part owner of the Baltimore Bullets.

But then the Baltimore team went bankrupt, and Clair lost nearly everything, save for his farm in Roscoe, New York. Clair refused to file for bankruptcy; his pride would not allow it. Instead he declared, "I'll pay back every cent." Clair went to his farm and started writing in an attempt to earn some money. The result was the famed Chip Hilton sports stories, classics of the sports-literature genre. One day in the early 1970s I got a call from Clair. "This is the happiest day of my life," he said. "I've now paid back every cent."

When I was at the Air Force Academy I read a book by Clair on the 1–3–1 zone, which gave Bob Spear and me the "seeds" for a new matchup defense that we called The Point. We used it at the academy, and it's still being used at North Carolina. Most of my former assistants who went on to head coaching jobs—except for those in the pros, which don't allow zones—also use it.

I learned something important from Clair Bee about creativity that had nothing to do with basketball. He told me that he once met Ernest Hemingway in a bar in Cuba. Clair asked Hemingway, "How do you learn to write?" Hemingway replied, "By writing every day."

Bob Spear encouraged me to go to clinics and hang around older coaches, picking their brains. In 1956 I chose to go to Spirit Lake, Iowa, to hear a lecture by Henry Iba, the Oklahoma State coach, who had one of the best minds in the game. I went up to reintroduce myself to Mr. Iba after he lectured, reminding him I had played for Kansas. "I remember you, Dean," he said. "Let's get some lunch."

He invited me back to his room, and I canceled a golf date. It was too important an opportunity to pass up. We went back to Mr. Iba's room for what was supposed to be a short visit—and talked basketball for the rest of the afternoon. I took notes on everything he said and after three hours had filled an entire booklet. It was an individual tutorial from one of the best basketball teachers of all time. Mr. Iba explained his fundamental philosophies to me. On defense, he preferred a soft-sagging help defense; any player who tried to go down the middle against an Iba team was pretty certain to get mugged. On offense, he believed in ball control and a low-scoring game. I asked him why he chose ball control, and he said he played on a team in Missouri once that was beaten by an embarrassing 50 points, and he had never gotten over it. He vividly remembered riding on the back of a truck after the game, thinking, *That will never happen to any team I coach.* And it didn't.

We used some ball control at Air Force as another way of equalizing things between us and the opponent, although we did fast break. We employed the Shuffle offense, which we borrowed from another terrific coach, Bruce Drake at Oklahoma. I had learned the Shuffle at Kansas while trying to prepare to play the Sooners. The Shuffle was an offense in which all five players played all five positions, making constant cuts with good ball movement. The Shuffle could drive the opposition crazy. It was a perfect man offense for Air Force, since all of our players could play inside or outside. Bob fell in love with the Shuffle and continued to perfect it until he resigned as coach. Also, it's not easy to force tempo on a team as well drilled as the cadets were. In 1960, a couple of years after I left the school, Air Force would upset national power Marquette, coached by the irreverent Al McGuire, with that bothersome Shuffle. Afterwards, Al joked that he would never schedule an academy match again. "Those cadets said 'yes sir, no sir' to the officials all day long," Al said, "and we never got a call."

The Air Force Academy was constantly upsetting higher-ranked opponents under Bob Spear. The cadets beat Pete Newell's UC-Berkeley team on the road, and lost by just 2 points to UCLA, coached by John Wooden. His philosophy was perfect for an academy, and Ben Carnevale later implemented much of it at Navy, where he too beat quite a few people, including our North Carolina 1959 team in the NCAA tournament. Bob believed in what we were doing so much that years later, when I was head coach at North Carolina, he got upset when I moved away from the Shuffle philosophically. But I promised him I would always keep our basic cut of the Shuffle, and I did.

One of the most memorable upsets Bob Spear pulled off came over Oklahoma State, coached by Mr. Iba, shortly after I left the academy to move to Chapel Hill. The game ended with a funny incident. My replacement as assistant coach was a captain named Joe Bradley, who had played for Mr. Iba. It was February 1961, and Air Force was in Stillwater to meet Oklahoma State. The cadets made Joe Bradley a bet: If Air Force could do the unthinkable and somehow beat that Oklahoma State team coached by the great Iba, then Bradley would have to shake hands with Iba afterwards and say, "Nice game, Hank."

I never met anybody in basketball who didn't have a respect bordering on reverence for Mr. Iba, and that's why everyone called him "Mister," just like we called Clair Bee "Mister" long after he had quit coaching. It was a show of respect and the natural way of addressing them, given their knowledge and experience. They didn't ask for that kind of formal address, but we wanted to give it to them.

Well, Air Force pulled off the upset, 52–46. All of the cadets, as well as Bob Spear, hung around to see what happened when Joe Bradley addressed his former coach and mentor.

Joe approached him slowly, extended his hand, and said, "Nice game . . . Mister Iba."

4

Coming to Chapel Hill

There was nothing in my first meeting with Frank McGuire that should have suggested to him that I was a young man with a future.

Bob Spear was always encouraging me to hang around older coaches, so he invited me to the 1957 NCAA coaches convention held during the Final Four in Kansas City. Those conventions were good opportunities for young assistants like me to make contacts and pick up ideas, but I had an even better reason for being there: My alma mater, Kansas, was in the Final Four along with North Carolina, Michigan State, and San Francisco.

I still felt a part of the Kansas program. I had coached three of the Jayhawks' senior starters—Maurice King, Johnny Parker, and Gene Elstun—when they were just freshmen. A fourth member of that team was a sophomore named Wilt Chamberlain, and the head coach was my former coach Dick Harp, who had replaced the retired Doc Allen.

Each year at the Final Four, the same four coaches roomed together: North Carolina's McGuire, Naval Academy coach Ben Carnevale, Air Force coach Spear, and University of Denver coach Hoyt Brawner. They were old friends and Navy veterans. McGuire and Carnevale were buddies dating back to World War II, when they were stationed in Chapel Hill together in the Navy V-5 training program. Spear had been stationed with Ben at the

Naval Academy as an assistant coach before he was sent to Europe. Brawner had also served in the Navy with Carnevale and McGuire.

At the 1957 Final Four, they shared a huge two-bedroom suite at the Continental Hotel. When Spear invited me to come to the Final Four, he told me I'd have to sleep on a roll-away bed in the living room, which was fine with me. All I wanted to do was watch Kansas and listen to the conversation. I found McGuire to be dapper and charming, but very much a New Yorker. "Whoever heard of anybody named Dean?" McGuire said. "Where I come from, you become a dean. You're not *named* Dean."

Circumstances grew complicated in the suite. Kansas beat San Francisco in the semifinals, while in the other semifinal Carolina survived three overtimes to beat Michigan State. So now Carolina was to play Kansas in the national title game. I still had deep emotional ties to the Jayhawks, and here I was sleeping in Frank's living room. Before the game McGuire asked me whom I would pull for.

"I'm going to stay with the alma mater," I said.

During the first half of the game I sat with Spear and Carnevale, but they were rooting for North Carolina because they were such pals of McGuire's. I couldn't stand it. I didn't see eye to eye with either of them, and we disagreed on every officiating call. I decided to change seats at halftime. "I'll see you guys later," I said disgustedly, and found a seat with the Kansas fans.

North Carolina won, 54–53, in triple overtime. Joe Quigg, a six-foot-nine center, hit two free throws with six seconds left in the third extra period to give Carolina the victory. I was crushed. It was a profound disappointment for me and anyone else who cared about the KU program, and I took it extremely hard. After the game I was so low I didn't feel like going out, so I went back to the hotel suite.

But when I got there McGuire had returned to the room too, and he had invited the whole Carolina team up to the suite for a postgame meeting. His players sat in the living room, freshly showered and shaved and wearing coats and ties, ready to go out on the town and celebrate. Frank wanted all of the coaches sharing the suite to say something to his players. Even me. It was the last thing I wanted to do.

"Coach, I really don't feel like talking to your team tonight," I said.

But he insisted. You can imagine the scene: the North Carolina players sitting there in blazers, itching to get out of there and hit the sidewalks, with me standing in front of them, a sour look on my face. First Ben said something, and then Bob and Hoyt. Then it was my turn.

"You guys had it at the end," I said. "Congratulations. But I certainly wasn't cheering for you."

I didn't know how Frank would react to what I said. But strangely, he seemed to like it. He just smiled and asked me, "What's the best place we can go get something to eat this late?" I told him the only place I knew of was called Eddy's, a nightclub two blocks away that was the most expensive in town. *At least let North Carolina pick up a big bill,* I thought to myself.

Frank said, "Great," and he got the Carolina contingent together, including the media, and we all went out and had a big dinner. Eddy's stayed open for the North Carolina party, and Frank told us to order anything we wanted from the menu. Later when Frank turned in his expense account for that night, North Carolina's athletic director, Chuck Erickson, questioned the size of the bill. "Can you believe forty-eight dollars just for the Roquefort dressing?" he said. "I'm not paying that part."

(Frank was still joking about that Roquefort dressing bill in New Orleans in 1982 after we won the national championship. John Swofford, our athletics director at the time, sent him a check for $48 to cover it.)

On the morning after the championship game, McGuire, Spear, Carnevale, Brawner, and I sat around a table in the suite and had breakfast together. I ate my eggs and tried to appreciate the fact that I had seen my team play in one of the more memorable championship games in the annals of the NCAA. Out of the blue, Frank looked up from his plate and said, "Dean, I've been talking to Ben, Hoyt, and Bob about you, and we're all in agreement. I would like for you to come to North Carolina to be my assistant coach. What do you say?"

I was dumbfounded. Frank explained that Buck Freeman, his longtime assistant, would be retiring in the next year. Buck and Frank went all the way back to 1936, when Buck was the head coach at St. John's and Frank was the team captain. When Frank became Carolina's head coach in 1952, he had hired Buck as his aide. Buck's whole life revolved around the game to such an extent that he thought players should give up their social lives in season. It wasn't unusual for him to check on Carolina's players in the middle of the night to make sure they were in their rooms. He was a guy who obviously didn't need much sleep, and he was set in his ways. He was tall, with snow-white hair, and he led with his shoulders when he walked, as if he were trudging into a head wind. Like Frank, he came from New York, and between the two of them they had an almost exclusive pipeline to players from the city. They genuinely believed they could coach New Yorkers better than other players because they understood them. Also they were wily. In those days there wasn't much scouting, and Buck liked to hold one good player back and sit him on the bench. Other teams would think that player must not be as good as the starters, when the opposite was true. He loved the surprise element of a sixth man.

Buck was ailing, Frank explained, and he was going to retire, if not this season, then next. I wasn't ready for the proposition and didn't know how to respond. I stammered that I would do whatever Bob Spear thought was best. "I don't intend to stay in the Air Force for a long period of time," I said, thinking aloud. Frank said there was no urgency. If Buck stayed in the job for one more year, the offer wouldn't be effective until 1958.

While I was happy at Air Force, I knew I didn't want to stay in the service. Bob Spear knew it too, and he encouraged me to take Frank up on his offer. "It's time for you to move on," he said. Coaching the defending national champions would be a great learning experience, he advised. But I wasn't particularly in the mood to hear that, given that they had beaten Kansas.

Frank and I stayed in touch. Buck Freeman did coach one more season at North Carolina, but it was a disappointing one since Joe Quigg, the hero of the championship game, broke his leg in preseason practice and missed the entire year. Carolina went 19–7 and didn't make it back to the postseason tournament. A year later, Frank and I met again at the 1958 NCAA Final Four. By this time Buck had indeed retired, and I was due to be discharged from the Air Force in August 1958. But I hadn't yet committed to Frank. The same group of five coaches went out to dinner, and Frank reiterated his offer. "I want you to come visit and I'll see to it that you're the highest-paid assistant coach in the country," he promised.

I agreed to come to Chapel Hill in early April to look over the university and the community. When I arrived I fell in love at first sight. The town was in its full springtime glory with dogwoods and cherry trees in blossom and petals floating in the breeze and dusting the footpaths. I was treated like royalty. Frank drove me around to look at houses and took me to dinner at Chapel Hill's best restaurant, The Pines, where the team often ate pregame meals. Leroy and Agnes Merritt, who managed the restaurant, were cordial people. They made sure I didn't want for anything. Agnes kept asking me, "Would you like another steak, Coach?"

Frank also introduced me to his graduating senior Tom Kearns, who was drafted by Syracuse in the NBA. Tom asked me if I wanted to play some basketball with him. Frank said to go ahead, since we had only one more appointment that afternoon. One good thing about writing a book: I can now finally tell someone I beat Tommy in a tough game of one on one. Frank had watched us play and needled Tom about losing to me. Tom replied, "I thought I should let him beat me since he is our guest this weekend." Coach then said, "I know Irish blarney when I hear it."

Frank offered me a salary of $7,500 a year, and I accepted. The money was of little consequence to me; I would have taken the job for $4,000 a year. What I didn't know was that Frank had to get the salary approved by the administration, which turned out to be more complicated than anyone might have suspected. In those days basketball wasn't yet a big revenue producer, and most programs had to skimp to make ends meet, so head coaches could afford only one assistant.

There were two giants in UNC's athletic department at the time, McGuire and football coach Jim Tatum. They got along well enough. Still, they were very protective of their own programs. When Tatum heard what McGuire had offered me he protested to athletic director Erickson. "You can't pay him that much," Tatum said, "because it'll mess up the pay scale on my staff."

I told McGuire the money was no big deal. I'd take less. But it had become a point of pride with Frank, who felt, rightly, that basketball needed to be treated with respect and looked on as important by the athletic administration. In those days there tended to be a bias toward football because most athletics directors had come out of that sport, and it received more attention in the sports pages. Feeling certain that Erickson would side with Tatum, McGuire decided to circumvent them both. He went straight to the top, to William Aycock, the dynamic university chancellor.

"I've found my assistant coach and we'll need to pay him seventy-five hundred a year," McGuire said. "I want to point out that he's a 'dean,' as in Dean Smith. And he's an American Baptist."

Aycock shrugged and said, "I don't know about the dean part. But there are already more Baptists than sparrows in North Carolina."

Aycock approved my hiring and called Erickson to tell him so. When Erickson spoke up about Tatum's concerns, Aycock said, "I've made my decision. I think Frank needs the money to pay this Dean Smith fellow. If Tatum gets mad, tell him he should be mad at me, not you; I'm the one who approved his salary."

It wasn't the last time Chancellor Aycock would stand up for me. But the irony of the situation was that my close friend Chris Fordham also arrived in Chapel Hill in 1958 to begin his first year as a member of the faculty at the university medical school—at a starting salary of $8,500. There was something inherently wrong in the fact that a young doctor and a young assistant basketball coach could arrive at the same time at the same university and make similar salaries. He later became dean of the medical school and chancellor of the university for ten years. He remains one of my best friends.

I moved to Chapel Hill in late August—and never left again. I had found what they call "The Southern Part of Heaven," and quickly understood why.

Frank McGuire was just slightly larger than life. Picture a guy with an easy charm and utter confidence who appeared to have stepped out of the pages of *Esquire* magazine, and that was Frank. His clothes hung on him just the way they did on the store mannequins, and his rich reddish-brown hair seemed to naturally fall into a swirl. He could have done anything he wanted, in any field. He *looked* like success.

McGuire had arrived to coach North Carolina in 1952–53, and success is exactly what he brought. I'll give you an example: Carolina had lost to nearby rival North Carolina State fourteen times straight before Frank came to town. N.C. State was coached by the great Indiana native Everett Case and was having its way with all of the schools in the state. But the very first time N.C. State met a McGuire-coached Carolina team, Carolina won, 70–69. In the next few years Frank won twelve of twenty-two games in competition with Case's teams.

Chapel Hill was an improbable home for McGuire, who was a New Yorker, but he came to love it. He had been smitten by Chapel Hill when he was stationed there during the war, and he thought it was a great town in which to raise his children, Patsyjeanne, Carol Ann, and Frankie Jr., who was born with cerebral palsy only one year before the move.

Frank made basketball important on the Carolina campus and refused to accept second-class citizenship. In fact, he brought class to everything he did. He traveled first-class, ate at fine restaurants, and insisted that his teams have the most handsome uniforms and best equipment. He dressed himself exquisitely for games. His handsome suits were shipped down from New York along with silk neckties. He cut quite a figure when he arrived in the bench area before tip-off. "It costs twenty-five cents more on the dollar to go first-class," he liked to say.

Frank enlarged my world in many ways. He made me less naive and introduced me to the real New York, the side of it I hadn't seen as a tourist. He taught me the value of always wearing a coat and tie to work. Whether it was July or January, we came to work in coats and ties, although the coat could come off at the office. Frank thought professional attire brought dignity to the profession. He said, "You never know who might drop in to see us, or when the telephone might ring for us to go across campus for a meeting. If we dress properly we'll be ready for any circumstance." I liked the sound of that, and to this day our standard of dress in the Carolina basketball office remains the same.

Frank had a distinct preference for New York players. He genuinely believed he had better rapport with them. The starting five on the '57 national championship team that beat Kansas were all New Yorkers: Joe Quigg at center, Pete Brennan and Lennie Rosenbluth at forwards, Bobby Cunningham and Tommy Kearns at guards, along with key reserves Danny Lotz and Bob Young. There were very few North Carolinians on the roster, but one of them, Ken Rosemond, later joined Frank and me as an assistant.

Somebody once wrote Frank asking why he only recruited New York players. "The reason I recruit New York players," he replied, "is because they have to be quick in order to dodge the eighteen thousand cabs that run around New York." That comment drew a quick letter from the head man of New York taxis.

I tried to suggest to Frank that the combination of North Carolina's academic reputation and its basketball success could allow us to recruit nationally, but Frank would say, "I feel more comfortable with New Yorkers. I know what they're thinking and how they feel about things. Especially the Irish." I had to beg Frank to look at a player out of Crystal City, Missouri, named Bill Bradley, whom I had seen play on a couple of occasions. We flew to St. Louis to meet with Bradley and his parents after lecturing at a clinic in Kansas. While Frank was intrigued by Bradley and by the midwestern landscape, his one memorable comment was, "I bet there are some New Yorkers on the lam hiding out in these small towns." Bradley put us on the list of schools he was considering, along with Yale, Princeton, Duke, and Kansas.

Frank's network of scouts and players in New York was labeled the "Underground Railroad" by *Sports Illustrated,* but his connections in New York ran far deeper than just basketball. It seemed as though he knew every alderman, precinct boss, and labor union rep in the city. One of his closest friends was Bill O'Brien, the city police commissioner. Frank always joked that he needed two sets of tickets so he could put the cops he knew on one side of the arena, the robbers on the other side.

He knew people such as Jack Curran, the Archbishop Malloy High School coach, who turned out scores of great players and who had been a star pitcher at St. John's when Frank was his coach. But Frank's best New York connection was Harry Gotkin, a passionate basketball fan and chief talent spotter for Carolina. The use of scouts would eventually be forbidden by the

NCAA, but for years Frank relied on Harry. The Gotkin Hat Company in New York was started by Harry's father, but Harry didn't care about hats. He cared about basketball and eating, not necessarily in that order. He'd watch kids play all over the city and call Frank and say, "This one's good, that one's good, that one's not." My first recruiting trip to New York came in April 1959 after my first season in Chapel Hill, and it was an eye-opener. Harry met me at Newark Airport and said, "Come on, Dean. I'm going to show you next year's North Carolina freshman team." He wasn't kidding either. We watched Larry Brown, Kenny McIntyre, Rich Brennan, Billy Galantai, and Art Heyman play together, and I could hardly wait for their arrival at Chapel Hill. Even though all of them said they were coming, there was no letter of intent to sign as there is today. Larry did come, but Heyman switched to Duke after announcing for Carolina in May. McIntyre, Brennan, and Galantai all enrolled in Wilmington Prep School, and then only Galantai came the following year. Billy earned his Ph.D. in education in later years.

One year later I went with Frank to recruit a skinny kid with an angular face named Billy Cunningham. Billy was the son of a New York fire chief, and his father and Frank knew a lot of the same people around town. Years later Billy admitted to me that he never had a say in where he was going to school. After McGuire and I left his home that night, his father told him, "That's it, Billy. You're going to North Carolina with Uncle Frank." Fortunately for Carolina basketball and for me, Billy came to Chapel Hill and stayed.

Frank loved New York so much that he had a provision in his contract that allowed him to spend every summer in Greenwood Lake, a retreat on the New York–New Jersey border, where he had a beautiful home. Frank's wife, Pat, was a New Yorker, a striking former model with a smart wit to go along with her slender brunette looks, and a style best described as elegant. Whenever Frank asked her if she wanted to go somewhere, she'd say, "Where's my hat?" When Frank would go to bed early at Greenwood Lake, the two of us would stay up discussing religion, current events, and Frank's welfare.

Frank was a generous boss who had a way of making you feel as though he couldn't get along without you. There was no question about who was in charge of his team and his program, but he had a casualness about him, too, that suggested he didn't want to sweat small stuff. He delegated responsibility, and from the start gave me plenty to do; he didn't like to handle the small organizational things, so it was up to me to make our practice plans and do a lot of the drills. Frank would stand up in the bleachers with a megaphone in his hands and supervise. I even answered his mail, dictating his letters and handing them to him for his signature.

Even when he was coaching he seemed like an urbane man-about-town. Frank was less into sideline strategy than he was a master coaching psychologist. On occasion he would stand up in the bleachers with his megaphone and chase a star player out of the gym just because he thought it made the other players feel good about themselves and their own abilities. It was his way of showing them they were important too.

In November of my first season as assistant, Frank suddenly took off on a recruiting trip to New York for five days, leaving the team in my hands. I was twenty-seven years old and suddenly in charge. The first day Frank was gone, I ran two players out of practice. When our future All-American Doug Moe didn't box out on a rebound, I yelled at him. On the next play, Moe was so "smart aleck" to show me he could box out that he whacked Danny Lotz, our team captain, so hard they almost got in a fight. So I tossed Moe out of practice. To this day Doug still apologizes to me for that. A little later I didn't think Moe's roommate, Lou Brown, was playing hard enough, so I ran him out of the gym too. But the next few days we had great practices.

By the time Frank got back I had installed a new defense, the point zone we had used at Air Force, which became our primary defense in the 1958–59 season. Frank asked the team before our opener which defense they liked better, the 2–1–2 that had been their staple, or the new point, and they were unanimous on The Point. Frank liked my initiative and encouraged me to speak up, even during games. "It'll be my decision," he advised me, "but throw out a lot of suggestions. Some of them I'll take, others I won't. Don't be offended when I choose to do something else."

That first year, as the only assistant, I had a lot of duties, what with answering Frank's mail, organizing varsity practice plans, and coaching the freshman team. Another of my jobs in the summer of 1959 was to serve as math tutor to Doug Moe, who would go on to become the ABA Player of the Year and the very successful coach of the NBA's Denver Nuggets, winning an NBA Coach of the Year award. Moe had a brilliant mind for math. An example: Once when he was playing for the Oakland franchise of the ABA, he made a bet with Rick Barry that he could multiply six numbers by six numbers in his head, right there in the middle of practice. He didn't have a very good practice, but he won the bet.

At Carolina, Doug didn't like to study and didn't go to class very often. Part of my job was to wake him up and make sure he went to his classes. I'd walk him up the hill to the math building. After I left he'd walk back down the hill and climb back into bed. There was one professor who was near retirement and famous for giving A's to everyone, but Doug was the only one who got C's, because he wouldn't show up often.

Doug was a special young man to me, and our close friendship continues to this day. A book of Doug Moe stories would be hilarious. When he talks to others about me I'm called "El Deano," but when the two of us talk he always calls me Coach. One of these days he will just call me Dean. Maybe I'm partial to him for helping me lift a washer and dryer in my new home when I arrived in 1958 and he was a rising sophomore who would become an All-American that year. There is only one Doug Moe!

In the summer of 1959, it was my job to get Doug through his trigonometry class in summer school. He needed a C to be eligible. We stayed up until 5 A.M. studying for an exam with an emphasis on oblique triangles. Believe me, I had Doug ready for that exam. He knew it perfectly. I sent him off to the exam with confidence, and then I set out for Greenwood Lake to visit Frank and Pat. Later Doug called with the disastrous news. "I made an eighteen," he said. "You didn't tell me I needed to memorize the theorems." The last time I had taken trig, in high school, the theorems were listed on the board for the class to see, and most college trig professors made it a practice to do the same. I since learned Doug didn't know the theorems, so there was no way he could solve the problems. Our All-American was ineligible for the first semester of his junior year. But Frank, typically, just shrugged it off.

When game time came, Frank was every bit the intense head coach. The way he worked the team up for a big game was fascinating. It was his habit to stay out of the dressing room beforehand, leaving the players alone. That way when he finally did enter, he made an impression on them, and they understood it was time to listen. I would write the individual matchups on the dressing room blackboard, and then Frank would make his entrance and go over them with the team. Then we would say the Lord's Prayer. But in typical New York style, Frank and the players said it fast. As a Baptist from Kansas, I have never heard it recited quite as rapidly as our team did.

Frank wasn't much for speeches, but he was a great motivator and always appealed to his players' tough natures. "We're from New York, and we're better and tougher than they are," he'd say. "Those guys over there just don't know how to play like we do." Unconsciously, Frank sometimes instilled a dash of paranoia too. Used sparingly and at the right time, it could unify the team and make our players feel it was us against the world. Later, a psychiatrist, my longtime friend Earl Somers, informed me that paranoia was a good short-term motivator but wears out quickly. Frank must have known that instinctively.

Some of Frank's best squads played with a chip on their shoulder, and things could get combative. In 1959 we were involved in a frightening melee at Wake Forest when hundreds of students poured out of the stands and onto the court. It started when a future New York Knicks, Dave Budd, a muscular player and a bruising competitor, mixed it up with one of our players. The riot was on. In the game film, you can see that one of our players, York Larese, literally had to fight people off as he left the court and tried to make his way to the locker room. It was a scary situation, and the result of it was that Wake wasn't allowed to play us on their home floor the next season. We had the game in Greensboro instead.

Years later, after Frank became coach at South Carolina, a dangerous fight broke out during a game against Maryland. Somewhere in the confusion, Maryland coach Lefty Driesell got hit, reportedly by South Carolina's John Ribock. Later when the press tried to piece together what happened, they asked Frank how Lefty got hit. Frank thought about it for a minute and said, "I think Lefty must have hit himself."

Frank had a great feel for the game and knew how to use a ploy. A typical Frank move came one December night in 1959 when we were getting ready to play Duke in the old Dixie Classic, a prestigious Christmas tournament. It was to be our first meeting with Vic Bubas, the newly named head coach of Duke, and Frank decided to try to shake Bubas up.

Thinking over our game plan, Frank suggested he might try a 1–2–2 zone. I balked, wondering what could be on his mind. We hadn't run a 1–2–2 zone since I had been there. In fact, we hadn't *practiced* it all year. "Coach, I don't think that's our best strategy," I said.

Frank said, "You put the matchups on the board. Now, once you start going over the matchups, I'll stop you. Don't be offended."

I did what I was told and wrote the matchups on the board. I began to go over them with the team, but pretty soon Frank interrupted me. "Coach Smith, hold it a minute," he said. "Vic Bubas is over there in the Duke dressing room, and he's getting ready to play North Carolina for the first time. I know he has to be scared to death. We haven't run a 1–2–2 zone all year, so I want us to start in a 1–2–2." Frank told the team he knew we hadn't practiced it, but he said, "We're ballplayers and it's simple. Just hustle and make sure the ball is covered."

After the players left the dressing room, McGuire assured me that if the zone hurt us we'd get out of it quickly. But it never did. Duke was completely taken aback by the change-up, and we beat them, 75–53.

In the three years I worked for McGuire, North Carolina went 20–5, 18–6, and 19–4, and I settled into a comfortable life in Chapel Hill. During that period I had two calls for leaving Chapel Hill. In the late spring of 1959 I received a call from Red Jacoby, athletic director at Wyoming. His longtime successful coach Ev Shelton had resigned and Red wanted me to come in for an interview. I had known Red the three years I was at the Academy, and he let it be known I would be his choice as head coach.

I told him I would call back in two days if I decided to interview. I had a huge problem about being a head coach after my first year as assistant to Frank. North Carolina was successful with a soft man and a zone defense; also a freelance, ball control offense. Kansas was successful with a man pressure defense and some set plays to use our personnel and, depending on the fast break, points off our pressure defense. These two schools of thought on how to play were 180 degrees apart. I wasn't sure which was the better way to play the game if I took the Wyoming job.

Fortunately, one day later the decision was made for me. Red called to tell me President Humphries at Wyoming had overruled him to hire Wyoming graduate Bill Strannigan, the very successful coach at Iowa State. "I think it is a great choice for Wyoming," I told Red and was surprised how relieved I felt. Then shortly after the 1960 season, my second as a Carolina assistant, my old coach Dick Harp had asked me to return to Kansas to join his staff. He said that he didn't want to coach more than four or five more years, and I would be in position to take over as head coach of my alma mater. I had to give the offer serious consideration because I considered Harp the man who taught me as much about the game as any coach.

McGuire knew I was struggling with my decision. Typically, he told me, "Come on, let's go to New York for a few days." We spent four days in Manhattan, visited a few high schools, and spent time with a group of Frank's closest friends. His longtime best pal, Jack LaRocca, had pitched in the Yankees farm system and still holds the Triple A Pacific Coast League record for hurling strikeouts. Danny Patrissy owned a restaurant in Little Italy and was a former student of Frank's at Xavier High School. Joe Powell was an old schoolmate and a longshoreman's union official. And of course there was Harry Gotkin. We had dinner every night at Patrissy's, argued baseball, went to music clubs like the old Bon Soir on Eighth Street and Basin Street East. By the end of the trip I realized I didn't want to leave Carolina.

I was loyal to both Frank and Dick. Frank allowed me to play a key role in decision making at Carolina, which I appreciated and enjoyed. Since I had played for Dick at Kansas, and held him in such high regard, I was afraid I would have trouble disagreeing with him on anything, which would have been a disservice to him. Coaches need assistants who are candid with them.

By 1960 the North Carolina basketball program came under investigation by the National Collegiate Athletic Association, which charged "excessive re-cruiting expenditures." According to the NCAA, "excessive" money was spent on entertaining recruits, although nobody could explain exactly what they thought Frank was guilty of, or provide a specific dollar amount, other than accusing him of extravagance and failing to keep receipts. In those days it was legal to take recruits to dinner and entertain them, and the rules on what was acceptable versus "excessive" were vague.

In the fall of 1960, Frank and Chancellor William Aycock appeared be-fore the NCAA Infractions Committee to respond to the accusations. Frank thought the charges were baseless and inspired by jealousy, and made his feelings clear in typical New York fashion. One of the committee members was a gentleman named Nicholas McKnight, a former dean of students at Columbia University. On hearing that Frank had spent $35 for three dinners at a New York restaurant one night, McKnight looked skeptically at Frank and said, "Coach McGuire, I am from Columbia University and I know many good restaurants in New York where I can get an excellent meal for three dollars."

"I wouldn't eat where you eat," Frank said.

Not long after that the NCAA found Carolina guilty of several violations of "excessive" spending. The university decided to appeal to the NCAA Council, but by then Frank, who continued to vehemently deny any wrong-doing, decided he was fed up with the whole process. He found it tedious and unjustified. He asked me to help Chancellor Aycock prepare the appeal so he wouldn't have to go before any more of those despised interrogations by committee.

In the meantime, he had to tell his old friend Harry Gotkin to stop talk-ing to prospects, because that was mandated by the NCAA. One night he took Harry and his usual group to Patrissy's in Little Italy. When Frank broke the news Harry was devastated. He didn't want to listen. He protested and complained and kept asking why. Finally, Danny Patrissy leaned over and grabbed Harry and exclaimed, "Harry, can't you get this through your head? Are you trying to hurt the man? He just told you that you can't help anymore!"

It was my responsibility to do the homework for our NCAA appeal. I had to plow through old expense accounts and financial records of 1956 and 1957 to prove that he hadn't spent money on recruits "excessively," whatever that meant. It wasn't an easy job. Back in those days we weren't a credit card society, so there weren't a lot of records. Most of Frank's expenses were paid for in cash, and he didn't like to ask for receipts because it was embarrassing to him. Also, it just wasn't in Frank's nature to worry about details. He didn't even do his own expense accounts; he turned them over to a team trainer or to Buck Freeman or later to me. What's more, it was Frank's style to invite anybody and everybody along for dinner and to pick up the tab. On one trip to Williamsburg, Virginia, to play William and Mary in 1957, he picked up the check for the team, staff, friends, and a few members of the press. Frank didn't have the receipt so I had to go back and trace all of the people on the bus to match what was turned in for reimbursement.

In the 1940s one of Frank's favorite places in New York was the Colony Club on the upper East Side. He enjoyed going there with a friend of his named Bob Fitzsimmons, a labor union attorney who was a regular. They would spend the evening, and when they were done they'd just get up and leave. They never even saw the check. Later on Bob Fitzsimmons would get a bill in the mail, with gratuity and the other charges included. That was the way Frank liked to operate, freewheeling and first-class. If he couldn't go first-class, he preferred not to go at all.

In January 1961, Chancellor Aycock, athletic director Erickson, and I flew to San Francisco to present our appeal to the NCAA Council. We had a great time the night before the meeting at the Blue Fox restaurant with Harvie Ward, the Carolina alum who was U.S. amateur golf champion. The meeting the next morning was run like a court proceeding, and Chancellor Aycock made our case like the brilliant lawyer he was. I simply stood by and handed him the documents to support his argument. Chuck answered some questions, and the chancellor went through every point, explaining financial details. He proved that no one was given cash of any amount, and showed that when you took into consideration the large numbers of people involved in Frank's dinner outings, the cost per person wasn't excessive. When he concluded, the council said, "Let the record show that this board has never heard a more thorough and detailed defense of a university's position than we did today."

I was certain there would be no penalty. The council was clearly impressed, and in an unprecedented decision, it sent the case back to the Infractions Committee for more study. Shortly afterwards the NCAA dropped a number of the charges—but it still accused us of excessive recruiting entertainment. I wanted to appeal that one too, but Aycock and McGuire decided to take the punishment and move on. "Don't fight it," Frank said. "We'll just serve it out."

We were placed on probation for one year and banned from participating in the NCAA tournament that was six weeks away. We were ranked in the top ten. It was a frustrating situation for our team; Larese and Moe were seniors and All-Americans, and we felt we would have done well in the tournament. The frustration of the sanction gradually wore on all of us, and we were involved in another nasty fight, this one at Duke. Fighting was almost commonplace in those days, but this incident was out of the ordinary. We had beaten Duke in the prestigious Dixie Classic, and the rematch was contested bitterly all evening, with intermittent scuffling that had to be broken up by the officials. With about nine seconds left, Larry Brown got into it with Duke's Art Heyman, who was a rival of his since their high school days on Long Island, yet a friend off the court. All of a sudden there was fighting on the floor among some players and spectators, among them a number of Duke football players. The result was that the ACC suspended two of our players, Larry Brown and Donnie Walsh, for the rest of the season. But since the fight was *at* Duke, we didn't think it was all Donnie and Larry. There should have been something said about their lack of crowd control, or so Frank and I thought.

Matters were about to get still worse. A gambling scandal hit college basketball across the country in 1961. No Carolina games were cited, but one of our substitutes was found to be involved with a gambler, and a couple of players from N.C. State were said to have altered the scores of games along betting interests. That prompted the president of the entire University of North Carolina system, William Friday, to abolish the popular Dixie Classic tournament. The Dixie Classic was a tournament in which the Big Four schools in the state—Carolina, N.C. State, Wake Forest, and Duke—along with four other prominent national teams, met between Christmas and New Year's for three days of intense basketball—four games each day. It was the most popular holiday tournament in the country by far.

In addition to doing away with the tournament, Friday and the chancellors at Carolina and N.C. State decided to inflict self-imposed sanctions on both state schools for the coming year of 1961–62. The penalties were prohibitive and indefinite. We were allowed to play only sixteen regular-season games, which allowed for only two games outside of the Atlantic Coast Conference. And we were only allowed to recruit two players a year from outside the ACC region—a particularly grave restriction since, at that time, we depended heavily on prospects from outside the area. North Carolina in those days did not have much of a high school basketball culture. The first blow to our recruiting fell as soon as the NCAA probation was announced in January. We got a letter from Bill Bradley's father saying we were no longer on his list of five schools. To me, it was unlikely we could have signed him anyway.

Chancellor Aycock went one step further in punishing Frank. In April he wrote a letter to Frank stating in no uncertain terms that things had to change. Frank's contract was due to expire in 1963, and Aycock said its renewal depended on several things. The NCAA was going to reinspect our program after the 1961–62 season, and "the results will be of great importance to me," Aycock said. Aycock concluded, "The number of games won or lost during the next season will not be a material factor in my recommendation" on whether to extend or terminate Frank's contract. Frank was deeply upset by the letter, and so was I. We didn't think it was justified.

That summer, Frank received a tantalizing job opportunity: to coach the Philadelphia Warriors of the NBA and their star, Wilt Chamberlain. The Warriors chief executive, Eddie Gottlieb, offered him a three-year contract at an annual salary of $20,000, almost double what he was making at Carolina. Frank vacillated; one day he turned the job down, the next day he was going. He had ties to Chapel Hill that would be hard to break. After nine seasons he was extremely popular with fans and alumni. His '57 championship had captured the state's imagination, and he had built the program into one of the best-known in the nation. His family loved it there, so much so that Frank told Gottlieb if he took the job, the Warriors would have to fly him back to Chapel Hill on his off days at the team's expense. Frank also demanded a fine suite at the Cherry Hill Inn, a beautiful place in New Jersey just across the bridge from Philadelphia. Frank kept waiting for Gottlieb to say no, but he acquiesced to every request.

One evening I sat with Frank and Pat outside of Kutcher's Hotel in the Catskills, and we discussed the situation. We had driven to Kutcher's for a basketball clinic from their Greenwood Lake home, and it was a gorgeous June night. We relaxed in a set of Adirondack chairs, and Frank said that he had made up his mind to resign at Carolina and take the job in Philadelphia.

Pat and I mustered every persuasive argument against it we could think of. Pat even said at one point, "You can leave if you want, but I'm staying." We talked until late. Finally, just before we retired, Frank said, "That's it. I'm not going to talk about this anymore. I'm staying in Chapel Hill."

But the very next morning Frank was having second thoughts again after visiting with his friend Clair Bee. He rested on the issue until early August, and then told me his decision was final: He was going to the NBA to coach Wilt Chamberlain and the Warriors.

"I'll recommend you for the job here because you're the man for it," Frank said. "But what you should do is go with me to Philadelphia and be my assistant. Things don't look too good here right now, and it will be difficult to turn it around."

But I told Frank right away I had always seen myself as a college coach. Also I had come to love Chapel Hill as much as he did, and so had my wife and three young children. I told him I sincerely believed we could rescue the program from the trouble it faced.

I drove Frank over to the South Building, the administrative center in the heart of the campus, and he walked into Chancellor Aycock's office to resign. I waited in the car. Frank wasn't gone long. He came out and got back in the car.

"Congratulations," he said. "Chancellor Aycock thinks it's a good idea for you to have the job. You won't be an interim coach or anything like that. You're the head basketball coach at North Carolina."

I drove us back to our offices at Woollen Gym. I was only thirty, I lacked head coaching experience, and I was taking over a program under difficult sanctions. I wanted the job but had some apprehension too. All coaches understand that if you mess up your first opportunity as a head coach, there may never be a second chance. But I wasn't smart enough to dwell on that back then. Naively, perhaps, I believed the problems would work themselves out in time.

I met with Chancellor Aycock in his office the next morning and formally accepted the job. He asked me what I wanted to be paid. A friend of mine, Joe Dean, who is now the athletic director at Louisiana State University, had once told me that a head basketball coach should be paid $100 more than the top assistant on the football staff. I suggested that to the chancellor. He picked up the phone and made a call to check on the salary of Carolina football assistant Emmitt Cheeks. When he hung up he said, "Your salary is ninety-two hundred dollars a year." We didn't sign a contract or confer with lawyers. We just shook hands. Aycock made it clear what he expected from me: Give the university a team of which it could be proud. He said, "I'll support you. Don't worry about the winning and the losing. If you do the things I've asked of you, you'll have a job here as long as I'm chancellor."

Not many coaches have the privilege of working for a chancellor who says something like that. Aycock was wise, strong, and supportive—the perfect man for a young head coach to have as his leader. He was so supportive, in fact, that when reports appeared in the press the next day calling me the "interim" coach, he called me at home that night to reassure me. "I never said anything about you being interim," he said. "You are the head coach and there's no interim about it. I'll straighten that out tomorrow in a press release."

Aycock wasn't someone who could be bullied by donors or pressured by alumni either. He had served with distinction in World War II, first training troops, including a battalion of Japanese-Americans, and then as a battalion commander in General Patton's Third Army, 87th Division. He was shipped overseas on the day that the Battle of the Bulge broke out and fought in Europe until the war ended there. He was getting ready to be shipped to the Pacific when the atomic bomb was dropped on Hiroshima. He arrived at Carolina in 1945 as a law student, and served as chancellor from 1957 to the summer of 1964, when he returned to his first love, teaching. He has won numerous Teacher of the Year awards, and remains an emeritus professor in the law school. At some point in the 1990s he wrote me a touching handwritten note. "You were the second best decision I ever made," he said, "next to marrying Grace."

When Aycock told me I had his full support, there was no doubt in my mind that he meant it. And we both knew I would need support, because there were some forces arrayed against me. Faculty members were understandably not enthusiastic about athletics in the wake of the NCAA probation, and some even wanted to deemphasize it. But Aycock persuaded them that it was important to maintain a top program. "I don't care who is governor, or who's on the faculty, or who's in the legislature. We're going to be at the top level of college athletics," he said to a faculty group shortly after he was appointed chancellor. "It is here and it won't go away. Since we have it, it's important we do it the right way. There is more press coverage of athletics than all other university projects combined, and the integrity of the university is reflected to a great extent by what happens with the athletic department. It's important for all of us to realize that if the athletic department has integrity, it reflects favorably on the entire university."

There was another faction, this one made up of university alumni, that wanted to conduct a national search for a head coach with a proven record. All of the other in-state schools had talented and experienced coaches: There was Everett Case at N.C. State, Vic Bubas at Duke, and Horace "Bones" McKinney at Wake Forest, who in addition to being one of the greatest game strategists and after-dinner speakers I ever knew, would become a good friend of mine. It was a tough crowd for any coach to break into, much less a young one under the formidable sanctions Carolina faced.

Athletic director Erickson was interested in hiring a former Carolina graduate named Dan Nimitz, who was coach at Mercer in Macon, Georgia. But Aycock circumvented him. One reason he named me so quickly was to stop the alums from pushing for a national search. He was certain he wanted me. He told me he had confidence that I could coach basketball. He knew me well. He was a decisive leader who wasn't afraid to make tough decisions.

Aycock was also willing to stand firm in the face of pressure by monied interests. A dramatic example was his backing of football coach Jim Hickey. Jim Tatum died suddenly of Rocky Mountain spotted fever in 1959, and Hickey, a former assistant, had the daunting task of succeeding him. Hickey was a man of warmth and intelligence, but he didn't go out of his way to court the alumni, and when his teams suffered from tough scheduling, some alums started agitating for his removal.

The story goes that two especially influential boosters marched into Aycock's office one day and demanded Hickey be fired. "Either that or we won't give another penny to the university," they threatened.

Aycock excused himself. He returned ten minutes later. "I'm sorry I was gone for so long," he said, "but it took me that amount of time to find Coach Hickey so I could inform him that I have just decided to extend his contract by another two years."

On at least one other occasion Aycock gave Hickey a raise just because some outside interests once again wanted him fired. He called me at home. "How do you like this one?" he said. "You've heard all this talk about how some members of the Educational Foundation are going to get together and get Hickey fired? I want you to know I just gave him a three-year contract."

Aycock said years later, "No one could have gotten rid of Dean unless they fired me first."

In the conversations leading up to my formal hiring, Aycock never once talked about winning or losing. He never said I had to win a certain number of games, or that I had to go to the NCAA tournament to keep my job. In those days, we had to win the ACC tournament to go anywhere. The ACC didn't allow teams to go to the NIT. Thankfully, Aycock understood what we were in store for, given the restrictions we would be operating under and the fact that our top players had graduated.

Shortly after I was named coach, Everett Case invited me over for dinner. Frank and Case and I enjoyed going to dinner together, and we always had a lot of laughs. But on this night Case spoke seriously and opened my eyes to the consequences of the sanctions. Case's nickname was the "Gray Fox" because of his shock of gray hair and his chess player's mind, the ability to foresee consequences two or three moves in advance of most other coaches. He had seen the effects of NCAA probation before at N.C. State and knew the harshest ones wouldn't be felt for a couple of years, when the recruiting restrictions had set in. He tried to tell me how tough it would be to rebuild our programs under the probationary measures we each faced, with reduced sixteen-game schedules (when other teams were playing twenty-five games) and only two scholarships to give to players outside our geographical area.

"Ole Bubas and Bones are licking their chops now," he said. "With the limitations we have on us, Duke and Wake will have it to themselves. We won't be able to recruit, and our real troubles will surface a couple of years from now when our current players are gone and we won't be able to replace them."

His theory was absolutely correct, but our players on those early teams had other ideas.

5

Uphill and
Around the Corner

O n the day I took over as head coach at North Carolina, the chances of my finishing out my career in that job were about a hundred to one. Most Division 1 basketball coaches are fired somewhere along the line. Some become athletic directors; others became TV commentators or enter a new vocation. Only a lucky few retire as coaches.

Back in August 1961, I was pretty certain I could coach, maybe too certain. Even so, I had already learned that no matter who you are, experienced players are important. We had lost five of our top eight players before the season ever started. Our starting lineup should have been six-foot Larry Brown, six-foot Donnie Walsh, six-seven Jim Hudock, six-six Ken Mc-Comb, and six-one Yogi Poteet. But McComb and Poteet were declared ineligible academically in late August, a serious blow. We had already lost two All-Americans and our starting center to graduation: six-six Doug Moe, six-four York Larese, and six-nine Dick Kepley, respectively. Our last two freshman teams won eight and lost fourteen in games against other ACC freshman teams. Certainly, we needed help from the 1960–61 freshman team and senior Hugh Donohue, six-eight, who had not played in 1961.

I asked much of the remaining players, and they turned out to be one of the hardest-working teams that I was to coach for the next thirty-six years. They were smart, they gave everything they had, and people loved them. I remember one day in an intrasquad scrimmage when nine guys dived for a loose ball. There was just one player left standing, Peppy Callahan, a six-two junior from Smithtown, New York, and I jokingly said, "We should run for Peppy." Peppy, a walk-on, was actually one of the hardest-working guys on the team, and he went on to become a colonel in the Air Force. For years afterwards I kept a copy of a film we had spliced together of that team as an example of a "hustle team." They set a North Carolina record for field-goal percentage (to date), which tells you what an intelligent team it was in shot selection.

We had an ambitious schedule, even though we were restricted to sixteen games. Forced by university sanctions to reduce our nonconference schedule to just two games, I chose to keep the toughest ones, Indiana and Notre Dame, and canceled games with a couple of teams we should have beaten.

Our first test was a closed preseason scrimmage against Belmont Abbey, a small college near Charlotte coached by Al McGuire. Al's teams were frequent scrimmage partners for us, and he, too, liked to look for talent in New York. Al brought in a guy named Jimmy Sparrow, a left-handed guard, by showing him pictures of the Duke campus. He told him that's where he'd be going to school. When Sparrow checked in at Belmont Abbey he went to Al's office and asked, "What about those pictures you sent me? Where's that part of campus?"

Al said, "You go there if you do well your first year here."

The team Al brought into Woollen Gym was as obstinate as ours was, and the scrimmage was intense. One of Belmont Abbey's players was really physical with Donnie Walsh and Larry Brown, but I decided not to interfere. I just watched, wondering how our guys would respond. The next thing I knew, Donnie and Larry set him up for some payback. We were running our shuffle cut, and Donnie set a back screen off the ball. Larry ran the Belmont Abbey player into the screen and Donnie leveled him. Right there I knew I had a couple of tough guys.

We ran a lot of pressure defense against Belmont Abbey, and it bothered one of their freshman guards from New York. Al was sitting up in the stands watching, and he yelled, "If you lose the ball one more time, I'm going to come down there and kick your —!" Of course, no sooner had he said that than the poor kid lost the ball again. The game stopped and all of us watched Al chasing that kid all around the building, and he caught him! Al had been a dash man in high school.

Before Frank left Carolina he advised me to make some visible changes in the program so that players would understand I was the head coach. He thought I should change our uniforms or move the bench to the other side of Woollen Gym to make the team my own. It was good advice and typical of the way Frank's mind worked, but I didn't take him up on it. I felt the team would accept me since I had been with the seniors for three years. I was a whole different proposition from Frank McGuire. He was dynamic and outgoing, and I was quiet and intense, a disciplinarian. The changes I made were on the court.

One of the first things I did was institute the "tired signal." When a player was tired, I told him he could pull himself from the game. All he had to do was hold up a clenched fist. The trade-off was that he could put himself back in when he was ready. Looking back on it, I realize that often when I did something differently or innovatively as a head coach, I did it as a reaction to other coaches I had known—because I disagreed with them. Much as I respected Phog Allen, I wanted to rest my own players more than he had rested his. I knew we were in good physical condition, but our pressure defense and constant movement off the ball made it difficult not to be tired. Also, there were just a few games on TV, thus no TV time-outs then. When fatigue sets in, execution breaks down. I decided I would rather have a fresh reserve on the floor than a tired starter, a philosophy I stuck to for the next thirty-six years and for which I would be criticized at times. But it would also win us a few games. I felt the best judge of whether a player was tired was the player himself. Of course, if we coaches saw someone not hustling, we would take him out of the game for several minutes. This surely encouraged a player to take himself out of the game, rather than have the coach make the decision.

The "tired signal" was not meant to be used away from basketball. When I walked toward the University Methodist Church for Donnie Moe's wedding, Donnie saw me through the window as he waited for the service to begin. He stepped out the side door and gave me the "tired signal." He wanted out of the game!

On December 2, 1961, we opened our season at home against Virginia, and I was only slightly apprehensive. I was looking forward to the game and felt very little pressure. I was a thirty-year-old whose only head-coaching experience was a dozen games as a player-coach in the armed forces. Before the game, I went to exhaustive lengths to plan everything, down to the last little details. For instance, I planned how our bench would be arranged during time-outs and where subs would sit when they came out of the game.

Finally it was game time. I took my seat on the bench in Woollen Gym, and our players took their places for the tip-off.

An official jogged over to me. "Where's the game ball?" he asked. I had forgotten it.

I sent team manager Elliott Murnick down to the end of the bench to pick out a game ball. Fortunately there was no TV coverage for the game.

Finally the game got under way. We found a good practice ball and the toss went up, and I became caught up in the action. For the first four minutes we were horrible. I took an early time-out, rare for me. I jumped them. "What happened to the new offense? We weren't running anything we had practiced, and we were impatient on offense." After that time-out, our players executed beautifully. I can still remember my pleasure as they created layup after layup. Defensively we were good from the outset. Virginia found it hard to complete a pass, much less find an uncontested shot.

Four or five times in the first half, I noticed players holding up their fists. I thought they were saying, "We've got them, Coach." At one point, Brown gave me a fist. I waved my fist back, as if to say, "Way to go, Larry!"

I had not only forgotten the ball, I had forgotten my own "tired signal."

We went on to beat Virginia, 80–46. But no sooner had we passed one test than another was in store for us. Our next game was at Clemson, and I didn't prepare the team properly for the press offense. We knew it because we had practiced it, but we didn't know it for a game on the road. I would never make that mistake again. From then on we practiced something until it was second nature, so that in the stresses of game situations, especially those encountered on the road, execution came off effortlessly. I hope. We did defeat Clemson in their small gym by 2 even though I did not have us ready to play on the road against a zone press.

I was learning that a head coach never relaxes. In December our only loss was to Indiana, 76–70, but we had only those three games. On January 6, 1962, we traveled to Charlotte to play against Notre Dame, and I was worried. The Fighting Irish were a good team coming off a big win over Illinois, and I respected their coach, Johnny Jordan, who was a friend from my days at the academy. He was such a good friend, in fact, that we had dinner the night before the game, which isn't done much anymore since there is so much tape to watch. Early in the day, Bob Quincy, our sports-information director and a friend, came by my room and said, "What are you so worried about? The line only has Notre Dame favored by six." The last thing I wanted to hear about was the betting odds after all we'd been through. "Don't ever mention a gambling line to me again," I said.

We were lucky to catch Notre Dame on a night when they were flat. We surprised everyone, including ourselves, by racing out to a 47–15 lead. Our defense was superb, we worked for great shots, and made the most out of our opportunities. I was so engrossed in the game that I was oblivious to the score. (Every coach should worry more about execution than the score.) When I saw the board I turned to my assistant, Ken Rosemond, and said, "Is that really forty-seven to fifteen, or is it supposed to be thirty-seven to fifteen?"

We were up 88–46 when I went to the bench, substituting four walk-ons and a scholarship player with about eight minutes left. I always believed in substituting when the game was safe, not just to keep from embarrassing the opponent, but also to give the hardworking subs a chance to play. Notre Dame closed the gap before the buzzer, and we won 99–80. After the game Johnny Jordan walked down to our bench to shake hands. "Thank you so much," he said. "Ninety-nine to eighty won't look as bad in the Chicago papers." Coach Jordan came to my room for some Chinese food late that night.

After eight games we were 6–2, and everybody was thrilled, including the head coach. But then the bubble burst, and we suffered consecutive beatings at the hands of Duke and Maryland. After the loss at Maryland, 79–62, I was really bothered. I didn't feel good about any part of the game. Not only had we not played well, but for the first time we were outhustled. Effort was something we could control. Frank McGuire's old friends and now mine, Buck Freeman, Jack LaRocca, Danny and Colleen Patrissy, and Lou and Florence Vine had all come to the game, and we went to dinner afterwards. They could see how disappointed I was. I couldn't get the loss out of my mind, to the point that I had no appetite. Buck said, "You played well. Maryland was just better." But I still wasn't hungry. After dinner Danny took me aside. "Dean, it's only a game," he said. "Don't let it get to you. You weren't supposed to be great this year."

I questioned my ability, feeling for the first time a chink in my confidence. I wondered if I had made the right decision in becoming a coach.

We went on to beat Maryland at home, and finished 7–7 in the conference, which today could get us an NCAA tourney bid. Our season ended with a 2-point loss to South Carolina in the first round of the ACC tournament, for an 8–9 mark overall. After it was over I put the season in perspective. I suspected that if I had been able to schedule some easy teams in a normal twenty-five-game season, we could have been 17–9. With Poteet and McComb in our lineup, we would have been very good. I felt a little better about my chosen livelihood, but I knew there was a great deal to do.

. . .

During my first season I had gotten an interesting call. "Dean," the caller said, "we need to get our two schools together and play. I'm a nineteen twenty-three graduate of Kansas, and you're a nineteen fifty-three graduate, and we played for the same head coach. Let's do a ten-year series, home and home, and that way neither of us will know what kind of team the other has." It was Adolph Rupp at Kentucky.

Rupp gave me some advice: He told me to beware of people who called up wanting to play one or two games right away. "That means they think they're going to be very good for a couple of years, and they figure you're going to be down," he said. Also, Rupp informed me, everybody called when they had great players. When Jerry Lucas went to Ohio State, suddenly the Buckeyes wanted to play Kentucky. Finally, he advised me, "As the flagship state university, don't play anybody from within your own state that you don't have to. You'll be the target and they'll be aiming at you, and you'll soon learn that the last thing in the world you need is any more rivals. You'll have plenty as it is." Coach Rupp wouldn't play Louisville or Eastern or Western Kentucky.

After I got off the phone, I went to Chuck Erickson and told him that Rupp had called to schedule a ten-year series between Carolina and Kentucky. Chuck said, "Oh, everybody's calling and trying to schedule us now. We're center cut. We've got a good name and no team." (We signed a contract for the series, and won seven of the ten even though I unwisely agreed to play six times in Kentucky to just four times in Carolina.)

But in 1962–63 I thought we had a team. Billy Cunningham, a sophomore, joined the varsity for what would be a 15–6 season. Billy came in as a six-foot, four-and-a-half-inch freshman, but before he graduated he grew to six six. He joined a team that included our alternately soulful and combative senior point guard, Larry Brown, a six-foot-four sophomore from Pantego, North Carolina, named Ray Respess, and a six-three walk-on, Charlie Shaffer, a son of Chapel Hill who was a great prep quarterback and originally recruited for football. His father happened to be director of development for the university. Charlie tore up his knee in football, so he came out for basketball instead and was a major surprise, playing so well with a knee brace. He was a marvelous multiple-sport athlete and would go on to become a corporate lawyer in Atlanta. He was also a member of the "Atlanta Nine" who were instrumental in bringing the 1996 Olympics there. In addition, we had Yogi Poteet of Hendersonville, North Carolina, who regained his eligibility, giving us a six-foot-one sharpshooter and a tremendous perimeter defender; and the six-three Mike Cooke of Mt. Airy, North Carolina, was our first man off the bench, followed by Bryan McSweeney. We had four Carolina natives among our first six players, which was a significant change in just one year. It wasn't intentional, but would please Chancellor Aycock.

The only other thing I could have asked for would have been for Ken McComb to return to school. McComb was six feet six, weighed 238 pounds, and I loved him as a player. As a sophomore substitute he had played in the last Dixie Classic, and hauled down eighteen rebounds in less than a half against Villanova. But Kenny never played again for Carolina after his academic setback; he got married and went to work as an electrician.

I not only took Rupp up on his offer to play Kentucky, I arranged for us to play at Indiana on the same trip. We would meet the Hoosiers on a Saturday, followed by the Wildcats in intimidating Memorial Gym on Monday. It meant we would face a slugger's row in one weekend. Indiana was led by Tom and Dick Van Arsdale, who were featured on the cover of *Sports Illustrated* that year as sophomore phenoms, while Kentucky had a virtuoso All-American in Cotton Nash.

I was naive in my scheduling, but I had an ulterior motive too. I was trying out an approach that I would adhere to for the rest of my career: Play tough games, and make sure some of them are on the road. In addition to Kentucky and Indiana, over the years we traveled to all but three of the Big Ten arenas, as well as UCLA, Houston, and Kansas, all before the conference season began. (In my first four years we never played more than ten home games, including those we played in Greensboro and Charlotte before home crowds. It's no secret that the home court is a huge advantage in basketball, and we sometimes paid a price for that scheduling.) When you play against strong teams your weaknesses are exposed, and then you have time to work on them before the tournament in March. For us the ACC tournament was critical. It determined the conference champion and which team would go to the NCAA tournament.

If your goal is to have twenty wins every season, that kind of scheduling isn't the way to do it. You can build a very impressive regular-season record by playing weaker teams while never learning much about your own basketball team. Building false confidence seldom works. But if your desire is to see a team genuinely improve, you have to play against challenging competition and learn from your losses.

We learned, all right. Indiana beat us, 90–76. All the way from Bloomington to Lexington on the bus I fumed in my seat. I wasn't angry just about the loss. Two of our players had come in late the night before, and I chewed them out. I wasn't certain I would even let them play against Kentucky.

We were all concerned about the Kentucky game. Memorial Gym was a tough place to play. Kentucky's losses at home were so rare they were listed in the basketball media guide. The Kentucky capacity crowd maintained a steady roar, and in the locker room before the game our team looked uncertain. Larry Brown actually broke out in hives all over his body. Back then there was no bigger basketball school than Kentucky, and no surer standard to measure our team against than the program built by Rupp, the Baron of the Bluegrass. But I wasn't nervous. The games that made *me* most nervous were the ones where I knew we were about to play a dangerous team, but our players, the fans, and the media were sure we'd win by 20.

In the locker room we listened to the crowd, and I told the team, "Look, when you go out there tonight forget about Kentucky, forget about the crowd. Pretend it's Tennessee. Just play forty minutes of basketball. Now this is how we're going to beat them." Then I outlined our strategy: Defensively we would use a point zone and one, with Yogi Poteet assigned the job of tracking Cotton Nash man-to-man. Yogi was six one to Nash's six five, but he was also our best defensive player when it came to staying between his man and the ball. Offensively we would work for the shots we wanted. If we got ahead, I said, we would try something: We would go to a delay, with Larry Brown holding the ball and looking to drive by his man to shoot or pass. "We can win," I said.

We stayed with Kentucky. Poteet played the game of his life against Nash, denying him the ball on many possessions. Shaffer was five for five. Everybody did his part. We held the ball against their aggressive man defense until someone got clear for a shot. We won, 68–66, and our players were euphoric. In the locker room afterwards, Shaffer came over to me and said, "That was the greatest game of basketball anybody ever coached." It wasn't, but I appreciated the sentiment because it meant that the team trusted me. It was as though a light had switched on, and everything suddenly made sense to them. I decided to walk back to the hotel with my friend and trainer John Lacey, so I could take a few minutes to appreciate what had just happened. I knew it was a benchmark for the program.

We went on to build a 15–6 record, and everybody seemed pleased with the team. What really made them happy was that we finished 10–4 in the conference. That team accomplished much: We beat Notre Dame at South

Bend on national television in overtime, and we were in every game we played. Had the guidelines been then what they are today, that team would have been a fairly high seed in the NCAA tournament.

There was one other interesting development that season. One afternoon we were practicing for a meeting with Duke. In the last game, Duke played a half-court zone press, and a typical strategy against it was to send four men to the corners with a center at the foul line. But we did something slightly different. Looking to score out of this set, we put our best ball handler, Larry Brown, at the foul line instead of a big man.

I huddled the defense and told them to show the zone press, but then switch into man-to-man. I wanted to see if Larry would recognize the change and go to our man-to-man delay game as he was supposed to. We were always working on things like recognition. Fortunately for all of us, Larry didn't recognize it, but he did know a scoring opportunity when he saw one. He drove right by his man, and passed to a teammate for a layup.

I told them to do it again. Larry said later, "I thought it was a conditioning drill." Brown's failure to recognize had opened up new possibilities.

It dawned on me that we could use this offense against a man-to-man defense, as well as the more common usage against a half-court zone press. It would work against any defense, for that matter. In fact, it would be an especially effective strategy if you had the lead. We would call it the Four Corners but didn't really begin using it as an offense until the 1965–66 season.

Tough times were ahead. I was about to enter one of the darker periods of my professional life. In my third season (1964) we dropped to 12–12, and a fifth-place 6–8 record in the ACC. We would never be worse than third place in the ACC after that. In thirty-one years, we would be as low as third place in the ACC only four times. To show the strength of the ACC in 1986, we were third in the ACC and eighth in the final AP poll nationally.

I did the worst coaching job of my career. Larry Brown had graduated, leaving us without a "true" point guard. After graduating, Larry went on to play for the Akron Goodyears of the AAU and then made the 1964 Olympic team under Hank Iba.

I did two things that weren't smart: I never settled on a starting lineup, and I tried too hard to make Billy Cunningham an All-American, which was achieved. Without Larry Brown, the point-guard spot was a revolving door of Ray Hassell and walk-ons Bill Brown, John Yokley, and Charlie Shaffer. Shaffer was a terrific perimeter player but I hurt him by trying to make him a point guard defensively. Yokley, who had been good enough for a scholarship out of high school, ended up starting at point guard in 1966. My shuffling of the lineup confused the players, and we ended up asking too much of Billy. It was, "Billy get the rebound, Billy bring the ball upcourt against a press." We had him doing everything, and I worried about conserving his energy. I even told him he could stop at midcourt if a shot went up on the fast break before he got down the floor. It was the last time we ever allowed such a thing at Carolina. On every subsequent team, when a shot went up our big men had to sprint for the rebound. I made a drill for our big men after that year. I would stand them at center court and an assistant coach would shoot a twenty-foot shot. The three or four big men would leave center court on the shot to rebound. If the ball hit the floor before one of them caught it, they would have to run sprints. I vowed I would never again lose sight of the fact that it's a team game.

Everett Case was right when he said our real problems would lie farther down the road than in our first couple of seasons. If you examined our old rosters, you would see that there were six walk-ons on that first squad, and on each of the next three teams there were four walk-ons. Our recruiting restrictions came at a time when we could least afford them.

I had no experience as a recruiter, and it was catching up with us. My only brush with selling a school had been at the Air Force Academy, where our principal competitors were the Naval Academy and West Point. Frank McGuire had done his own recruiting. The bottom line was that I had no idea about the persistence it took to recruit at this level. To give you an example, during Christmas of 1963 we had a two-week break before we were scheduled to play again against Notre Dame. My assistant, Ken Rosemond, and I should have been out recruiting—visiting and scouting prospects. Instead we used some of the time to go to Jacksonville, Florida, to see North Carolina play Air Force in the Gator Bowl.

Between the recruiting sanctions, our limited schedule, and my status as a relative newcomer, we had some handicaps. But as a recruiter I was honest and sincere, and I had one great asset: the beautiful campus of North Carolina with its wonderful college-town atmosphere and academic reputation. Believe me, Ken and I made sure each prospect had our academic rating and pictures of our campus, and we pointed out that there should be an opportunity to play.

In 1963, we won our first "name" player, the highly sought after Bobby Lewis from St. John's Academy in Washington, D.C., a gazellelike leaper and great scorer inside who we thought would play guard one day. Bobby revered Billy Cunningham after watching him knock down a long jumper to force overtime and win at Notre Dame in one of the few nationally televised games in 1963. When Bobby visited the campus, Billy served as his host and showed him around. But what got him was our campus, which he saw in full spring bloom. "Bobby made the best decision and the one we hoped he would," his parents told me.

The very next year, 1964, we secured one of the top high school players in America, a young man named Larry Miller from Catasauqua, Pennsylvania. Ken Rosemond persuaded Larry to visit our campus. Miller was six foot four and built like a wall, and he had played on a summer league men's team when just an eighth-grader. Ken went to the Miller home to visit with Larry and his family three different times. He would sit and drink a beer with Larry's father, Julius. Never once did they suspect the truth: that Ken Rosemond *hated* beer.

Miller was supposed to be all wrapped up by Duke. But Ken kept showing up, and one afternoon when he was sitting around with the Millers he told him, "You know, Larry, the saddest thing is that if you went from here down to Duke, you'd be going all that way and you'd still be five minutes from heaven. Come down to see for yourself."

Miller liked Ken for saying that. And he liked another suggestion by Ken about being special as the only high school All-American on our freshman team. Larry could be the one to turn it all around, whereas Duke had already signed six other freshmen, including a few high school All-Americans. As recruiting wore on, Miller became uncertain; now he wasn't so sure anymore about Duke after he came to visit Chapel Hill. Cunningham and Lewis, along with Charlie Shaffer, and his future wife, Harriett, drove him around campus and showed him every leaf and blossom. The very next day Duke's persuasive Vic Bubas and his assistants showed up at Miller's door with a formal offer of scholarship in hand, but Miller refused to commit. When he was ready, he said, he would let us all know his decision by inviting the chosen coach to his high school graduation.

Larry's parents had also driven down to Chapel Hill when he visited. In those days, in order for the parents to have a good time, I would have close friends Mary Frances and Guy Andrews, along with Tassie and Jimmy Dempsey, help me entertain, since they were likely to be the same age as the parents and have more in common with them. They were all Carolina people and made a good impression. I'll never forget Mary Frances "cutting in" to dance with Peggy Miller in my small basement recreation room. Mary Frances didn't drink, but I've never seen a more vivacious personality. The Millers also enjoyed their visit to Chapel Hill.

In the middle of all this, I went up to Pennsylvania and took Larry and his family to dinner at a local stop that Mr. Miller liked. Duke assistant Chuck Daly had been up there recruiting Larry and had eaten with the family at the very same place. Daly raved about the food, Mr. Miller told me with pride. "He said he has traveled all across the country, but this place served the best steak he's ever eaten anywhere." I looked down at my plate, at a T-bone that had been pan fried. I knew I was supposed to say something similar, but I just couldn't.

"What do you think?" Mr. Miller asked.

"That really is some steak," I said.

We waited for Larry's answer until June. One Saturday afternoon I was playing golf at the Country Club of North Carolina with our usual foursome, Dr. Chris Fordham, Simon Terrell, husband of my secretary, Betsy, and the head of high school sports in the state, and Dr. Earl Somers, a local psychiatrist, all of whom were Carolina alums, but hardly ever talked about basketball. My friend Buck Adams, the golf pro there and a huge Carolina basketball fan, came driving out in a cart to the number-eight green to tell me that Larry Miller was on the phone. Buck was so excited he was waving his arms over his head. Driving back I said, "Buck, he could be calling to say he's not coming." Buck, crushed, said, "Oh." I took the call in the pro shop. Larry said he wanted to ask me some more questions. We chatted for a while, and then Larry said, "I'll call you tomorrow night to let you know what I'm going to do. Where will you be?"

I told him I would be running a basketball camp in Woollen Gym, but to leave word with my wife. The next night was hot, so during the clinic we left the doors and windows of the gym open to let in a breeze. I saw my wife, Ann, come through the doors. She had jumped in the car and driven up to tell me the news. Larry Miller had called, she said. He wanted to know if I would attend his graduation. We had beaten Duke in a head-to-head recruiting battle for the first time since I became coach.

Inflated expectations turned out to be our biggest problem in my fourth year. Cunningham would be a senior. Bobby Lewis had averaged right at 37 points a game for our freshman team as a post man. In one outing against Elon's junior varsity, Bobby hung 50 points up. The idea of Cunningham playing on the same team with Lewis gave everyone sky-high expectations. But I was more realistic. I looked at our schedule and saw no sure wins, except for possibly a visit from Tulane. We had only two home games in the first thirteen, plus meetings with Kentucky in Charlotte and an excellent Vanderbilt team in Greensboro. We managed to win those four games, thanks in part to the home-court advantage.

For the first time since I had become head coach, fans and media made it clear we were supposed to do better than we had in the previous rebuilding period. But I knew that Bobby would have trouble adjusting to the varsity, even with Cunningham to help him. He was still just a skinny six-three sophomore, and while he was extremely talented, he had to make the transition from playing the post to the perimeter. What few people realized was that we were still thin in numbers and size, and four of the twelve lettermen were walk-ons. Billy, who by then had grown to six six, was our second-tallest player after the six-eight Bob Bennett.

The season started out well enough. I must have thought our prospects looked pretty good, because I began building a house in the spring of 1964 for my family in the Morgan Creek section of Chapel Hill. In December we embarked on a two-game road trip to Georgia and South Carolina, and while we were away I received another job offer.

During preseason practices, I had an impromptu and interesting visitor. Joel Eaves, the Auburn head coach who, unknown to me, was about to become athletic director at Georgia, came to Chapel Hill to watch us practice for a couple of days. I thought the visit was a little strange, but knew he was running the Shuffle offense at Auburn and had visited Bob Spear and me a few years earlier. As it turned out, it wasn't so impromptu. By the time we arrived at Georgia on that road swing in early December, Joel had taken over as Georgia's athletic director. We lost the game 64–61, but afterwards Joel and his wife, Wealthy, asked me to come over for a postgame meal, and over dinner Joel asked me to come to Georgia following the season as the new head coach. He had a plan: He wanted me to be the basketball coach and had just hired Vince Dooley as the football coach. I was honored by the offer, especially in view of the fact that our team had just lost a game. But I told Joel that he should continue his search, because I didn't want to leave Chapel Hill. I suggested he might want to look at my assistant, Ken Rosemond.

On December 5, 1964, we traveled to South Carolina, where Frank McGuire had just taken over as head coach. Frank ended up spending just one year in Philadelphia with Wilt Chamberlain. When the Warriors went to California he refused to move west. (Once, when he was asked the major difference between the pro and college game, Frank joked that in the pros his biggest responsibility was "to see that Wilt made the plane on time.")

After sitting out in the business world a couple of seasons, Frank had accepted the job of building South Carolina's program.

We won the game, and afterwards I felt so good about the future that when I got home to the newly built house on Morgan Creek I said to Ann, half joking but also with relief, "It looks like we'll be able to keep the house."

We followed the South Carolina win with a 15-point victory over a Kentucky team that included a guy named Pat Riley. But then we had a major setback at Indiana. The Van Arsdale twins along with Jon McGlocklin were seniors, and the Hoosiers were ranked number one in the country. They whacked us, 107–81, in a televised game. I was so upset with the team at halftime that I decided to let them stew in the locker room by themselves for a few minutes. Ken Rosemond and I stood in the hallway talking. "I think I'm going to let them sit before blasting our impatience," I said. Suddenly, an official walked up and told me it was time to get back on the court. In the Big Ten, the intermission period for televised games was only ten minutes instead of the usual fifteen, and no one had told me. We took the court without much talking at all—not that it mattered—but I would hear about the incident later.

On December 21, we embarked on a four-game road trip, and much as I believed in testing a team with tough scheduling, this time I overdid it. We lost three straight road games to a strong Florida team coached by Norm Sloan, to Maryland by 8, and to Wake Forest, 107–85. A loss to another in-state school is never a popular thing on the Carolina campus, but the margin of the Wake defeat rankled. Our record was now 6–6.

The discontent had been slowly building in Chapel Hill. I had heard comments on campus, and I was openly criticized in some papers. The talk was that if Carolina wasn't winning with Cunningham and Lewis, the problem had to be the coach.

It was a long ride home that night after the Wake loss. I sat in the front of the bus, thinking of how we could get ready for Duke in only two days. Finally, we pulled up in front of Woollen Gym. I noticed some students gathered across the street, about a hundred or so of them, and then Ken Rosemond said, "Look, they're hanging you in effigy over there."

A dummy hung from a noose in front of the gym. I could tell it was me was because of its long nose. Students were leaning out of their windows from the dormitory across the street to watch. I didn't make a move. As a matter of fact, I don't recall my exact emotion at that moment. Billy Cunningham remembers being simmering mad.

I stood up to address the team. I knew the players were tired. I decided to give them a day off. They had played two games in three days, and now we had just forty-eight hours to prepare to play at Duke—another horrible piece of scheduling on my part. "There will be no practice tomorrow," I said, "but I want to meet with each of you individually. See a manager for the time, and be sure to be in class tomorrow."

When I was done speaking, I left the bus and went to my car. I didn't see what happened next, I only heard about it later. Billy Cunningham leaped out of his seat and ran down the steps of the bus. He grabbed the effigy and tore it down. I heard Billy Galantai helped as well. The rest of the players filed off the bus and walked by the effigy, ignoring it.

The incident has become part of Carolina lore, and it certainly isn't an experience I would wish on anyone. You never forget a thing like that, ever. But it wasn't as traumatic for me as it has been made out to be over the years, and my standard comment on the subject ever since has been that I was pleased there was interest in basketball here and I'm just happy they used a dummy and not the real thing.

Quite frankly, I didn't dwell on the episode or worry too much about my job. I did know some people were calling for me to be fired. If one hundred students were there that night, I figured several hundred more felt the same way. But I also knew I had the backing of my administration, and that if I ever lost that backing, I could find another coaching job. I was also confident that the players were with me. If you've got your team behind you, that's a big part of it.

I drove home to the house on Morgan Creek and to my sleeping family. It was very late. I checked on each of the children and then called my sister, Joan, who was living in St. Louis at the time. Joan can tell you that I wasn't unduly upset that night. I usually alternated calls to Joan or my parents after games to tell them the score, and this night was no different. I told her we had lost to Wake Forest, and briefly summarized the scene waiting for me at Woollen Gym. "There was an incident," I said, and described it for her, but I didn't go into it at length. Joan was more disturbed by it than I was. I reassured her. "It's not the end of the world," I said. After I got off the phone, my minister and good friend from Binkley Baptist Church, Bob Seymour, called because he had heard about the effigy. We talked for a few minutes, and I told him what I had told Joan.

"We'll overcome it," I said. "It's not the end of the world."

The second-guessing continued the next morning. First thing, I got a call from Chuck Erickson and his assistant athletic director, Walter Rabb. They wanted to meet with me. I said fine, but it would have to be brief. "I have the players coming in for meetings, and I don't have long to talk," I said. "We've got Duke on the road in two days."

Erickson went right to the point. "We got a problem here," he said. After getting drilled by 22 points just eleven hours earlier, I probably could have figured that out on my own. Sometimes, I felt that Chuck let some old ill will affect his relationship with me. Chuck and Frank McGuire hadn't gotten along, and I certainly wanted to fight some of Frank's ancient battles with him. Still, the only real differences I had with Chuck involved funding for the program. I knew he thought I was a good coach. Nobody threatened to fire me in that meeting. Chuck just said, "You've got to get things straight." Chuck brought up the halftime mixup at the Indiana game. "I understand you were only in the dressing room for one minute at the Indiana game," he said. I explained what had happened as best I could, and Chuck accepted the explanation. Then he simply said, "You need to get it going." Chuck and I talked often after he retired and became good friends.

People have often asked me if I was afraid for my job. The answer is, not really. My biggest supporter, Aycock, had left the chancellor's position the previous summer, but he was still an influential figure on campus. Years later, I learned that a couple of alumni went to Aycock to talk about firing me, but true to his word, he had just laughed and told them, "You handle your business, I'll handle mine." Ironically, I ran into one of those men many years later. I was in a restaurant in Chapel Hill when the man stuck out his hand, introduced himself, and told me what a great job we were doing. I shook his hand. "I'm sure glad your talk with Chancellor Aycock didn't do any good," I said. We both laughed.

When Aycock left the chancellor's seat, he made it clear that he felt I should remain the head coach, and his successor, Paul Sharp, agreed with him. I never heard a word of criticism from South Building. I had several close friends on the faculty, and I knew if I was in trouble they would tell me.

Chancellor Aycock knew that any coach he could have brought in from the outside would have needed three or four years to get the program going again. "I knew at some point we were going to have to win," Aycock has said of that period. "But the reason I wanted Dean had nothing to do with winning games. I thought he was a teacher, and I think he thought of himself as a teacher." He had told me from the beginning to go at it with everything I had, and he would back me. And he did.

While I appreciated the support from the administration, what we really needed was a win. But there was no tougher assignment than Duke. The

Blue Devils were 8–1 and ranked number six in the nation behind the play of Steve Vacendak and Jack Marin, and they had made the national finals the previous year. We were 6–6 and struggling. With all that was going on and my poor scheduling, we didn't even have time to practice much before making the drive to Durham. Nobody gave us a chance.

But we were a fired-up group when we got there. I would prefer not to have to be hung in effigy to motivate a team, but that incident helped. I gave a pregame speech that, for me, was rousing. I told the team, "We're going to spread out and move and keep on moving. We will hold the ball until we get *exactly* what we want. Don't worry about executing plays, just stay on the move." Defensively, we keyed on Vacendak and Marin.

We executed our plan almost to perfection. Duke played into our hands and did what we wanted them to, which was put up hurried shots. Meanwhile, our players waited for the right opportunity. We won, 65–62. It was an enormous upset. For the game, Duke took 66 shots and made just 26, while we took just 49, but sank 27. We held Vacendak and Marin to 11 and 10 points respectively, and controlled the tempo throughout.

The short bus ride back to Chapel Hill was in stark contrast to the one home after the Wake Forest game. We were a happy group of players and coaches on that bus, and when we arrived at Woollen Gym a different sort of demonstration was waiting for us. A large group of students had gathered to celebrate the victory and welcome the team. They urged me to say a few words, but I declined.

"I can't," I said. "There's something tight around my neck that keeps me from speaking."

By then I should have become accustomed to the tight fit, because our celebration didn't last long. North Carolina State visited Chapel Hill four days later and came from behind to beat us, 65–62. I've never heard this talked about, so I don't think it's common knowledge, but there was another effigy burning after that game at Woollen Gym, although this one was smaller. A dummy was strung up, and someone played taps. Two effigy hangings and one huge victory celebration! It was a full week. I can remember thinking, *Who needs this? I would be happy coaching high school and teaching math.* I was going to do my best, and if that wasn't good enough, I wasn't going to spend any more time worrying about it.

Next we beat Virginia on the road, only to lose at home to Maryland. We were 8–8, and we had a week off before we were to play New York University at Greensboro Coliseum. I spent the off week doing some very serious reading and thinking, in addition to holding some excellent practices.

I had a small study in our house on Morgan Creek Road where I would go to watch game film. It was a simple room with a film projector, and a desk over which there were three shelves of books, most of which dealt with philosophy and theology. My sister, Joan, who had completed a master's degree at the University of Chicago's Divinity School, had interested me in those subjects and afterwards given me her books. While visiting her at school there in 1954, I had gone to a lecture by the famous theologian Paul Tillich. I didn't understand much of what Dr. Tillich said that day, but his remarks provoked an interest and I wanted to learn more. "Man is man because he is free," Tillich said. What did he mean by that? I wondered. One professor claimed that Tillich "had answers for questions which haven't been asked," so at least I wasn't the only one having trouble understanding him.

It was a habit of mine to do some reading late at night in my study after watching film. I would leaf through various volumes. I read Elton Trueblood, who later became a good friend, and I read Christian psychologist Paul Tournier from Switzerland, whom I had heard speak in Chapel Hill, and also Robert McAfee Brown, who had put together the Layman's Theological Library. This library introduced me to theologians and philosophers such as Barth, Bultmann, Buber, Bonhoeffer, and Kierkegaard. I guess I was searching for the meaning of life through these authors, and still am. Outside of these kinds of books I did very little reading.

One night after the usual late dinner and goodnight rituals with Sharon, Sandy, and Scott, I decided against watching more film and perused the bookshelves. I remembered that Joan had given me a book for Christmas by Catherine Marshall. I had read her excellent memoir of her husband, *A Man Called Peter*. Peter Marshall was chaplain for the U.S. Senate and pastor of the New York Avenue Presbyterian Church in Washington, D.C., before his untimely death at age forty-nine. I decided to thumb through her latest book, *Beyond Our Selves,* before retiring.

The first chapter, entitled "Something More," made me keep reading. She wrote, "If you are satisfied with your life and feel no need for any help outside yourself, this book is not for you. The search for God begins at the point of need."

I read past midnight into the early hours. When I reached chapter ten, "The Power of Helplessness," I sat up straight and alert. I was feeling helpless. I had to admit it: I was struggling, no matter how often I had told others the events of the last several weeks weren't the end of the world and I would overcome them. Catherine Marshall wrote, "Crisis brings us face to face with our inadequacy, and our inadequacy in turn leads us to the inexhaustible sufficiency of God. This is the power of helplessness, a principle written into the fabric of life."

Having been raised by two parents who were professing Christians, I had heard all of my life about the Holy Spirit, an inner counselor in every human being. Although it is called by various names, I believe the basic concept of a Holy Spirit can be found in a variety of belief systems. In the excellent twelve-step program outlined by Alcoholics Anonymous it is often referred to as "The Higher Power." My close friend Dr. Chris Fordham prefers to call it the Human Spirit. We both believe our Creator planned the spirit for each human as a gift, so I can go along with his term too.

I had always been aware of the Holy Spirit, I realized, but I had never truly given myself over to it. So often in my life I thought I was self-sufficient. The key, I suddenly understood, lay in surrendering my life and my daily choices to the gift of power within. Every word Marshall wrote seemed to have particular relevance for me. "No sinner is hopeless, no situation is irretrievable. No cause is past redeeming," I read. A setback, Marshall wrote, "is actually the crucible out of which victory could rise." Finally she quoted Jesus in John's Gospel, "I am the vine; you are the branches. Apart from me you can do nothing."

Catherine Marshall's chapter on helplessness gave me clarity, and more important, the conviction that I could give up control of my life choices and allow my Higher Power to take them over. Bob Seymour said it more simply in a sermon he delivered, entitled "Discipline's Paradoxical Promise." Bob said, "We are most happy and free with God in control of our life." Now I understood the meaning of his words. When I closed *Beyond Our Selves,* I thought to myself: *I give up. You take over.* As soon as the words formed in my mind, I immediately felt a letting go and a peace.

I should say two things at this point. One, simply because I decided to surrender my daily choices to that Power didn't mean I never messed up again. Each day, I make the same old mistake of trying to control my life. It's hard to let go. An example: After surrendering in my morning prayer, I get in the car and drive to the office, feeling at peace. As I come around a corner, another driver doesn't yield. I slam on the brakes, lean on my horn, and descend into pettiness. I yell, "What are you doing?" That's why I say it's a daily surrender, and sometimes a moment-to-moment surrender. It's only human to want to take charge of your own life. But when I "give up" choices to the spirit within me, that's when I am most happy and free.

Two, this experience should not imply that God was now on my side to help North Carolina win basketball games. I would think a loving Creator wants all individuals and teams to do well and enjoy playing. It bothers me when a church invites the star quarterback to speak after throwing five touchdown passes. Actually, I think it would be more appropriate to invite a quarterback who threw five interceptions. He might talk about how he regained his peace of mind by surrendering to the spirit. He might also say that no human is in charge of the universe, but each of us can have contact with the One who helps us make our decisions.

That evening of study and reflection brought a certain calm to my life. It made me less anxious. Although I never talked to the team about my realizations, I do think they sensed something, a change in me. They seemed to relax too, and we started a streak of some very good basketball. Things didn't improve overnight, of course, but almost. When we went to Greensboro Coliseum to play New York University a few days later, I was soundly booed during the team introductions before tip-off. But we went on to beat NYU, 100–78, and by the end of the game the boos had turned to cheers. It was a huge win to my way of thinking, since NYU was considered an excellent program in the early '60s under Lou Rossini.

We didn't lose another regular-season game. We won seven straight, and eight of our last ten to finish at 15–9 and 10–4 in the Atlantic Coast Conference, which was second only to Duke (even though we beat Duke in both meetings). In the end, Cunningham averaged a magnificent 25 points and fourteen rebounds a game, while Lewis averaged 21 points. That team, too, would have been an NCAA tournament team under today's rules.

We had turned the corner but I probably didn't realize it then.

A couple of important things happened in the next year. We moved from Woollen Gym, which seated 4,000 at most, to brand-new Carmichael Auditorium, with 8,800 seats for basketball, and christened it by going 16–11 and 8–6 in the ACC, a third-place finish in the league. "The L&M Boys"— Lewis and Miller—gained renown; Lewis fulfilled all the promise he had shown, setting a Carolina single-game record with 49 points against Florida State, and Miller had an outstanding sophomore season. Ken Rosemond had departed to take the head coaching job at Georgia under Joel Eaves. And I made my first coaching hires, bringing in Larry Brown and John Lotz as my new assistant coaches. With John and Larry as my assistants we could enjoy being a three-man staff for the first time.

With Billy Cunningham gone—he graduated in 1965 as a two-time All-American and the school's all-time leading rebounder—we needed to find a way to make more use of Lewis and Miller offensively as six-three forwards. We didn't have much size on the team, so we would try to spread people out and to take them one on one in the Four Corners, especially with a lead. Bob Bennett was a six-eight senior who could handle the ball and shoot pretty well, which allowed us to use Lewis and Miller in one-on-one situations to drive or post up. In fact, Lewis and Miller combined would shoot 54 percent from the field during the season.

We upset Ohio State in Columbus with the Four Corners early in the season, 85–72, using it to protect a large first-half margin, as Miller had 33 points and Lewis had 31. Then we used it for an entire game in a now-famous ACC tournament meeting with Duke to end the year. The Duke game is when it really came into its own. Duke had beaten us in two regular season meetings using a zone defense. I decided our best chance to control the pace of the game was to go to the Four Corners and make them come out to chase us in man or a zone press defense. But Vic Bubas told his team to be patient and don't gamble.

The halftime score was 7–5, in favor of Duke. We took just five shots in the half, waiting for a wide-open opportunity. We heard a lot of boos, and some debris was even thrown on the court; it wasn't the most popular piece of bench coaching I've ever done. But as I said later, "We didn't want a good game. We wanted to win." As the clock wound down we were tied at 20. Duke got a rebound with 1:40 to go, and held the ball for the last shot. Duke's Mike Lewis sank a free throw for a 21–20 lead, we never got another shot off, and we lost by a point. But I decided the Four Corners had been the most effective strategy, giving us a chance to win in the last minute against this Duke team, which moved on to the Final Four.

Ever since that game, I have been wrongly credited as the sole creator of the Four Corners. I've heard of a number of coaches who ran something similar. John McClendon, a good friend of mine who coached at North Carolina College and Tennessee State among other places, tells me they ran a delay game that he called Two-in-the-Corner. Chuck Noe, while at South Carolina, used three men out by the ten-second line, with his best two players down low near the basket, and called it The Mongoose. A major contribution to the evolution of Four Corners came from our Air Force team under Bob Spear during a game against New Mexico in 1957. The rules then stated that the defense had to force action by being within three feet of the ball handler. We put three players across the ten-second line and two in each corner. Our smaller team had a field day, driving past the New Mexico defenders in Albuquerque for a big win.

If there was an "innovation" at Carolina, it was to put our best ball handler in the middle, rather than a big man. Over the years we realized how frustrating the Four Corners could be to the opponent, and we refined it even further, adding flourishes like backdoor plays. We really got too much attention for it, and we were mislabeled a stalling team when in fact we were very much a fast-breaking team and routinely among the top scoring teams in the nation. Often the effect of the Four Corners was psychological, to show that we were in command. Of everything. We would spread our players to the four corners of the floor and dribble interminably, daring them to come get us—and we taught the players to smile while they were running it. Sometimes a smile could really frustrate the opponent, but more important, it showed what kind of confidence we had.

So ended my fifth season as head coach at Carolina. Ironically, when people talk about those first five years, they almost treat them as hardships, which I had come to believe until writing this book. But in retrospect, they were some good years. If you went by current standards, three of those five teams surely would have qualified for the NCAA tournament. They won some big games under tough circumstances, despite the fact that many of them were on the road. The five-year record reads sixty-six wins and forty-seven losses. Even in the well-balanced ACC we won forty-one while losing twenty-nine, which is the third best in the league for those five years, coming within one game of Wake Forest for second place in that period. I will always be grateful to the men who played on those teams, and when I look back on that early time, I see that we had not just great players but great students, who were very much a part of the student body. Earl Johnson, Richard Vinroot, and Charlie Shaffer were class presidents. Larry Brown was a class vice president, and a number of others served in student leadership capacities. Of the forty players who lettered on those first five teams, an unbelievable twenty-seven (68 percent) have at least a master's degree. Sixteen master's degree recipients (master's degrees in business lead, with six), seven lawyers, and four with doctorates are among the twenty-seven. More important, 100 percent of our players did receive their undergraduate degrees.

Not only was the record of those first five teams better than has been generally acknowledged, their accomplishments came amid much turmoil that was not of their making. They laid a foundation that helped our later teams win some very big games, and brought a lot of excitement to the school.

And they made sure a change in head coaches would not be necessary.

6

Hitting Our Stride

I liked the '60s, but I liked them a lot better after we won a few ball games.

Before the decade was out there would be campus sit-ins and marijuana smoke-outs. Discussions about hair. Vigils, rallies, protests. Our campus was an active one, and I thought the changes on it were great, even when I had to run players out of the gym on occasion. It was a fascinating time to be at a university, although the questions could be perplexing. How to impose order on a group of young people in an era when they were more concerned with personal freedoms? Striking a balance between team obligations and individual rights seemed to go to the heart of what was happening around us on our quadrangle and in society at large. So it was all the more gratifying to think of what we accomplished in that era of social upheaval and campus unrest. Between 1967 and 1969, our team went to three straight NCAA Final Fours, won three straight ACC regular season titles, and three straight ACC tournament titles. It was quite a run.

It began with a single recruiting class to complement Larry Miller and Bob Lewis. In April 1965, I hired Larry Brown, and two months later, John Lotz, giving me two extremely competent assistants. It was fun to have my former captain Larry with me again, plus an experienced high school coach,

John. I gained two excellent recruiters who loved our university and were loyal to the head coach. Larry lit up every room he walked into, and people immediately took to him, just as they do today. Larry got to Carolina just in time to help finalize our recruiting efforts for what would be the class of 1969. John was a great motivator with our players as individuals, with a lifestyle all respected.

Our basketball office was still a relatively small operation. When Ken Rosemond went to Georgia, my secretary, Betsy Terrell, and I were left alone in the office. Betsy was indispensable. Early in my tenure Chuck Erickson had given me a choice: I could hire two assistant coaches, or I could hire one assistant and a secretary. I opted to have a single assistant and asked Betsy to work for me. Betsy came from the Carolina ticket office so I knew she could handle a variety of pressures and responsibilities, and she was full of basketball savvy. Her husband, Simon, helped run the North Carolina High School Athletic Association and was a golf buddy of mine. Betsy was a secretary in name only; in reality she became virtually an assistant coach. She talked to players about their grades, helped them make their schedules, and ran the office. She held down the fort while I hit the road to doggedly recruit a class of prospects that became known as our first true "nucleus class."

Back in 1965–66, there were fewer NCAA rules than now and you could write, call, and visit a recruit as often as you liked. I was making frequent trips to Schenectady, New York, to see a young man named Dick Grubar, but so were coaches from Boston College, Notre Dame, and Kentucky. Grubar was a post player at Bishop Gibbons High School. He was six foot four, and while some college coaches didn't know quite where to play him, I felt he could be a point guard, because he had quick feet and was a gifted passer, but most important, he had much basketball savvy. On top of those attributes, he was a special competitor, plus an A student. I really wanted him after seeing him play in December of his senior year.

I was just as eager to sign the six-foot-eleven Rusty Clark of Fayetteville, North Carolina. He would be a breakthrough for us, our first big man and true center. Rusty, who wanted to go to medical school, committed to us when he won a Morehead Scholarship, which was the most prestigious grant offered by the university and patterned after the Rhodes Scholarship. Davidson College turned out to be our main competition for Rusty. His brother graduated from Davidson and both parents from Carolina.

Although Rusty was definitely coming, I wanted Larry to travel the ninety-minute drive to meet the Clarks. The first time Larry walked into the

Clark house he stared upward at Rusty, all six eleven of him. Larry is five foot ten so Rusty loomed over him. Next Mrs. Clark walked into the room, a very tall woman. Then the family dog, Montgomery, trotted in.

He was a mammoth Saint Bernard.

Larry looked around the huge living room for a place to sit down and realized that even the furniture was big. He took a seat, and the couch swallowed him. "I sort of sunk in," he says. "I sat there feeling like Alice in Wonderland."

Bill Bunting, a six-eight forward from New Bern, North Carolina, was another prospect we wanted very much, but so did Duke late in the recruiting process. Bill's father was a Duke alum, so we knew it would be hard to sign him. When Larry began visiting with Bill they appeared to mesh well. Fortunately, we had some other natural inroads. Bill's brother was a student at Carolina, and one of Bill's neighbors was a doctor named Simmons Patterson, who came from a family that was very loyal and important to UNC (among the most coveted athletic awards at UNC is the Patterson Medal). Fortunately, Bill resolved his divided family loyalties by signing with us, and I'm certain Larry's help was crucial.

We had already signed the six-five Joe Brown of Valdese, North Carolina, who had been in our summer basketball camp along with Clark and Bunting, which helped recruiting. For good measure we added Gerald Tuttle, a six-foot guard from London, Kentucky. It was Larry who convinced me to sign Tuttle, whom I had never heard of. Larry had played with his elder brother, Cecil Tuttle, on the Goodyear AAU team. Late in our recruiting period Cecil called up and told Larry that his younger brother had taken a small high school team all the way to the semifinals of the Kentucky state championship. Gerald was not recruited by NCAA Division 1 teams, but he was obviously a competitor who helped his team win games.

Every year, the freshmen played the varsity in a preseason scrimmage, and this year the game took place before a particularly large crowd. Interest in the freshmen was high. The annual scrimmage was part welcome and part wake-up call for the freshmen, a way of demonstrating to them exactly how much they had to learn. The varsity always won, and the freshmen invariably went away knowing they had work to do.

But this game produced an upset. The freshmen actually *beat* our upperclassmen. Anytime you have freshmen playing against upperclassmen the crowd will root for the freshmen, and that's what happened. Also, if freshmen had been eligible to play at that time, two or three could have been starters.

I didn't like the results the scrimmage produced. Can you imagine how Bob Lewis and Larry Miller felt with their own fans pulling against them? It was like a road game! The freshmen didn't need to get cocky; they needed to understand they had a long way to go. We set up a rematch so the varsity could get revenge, which they did, predictably. Miller, Lewis, seniors Bob Bennett, John Yokley, and the others weren't about to let the matter drop. Then just to make the point clear, we had another rematch so the varsity could win *again*. Afterwards, with everything back in its proper place, I abolished the game, and from then on instead of a varsity-freshman game, we had a full-team scrimmage with upperclassmen and freshmen mixed together and called it the Blue-White game. I watched from the scorer's table, and fans pulled for both teams.

The good news was that it demonstrated what kind of help was just around the corner. When those freshmen joined the varsity to make up the 1966–67 team, the result was perfect harmony and a complementary, balanced team. The prolific scorer Bobby Lewis and the adept passer Dick Grubar were in the backcourt, Larry Miller and Bill Bunting made a one-two punch in the frontcourt, and Clark was a true center. Tom Gauntlett, a former starter as a junior, was relegated to a sixth-man role. It wasn't easy to make that kind of adjustment, but he did it gracefully. The chemistry was just right; the upperclassmen didn't feel pressure to do too much, while the sophomores provided a great supporting cast. Most important, we could be a solid rebounding team for the first time since 1961.

We won nine straight games to open the 1966–67 season, and rose steadily in the national rankings to number five. We gained notoriety when we traveled to defending national runner-up Kentucky on December 13, 1966, and won, 64–55. The Wildcats had played predominantly black Texas Western the previous year for the NCAA title in a famous confrontation, and were back with possibly another great team, featuring players like Pat Riley and Louie Dampier. The win meant a lot to Grubar because he and Riley were both from Schenectady.

But living in that kind of rare air made me catch my breath. All of a sudden I felt a kind of pressure I hadn't felt since the effigy incident in my fourth season. In late December we went to Tampa for an invitational tournament. We were getting ready to play Florida State for the championship when the pressure hit me. I had stayed in the locker room while the team took the floor to warm up. That was the way Frank McGuire always did it. He would loiter in the dressing room until two minutes before tip-off, when he finally made his entrance.

I was standing back there in the dressing room by myself, reading the game program and killing time, when, out of nowhere, negative thoughts began to rush through my mind. *What if they beat us?* I thought. I felt pressure, that claustrophobic sensation that sits on your chest and creeps like cold water into your stomach. For about ten minutes I stood there in the grip of it. Then all of a sudden I thought, *This is ridiculous.* Back when I was hung in effigy, I had come to a peace with these feelings, or so I thought. I had vowed to do the best I could with every team, and if that wasn't enough, then I'd do something else. *Don't worry about it,* I told myself. *It's not that important.*

We beat Florida State, 81–54, and from that night on, I always went to the court with my team for pregame warm-ups. Sitting in the locker room was a miserable way to spend time before the tip-off, at least it was for me. I already knew our game plan and certainly didn't need to review it. Interestingly, the only ACC coach I ever remember coming out for pregame warm-ups is Dave Odom, Wake Forest's outstanding coach. We usually had a nice chat before our teams played each other. That night I learned once and for all how to cope with pressure and how to disarm it: You had to accept the potential consequences in advance and put them in perspective. The realization may have accounted for my so-called casual demeanor in pressure situations in the coming years. Everyone had job pressure, I decided. A mother with three young children has pressure.

My confrontation with myself in Tampa was good preparation, because even more pressure was yet to come. By February we were 19–4 and ranked number four in the country. But it didn't mean a thing. In those days if you didn't win the ACC tournament, you didn't go anywhere. Your season was over. You could go undefeated, and still you had to prove yourself all over again in the three-day sudden-death ACC tournament, with an NCAA berth going to the winner only. It was an idiosyncratic way to determine a champion (no other conference except the Southern operated that way), and it meant that the ACC tournament was the most important event of the season for the eight conference schools and their fans. A berth in the NCAAs was merely gravy. If you didn't win the ACC tournament, the NCAAs were irrelevant because you didn't go (not even to the NIT in New York).

Unfair? Without a doubt. Exciting? Certainly. But for the best teams, it meant great pressure. ACC showdowns often resulted in upsets. One misstep could ruin your whole year. We proved in the regular season that we had the best team—but we also knew that in the ACC tournament the best team didn't always win. A famous example was Carolina's undefeated 1957 championship team, which almost didn't even make it into the NCAA tournament. Lennie Rosenbluth had to hit a fourteen-foot hook shot with less than a minute to play to beat Wake Forest in the ACC semifinals.

I don't think anyone thought it was a fair way to decide an NCAA berth, but that in itself created heightened interest. It was a high-risk, sudden-death scenario, and it was a huge story when a low seed knocked out a favorite. The formula created borderline hysteria among the teams and fans. We now see all of this happening in the NCAA tournament known as "March madness."

Because of the dog-eat-dog nature of the ACC, the tournament was covered by the national media, and it was a tough ticket, a scalper's heyday. To buy tickets, fans had to make contributions to their schools. To this day the UNC Educational Foundation's Ernie Williamson ("Mr. Carolina Athletics" should be his title) credits our 1967–69 teams with saving the foundation that supports all athletic scholarships. Our football program was struggling at the time, so the winning basketball teams kept the money coming in and the foundation strong.

These days you have to give at least $70,000 to the UNC program to be eligible to buy two ACC seats, but back then you could give as little as $100 to Clemson and qualify to buy two tickets. So there were North Carolina fans giving money to Clemson in order to get tickets. It remains legalized scalping, really.

We planned all year long for the ACC tournament. Everything rested on those three days in March. I think winning the ACC is harder than making the NCAA Final Four. The ACC was such a deep conference that you had to beat three excellent teams to win the tournament. Also, if you were favored, you often had the fans of all seven other schools cheering against you. You couldn't take a single win for granted. Complicating matters was the fact that it was the third meeting of the year with your conference rivals, which meant you knew each other very well. It was extremely hard to beat a good team three times in a row.

We built long-term strategies for the ACC tournament. We held things back, things we didn't want to show other conference teams. If our best chance to beat an ACC rival meant holding the ball, we'd wait until the tournament to reveal that strategy. If a team didn't like to play against a zone, we wouldn't show zone against them in the regular season—and then make them play against it in the tournament. Sometimes, we would throw out a look in the regular season just to give our opponents something to think about. We would play a triangle-and-two for a few possessions, even if we didn't plan to use it in the tournament, so that at least our opponents would have to waste some time practicing for it.

College basketball is a tournament game; preparation time is nil. The ACC tournament is played on consecutive days. My goal was to force other teams to react to what we were doing, while instilling some principles that would minimize our own preparation. That's one reason we used pressure man defense with some traps: It made the other team react to *us*. By forcing them to cope with our changing defenses, we didn't have to worry about every play they might run against us. Our *principles* should take care of it. Furthermore, our defense was predicated on not allowing the opponent to run its set offense in the first place.

That was our hope, anyway, as we went to Greensboro for the '67 tournament. Some of the pressure was taken off us the day we arrived when a respected writer named Smith Barrier of the *Greensboro Daily News* picked Duke to win. The headline read: DUKE TO WIN TOURNAMENT. Larry Miller cut out the column and kept it in his locker for the duration.

We beat N.C. State, Wake Forest, and Duke in order. Keep in mind we had beaten each of our three rivals twice already during the regular season, which made those wins even more difficult to come by. It's tough psychologically to play a rival that often. We struggled past eighth-place N.C. State by 3 points, which was a good win over a team that had lost in overtime to the SEC champion, Tennessee, just a few days earlier. We had an easier time with Wake, 89–79. In the championship game we were at our best, defeating Duke for the third time, 82–73.

Afterwards Miller, who had 32 points and eleven rebounds against Duke and was named the tournament's MVP, showed the press how he had saved the Smith Barrier article right up there in his locker. Smitty laughed when he saw it.

We were in. We were going to the NCAA tournament for the first time since 1959—but we were mentally and physically exhausted from the effort it took to get there. Fortunately we had a bye in the first round before we would go to College Park, Maryland, for the NCAA East regional. We had a week to practice, but it was equally important to somehow refresh ourselves and decompress from the ordeal of the ACC. I wanted to get our players' minds off basketball while at the same time giving them some exercise, so I came up with an offbeat idea. We began the week by playing volleyball instead of basketball. When the players arrived at the gym I had strung up a volleyball net. Maybe it helped. In the NCAA East regional we met Princeton again, and this time we beat the Tigers, 78–70.

After the game, Bobby Lewis asked me for permission to practice shooting with Coach Lotz the next morning, since he hadn't shot well at College Park. We had less than twenty-four hours before our next game and I felt he was too conscientious about it and, in fact, was overworking. "You can't shoot," I said. "Just *picture* how well you're going to shoot tomorrow."

We played better and more confidently in a convincing win over Bob Cousy's Boston College team, 96–80. Lewis did shoot well, with eleven of eighteen field goals and nine of ten foul shots for 31 points. He had six assists. His teammates shot 53 percent. That sent us to the Final Four, with a potential meeting in the championship with the great UCLA and its seven-foot sophomore Lew Alcindor, now Kareem Abdul Jabbar. Scores of North Carolina fans followed us to Louisville, excited at having a team in the Final Four for the third time in the history of the NCAA (1946 and 1957 were the others).

UCLA was an inescapable reality of college basketball in the '60s. If you wanted a title, you had to go through them. The Bruins were all we heard about or thought about—and that should have been a danger sign. First we had to play Dayton in the semifinals. Our team wasn't worried, but the coaching staff surely was. We knew Dayton was extremely capable, and we racked our brains as to how to keep our players from looking ahead. But that proved impossible. As early as February, the Carolina writers had started talking about a matchup of our sophomores versus the UCLA sophomores.

Our players fell into the trap. After all, Dayton had lost to Virginia Tech, and we had thrashed the same team by 32 back in February at home. Never, never go by comparative scores!

We took an early lead and then we lost, 76–62. Dayton was a hot team that starred Donnie May. Dayton, well coached by Don Donoher, would go to the championship game against UCLA, and we were in the consolation bracket against Houston. As I was leaving my postgame press conference I ran into my friend Abe Lemons, the hilarious former Texas coach. Abe put his arm around me. "Look, you're lucky to be here," he said. "Any coach is. Enjoy it, whether you win it or not. Some of us have never been able to bring teams here." It may have helped my attitude.

We were so devastated that we didn't even practice for the consolation game. It meant nothing to us—it was a disappointing and unnecessary tribulation—and I would eventually lead the fight through our coaches association to have it abolished. I wrote to every living coach who had a team in a consolation game and asked two questions. One, did the players enjoy the game? Two, did you enjoy coaching the game? I got one yes. The replies were otherwise unanimous against it. Nevertheless, a consolation game in the Final Four survived until 1981, although regional consolation games were abolished in 1976.

Before the game I told our guys, who of course were disappointed, "Just go out and shoot it up and have some fun." We lost to Elvin Hayes and Houston, 84–62. But with five minutes to play, we heard something that revived our spirits. That night our fans paid us a wonderful tribute, one I've never forgotten.

"We're number four!" they chanted.

It was the greatest chant I ever heard. After all, when two teams play a game there has to be a loser. You can't both win. But for the loser to be made to feel so horrible by the rest of society is not what games should be about. The "number one" syndrome in our society says: If you're not number one, then you're a "loser," and being a loser is considered the ultimate put-down in our culture. So when those fans chanted I felt a rush of gratitude. I'm not sure any school has celebrated a number-four finish, before or since, in quite that way. It's really okay to be number two, or number four or number six. But very few people agree with me on that.

Under the pioneering leadership of President Frank Porter Graham, the University of North Carolina was widely recognized as a major liberal voice in the South. By 1951 it had cautiously opened its doors to a few black students, and that number steadily increased. The changing policy in race relations raised the legitimate question about the recruiting of black athletes. For me, integrating basketball was an obvious thing to do. I did not see it as a political issue but primarily as an ethical one. It was the right and fair move to make. I recalled the precedent of my own alma mater, the University of Kansas, where a black athlete was recruited on the team in 1951. At Carolina, this was overdue, as it was at Kansas.

I have been called "courageous" for leading the way in the South toward the integration of collegiate basketball, but I never considered it a matter of courage. It was simply the correct thing to do. In fact, I was annoyed that it was regarded as so earthshaking and newsworthy. I saw it as only one small example of what was beginning to happen all over the country.

In athletics, black and white teammates live together constantly, and it doesn't take long for color to seem totally irrelevant. In fact, we cease to see each other in racial categories. Color seems more like a disguise, for as we become better acquainted, we affirm each other as fellow human beings with a common goal. One thing I have greatly enjoyed as a coach is attending the weddings of many of our players because all such events bring blacks and whites together in such a beautiful way. There you see how friendships transcend everything else.

The very word *integration* seems too abstract for me. Whenever I hear the word, it calls to mind our first black player, Charles Scott, whose strong and animated personality symbolizes the best of humanity. I must also acknowledge that my perspective was significantly shaped by my Christian faith, as indeed much of the civil rights activism of the time emanated from the church, with the leadership of Dr. Martin Luther King, Jr.

But I am getting ahead of my story. Let me tell you more about my background and how this played out in North Carolina. Since Kansans tend to identify themselves as northerners when it comes to racial matters, I was not sure how I would adjust to a more overtly segregated culture, and in 1958 even Chapel Hill was a very southern town with the traditional racist mores. Since I had lived only in Kansas, Colorado, and Germany, I expected some discomfort, and I must say that I recall well how shocked I was when I first saw dual drinking fountains, one for "whites" and the other for "coloreds," at Pinehurst. However, I never forgot that racism in America is a national phenomenon and perhaps is more insidious outside the South. I also had heard the ubiquitous racist jokes in Kansas, New York, and elsewhere.

As a midwestern "northerner," I felt I had an obligation to understand the prevailing attitudes in the South. I recalled a radio editorial about a freak southern snowstorm and the danger it posed for locals because of all the Yankee drivers who had come "down here." As expert winter drivers, they crashed into everyone because they failed to realize that the roads in the South seldom receive the same treatment as in the North due to a lack of snow removal equipment.

Race was also a frequent topic of conversation. I remember an initial one, shortly after I arrived in late August, when things were slow at the university, which back then did not resume classes until mid-September. I was alone in Frank McGuire's office in Woollen Gym while Frank was on vacation. An older gentleman would stop by to chat, and our casual discussions about race would often end up as spirited debates. He had grown up in the South and insisted that the majority of southern whites had warm and sincere relationships with black people. "We consider our black maids as members of the family," he said. But I asked, "How can you talk about 'loving' black people when you are not on an equal footing and legislate 'keeping them in their place'?"

One of my first orders of business upon arriving in Chapel Hill was to find a church home. As the saying goes, we "shopped around." I was reared in a strong churchgoing family and often spent at least four hours on Sunday in church-related activities. My church back in Kansas had nurtured my inquiring mind and convinced me that I did not need to forfeit my intellect to have faith, so I steered clear of some churches. Also, the Christian education program for our young children was important in making the choice. These preconditions reduced my options in Chapel Hill in 1959.

I was an American Baptist, but in the South, Baptists come in many variations, though the majority were under the Southern Baptist Convention umbrella, a largely conservative body and slow to speak out on social issues. I attended one such local congregation and was offended by the prevailing practice of voting new members into the church ("All in favor, say aye"), which we did also in my Kansas churches. We visited congregations of other denominations. Although Ann was an Episcopalian, she was willing to go with me wherever I wished. It was Jim Cansler, the Baptist student chaplain at UNC, who directed us to a new church, which had only recently been organized and which was meeting on the university campus. It had only eleven founding families but represented a nice blend of both community and university folk. They were restless Baptists who were eager to move out into new directions and were especially committed to racial inclusiveness.

I recall so vividly our first visit to the Olin T. Binkley Memorial Baptist Church, meeting in Gerrard Hall. (The last scene in the recent movie *Patch Adams* was filmed at Gerrard.) A young man by the name of Robert Seymour had just been called as the first minister and was preaching his initial sermon. He was no ordinary Baptist pastor, for none of his credentials were from Baptist institutions. His bachelor of divinity was from Yale, and he had a Ph.D. from the University of Edinburgh, Scotland. Bob became my lifelong friend and mentor, and he served the same congregation for thirty years. He emerged as a leader in the community, as the first president of the Interfaith Council for Social Service and as a member on nearly every board and agency in the town. He retired over a decade ago and has since written two books, *Whites Only* and *Aging Without Apology*. His current regular column in *The Chapel Hill News* addresses many serious issues, with an occasional tongue-in-cheek piece, such as his defense of the southern custom of drinking sweet tea!

The church was named for Dr. Olin T. Binkley, who is recognized among Southern Baptists as a liberal voice and who was at one time the minister of our sister congregation in Chapel Hill, the University Baptist Church. The first controversy of the new congregation was over membership policy—not about race but about baptism. This was resolved by the congregation's breaking ranks with the denomination and becoming what is known as an open membership church, one which respects whatever mode of baptism new members may have received elsewhere without requiring baptism by immersion. Bob and I became good friends even though he had little interest in basketball; I was grateful for someone who would talk to me about other things. However, his beautiful musician wife, Pearl, enjoyed basketball games when she had time away from being the organist at Binkley.

Seymour was deeply committed to ending segregation in the South, and so the congregation was very actively involved in fostering integration at many levels in our community, especially in the public schools. In the early '60s the congregation was invited to participate in a foundation-supported program called Summer Interracial Ministry, which placed white seminarians in leadership positions in black congregations and vice versa. Binkley welcomed a charismatic young black man from North Carolina who was a senior at Union Theological Seminary in New York City. His name was James Forbes, and he is now the minister of Riverside Church in New York, one of the most prestigious congregations in our country. At the time he came to Binkley, it was unheard of for an African-American to be on the staff of a white church in the South. It was regarded as highly controversial, but it was a transforming experience for the congregation.

After the Public Accommodations legislation was passed by Congress, our pastor felt it was imperative to make sure that all local restaurants complied with the new law. Bob called me and asked if I would accompany him and a black student to the Pines restaurant for dinner. I was an appropriate one to go because it was a tradition for the basketball team to eat pregame meals there. The Pines was an excellent restaurant on the edge of town but had been a holdout for segregation. Frank McGuire had introduced me to it when I was invited for the interview to be his assistant coach. Thereafter, I became a regular. "If you come with us, I am certain they will serve us," Bob said. I of course agreed to go and did not really consider it a big deal. Years afterwards, some reports have made it sound like I personally integrated every restaurant in Chapel Hill! The truth is, I was just an assistant coach, and hardly the most influential person in town, an unlikely standard-bearer for integration. But Bob knew that I knew the management and that they valued the business of the basketball team. My presence would make the point. A touch of familiarity might make the situation easier for everybody, we thought.

The three of us walked in and took a table. If the patrons or staff were shocked, I do not recall it. I have read accounts that claim we were received with stunned silence and glares, but I do not think that was the case. The only thing a little awkward was a slight delay in seating us as the hostess sized up the situation and looked to the manager for a signal about how to proceed. We ordered, were served, visited, and ate without incident. That was it. How ridiculous it all seems now!

You have to understand this small act in the context of events going on all around us. The civil rights movement had been gaining momentum ever since the Alabama bus boycott in 1955 and the North Carolina lunch counter sit-ins in 1960. Four freshmen from Greensboro's AT&T had walked into Woolworth's and taken seats at the all-white Formica counter-top, and were refused service. They sat there all day and returned the following day joined by eighty-five volunteers prepared to maintain an open-ended siege. Binkley Church was caught up in trying to respond to all of this as similar protests and sit-ins spread across the state. Although I never had the opportunity to meet Dr. Martin Luther King, Jr., he came to Chapel Hill and said in support of the demonstrators, "The underlying philosophies of segregation are diametrically opposed to democracy and Christianity, and all the dialectics of all the logicians in the world cannot make them lie down together."

In the years following the turmoil of the civil rights struggle, I talked often to my players about Dr. King and quoted him frequently. It became a tradition in our program to have a Thought of the Day, and frequently I borrowed these from him. Two that come to mind are "Those who sit at rest buy their quiet with disgrace" and "Injustice anywhere is a threat to justice everywhere."

Though there were many liberal voices in Chapel Hill, prejudice was also deeply entrenched. The town board had hoped to pass a public accommodations law before the federal government did, but the effort failed. There was also considerable maneuvering to delay the mandate to integrate the schools "at all deliberate speed." Even so, it was surprising to me that there was not then a single black athlete in the university. I talked to Bob Seymour about this and also Frank McGuire. Frank had previously coached a young black athlete at St. John's in 1962 named Solly Walker who experienced a brutal taunting on a road trip in Kentucky. "I wouldn't wish that kind of treatment on anyone," Frank said. But the university administration was very open to integrating athletics. I knew Chancellor Aycock was wholeheartedly in favor of it.

On the very day I was named head coach of UNC, Bob Seymour called me. His first question was about recruiting a black player. At the time I was serving as the chair of the Student Affairs Committee of our church, and Bob said, "Now that you are head coach your primary church work is the opportunity afforded by your vocation. Go find a black basketball player for the university." Our congregation was committed to the principle that "church work" was not inside the institution but was out in the world in one's day-to-day activity.

Again, people saw this effort to break the racial barrier in athletics as a "courageous" move, but I disagree. That is why I was reluctant to accept the Arthur Ashe Award for Courage at the ESPYs at Radio City Music Hall in 1998. Looking back on it, if I had truly been courageous, I would have gone to every black high school gym in the state looking for players. That would have taken real courage, to let the people in those schools know that we were there and would welcome them. Instead, I just followed leads through occasional hearsay, and it wasn't until 1965–66 that we successfully recruited Charles Scott. I wasn't the only coach who was looking either. I knew that Bones McKinney was doing the same thing over at Wake Forest and Lefty Driesell at Davidson. Bud Millikan at Maryland already had a black player.

In 1962, I got a letter from a gentleman named Frank McDuffie, Jr., who was the headmaster and coach at Laurinburg Institute, an all-black academy his father had founded about ninety minutes south of Chapel Hill. "I've got three players on my team who are better than anybody you have," he wrote. He may have been right. One of the players was Jimmy Walker, who was All-American at Providence and also played in the NBA.

As was our custom when people wrote recommending players, we wrote back thanking him for the letter, and requested information on their transcripts. I added that if the student with the right academic background came along, we'd certainly want to see him play and visit with him. I never heard back on those students and let the matter drop. But it was the start of an important correspondence.

One afternoon in 1963 or 1964 I got a call from an acquaintance named Willie Holderness, whose wealthy family was an important part of the Jefferson Standard life insurance company. Willie was an attorney in Greensboro, and his brother Chick, whom I knew even better, was an officer at Jefferson Standard. Willie had a simple question for me. "Dean, if I send a student down there on a Jefferson Standard scholarship and he's good enough to play, are you going to play him?" he asked.

"Certainly. No doubt in the world," I said. "Why?"

"This is a Negro youngster from Dudley High School."

I said, "I've heard of him. He'll play."

Lou Hudson was ranked third in his class of over three hundred students, with an excellent academic record at Dudley, in addition to being a splendid ballplayer. He seemed like the perfect student-athlete for Carolina, exactly what we were looking for. But it turned out Hudson's SAT scores were barely shy of Carolina's standards, which had gone up dramatically. The ACC had a standard minimum score of 800 for many years, but Carolina, Duke, and Virginia were even more difficult to get into. Some said the 800 minimum was adopted in an attempt to hurt admissions for disadvantaged youngsters. That was just one of many instances over the years in which I would disagree with standardized tests as a measure of classroom aptitude. I became certain the SATs were culturally and economically biased—a suspicion that was confirmed by the U.S. Supreme Court not long ago. I knew too many absolutely brilliant young men whose scores were low, who then excelled in college. By the same token I knew plenty of young men with high test scores who did not perform well in the classroom. I specifically remember one player who scored more than 1,200 on his SATs, yet struggled to graduate. I knew another young man from a rural southern background who scored only 690, but excelled in his classes, graduated easily, and went on to graduate school for a master's degree.

Although we may not have successfully recruited Hudson anyway, reluctantly, I had to abandon the idea of his wearing Carolina blue. He was a classic example of the SAT's inaccuracy. He went to Minnesota and became an honor roll student. Then, of course, he became an All-Pro with the Atlanta Hawks.

I kept looking for players and took suggestions from anyone and everyone. One afternoon a student and fan named Reggie Fountain said to me, "You ought to see the Negro team at Elm City. They have some players." It was a good lead. The head coach there, Harvey Reid, became an invaluable contact and friend over the next several years, and through him I met a history teacher at Elm City High named Phil Ford, Sr., whose son became inseparable from Carolina basketball. Harvey was a smart coach who ran a tight ship, and I trusted his judgment and appraisals of players.

The day I called him I said, "Be on the lookout for a good student and a good player, because we want to do something." Harvey told me about a young man named William Cooper. He said he had one player who was better but who probably couldn't get into Carolina academically. Reggie Fountain went down to Elm City and brought us back an eight-millimeter game film with footage of Cooper. In 1964–65, William Cooper came to Carolina. We intended to surprise some people. The idea was to bring William in with no fanfare as just another student, have him play freshman basketball, and then invite him to walk on the varsity basketball team.

At first everything went according to plan, but then it turned out that William, a good student in high school who continued to do excellent academic work in college, had his priorities in order. William played on the freshman team in 1964–65 and was a crowd favorite. But in the first week of varsity practice his sophomore year, he came to me after practice. "Coach, I flunked an accounting exam, and I want to be a business major," he said. "I just don't see how I can play basketball and maintain my grades at the level I need to. I've got to go at it hard this next semester." I tried to talk him out of quitting the team. "Don't make a quick decision," I said. "Take a couple of days off and think about this."

But two days later he came back to me and said he had made his decision: He was going to give up basketball so he could devote full time to his studies. Had he remained on the team, he would have been on the 1965–66 varsity, and therefore would have been the first black athlete ever in the Deep South at a predominately white university. Instead, he graduated in good shape and became an officer in the U.S. Army. Years later he sent his two children to Carolina. His daughter, Tonya Cooper, played basketball for the Carolina women's team from 1992 to 1996, and his son, Brent, was a member of our junior varsity in 1991–92.

I had never heard of Charles Scott until January 15, 1966, when I was riding back on the team bus after we had lost a heartbreaker at Virginia, 70–69. Bill Currie, our radio play-by-play announcer, said to me, "Old Lefty's got himself a black player coming in next year. He's visiting Duke this weekend."

I said, "If he's going to visit Duke, he must not be all set for Davidson."

Currie started telling me about Scott, a six-foot-five forward who was tearing up the court at the Laurinburg Institute. Charles had received financial aid for academic readiness at Laurinburg prep from New York when he was fifteen, and in addition to being a great prospect, he was the top student in his class. In fact, he wound up valedictorian. It was no wonder that he had his choice of schools, eventually choosing from among Davidson, Duke, Carolina, West Virginia, and others, including Ivy League schools.

Immediately I sent John Lotz to study the ability of Charles Scott, while Larry went off to Indiana to see a player who was considered the premier high school player in the country, Rick Mount. Later they talked. "I bet mine is better than the one you saw," Lotz said. Larry decided to go see Scott for himself and came back to the office saying John was correct.

We had a rule that I had to see a player play before offering a scholarship, so I drove down to watch a game and brought along some friends to help recruit when meeting with the McDuffies and Charles after the game. Accompanying me were Frank Klingberg, a Carolina history professor, Thal Elliott, an African-American and a member of Binkley Baptist and a medical student at the university, and Dan Pollitt, a Carolina law professor who at that time had just been featured in *U.S. News and World Report* as one of Lyndon Johnson's "idea men." Frank and Mrs. McDuffie welcomed us to their home and were most hospitable. McDuffie said that while Charles had made an initial commitment to Lefty Driesell at Davidson in September, he had since backed away from it and was open to recruitment. Mrs. McDuffie, who was dean of students, was covering the academic situation while Mr. McDuffie talked basketball. Still, most of the ninety minutes was spent discussing black-white relations at the university and in the town of Chapel Hill.

Months later, I learned that when Charles visited Davidson, Lefty took him out to eat in a nice restaurant and they had a pleasant meal together. But on a later visit to a Davidson restaurant, Scott and the McDuffies took their seats and were told by a waitress: "This is for whites only over here." Charles had trouble getting past the incident, and began to doubt whether Davidson was the right place for him.

Charles and the McDuffies felt it could be an important step to be the first black player at North Carolina, because it was the state's oldest university, chartered in 1789. Charles agreed to visit and came down on our annual Jubilee Weekend, which celebrates the spring season. Once again I understood the importance of showing off Chapel Hill in bloom. As part of the Jubilee Weekend there was a huge concert, with Smokey Robinson and the Miracles, and the Temptations.

Charles said later that we did things differently from other schools he visited. We didn't set out to separate him from the other players. We gave him a lot of attention, introducing him to just about every influential person on campus and in the town, but we were also natural and ourselves. We tried to give him an uncensored look at Chapel Hill. Freshman Dick Grubar was his host, and he hung around with players close to his age, the guys with whom he would be playing and spending most of his time. That was apparently a departure for Charles. "At the other schools they only introduced me to one player, usually a senior who would be long gone when I arrived," he said.

At one point during his visit I sat Charles down for a talk. "What do you want to be called?" I asked him. It was a policy of mine to always ask, because you could never be sure. You'd hear a guy called William by his father, Billy by his mother, and Bill by his friends. I wanted them to go by the name they chose for themselves since that would be the name in the newspapers. Charles appreciated that. "Other coaches called me Charlie Scott," he says. "Well that was never my name." He was always Charles to me.

I took Charles to church with me at Binkley Baptist and introduced him to members of the congregation, one of whom was Howard Lee, who taught in the school of social work and went on to become the mayor of Chapel Hill, the first black mayor that I know of in a predominantly white southern town. Howard's charming and vivacious wife, Lillian, was an instant hit with Charles and has continued to be close to our student-athletes to this day. Also, at church, Charles could say hello to Thal Elliott again and meet his wife, Edith, who would become dean of women at Carolina. Charles also met with the chancellor of the university, Carlyle Sitterson, who told him he should pledge the fraternity at St. Anthony's Hall, where the chancellor's own son was a member. When Charles told me he wanted to major in premed, I took him to meet my friend Chris Fordham, who was then an associate dean of the medical school. Fordham took charge of Charles for a few hours and let him watch an operation.

But toward the end of his visit, Charles slipped off. We couldn't find him for about two hours. He was out looking around town on his own, going into places by himself to see how he would be treated. If he was with a coach, he reasoned, he might be treated differently.

When Charles's visit was over, I was confident that he would commit, which he then did. Bob Quincy, our sports information director, and I drove down to Laurinburg for his official signing. But as soon as we walked into the academy we saw Lefty Driesell in the hallway. Lefty had come to Laurinburg hoping to talk Charles out of his decision. I said to myself, *My gosh, I thought this was over.* We had to walk right by Lefty, so I said hello. Then Mr. McDuffie summoned us into his office while Charles signed his scholarship papers. Afterwards, Mr. McDuffie had to go outside and tell Lefty that Charles couldn't see him because he had just signed with North Carolina.

Everyone at North Carolina was thrilled with Charles's signing, with the exception of a single person. We received a solitary letter of complaint from a booster, protesting that when we gave Charles a scholarship we took one away from a white kid. Chuck Erickson was worried about it, so I suggested,

"Why don't you check and see how much he contributes?" Chuck looked into it. He found out the booster contributed exactly $25 annually, but it could have been five million dollars and it wouldn't have changed anything.

I wasn't worried about Charles fitting in on the Carolina campus. Charles would tell you that he was wholeheartedly accepted on our campus and on our team. John Lotz was particularly close to Charles and was chosen to be best man at his wedding years later. Charles did pledge St. Anthony's Hall, although he said later he wasn't a fraternity type. Our team, he said, was his fraternity.

It helped that Charles had to play freshman ball for a year, along with our other recruits, Eddie Fogler and Jim Delany, which quieted the attention he was receiving. But when word got around what a great player he was, the crowds grew so large for the preliminary game that we scheduled two separate games for freshmen only. Charles told me later, "It was the first time I had played with white players, but it was also the first time some of them had ever played with a black player. We were genuine in our feelings, and we felt our way along, and we grew closer over time. There was an openness and a friendliness about it."

I told freshman coach Larry Brown, "On the court he's like everybody else. Don't baby him." Like any freshman, Charles had to learn shot selection and our defensive principles, and sometimes he learned the hard way. He tells a funny story about my disciplining him one afternoon in practice, which I didn't remember. He must have been late or committed some other violation, because I told him to run the Carmichael steps for ten minutes wearing a weighted vest. Well, he ran and ran and I never stopped him. After fifteen or twenty minutes he came to me exhausted and asked he if could stop now.

"Oh, I forgot about you," I said apologetically.

Charles stared at me in amazement. "How can you *forget* about me?" he said. "You've only got one black player on the floor. It's hard to miss me."

Ever since then I have assigned a manager to keep track of the amount of time a player runs and tell him when to stop.

Recruiting was proving to be a never-ending job, a constant source of anxiety, and at times, a heartbreaker. In the spring we lost two great prospects to rival schools in a single day. We had spent the better part of a year recruiting Dick DeVenzio of Ambridge, Pennsylvania, and that December we had also begun to recruit Austin Carr of Washington, D.C., when his SAT scores came in very high. They were possibly the two best high school guards in the country, and we thought we had good chances of getting both.

Carr had already announced he was going to Notre Dame, but he hadn't officially signed and he told a friend he'd be interested in looking at Carolina. We invited him for Jubilee Weekend, which included a Dionne Warwick concert at Carmichael. I sent Larry Brown to Washington to fly back on the plane with him. However, their flight out of Washington National was canceled. Larry rented a car and drove illegally on the shoulder of the crowded Baltimore-Washington freeway to BWI and arrived at the airport in time to make the flight and get to Chapel Hill for the concert. Carr had a great visit, and our chances looked good.

On the Sunday night following his visit, I called Carr to see if he had enjoyed his visit. When he told me he'd like to come to Carolina, I was thrilled. I said, "Coach Brown and I will be there tomorrow night, and we're excited." Since Carr was a guard, I took Larry rather than Coach Lotz.

I had another call to place, to DeVenzio, who had won a state championship and was wavering between Duke and Carolina. When I called Dick, he said he had made his decision. He'd like to come to Carolina. I said, "Are you free Tuesday night? Coach Brown and I will be up there and we're really excited." Then I called Larry Brown. "We're leaving tomorrow," I said. We would fly to Washington first and sign Austin Carr, and then continue to Pittsburgh on Tuesday to sign Dick DeVenzio, I told him.

But things didn't go as planned. On our arrival at Austin's home in Washington, he wasn't there. His dad told us that he was out visiting someone, who I understood to be "Father Collins." We sat around and waited and waited. Finally, I said, "Is Austin coming?" The reply I got back was, "We thought he'd be coming, but Mr. Collins was really upset." All that time, I thought Father Collins was a priest, but later on I discovered that he was a Notre Dame alumnus. Larry and I waited some more, until his dad said he talked with him and he was going to Notre Dame. We went out to dinner.

Meanwhile, my secretary, Betsy Terrell, tried to reach us Tuesday before we left for the airport to tell me that Dick DeVenzio wanted to speak with me. But I didn't get the message. Larry and I flew to Pittsburgh and drove to the DeVenzio home. We knocked on the door, and Dick opened it with tears in his eyes. "I'm going to Duke," he said. He was obviously under some pressure. We had become very close to him and his family, and to tell us no was difficult for him. I hated to see a young man so upset over his choice of college, and I thought, *We're not going to be a part of this*. I wanted to make it easier for him, not harder, so I said, "It's okay, it's not worth all this." Interestingly, his father, who coached him, and his mom had both told me two weeks earlier they wanted him to go to Carolina. Perhaps that is why Dick was home by himself when we arrived. We remain friends with the DeVenzio family today. Dick recruited Randy Wiel for us in 1975 after coaching him in Aruba.

As we got in the car at the DeVenzios' home, I said to Larry, "You know what we're going to do? It is too late for the last flight home, so we're going to my favorite restaurant and having a great meal."

Vic Bubas, of Duke, had flown in to visit Dick on Monday night when Dick told him Carolina was his choice. We should have gone to Dick's house on Monday.

Shortly after that, Larry left Carolina to finally play pro basketball for the New Orleans Buccaneers in the old American Basketball Association, which was his dream. This was the inaugural year of the ABA, and Buccaneers coach Babe McCarthy was looking for players. He signed Doug Moe, who had been overseas playing in Italy, and Doug told McCarthy of Larry's dream to play pro and that he would leave the Carolina coaching staff to do it. The Buccaneers got a package deal: In that first season Doug became the Most Valuable Player in the ABA, while Larry was the MVP of the all-star game.

I was sorry to lose Larry, and felt he would be an excellent coach one day. At the summer camp where he was a counselor while a student at Carolina, kids would follow him around because they were so attracted to him. He put in the Shuffle offense, and won two camp championships.

Later, when I declined an offer to become head coach of the ABA Carolina Cougars, I strongly recommended Larry Brown for the job. Ted Munchak, the team's owner, and Carl Scheer, the general manager, hired him—as well as Doug Moe as his chief assistant. Doug had played for the Cougars. When they traded for him unsigned, I told Doug to hold out for what was a huge salary at the time. Doug didn't have an agent, so his wife, Jane, and I persuaded him to stick to the figure I had recommended. They called Doug into the Cougars office and offered half the amount Jane and I suggested. Doug said to them, "Okay!" Jane told me to go with him next time. Doug and Larry asked me to come up to Boone, North Carolina, for the Cougars' first training camp, and I watched them install a great deal of what we ran at Carolina. I cautioned them that much of it might not be suited for the pros, but Larry and Doug felt that our baseline trap pressure and our passing game would work. It did, much to my surprise, since the rules for the ABA and NBA game are so different from college rules.

With Larry's departure, I gained a lifelong friend and partner in the man who replaced him, Bill Guthridge, who would be my assistant for the next thirty years. John Lotz, a coassistant with Larry, also immediately approved of Bill. I had known Bill slightly before he arrived at Chapel Hill. He was from Parsons, Kansas, and in my senior year of college, I had dated his sister for a few months. Bill played for Kansas State's 1958 Final Four team, and Tex Winter hired him as an assistant coach at K-State. When I offered Bill the job at Carolina, Tex hated to lose him but understood it could be a good move for Bill. Bill was *much* better organized than Larry, John, or I. I think Betsy was relieved when she found this true.

Bill was an honor student at K-State, and was named one of the university's thirteen most outstanding all-around seniors in 1960. Bill would also coach the freshmen since John liked being on the road. The summer I hired Bill, he was coaching in Puerto Rico, and was so successful that he was named Coach of the Year there. In 1968 he was invited to coach Puerto Rico's national team in the Olympics but declined.

At Carolina I asked my assistants to handle a number of duties so they would have good all-around preparation for becoming head coaches in their own right. The one exception was shooting; I wanted only one voice instructing our players on their shot because too many opinions could muddle a player. I did reserve the right as head coach to step in and correct a shot. John Lotz was our shooting coach during his seven years in Chapel Hill, but when John left to become head coach at Florida, Bill assumed the role. Bill had great judgment in picking talent and a terrific grasp of basketball mechanics. He was quiet, patient when I was not, and his subdued style hid a dry wit. Bill and the gifted John Lotz provided me with a tremendous staff for many years.

As sensational as the previous season had been, we all felt we could reprise it in 1967–68. From the very outset, expectations were high. We lost All-American Bobby Lewis, as well as Donnie Moe, Mark Mirken, and Tom Gauntlett to graduation. But Charles Scott came up from the freshman team along with Eddie Fogler and Jim Delany. Larry Miller was a senior All-American, and that great sophomore class now had a Final Four experience behind them.

We built a 28–4 record and were ranked number two for much of the season, behind the inevitable number one, UCLA. Ava Gardner even came to one of our games. She was a friend of Jim and Tassie Dempsey, a couple from nearby Wilson, North Carolina, who were huge supporters of our team, and whom I had met through Joe Dean, a Converse representative and later the athletic director at LSU. Jimmy Dempsey had been a pilot in World War II and at one time was the youngest major in the Air Force. Jimmy kept a single-engine plane, and NCAA rules at the time allowed for an alumnus to bring a prospect to campus for an unofficial visit, so Jimmy had flown Dick Grubar from Schenectady to Chapel Hill when we were recruiting him. Johnny Dee, the coach at Notre Dame, called me up and asked how we could do that. I told him it was no different from a Fighting Irish alum driving a prospect from Chicago to South Bend, according to the NCAA people with whom I checked.

The Dempseys became great friends of our program. Tassie was known to our players as "Ma" and always brought her fried chicken to tailgate parties before football games. If you asked our players what their favorite food was, they often replied, "Ma Dempsey's fried chicken." As a girl, Tassie had gone to school with Ava Gardner, and they had kept in touch. During December 1967, Ava came to visit her old friend for a few days, and Tassie brought her to a ball game. Afterwards I had a small group of people, along with our staff, come to my house on Morgan Creek, and Ava decided to come along to the party with the Dempseys. I'm afraid I wasn't a very good host that night, because I spent most of it talking to Ava, whom I had admired for some time.

As successful as we were, no season is ever easy. This one had its trials too. On December 8 we lost to a good Vanderbilt team on the road, 89–76. It marked the last time in my career I ever kept a team in the locker room and talked to them as a group after a game. I didn't think we had played very well, and I jumped all over them. I had started Joe Brown over Bill Bunting to try to fire Bill up, but the result was that neither played well because it made them both tentative. I was so upset with the loss and the way we had played that I stayed on the team, criticizing them for close to twenty minutes. "I'm disappointed in your effort," I said, among other things.

I was still upset when I left the gym. I had to get back to Chapel Hill to do our TV show, so I hopped on a single-engine, four-seat plane with my co-host, Bill Currie, despite the fact that it was sleeting outside. I sat on the plane and brooded over the statistics, so low that I didn't even notice that the plane was bouncing all over the place and it was sleeting outside. One of the TV-show staffers, Richard Raley, was so nauseated he begged the pilot to land, and we set down somewhere in the mountains on a tiny airstrip so he could be sick. That's when I finally calmed down.

Back in Chapel Hill, when I looked at the game film, I realized it wasn't a case of Carolina playing so badly, it was a case of Vandy playing well. Also, the situation with Brown and Bunting was more my fault than theirs, I realized. I made up my mind that I would never again talk to a team after a game as a group. From then on we would simply say a quick prayer after the game, and then I would walk out. That way I would be sure I knew what I was talking about when I analyzed a performance.

We went on a twenty-game winning streak. In late December, we traveled to Portland to play in the Far West Classic, a prestigious tournament in which we would meet three of the more accomplished teams in the region: Stanford, Utah, and Oregon State. We arrived late in the evening before the tournament was to begin, and went right to practice after we landed. But on the way the airline lost our luggage. All of our game and practice gear was in the lost luggage. We didn't have shorts or jerseys or sneakers.

We needed the workout anyway, I decided. Since we didn't have shoes, we wore socks. We didn't have jerseys, so we wore T-shirts. We didn't have shorts, so we wore our boxers. You can imagine what a sight it was. Larry Miller was renowned all over campus for his good looks and cool persona, but that night he practiced in a pair of plaid undershorts. Later, *Sports Illustrated*'s story about the tournament labeled us "The BVD Boys."

We went almost three months without losing a game and locked up the ACC regular season title, before we dropped our last two games by the identical score of 87–86. We lost to South Carolina when a scrappy player named Bobby Cremins scored 25 points, including six free throws in the last ninety seconds, and was in double figures in rebounds. Then we lost at Duke in triple overtime. But the defeats were harmless, and perhaps even a blessing, because they helped us regain our concentration for the ACC tournament.

Once again, unless we won the ACC tournament we weren't going anywhere. When N.C. State trailed us by just 31–26 at halftime of the ACC championship game, we had to face the very real possibility that our season could end. Upsets were all too common in the ACC tournament, and we were in danger of one now, struggling against a team we had beaten by a dozen points in the regular season. In the locker room I confronted our team after the usual adjustments were made for the second half. "This is where we want to be, so you guys decide how important it is to you," I said. "Talk it over among yourselves, and when you get ready come out and we'll see how you play. I'm going to sit there and watch."

I walked out. They were in there four or five minutes by themselves. I was told a few years later that Larry Miller and Rusty Clark took over where I left off and did a great job. When Larry and Rusty talked, the team listened. Rusty Clark couldn't bear the thought of losing to N.C. State because one of the Wolfpack players was his old high school teammate Vann Williford. Rusty was so fired up he threw a punch in retaliation at Williford and was tossed out of the game after we were ahead by 20. It was uncharacteristic behavior for the future trauma surgeon Clark. But we scored 56 points in the second half while holding N.C. State to 24. The final score was the most lopsided in ACC championship history, 87–50.

We went into the NCAA tournament with no intention of being stopped short of the championship this time around. But there were some major obstacles in our way. Our first-round opponent would be St. Bonaventure, undefeated at 23–0 and ranked third in the nation. We were ranked fourth. It was a ridiculous pairing. I told the press, "They're ranked third and we're looking up at them, so this ought to be interesting." The NCAA seeds teams today, and you would never have two Top Five teams meeting in the first round. But back then it was prearranged before the season that the ACC champion would play an eastern independent team in the first round of the regional.

St. Bonaventure was unbeaten for the first time in school history and was led by their All-American center, Bob Lanier, who was averaging 26.2 points and 15.5 rebounds as a sophomore. But Rusty Clark did a great job on Lanier, and we played very well defensively to win, 91–72. Next we met Davidson in a dangerous game; Lefty Driesell was still hot about Charles Scott, and his Wildcats led us by 6 at halftime before we went on to a 70–66 victory, to reach the Final Four in Los Angeles. Clark was MVP of the regionals.

This time nobody was looking ahead to UCLA. All five of our starters were in double figures as we defeated Big Ten champion Ohio State in the national semifinals, 80–66. Finally, we were going to play for a national championship in Los Angeles.

But there was one problem: Our opponent, UCLA, was without a weakness. The Bruins—Lew Alcindor, Lucius Allen, Mike Warren, Lynn Shackelford, and Mike Lynn—had outside shooters, great depth, and coaching, and pundits were already placing them among the great teams of all time. They had gone 30–0 in 1967, and they arrived at the '68 Final Four just as hungry since they had lost to Houston before 68,000 people in mid-season. Alcindor so dominated the collegiate ranks that the NCAA had even instituted a no-dunk rule before the season began. But we were hungry too. Our team really believed they could play with UCLA, especially Charles Scott, who had gone against Alcindor when they were just youths at the 134th Street Kennedy Center in Harlem.

No one expected us to win—except us. After we beat Ohio State, I allowed our players to stay in the arena to watch Houston and UCLA. It was the only time I ever let our players scout an opponent in person. I didn't want them to be overconfident against either Houston or UCLA. We watched UCLA beat Houston and Elvin Hayes by the remarkable score of 101–69. The well-coached Bruins had a complete team: offense, defense, rebounding. What's more, we would have to play them before a packed crowd in the L.A. Sports Arena, which was really like a home game for them since their fans had virtually all of the tickets. I decided our best chance to win would be to shorten the game. I'm sure it wasn't a popular decision among our confident players, but it was still our best chance to win against a truly great UCLA team.

We successfully started out in the Four Corners. We slowed the pace, and they went to a 1–3–1 trap defense, which was perfect for us. Unfortunately, the "one" under the basket was Alcindor. Still, we trailed by just 7 points at halftime. But along with the rest of college basketball, we had no answer for Alcindor. He scored 34 points, hitting 17 of 21 from the field. He was also an intimidating force under the basket, making it hard for us to get any uncontested shots within ten feet of the basket. Along with that, he had most of the defensive rebounds. We played excellent defense on their great guards. In the second half, we abandoned the Four Corners, which may have been a mistake on my part, but UCLA had the talent and the coaching to answer any challenge. The final score was 78–55, and afterwards I said: "UCLA has to be the best basketball team ever assembled."

The next morning I went to church. I took my parents to services at the Bel-Air Presbyterian Church. The pastor there was Donn Moomaw, a former All-American linebacker for UCLA from 1950 to 1952, whom I met when we served together on the board of directors for the Fellowship of Christian Athletes. After the service, Donn said there was someone he wanted me to meet. He introduced us to the governor of California, Ronald Reagan. My father left the church saying, "I shook hands with Ronald Reagan. I won't wash my hands for the rest of the day, and maybe for the rest of the week."

My father, of course, was a Republican, but I was a Democrat. The curious thing is that even now I get a lot of Republican mail, because I registered

Republican for one year back in 1958 when I moved from Colorado. In that mail, the term *liberal* is thrown around like a dirty word, or an un-American one. I once counted it used twenty-three times in a single piece of campaign literature. It cited the "liberal" media, "liberal" politicians, the "liberal" agenda, until the word became meaningless. I'm not sure how liberal I truly am. I think we should be free and tolerant as a society. Does that make me liberal? Maybe so. Mainly, I hope I'm sensible.

But in the 1960s, the word *liberal* had meaning, especially to some of us at Binkley Baptist Church. One of the things it meant was that you disagreed with the Vietnam War.

When Richard Vinroot was in law school we had a lot of conversations about the war. Richard was a former player who had graduated in 1963 with a degree in business, and by 1966 he was on the verge of completing his law degree at Carolina. He was also a member of Binkley Church. The topic of Vietnam was becoming more divisive, and Richard and I were each troubled in both our intellectual capacity and our moral sense by the events in Vietnam. We differed, however. He believed in the war and felt he should serve in Vietnam. I was against the war.

Richard felt deeply that if Americans were being sent to Vietnam, we were honor bound to support them, as did I. But Richard went a step further. The fact that his peers were being killed gave him deep pangs of conscience. Young men his age were being exposed to combat while he was tucked away in Chapel Hill.

"I need to serve," Richard said.

"You have to do what your conscience says," I said.

Richard decided to do exactly that. After he finished law school he enlisted—as a buck private. At first I tried to discourage him. Richard had a deferment because of his six-eight height, but he declined to exercise it. Nor did he want limited duty. He volunteered for the draft, and after basic training at Fort Jackson, North Carolina, he was sent to Vietnam and served there in the First Signal Brigade. He was initially stationed at Longh Bin outside Saigon, which was the largest military installation over there, practically a city of twenty thousand troops. But he traveled all over the country.

I wrote him as often as I could. I sent him accounts of our games and news of what was going on back home. I kept him abreast of the latest funny stories involving his buddy Larry Brown. We corresponded back and forth on a regular basis. Despite the fact that I opposed the war, I wanted to support him personally. "You did the right thing," I wrote. "Don't look back." Richard said later that after his mother and his wife, the most letters he got were from me. In Richard's letters home, he never questioned his obligation to serve, or even believed the matter fell into the category of a "question."

By the spring and summer of 1968, the North Carolina campus was in a state of upheaval. Civil disobedience was the order of the day. First, Martin Luther King, Jr., was killed, and then Bobby Kennedy was assassinated in the Ambassador Hotel, where we had stayed during the Final Four. I watched police clubbing student protesters at the Democratic National Convention in Chicago. When Kent State erupted in 1970 we worried about a similar outbreak at Carolina.

That summer Charles Scott made the Olympic team, coached by Henry Iba, in Mexico City, where he won a gold medal. We all watched as Tommy Smith and John Carlos raised their black-gloved fists in a black-power salute and lowered their heads on the medal podium after the two-hundred-meter race.

The mood of protest wasn't always compatible with the concept of team. It was a potential conflict—order and discipline were not in fashion. But among our players I never felt dissension or disquiet. I wanted our student-athletes to follow their convictions and to have a certain amount of freedom of self-expression. They, in turn, always understood they were representatives of the university while on the basketball court. There was a fair exchange.

A little flexibility helped. One afternoon Rusty Clark came to me and wanted to know if we could change our travel plans to go to the ACC tournament. We were scheduled to leave in the evening and get to Greensboro in time for dinner, but Rusty wanted to know if we could delay the trip until early the next morning. Greensboro is only fifty miles away, but by going early, we could focus better on the all-important tournament.

"What's going on?" I asked.

"The Supremes are in town," he said.

I told him that he'd better be ready to play when we did go to tournament.

One afternoon Bill Chamberlain, a six-foot-five sophomore from New York, asked if he could miss practice for political reasons. Chamberlain had turned down Princeton to follow Charles Scott's trail to Carolina. He was our second black player, and he was, if anything, even more politically aware than Charles. Ordinarily, missing practice was out of the question.

Our rule was that if you had a class requirement such as a lab, or if you were seriously in arrears with an assignment due, you could miss a practice. But it had better be good (and don't come in on a Monday after you'd had all weekend and claim you needed to study instead of practice). But Chamberlain didn't want off to study, he had something else in mind. I could tell he was worried about asking me. Finally he came out with it.

He wanted to go to a rally for the campus cafeteria workers. A civil rights demonstration was being staged over the low pay and working conditions for cafeteria workers, and he had been asked to speak.

"Great," I said. "Go do it."

It was difficult for me to tell a student not to be politically active on his campus when I felt the chief reason they were there was to ask questions and develop their own convictions. In determining what, if anything, our policy would be when it came to players' activism, the answer was clear to me: While the team came first in season, it should never infringe on an individual's beliefs.

Many young men on our campus wanted to wear their hair long, and some wanted it to touch their elbows. That was in style, the only thing to do. I understood that. I wore white bucks when I was in college because everybody else did. I definitely wanted our players to be a part of their peer group. But it was a fine line. When the players appeared on television they represented not just themselves but the team, and a much larger entity, the university. Their image would reflect on the entire school, so it had to be moderate, neat, and presentable.

But I didn't want to force a lot of rules on players. That would have been bad policy and bad for morale. Instead, each fall I sat down with our seniors and we started over on team rules. They made the rules, and I enforced them. Once a rule was discussed as a team, it became *their* rule and not mine. When it came to, say, hair length, we discussed it, and the seniors determined what was acceptable.

I was less yielding on the subject of a dress code. We always wore blue blazers and ties on road trips. When we traveled as a team, we stayed at great hotels and ate at great restaurants, because I felt the players deserved that in exchange for such hard work and commitment. I was sorry when the NCAA did away with the team blazer policy in 1972 as part of cost-cutting measures. The reason I was sorry to see the blazers go was because they were a great equalizer. In team blazers no player looked more important than any other; you couldn't tell who was rich or who was poor. In fact, one player told me his Carolina blue blazer was the only dress coat he had ever owned.

I believed in the same kind of consistency in their uniforms. I didn't want a mishmash of jersey styles and sweatbands, with players trying to set themselves apart with clothing. In 1970 our seniors asked me to allow each individual to select his own playing shoes. Our players wore various styles of sneakers, and I didn't like the way it looked. At the same time, however, I tried to make sure that they were always in fashion. When we got new warm-ups, we ordered bell bottoms, and we were probably the first team to wear V-necked jerseys.

Perhaps because we discussed all of these issues openly and dealt with them firmly, I don't remember discipline being a big deal in those years. We avoided any serious unrest. If the head coach has conviction, the most naturally disciplined group on any campus will be his athletic team because team members are used to sacrificing a certain amount of peer acceptance in seeking excellence. I'm convinced that our work habits and tough practices instilled a certain mind-set and mental toughness in our players, and that's why we avoided problems. From 1967 to 1969 we had so many close games—and generally won them in the last minute—that our players developed a deep pride in the program. They were committed, they worked awfully hard, and they had high expectations. I think it prevented a lot of dissension.

"The really free person in society is the one who is disciplined," I told our players. What I meant was, true freedom results from having choices. The person who is more disciplined is the person who creates options for himself. An example: Suppose there were two players who liked to indulge themselves off the court. Both players were told that to make it with their NBA teams, they needed to lose twenty pounds. One player didn't bother to lose the weight and got cut. The other player didn't just lose twenty pounds, he lost twenty-five, and made the team. So which of them was more free? The disciplined player had a choice—to gain or lose weight.

I believe the disciplined person can do anything, although in many ways I didn't have a great deal of self-discipline. He can exercise restraint and make sacrifices, or he can choose to stay up late and smoke ten packs of cigarettes. Usually a player who came to North Carolina had some discipline or he wouldn't be there in the first place. He said no to a lot of things to work on his basketball. Of course, the average Carolina student was disciplined too, and had made sacrifices in high school to make the grades required to be admitted to the university.

I wanted our players to be involved in the issues of the day and to feel they could talk freely about them to me. I was eager to know their opinions, so I often mentioned current events in individual meetings. In a one-on-one meeting with a player I would ask his opinion on a current event. I rarely gave my own opinion; I would just try him get he to talk so they would feel he had the same freedom of expression as other students.

My relationship with the players was a paradox in some ways. On the court I was a benevolent dictator, but in the spring and summer I hoped I was a servant to some degree, and a counselor. When it came to participation in demonstrations or protests, I tried to make sure they understood the implications of their appearance. We had to be realistic: They carried more weight at a university rally because they were Carolina basketball players and public figures on campus, as are the coaches. "Understand that you are being used because you're a name," I said. "That's why they want you to be there. But now tell me what you're being used for. And do you believe it yourself?"

I applied the same rules to myself. It helped, I think, that I was still a fairly young man. I was over thirty, but I wasn't yet forty, and I had my own views on the events of 1968. I twice attended the Friday-noon antiwar vigils at the local post office. They were quiet events, and I went with a professor friend of mine. I can remember standing in long lines with some of the members from Binkley. I wasn't the kind who wanted to be a leader on the Vietnam issue or out front at a protest. A vigil or putting my signature on a petition was the most I felt comfortable with. I lent my presence because it was what I believed.

I think we're human beings first, coaches and players second, and in the '60s we had to strike an extremely delicate balance between the two. Sometimes there was a dichotomy at work. But I was aiming to show our players that there was nothing wrong with that because complexity is part of life. There is something to be said for having your own convictions and views and your own way of living, regardless of your vocation.

Charles Scott may have understood that as well as any of us. He was particularly active on campus and in the area, because he felt a responsibility to be visible on the civil rights front. There were no other black basketball players in the other major conferences in the Deep South—except Perry Wallace, who entered Vanderbilt when Charles came here. There were no others in the Southeastern Conference, none in the Southwest or in the Southern. None of those same major conferences had black football players either, and in fact, Scott played host to a quarterback recruit named Ricky Lanier, who became the first on the gridiron at Carolina the year after Charles arrived.

To me, the presence of Charles Scott on the court for us was nothing to commemorate or remark on. It was simply past due. It *should* have happened, no more and no less. But the unfortunate fact was that Charles still faced bigotry and even heard racial slurs from crowds when we played on the road. He put up with it gracefully. But matters reached a personal crisis for him in the 1968–69 season.

We felt our '69 team had every chance of being as good as the last two. I remember walking up the steps from the Carmichael floor to our office and saying to Bill Guthridge and John Lotz, "Boy, we're good." Larry Miller had graduated, but Clark, Bunting, Grubar, Brown, and Tuttle were still with us, Scott was coming into his prime as a collegiate player, and we had promoted Eddie Fogler to point guard. Our six-ten sophomore Lee Dedmon came off the bench to spell the frontcourt. By February we were 19–1.

On February 14, we met South Carolina in Charlotte as our home game in what was becoming a strong rivalry. They won, 68–66. But the more significant event was that a sophomore guard named John Roche scored 30 points. It didn't seem all that important at the time, but the truth is that it allowed the last remaining prejudiced people in the ACC to use it against us.

When we went to South Carolina a few weeks later to renew the rivalry in Columbia, things got ugly. Some South Carolina fans hurled the worst possible racial epithets at Charles, taunting him as he warmed up. Then early in the game one of their players hit him hard. Despite that behavior, we won, 68–62.

If we were angry that day, we were about to be even angrier. When the all-conference awards were released, there was a shock. Most people who knew basketball considered Charles Scott the best player in the league. He had a quick first step, was a great defensive player, and had a soft jumper with which he averaged over 22 points and 7 rebounds a game. His team won the regular-season ACC championship. He was an Olympian, and his talent and contributions were inarguable. But then came the announcement: Scott had lost the ACC Player of the Year award—to John Roche of South Carolina, a sophomore whose team finished second place to UNC in the league.

It was transparently racist. The awards were voted on by ACC sportswriters, sportscasters, and media relations directors for the schools, all of them, of course, white. The vote wasn't even close. Roche had won by 56 to 39. The real telltale sign of what happened was that five voters did not even put Charles on their all-conference team—*despite the fact that he was an Olympian and a first-team All-American*. It was a clear insult. In the coming days there was even some acknowledgment among sportswriters that an injustice had been done.

We were upset. But it fueled us too. Playing with a vengeance, we reached the championship game of the ACC tournament for the third straight year and met Duke again, as we did in 1967. Early in the game Dick Grubar went down clutching his knee. With Dick on the sidelines, Duke led us at halftime by 9 points. We regrouped in the locker room, and Grubar came out and tried to play in the second half, but it was immediately apparent his knee wouldn't hold up. Then Bill Bunting fouled out with 9:26 left. We were without two starters, and a comeback seemed impossible. Duke extended its lead by 11.

What we did next has become part of Carolina lore. We worked steadily at the deficit, erasing it a little bit at a time. Charles Scott was hot and the players were looking for him. Charles scored 28 points in the second half, knocking down shots from everywhere. In the end he made 12 of 13 in the second half (some of which were beautiful drives out of Four Corners), and 17 of 23 for the game, for a career-high 40 points. We won handily. Final score: 85–74.

Afterwards, Charles was the unanimous choice for MVP of the tournament, and he was also named ACC Athlete of the Year, a possible concession from voters. Charles said later that despite the occasional epithet he had heard from crowds, that voting miscarriage for Player of the Year was the first time he felt genuinely slurred. "They put a guy ahead of me because I'm not white," he told *The Washington Post*.

The ACC voting provoked a controversy in the midst of the NCAA tournament. Without Grubar, who was out for the duration of the season with a knee injury, we barely beat a strong Duquesne team, 79–78, in the East regional semifinal, and afterwards, Charles, who had lit up the scoreboard again for 22 points, told the national media exactly how he felt. I stood by him. I called a team meeting and told our players that the ACC vote had become a hot media issue, and that Charles had every right to protest it publicly. But I added that we needed to maintain our focus for our next opponent.

Lefty Driesell's Davidson team came to the NCAA East regional final at Maryland's Cole Field House determined to upset us. "I'd rather die than lose to Carolina again," Lefty said. It would be an emotional game, Lefty's last for Davidson, because he was about to be named head coach at Maryland.

Neither team could gain the upper hand, not until the last two minutes. Charles tried hard to duplicate his feat, hitting 10 of 14 from the field, but still we trailed by 2 with 1:30 to play. Then Charles buried a jumper to tie the score at 85. Davidson's Jerry Kroll held the ball, waiting for the last shot of the game. He dribbled hard—and ran right into Gerald Tuttle, who took a heroic charge.

I called time-out with thirteen seconds remaining and told our players that Davidson would probably converge on Charles. "Charles, we're going to run 'penetration,' but Lefty is going to have them key on you. We should have guys open all over the court when they converge. If we miss, rebound it. At worst, we will win in overtime."

We inbounded the ball to Charles. He didn't look at anything but the basket. He took the ball thirty feet from the basket, dribbled twice, held it to let the clock go down, and rose in the air. He soared above the defenders and put up an arc with three seconds to play. It settled through the net as the buzzer sounded—and we exploded off the bench. We were going to our third straight Final Four.

But our season lasted a week too long. The team that showed up in Louisville for the Final Four wasn't quite the same team that had played in the ACC tournament, with the loss of Grubar. Still, Purdue was simply better than we were in the national semifinals even if Grubar had played. In the consolation game against Drake, I told the team to just have fun and shoot it up, and we lost, 104–84. We finished with a record of 27–5.

Generally, that Final Four is regarded as the end of a marvelous three-year era. But the truth was, we would go on to win the NIT in 1971 and return to the Final Four in 1972, so actually it was a six-year period. I still marvel at what those teams did. The class of '69—Clark, Grubar, Bunting, Tuttle, and Brown—graduated with an 81–15 record in the three years. When we reached the Final Four in 1969, I realized something else: Our starting lineup included five men who had scored better than 900 on their SATs. I don't think that's been true of a Final Four team since. To win three straight ACC regular season titles, three straight ACC tournament titles, and reach three straight Final Fours, while maintaining the highest academic standards, was a rare thing.

But more important, in those years at Carolina we gained a clear and vital understanding of the place of collegiate athletics on a campus. The team was a small part of a university community in which people argued politics, passed and failed classes, followed changing fashions, attended church, and lived their lives. By the close of the decade I realized how lucky I was to live and work on such a beautiful, thriving campus where open debate was not just tolerated, but encouraged.

While things were going well on campus and with our program, my marriage wasn't doing well, nor was I taking time away from my work to help the situation. Ann and I didn't argue or even talk much except to discuss the children.

In 1970, I moved in with John Lotz, who was still single. I would see my children daily, but this nevertheless was a difficult time in my life and also for Ann. In 1973, the divorce was final. Ann still lives in Chapel Hill and we remain friends.

7

The Carolina Way

Our philosophy at North Carolina was clear from day one. Each year we had the same goals: (1) Play together; (2) Play hard; (3) Play smart. Together meant unselfishly, hard meant with effort, and smart meant with proper execution.

Beginning in 1971, we would average just under twenty-seven wins a season for the next twenty-seven years. As we developed a reputation for unparalleled consistency and appeared on television all over the country, we acquired a distinct persona. Our collective demeanor was modest and neat. We wore sleeveless V-neck jerseys, boxy shorts that were neither too short nor too long, high tube socks with stripes of Carolina blue, low quarter shoes, and uniformly white wristbands.

It was my hope that our appearance would bespeak achievement without shouting it. The first time I saw a player "showboat" after making a play, I said, "Try to act like you've done this before." If you had to call attention to yourself or celebrate excessively, you must not be very good. It was just like a hole in one in golf. Now this would be cause for celebration because it only happens once or twice in a lifetime, if at all. Two points was hardly a reason to be demonstrative. Why not appear accustomed to making great plays?

Perhaps it was that particular Carolina brand of understatedness, combined with our consistency, that made one writer label our program "the IBM of college basketball." We began hearing references to the Carolina "system" and the Carolina "image," and a book was published analyzing our success, called *The Big Blue Machine*. But I disliked those terms because I felt they were inaccurate. We had a philosophy of basketball, not a system.

A "system" would imply that we used the same offensive and defensive strategy every season. Actually, we were very flexible in our strategy, and it changed from year to year, depending on the individuals in our program, who were diverse in their weaknesses and strengths. But while our strategy was flexible, our overall philosophy and methods were fairly constant. In fact, our assistant coaches carried them on after they left here. Even as you read this book, a number of former Carolina assistants are active head coaches enjoying great success using team goals, practice plans, and even small rituals that are very similar to the ones we employed at Carolina. (Still, each of them has different personnel, and they must adapt their own approaches based on individuals, trying to hide the weaknesses while using the strengths.)

Our goals—to play together, play hard, and play smart—were our mission statement. If we met those goals, then we probably would win. But winning was merely a by-product. Our coaches seldom used the word *win*.

Ideally, as a head coach I should have been pleased if the team played well, win or lose. But I struggled with that part. Other people made judgments based on who won the game, and it did affect me. There were times, I'll admit, when losing bothered me no matter how well we played, and there were times I was happy to win even if we executed poorly. If we failed to execute and played selfishly, and yet somehow managed to pull off the victory, I should have been upset. And I may have been, but I probably felt better than if we played hard, played smart, and played together—and lost.

To make winning an end in and of itself seemed neither realistic nor good teaching. Too many factors in the game of basketball were beyond our control. Talent fluctuated wildly from year to year, depending on how we fared with recruiting, how many players we lost to the pros, and what new players brought to the team. Injuries, bad luck, a poor referee's call, or any number of other unpredictable circumstances could influence the outcome of a game or an entire season.

Therefore, we chose to measure our success in different terms. We asked ourselves: (1) Were we unselfish? (2) Did we play hard on every possession? (3) Did we execute the basic fundamentals well offensively and defensively?

There was a fourth principle at work in our program: to have fun. Often during time-outs at critical junctures in games, I would smile at our players and say, "Isn't this fun?" If we met our first three goals, listed above, then we would indeed have fun.

The question was how to convince a team to do those three things, to play together, play hard, and play smart.

I began my talks to our team each season by explaining what I meant by playing together. Basketball is a game that is dependent on togetherness. In my individual sessions with players, I pointed out that seldom, if ever, had there been a leading scorer in the country who played on a ranked team, and certainly not a championship team. Also, I pointed out the importance of helping each other in various other ways, whether in playing "team" defense, setting an offensive screen to help a teammate, or passing the ball to the open man.

Second, I talked about playing hard. We began by suggesting that everyone could control his own effort. There was a lot in basketball beyond our control, but a player should never let anyone try harder than he does. There was no excuse if another team played harder than we did, and we constantly pointed out in practice sessions when we didn't think our players were giving the maximum effort. If they were tired in games, they should give the "tired signal" and we then substituted. We would stop practice and have the team run a quick sprint for any player who failed to sprint back on defense, or when there was any other indication that someone was not playing all out. It was important to notice when someone was not giving full effort and penalize him right then and there. It did wonders in getting the point across to the other players.

When it came to playing smart, we used practice and repetition to teach our players what we wanted, drilling them so that we would have good execution in the fundamentals offensively and defensively at game time. In fact, our entire program was built around the practice session. The teaching I did in our practices was what I really missed the most when I retired. I did love practice because it was my classroom. (Although I also loved late-game situations, especially when we won, and we certainly practiced the last five minutes of game situations almost every practice.)

In teaching I tried to be thorough. I would ask questions and expect correct answers on the practice court. In order to achieve execution, or "play smart," we did a great deal of part-method teaching. We would break down into "stations," with a lot of two-on-two work offensively and defensively.

I was very demanding, but the role of a head coach is that of a demanding teacher. Those of you who are reading this book can probably all look back on a tough teacher you had, and if you're lucky you think of him or her with affection. Demands must be coupled with true caring for the students. A demanding teacher is quick to praise action that deserves praise, but will criticize the act, not the person. The coach's job is to be part servant in helping the player reach his goals.

Certainly, coaching was not a matter of manipulating people to do what would help us. I never did like the term *handle* people, which to me meant conning people. The life insurance salesman who genuinely believes someone needs life insurance is different from the one who tries to manipulate or con them into buying something they do not need.

I believed a demanding teacher should treat each player as an important part of the team, which, of course, he is. The least skilled player received the same attention from me as the best player. When their careers drew to a close, I always had what I called an "exit meeting" with each young man, to discuss what his goals had been and what they were for the future.

To me, the players got the wins, and I got the losses. Caring for one another and building relationships should be the most important goal, no matter what vocation you are in.

Our 1971 team was a good illustration of what could happen when a group of players focused on these goals rather than on winning. Few expected us to have a great season, yet that is exactly what we had. We were unranked in the national polls in preseason, and picked to finish anywhere from fourth to seventh in the league.

We were also in what is commonly known as a "rebuilding phase" and at a crucial juncture for the program. The previous season we had gone 18–9 and were on the verge of being written off. We had lost All-American Charles Scott and key contributors Jim Delany and Eddie Fogler to graduation. Also, we had just suffered a demoralizing recruiting loss when Tom McMillen, the future Rhodes scholar, NBA player, and congressman, chose to go to Maryland after we had spent years pursuing him and he had chosen us before switching.

McMillen, a coveted six-foot-ten prospect from Mansfield, Pennsylvania, had attended our summer camp when he was fourteen, but by his junior year he was being recruited by as many as three hundred colleges. He described in his own book what an emotionally trying time it was for him and his family. After meticulously studying fourteen schools, Tom narrowed his final choices to three: Maryland, North Carolina, and Virginia. But that didn't simplify matters. Instead, things only got more complicated. Tom came from a close-knit family, and each member had a different opinion about where he should go to school. Tom was leaning toward North Carolina, but as he describes in his own book, there were several factors to consider, and he was having a terrible time making a decision that would please everyone.

His mother liked Virginia, in part because coach Bill Gibson was originally from their hometown of Mansfield and remained a close friend to their entire family. But one of Tom's older brothers, Paul, was a banker in Chapel Hill and preferred to see him at Carolina. Another brother, Jay, was a former all-ACC player for Maryland and had just enrolled in dental school there. Tom's father also favored Maryland, because he was in poor health and it would be an easier drive for him. Moreover, Maryland coach Lefty Driesell had hired a young man named Joe Harrington as an assistant coach—and Harrington was a dear friend of Jay and Tom's. Lefty made no secret that he had done so in part to help in recruiting Tom.

Tom called all three head coaches and told us that he would entertain one more visit from each of us and then make his decision. We each went to Mansfield on successive days and made our final presentations, and afterwards Tom sat down with his high school coach, Rich Miller, and reviewed his choices. Finally, one April night, he picked up the phone and called me. He was coming to North Carolina.

I assumed he had discussed the decision with his parents, as I was aware that they each favored different schools. I allowed myself to get excited. It was a huge mistake not to contact his parents immediately.

The next day Tom's mother indicated to the newspapers that neither she nor Dr. McMillen would sign his grant-in-aid papers, without which we couldn't extend him a scholarship. They would not give their permission for him to attend Carolina. I called them to see if we could resolve the situation. They invited me to their house for a cookout, at which they informed me they wanted to think about the situation over the summer and would see if the family could come to a decision.

Collegiate recruiting was not an enjoyable experience for that family, I'm sure, and I really did feel bad that it had caused a problem for them. They received all sorts of mail, including some anonymous letters leveling false accusations at the North Carolina program. Tom would call and read me the letters, and we even laughed about some of them. Knowing what sort of pressure they were under, I tried to let up. Tom went to Europe to play in the

University Games, and he wasn't scheduled to return to the States until just a few days before the start of fall classes. Bill Guthridge and John Lotz stayed in touch with him, and we could only assume that he would arrive on campus with the other freshmen. Meanwhile, I went to Switzerland to give a basketball clinic.

But the day before Tom was supposed to leave home for college, he sent a wire to our offices. Coach Guthridge and Coach Lotz reached me in Switzerland and read it to me. "Very, very sorry. Hope you understand. I am going to Maryland for reasons you know."

When I got back from Switzerland I called Tom to wish him luck, and we have remained friends ever since. Three or four years after Tom graduated from Maryland, Coach Guthridge and I visited with his mother, and we had a nice conversation.

After the McMillen reversal, everyone was watching to see which way we would go, up or down. Scott and the players from the class of '69, who brought the program so much national attention, were now alumni. Would we bounce back, or fade from prominence again? The '71 team answered every question and upset every prediction. They finished first in the ACC regular season, won the NIT, ranked number thirteen in the final national poll, and stamped us again as a national contender.

Steve Previs was a six-two junior guard from Bethel Park, Pennsylvania, who would spill his blood to get to a loose ball. Sophomore George Karl, six one, was a similar headlong type of player and a crowd pleaser. Bill Chamberlain, the six-five junior from New York, had a quickness around the basket, while six-six Dennis Wuycik, from Ambridge, Pennsylvania, could score and rebound. Senior Lee Dedmon, our six-ten center, had shown vast improvement, and Kim Huband, Donn Johnston, Dave Chadwick, and Dale Gipple gave us solid minutes off the bench.

That team practiced unselfishness day in and day out. The result was that while we had no great individual scorers, we were one of the hottest shooting teams in the country, averaging 52.2 percent from the field for the season (with Wuycik shooting 60.7, Chamberlain shooting 57.2, and Karl 52.4). It was simply a matter of good shot selection and fast break baskets off our outstanding defense. Defensively, Previs and Karl could put pressure on any guards in the country.

We won the ACC regular season title with an 11–3 record—in a year when South Carolina was picked as number one in the nation in preseason. We split with Frank McGuire's team in the regular season, and the signature game for our team came on January 4 in Carmichael Auditorium against the unbeaten number-one Gamecocks. Our players, attacking with poise and confidence, led the entire game and won, 79–64. South Carolina then beat us in a war in Columbia, 76–72, setting up the rubber match in the finals of the ACC tournament.

The ACC tournament game would decide the NCAA representative, and the loser would in all likelihood be invited to the NIT. The pressure was on South Carolina, what with its preseason ranking and its disappointing second-place finish to us in the ACC regular season. I knew Frank McGuire didn't particularly like the tournament, and I agreed that it wasn't the best way to decide the champion. In Frank's nine years at North Carolina, his team won one championship, in 1957. He was now in his seventh year at South Carolina and still frustrated by the tournament format, as I was.

It was a great game for the spectators; both teams fought hard to the bitter end, and with a little over a minute to play, neither team was able to gain the upper hand. We led, just 51–50. Each possession became extremely important. When a jump ball was called, I took a time-out to be sure we gained possession. We put one of our biggest players, Bill Chamberlain, on the circle, and I said, "Tip the ball to Bill." Which we did. Bill took it down like a rebound. But then we missed a free throw, and South Carolina regained the ball. South Carolina's Kevin Joyce tried to drive the baseline, but our Lee Dedmon tied him up for another jump ball with just *three* seconds to play. Again, possession was everything. I called another quick time-out.

During that time-out, I made a decision that I later wished I could take back. In the huddle I told our players, "I know Coach McGuire will think we are going to tap to Chamberlain, so let's use Chamberlain as a decoy." The jump situation was at South Carolina's end of the court, in front of their bench. I turned to Lee Dedmon and said, "Lee, I want you to tap to George Karl." My intention was to have George leave the circle and run toward the South Carolina bench. Lee would tap it to him, and we would go on to the NCAA tournament. I told everyone else where to line up—but I failed to make it clear to one player. When a player doesn't know where to go, it's the coach's mistake.

South Carolina's Joyce, a great leaper, got a break on the timing of his jump. He flicked the ball to the Gamecocks' Tom Owens—who scored at the buzzer. It was a heartbreaking loss. It certainly wasn't Lee's fault. It was nobody else's but mine.

We wouldn't be going to the NCAAs, but at least South Carolina would. It was difficult to compete against a very close friend and my former boss, Frank McGuire, and I was happy for him to go on to the national tournament if we couldn't. In the end, South Carolina lost in the East regionals to Pennsylvania and later that year left the ACC for good. But that didn't end the rivalry. We met South Carolina in the NCAA tournament the very next year, 1972. We had all of our players back except for Dedmon, and our players were fired up. We won, 92–69. We still went up against Frank in recruiting every year too, until his resignation in 1979. We pursued many of the same New York players, and Coach McGuire got virtually all of them. Eddie Fogler of Flushing was an exception. Another was John O'Donnell of Fordham Prep, who was one of two New Yorkers recruited by both of us in 1971, along with Brian Winters. We split on those two: Winters went to South Carolina, and O'Donnell came to North Carolina and became a Rhodes scholar nominee and later an orthopedic surgeon.

Back in 1971, the NIT was extremely prestigious in New York, and I was impressed with the way our team put the loss to South Carolina behind them and refocused on winning a title. We defeated a Massachusetts team starring Julius "Doc" Erving in the first round, after he got in quick foul trouble. These days when I play golf with Julius, I like to needle him about the final score, 90–49. But he rightly points out that he fouled out early. I answer that we lost our leading scorer, Dennis Wuycik, for the season to a knee injury. Dave Chadwick did a marvelous job of filling in for the injured Wuycik, and we got by a good Providence team in the second round, and then beat Duke for the third time that season in the semifinals. In the final, we defeated Georgia Tech convincingly, 84–66, to leave New York as the NIT champions. Bill Chamberlain was named the tournament MVP.

I have often said over the years that the 1971 team really sustained the Carolina program. Those players understood that when we committed to our philosophy wholeheartedly, as they did, we were an outstanding team. Eight different players alternated on the floor during that season, and five of them finished with over 80 assists apiece, while four averaged in double figures, and each of our starting five was our leading scorer in at least one game. With our team hustle and togetherness, we looked as if we had the home-court advantage in every game.

We had more than a winning team. We had a winning program.

Practice was the foundation of everything we did. Our practices were tough, carefully planned, and meticulously organized. We believed that doing the small things right helped us to do the big things right.

"Practice is a privilege," I told our players. "If you're not here to work, don't come. After all, this isn't a required freshman English course. This is fun and it's an elective. Not only that, it's easier than football."

Each day, players received a typed copy of our practice plan. They would come into the locker room, and while dressing they would leaf through the plan, which would give them a precise schedule of what we would be working on that day.

At the top of the plan was a Thought for the Day, which was usually a quotation that had nothing to do with basketball. Rather, it was a philosophical remark that, we hoped, put basketball into a larger context. We used the Serenity Prayer on occasion. Or we might use something taken from the Bible, or something Islamic or Judaic. The players were asked to memorize it. As they went through their prepractice stretches and routines, you could see their lips moving as they repeated it over and over.

You can tell more about a person from what he says about others than what others say about him.

Don't let one day pass without doing something for a person who cannot repay you.

Never judge your neighbor until you have walked in his moccasins for two full moons.

The Emphasis of the Day was a basketball thought. The idea for it came from Larry Brown and Doug Moe when they were living in Chapel Hill and coaching the Carolina Cougars of the ABA. They had played for coach Alex Hannum in Oakland, and he had an Emphasis of the Day, not every day, but often. When they did have it, it was stressed. Larry and Doug told me the Oakland players would run laps if they messed up the Emphasis of the Day. That's when I thought it would be a good idea for our program.

Only about twice a year would one of our players fail to get it right when I asked him for our Thought for the Day or Emphasis of the Day. They didn't want to cause their teammates to have to run for their mistake, so they were careful to learn it.

Sometimes it was a strategic emphasis, other times it involved team building. It might be *Sprint back on defense,* or *Catch the ball with both hands if possible.* We wanted players to remember their fundamentals. We didn't want to see them jogging up the court or reaching out lazily to grab the ball with one hand.

To start practice I would blow a whistle, and players would sprint to join me at the jump circle. As they gathered around me, I would say what I wanted to about that day's practice. Then I'd look to see if any player was trying to avoid eye contact with me. If so, I'd probably call on him for the offensive Emphasis of the Day. I'd often pick on a freshman for one of these. Then I'd ask for the defensive Emphasis of the Day, then for the Thought of

EMPHASIS OF THE DAY: Offensive: MOVE INTELLIGENTLY AND QUICKLY WITHOUT THE BALL!

Defensive: MOVE WHEN BALL MOVES, WORKING FOR PROPER VISION OF
SEEING YOUR MAN AND THE BALL!

THOUGHT FOR THE DAY: "THE LAST OF THE HUMAN FREEDOMS IS TO CHOOSE YOUR ATTITUDE IN A
GIVEN CIRCUMSTANCE; TO CHOOSE ONE'S OWN WAY!"—Victor Frankel

STATIONS: 1. Stretching
2. Jump Rope
3. Individual Baskets, Shooting Form
4. Big Men & Perimeter Men – Shooting & Individual Work

TIME		SUBJECTS
3:30		MEETING – LECTURE AND TAPE –
4:45		ASSEMBLY –
4:47		FAST BREAK DRILL #2 – 12 MADE JUMP SHOTS – USE BOARD FROM WING – (Inside 15')
4:49		ONE-ON-ONE – BOTH ENDS – BALL ON SIDELINE – BALL IN MIDDLE – POST MOVES
4:55		OFFENSIVE – DEFENSIVE STATIONS: A) SCREENING WORK – COACH WITH BALL
		:03 per group- B) DENY PASS, SUPPORT ON DRIBBLER
		rotate AND RECOVER
		C) SCREEN AT BALL – DOUBLE, FAKE DOUBLE –
5:05		SHOOTING STATION – GROUP B –
		4-ON-4 DEFENSE WORK – GROUPS C & A –
		"SHELL" – ONE MAN FRONT – TWO MAN FRONT
	*	BASELINE DRIVE INTO FREE-LANCE – SOLID DOUBLE! TALK & PICK-UP –
	*	SCREEN AT BALL INTO FREE-LANCE – SOLID DOUBLE! TALK & PICK-UP –
5:13		ROTATE GROUPS –
5:21		ROTATE GROUPS –
5:29		LOSERS RUN –
5:30		HALF-COURT DEFENSE WORK – DEFENSE BREAKING MADE OR MISSED – UNTIL DEAD
		BALL – MORE SCRAMBLE (32 – 42) THAN MAN (22) –
5:42		WATER BREAK –
5:44		OUT-OF-BOUNDS SITUATIONS – REVIEW – ENDLINE, ¾ COURT, ½, ¼, BASELINE
		DEFENSES 24, 33, 43, 42, #1, #3 –
5:54		#3 OFFENSE WORK – MUST LOOK TO SCREEN FOR MAN WHO JUST PASSED BALL!
		DEFENSE BREAKING UNTIL DEAD BALL OR DEFENSE STOPS BREAK –
6:06		INTRODUCE #2 – ZONE OFFENSE (Dummy) – BOTH ENDS –
6:11		HALF-COURT ZONE OFFENSE – #5 FREE-LANCE – #2 "T" GAME –
		AGAINST POINT ZONE AND SCRAMBLE OUT OF POINT –
6:21	*	CONTROLLED SCRIMMAGE – BOTH TEAMS – ZONE CALL ON MADE – MISS SHOT – 22 – MAN –
		SCORE 30-30 – 5 MIN. IN 1st HALF –
6:31		SCRIMMAGE 3:00 3 MIN. LEFT IN GAME – WHITE 68-BLUE 75 – BLUE'S BALL – WHITE –
		IN "CATCH-UP" – FOUL REBOUNDER IF YOU MISS SHOT –
6:37		SCRIMMAGE 3 MIN. LEFT IN GAME –
		WHITE 73 - BLUE 68 – WHITE BALL – WHITE #1 "BURN" INTO 44 SERIES OFFENSE –
6:43		WINNERS-LOSERS-SPRINTS –
6:45		CONDITIONING ??? OR SHOOTING GAME – 30 SEC.-
	*	COMPETITIVE

WHITE	BLUE
(1) PHELPS (RÖDL)	(1) CALABRIA (CHERRY)
(2) RÖDL (WILLIAMS)	(2) DAVIS (CHERRY)
(3) SULLIVAN (RÖDL)	(3) CHERRY (STEPHENSON)
(4) LYNCH (SULLIVAN)(SALVADORI)	(4) WENSTROM (GETH)
(5) MONTROSS (SALVADORI)	(5) ZWIKKER (WENSTROM)

(Injured – Reese; Exam – Zwikker – Leave at Break)

You will notice from the two practice plan examples I have given that one is for a November date in our 1993 championship season and the other for a March date in the championship season of 1982. In November we generally practice much longer than we do in March but still seldom over two hours.

We begin practice with something that includes the entire team, to create some enthusiasm. We then go to offensive or defensive "part-method" drills before the heart of the early practice, which is our four-on-four defensive work. When the whistle blows to rotate groups, players must

EMPHASIS OF THE DAY: Offensive: NO UNNECESSARY DRIBBLE!
Defensive: PRESSURE ON BALL – DON'T FOUL DRIBBLER!

THOUGHT FOR THE DAY: "WE MAY BE ON THE RIGHT TRACK BUT IF WE STAND STILL, WE WILL
BE RUN OVER! IMPROVE TODAY!"

STATIONS: INDIVIDUAL WORK – A COACH WILL ASSIGN

TIME		SUBJECTS
4:15		ASSEMBLY –
4:17		FAST BREAK DRILL #1 – ENTHUSIASTIC! –
4:19		FAST BREAK ORGANIZATION – BOX OUT FROM MAN AND POINT DEFENSE –
		BLUES SHOOT QUICKLY! –
4:25		DEFENSIVE STATIONS: A. GUARDING SCREEN AT BALL – GOOD DOUBLE! SPRINT OFF. –
		B. GUARDING SCREEN AWAY – DOWN AND REAR –
		C. GUARDING LATERAL SCREEN ON BLOCK –
4:28		ROTATE GROUPS –
4:31		ROTATE GROUPS –
4:34		SHOOTING STATION – GROUP II – RECORD SHOTS – USE TOSS BACKS –
	*	4-ON-4 DEFENSE – DEFENSE – GROUP I – GROUP III FREE-LANCE PASSING GAME –
4:41		ROTATE GROUPS – SHOOTING – GROUP I –
	*	DEFENSE – GROUP II – GROUP III OFFENSE –
4:48		HALF-COURT DEFENSE – DEFENSE FAST BREAK – MISS OR MADE –
		#22-#32-#42 – ON MADE – INTO SECONDARY BREAK –
5:06		WATER BREAK –
5:08	*	ZONE-OFFENSE-DEFENSE GAME – GROUPS I & II –
		SIX POSSESSIONS WITH FAST BREAK –
5:18		FULL COURT PRESS OFFENSE – AGAINST 6 DEFENSIVE MEN IN ZONE PRESS –
5:22	*	PRESS OFFENSE-DEFENSE GAME – FROM FOUL SHOT DEFENSE – 54-43-33 – SPRINT TO
		FOUL LINE –
5:30		PART METHOD OFFENSE – 1,4 & 5'S – ONE END – 2 & 3 – OTHER END – B-1, B-2, B-3, #3 –
5:35		HALF-COURT MAN OFFENSE – EXECUTION – WHITE BALL – B-1, B-2, B-3, B-23 INTO FREE-LANCE
		PASSING GAME – NO BREAK BUT CHECK DEF. BALANCE –
5:45		#4-#4C DELAY OFFENSE – 3:00 MIN. TO PLAY – 66-62 WHITE BALL –
		– 1:00 MIN. TO PLAY – 69-68 WHITE BALL –
5:55	*	FOUL SHOOTING – SEVEN WHITES VS SEVEN BLUES –
		ONE ON ONE – POSSIBLE 14 POINTS –
		WINNERS – LOSER SPRINTS –
5:58		WINNERS – LOSER SPRINTS –
6:00		PRACTICE CONCLUSION –
		*COMPETITIVE (Winners-Losers) –

WHITE	BLUE
(1) BLACK (BRADDOCK)	(1) ROBINSON (PETERSON)
(2) JORDAN (BRADDOCK)(PETERSON)	(2) EXUM (PETERSON)
(3) DOHERTY (JORDAN)	(3) BARLOW (EXUM)
(4) WORTHY (BRUST)	(4) BROWNLEE (MAKKONEN)
(5) PERKINS (WORTHY)	(5) MARTIN (BROWNLEE)

sprint to their new position. The personnel in the drill groups are changed every two weeks throughout the season to avoid forming cliques. Groups by size obviously remain the same.

After the water break in each practice, we move to some type of work in the five-on-five situation. However, in November we are still introducing team offense and defense, so there is not as much five-on-five scrimmage as we do later in the year. Throughout the year we end practice with work in close-game situations. When there is an asterisk beside one of the planned activities, it means it is competitive, and the losers will run sprints. We will not make it competitive until each of the players knows the drill very well. When we are learning new things, we never make it competitive.

Although the manager tells me when time is up, the times are flexible if I choose to spend more time on what we are doing.

the Day. Those were the three things a player had to learn before practice. If the one on whom I called missed it, they all had to run.

A couple of years ago, Matt Wenstrom, a member of our '93 national championship team, returned to visit campus after spending two seasons playing basketball in Germany. I invited Matt to watch practice. As we were getting started I said, "Matt, tell them the Thought of the Day concerning what to to with a mistake."

Without hesitation Matt shot back, "You recognize it, you admit it, you learn from it, and you forget it."

After we met in a circle, we began practice. The workouts tended to be longer in preseason, perhaps even as long as two and a half hours, and gradually decreased in length, as the season progressed, to ninety minutes. Regardless of length, there was no horsing around. Practice was a classroom, and I required their complete attention. Also, our practices were closed to the public. I didn't see any of our English professors letting strangers in off the street to watch them teach. I insisted on an atmosphere that was conducive to learning. If special guests came to practice, they were required to get a pass and were asked to sit at the top of the arena, where they wouldn't be distracting.

Players sprinted from station to station for various drills with a blow of my whistle. Even water breaks were carefully timed—for exactly two minutes. Our drills were very specific, and after the players had learned them they became competitive.

Virtually everything we did in practice was graded, and grades were based on execution. Pure scoring was irrelevant to me; I was more concerned with whether the player had looked for the right pass, made the right judgment, taken the proper shot. Players earned points for steals, good passes, and drawn charges. We kept careful count—not just for a single practice, but for their entire careers. At the end of the practice your point total determined whether or not you ran sprints. Enough points meant a player didn't have to run. Two points got you excused from one sprint.

Eventually, we allowed graduating seniors to "will" their points to returning players, which resulted in a strange apprentice system. Younger players would run all kinds of errands for upperclassmen, making trips to Taco Bell or McDonald's to pick up hamburgers in hopes of inheriting their points.

As we moved from station to station, we drilled players in the specifics of our basic philosophy. Our players always felt that our practices were harder than games, and that's the way it should have been.

I certainly enjoyed having many high school coaches attend our practices at Carolina. It was exciting to me when they saw something in our sessions that they could use successfully in their own programs. I will always remember coach Jack Greynolds of Barberton, Ohio, calling me after his team had won the state championship to thank me for the run-and-jump defense idea he got from watching us practice in the early 1970s. Whereas we used the run-and-jump as a surprise, he took it a step further by using it every time. It created havoc with players with high school ballhandling skills. Jack was highly successful his entire career.

I enjoyed coach Don McCool and his group of fellow coaches coming each year from northern Virginia. They came with great enthusiasm. They used what they learned, along with many of their own ideas, and won many games despite not having Division 1 college basketball prospects. Also, many years ago Stu Vetter came with his assistants to study our practice organization, which they implement well with Stu's teams.

We've also had many college coaches come by over the years in the off-season to talk basketball and look at tapes. These were great learning sessions for our staff as well as the visitors.

I received a call in the summer of 1987 from Gregg Popovich at Pomona College in California. "Popo" had played for Bob Spear at Air Force and had married my good friend Jim Conboy's daughter. He asked to spend a year with us while on sabbatical watching practice and sitting in on staff meetings. After three months I suggested (as did Bob Spear) that he should go with Larry Brown to watch Kansas practice and play for the next three months. Kansas won the 1988 NCAA Championship and then Larry took "Popo" to San Antonio when he switched to the NBA. Now "Popo" just finished 1999 as head coach of the NBA champions. He is an excellent coach and went from Pomona to the NBA.

When K. C. Jones was coaching the Boston Celtics, he and his wife and child came to Chapel Hill for three days to talk basketball. That was a great time for us. K.C. wanted to put in our secondary fast break along with our offensive sets, which we called B-1, B-2, and B-3. After he went home to begin practice with the Celtics, he was really excited about Larry Bird setting those back screens and then receiving a pass. But he called after a week of practice and said Bird was getting beaten up setting these screens, so K.C. had to drop the idea. I completely understood. The NBA and college basketball are two entirely different games.

Friends such as former NFL coach Bud Carson and NFL coach Al Groh also enjoyed our practices. Another practice visitor was Anson Dorrance,

Carolina's women's soccer coach, whose teams have won ten of the past twelve NCAA championships.

Our practices were highly organized and the players gave great effort, which helped our annual fall clinic in Chapel Hill be successful. Junior high, high school, and college coaches would bring a couple of their players to these clinics just to show them how much effort it takes to play at this level.

These practice sessions, along with the big games, were what I liked best about coaching. Some important principles of coaching here are:

Defense as our program's cornerstone: Having a true team defense helped bring about the three goals of playing together, playing hard, and playing smart. By *team defense* we meant having a solidarity that required each player to trust his teammates. Our defense would not work if one player was out of position. Also, we told our players to always encourage their teammates, unless they themselves were perfect.

We tried to show our players that it is much easier to play team defense five-on-five than it would be two-on-two. The fewer people on the court, the more advantage the offense has. Sometimes we even demonstrated the value of team defense by having a fourteen-man squad, with seven playing seven in half-court. They quickly understood how important team defense is.

Moreover, team defense promoted team offense. When players bought into a team defense it went a long way toward guaranteeing unselfish play on offense. We talked all the time about "shot selection," because taking good sound shots usually meant that a team was playing unselfishly on offense. As an example of shot selection, twenty-four of the last twenty-seven Carolina teams have shot higher than 50 percent on field goals for the season.

Pitching to the man ahead: It was an absolute must in our program. If a player stole the ball and was headed toward an open basket, but had a team-mate in front of him, we insisted that he pitch the ball ahead. That seems a little thing, but it was an important part of our philosophy and went straight to the point of building an ethic of unselfishness throughout the team. If a player failed to pitch the ball ahead, we removed him from the game.

But we also point out that you are being selfish if you pass up a great shot to force a pass in order to make yourself look good. A player can be just as selfish by passing up a good shot to make a spectacular pass that shouldn't have been attempted in the first place.

The Honor Roll: Our coaching staff graded each game on tape, posses-sion by possession. The entire process took about five hours, and we devoted so much time to it because we wanted to be absolutely sure we were accurate in our grading. Statistics can cause all kinds of problems if they aren't accurate. We thought the time was well worth it because we wanted our players to know that we appreciated the little things they did to help their team win.

Based on our grading of the tape, we chose an Honor Roll for each game, and each category was for unselfish play. The Honor Roll began in my first year at Carolina with just one category—drawing a charge—but by my last year as head coach we had several: defense, assist/error ratio, offensive rebounding, drawing charges, screening, good plays, blocked shots, and deflections. We wanted our players to depend on the Honor Roll as an appraisal of who played well, rather than the traditional postgame statistics. In fact, we didn't even let the game statistics in our locker room after the game. I think the Honor Roll was another part of our philosophy that helped bring about unselfish team play and it is made public.

Shot selection: Sometime in the last ten to fifteen years of my career, I came up with the idea of scrimmaging without keeping score. The idea was to teach our players shot selection. I would stand by the scorer's table and award points based on how good the shot was, not whether it went in the basket. The scoring was done confidentially with me and a manager until the end of the ten-minute scrimmage, at which time we would announce the winning team. For instance, if someone hit a tough 3-point shot when he should not have taken it, with a defensive player guarding him and no rebounding coverage, I would tell the manager to put down "0 points," whether it went in or not. If someone had a layup opportunity with no one guarding him and he took but missed the shot, I would tell the manager to mark down the full 3 points, because he had taken the best shot.

The scoring system went like this: 3 points for the best shot (you could also get a 3 if you were fouled in the act of shooting a great shot); 2 points on a good but not a great shot (you earned points when you were fouled on a drive even if you missed the foul shots); and 1 point for a shot that was acceptable but perhaps could have been better. Loss of the ball without a shot was minus 2.

A good shot, to us, was one the shooter could make at a high percentage that was also taken with rebounding coverage if it was an outside shot. If you got an unguarded layup, we didn't care if you had rebounding coverage.

We didn't do this type of scrimmage often, but I wish we had done it more. Our players knew that the way to win, and to avoid running, was to be sure they took the kind of shot we wanted. We felt it brought about better

HONOR ROLL

GAME SCORE	DEFENSIVE AWARD	ASSIST ERROR	OFFENSIVE REBOUNDS	DRAW CHARGES	SCREENER AWARD	GOOD PLAYS 1st to loose ball Savvy draw focus	BLOCKED SHOTS	DEFLECTIONS
BLUE 89W WHITE 69	LYNCH	LYNCH	MONTROSS	CALABRIA	MONTROSS	LYNCH	WENSTROM	PHELPS
UNC 121W HIGH FIVE 74	RÖDL	LYNCH	LYNCH	MONTROSS SULLIVAN	SULLIVAN SALVADORI WILLIAMS	SULLIVAN	SALVADORI	LYNCH RÖDL
UNC 103W VICTORIAN ALL-STAR 75	LYNCH	CALABRIA	LYNCH	REESE	MONTROSS	LYNCH	MONTROSS RÖDL SALVADORI WENSTROM	LYNCH
UNC 119W OLD DOMINION 82	RÖDL	RÖDL	SALVADORI	WILLIAMS	——	RÖDL	SALVADORI	LYNCH
UNC 108W SOUTH CAROLINA 67	MONTROSS	PHELPS	LYNCH	LYNCH WILLIAMS	REESE	LYNCH	SALVADORI	LYNCH
UNC 104W TEXAS 68	PHELPS	PHELPS	WENSTROM	SULLIVAN PHELPS	REESE	PHELPS	SALVADORI	PHELPS
UNC 78W VIRGINIA TECH 62	PHELPS	PHELPS SULLIVAN	LYNCH	——	LYNCH SALVADORI	CHERRY	SULLIVAN MONTROSS	RÖDL
UNC 84W HOUSTON 76	PHELPS	PHELPS	LYNCH	PHELPS	LYNCH	PHELPS	RÖDL	PHELPS
UNC 103W BUTLER 56	PHELPS	CALABRIA	LYNCH	REESE CHERRY	WENSTROM	PHELPS	MONTROSS	LYNCH
UNC 84W OHIO ST. 64	PHELPS	SULLIVAN	LYNCH	REESE PHELPS	MONTROSS	RÖDL	SALVADORI	PHELPS
UNC 80W SW LOUISIANA 59	PHELPS	RÖDL	LYNCH	PHELPS	SULLIVAN	PHELPS	SALVADORI PHELPS	PHELPS
UNC 78L MICHIGAN 79	PHELPS	SALVADORI	LYNCH	PHELPS	MONTROSS	RÖDL	MONTROSS	PHELPS
UNC 101W HAWAII 84	PHELPS	RÖDL	LYNCH	PHELPS CHERRY REESE RÖDL	MONTROSS	SALVADORI	SALVADORI	PHELPS

The honor roll for the beginning of the 1992–93 season.

shot selection in games—and as proof, we usually led the ACC in field-goal shooting and were generally in the top ten nationally. Our scramble defense provided some easy shots off interceptions as well.

Being honest with players: I believed in being candid with players, whether we were talking about their role on the team or explaining to them what they were doing well and not so well. Many of my conversations with our players would be one-on-one in my office. To break the ice, I'd say, "You aren't playing as much as you'd like, are you?"

But I thought it was crucial when talking to one player never to discuss another player. I certainly wouldn't say, "You're not quite as good as Johnny," or, "This is what you must do to beat Johnny out." I didn't want my players to make rivals out of their own teammates; that would have been counterproductive. We would talk about what it would take for him to make the top seven, as opposed to what he had to do to beat a certain player. If a player wasn't in the top seven and wasn't going to get there that season, we would talk about what he could do to help the team. But we tried not to define roles for players until it became necessary because we preferred them to fall into their roles naturally. Also, I didn't want players to grow *too* happy with their roles and lose the incentive to improve in practice.

One player who was struggling came to my office to talk. I got up and made him sit in my chair. We reversed roles. "If you were coaching this team, would you play you?" I asked.

Often players would come to me and ask, "What can I do to earn more playing time?" I would tell them as specifically as possible what they needed to work on. But sometimes I told them, "These are things you should have worked on last summer. We're in season now."

Demanding unselfish play: College basketball is a game that absolutely demands unselfish play. At least that's the way I always tried to teach it. In baseball you have the sacrifice bunt, but in most other cases you're expected to be essentially selfish; you try to be aggressive at the plate and to catch every ball that's hit. In football, if the ball was on the one-foot line, and all eleven players could score, you might have a fight to see who carried the ball. In an individual sport such as golf, you're expected to be as selfish as you want. But all of that suddenly changes in the Ryder Cup, when players are playing for their teammates and their country, not just for themselves. Golfers are not used to playing for a team. Because of that, I'm sure professional golfers would tell you that playing in the Ryder Cup carries with it more pressure than playing in the U.S. Open or the Masters.

Recruiting unselfishness: We checked carefully in our recruiting to be sure the players we brought in were compatible with our philosophy. Freshmen came into our program used to having the ball and being the centerpiece of the offense. I could understand a high school coach wanting the ball in the hands of his best player, because he might not have anyone else who could score from outside of five feet. In that case it was in a team's best interest for one player to shoot a lot. But at North Carolina we wanted to win as a team, and freshmen had to learn that what they did without the ball was just as important as what they did *with* it for the success of the team.

Because of the type of people we recruited, we were able to make that happen. Often you can say right away whether a young man is unselfish. The first time I saw Matt Doherty play, I knew he was completely unselfish. The same with Dick Grubar. But we talked to a number of people about a young man before we offered him a scholarship, and in recruiting we never paid the slightest attention to a player's scoring average—but we did look at his shooting percentage.

In fact, a high scoring average could be a danger signal because it meant that player was used to taking so many shots per game and might have trouble sharing the ball with teammates. Frequently, I'd be more interested in a guy who was living on the foul line than I would be in the high scorer. How'd he get there? It meant he was taking the ball inside and doing things right. I would recruit him harder than someone who shot the ball forty times and made ten baskets.

One way I taught freshmen my philosophy on scoring was to start preseason by saying they had to make at least three passes before they could shoot anything but a layup. It made them learn to play offense away from the ball. In high school they either had the ball or were chasing to get the ball, rather than screening for a teammate. Our passing game was designed to move the ball and move without the ball so the defense would eventually break down. Against a good defense, the offensive team must move the ball, and themselves, to take away the "vision" of the defensive players, with the aim of penetrating the defense by pass or dribble. To teach movement without the ball we had a fine drill: No dribbling was allowed, and the team that could make the most number of passes without losing possession won. The only shot allowed would be a wide-open layup.

Putting statistics in proper perspective: On statistics we listed players alphabetically, rather than by high scorers. We weren't about to preach "team" to our players, only to issue statistics suggesting that our high scorer was our most important player. We all want approval, but at Carolina we were determined to earn it as a team.

The truth is, you can stop anybody from scoring in college basketball. Our rules guarantee that. Just put three defensive players on him and force someone else to shoot. It would be a dear price to pay, but it could be done if your only objective was to stop the high scorer.

The amount of attention given to how much a player scores is wrong. I even heard a respected TV announcer say once that a player "had" to get 25 points for his team to win. But team field-goal percentage, ballhandling, and rebounding—not a single player's scoring average—determines how potent your offense is. We never worried unduly about high scorers we played against. Sure, we tried to limit the number of shots they might get, but if they wanted to force the ball up, that was fine with us. It didn't bother me if a guy scored 30 points on us if he had to take forty shots to get them. That meant he was taking bad shots and hitting a low percentage, and we'd get the rebound and be off and running.

(But it was a funny thing about my principles on high scorers and proper shot selection. Once our players got to the pros, I was like a nervous parent who just wanted them to do well. Sometimes I'd catch myself yelling, "Shoot!" I told our players who were pros in Europe and the NBA to be conscious of their shots and the number of their rebounds because their owners were.)

Training freshmen: We didn't penalize players because they were freshmen, but we had to teach them basketball was a team game. In high school they had been the center of attention as well as the center of their coach's strategy. Often they didn't know how to defend, which was the foundation of our program. They had to earn their way as freshmen. They shagged loose balls, carried our gear, lugged the film and video equipment, and performed various other chores. (Michael Jordan spent his freshman year carrying a heavy projector through airports.)

In 1973 the NCAA voted to make freshmen eligible for varsity play. I disagreed. I thought it was a terrible decision. There is a simple, obvious way to reorder academic priorities: Make freshmen ineligible again. The decision was made strictly to save money, because schools didn't want to support freshmen who weren't competing on the varsity. Administrators said, "Why should we pay for their scholarships when they aren't even playing?"

There is no question in my mind freshmen were better served by sitting out for a year. Almost all of the ailments of intercollegiate basketball would be improved if freshmen and transfers from junior colleges were required to spend a year in residence before playing varsity basketball. If we are serious about wanting to minimize those problems and doing what's best for the student-athletes, we would make them spend a year getting academically and socially oriented before they play anything but a freshman schedule. As members of a freshman team, they would be playing with nonrecruited students who would become close friends. It would help them become a part of the general student body.

As members of the varsity, freshmen miss class. They miss vacations. They have to spend more time in practice than they did on the old freshman teams. And they have to attend film sessions, frequent squad meetings, and put in travel days to and from road games and media commitments.

Making any new student ineligible until he or she has completed a full academic year would be a clear statement by universities. It would say unequivocally that their commitment is to the academic well-being of athletes. It would reduce the intensity of recruiting and the "quick fix" psychology that is so conducive to cheating.

What's more, there is no evidence that freshman ineligibility would impair the careers of future pros. On the contrary, a year of apprenticeship enhances their ability to learn fundamentals, which should in fact improve their chances for having long, healthy careers. Sitting out as freshmen certainly didn't appear to hinder the development of Kareem Abdul Jabbar, Bill Walton, Charles Scott, or Billy Cunningham. Rather, it served to produce some of the most intelligent and well-schooled men in the game.

Meting out punishment: We would discipline players for being late, for missing class, and for other reasons. But anytime you discipline someone in a team environment, you must go to great pains to be completely fair. I would make sure Coach Guthridge wrote down what disciplinary action we took in each instance, so the next time something arose, we were consistent in handing out the punishment. Don't think for a minute that the offending player didn't know what disciplinary action had been taken for a similar violation. Also, we believed the players should know in advance what the punishment should be for violating team rules.

On the court we punished as a team, not individually. For instance, if one player didn't hustle in practice, the whole team ran sprints. We found the peer-pressure method far more effective in building habits and morale than motivation created by fear, reward, or any other means. My old friend from high school and the University of Kansas, Bill Bunten, had been to Marine leadership school where he learned a good disciplinary technique: If one rifle wasn't clean, the entire platoon was disciplined. Another dear friend, Dr. Earl Somers, told me that during World War II a psychiatric study found that men who were being fired at in foxholes were obviously frightened, and as human nature dictates, didn't want to get fired at. Their motivation under duress wasn't that they were fighting for the United States, but that they didn't want to let their buddies down.

Respecting the players: I always felt that it was important not to embarrass the players in public. My college coach at Kansas, Doc Allen, at times would substitute a player because of a mistake, and some of us who were not star players would play tentatively as a result—we were afraid of the repercussions. I wanted our players to be comfortable trying a pass that could lead to a layup. If you have ten of those situations and the player completes seven passes for layups and throws three away, you're way ahead of the game. It's about risk-reward. Now, our players knew that I would substitute immediately if they weren't playing hard or if I knew they were playing selfishly. Overall, however, I did not substitute on mistakes.

Silencing the crowd: Our North Carolina teams played extremely well on the road. Between 1967 and 1997 we were 140–76 on the road in the ACC—a rate of 65 percent. The next best road record during those years was held by Duke, which was 89–125, or 42 percent. Third best was N.C. State, with a road-winning percentage in the league of 36. We liked to talk to our players about having the ability to silence the crowds at N.C. State, Clemson, Wake Forest, or Duke. We discussed the challenge of concentrating on execution in a hostile environment. Just think how much fun we could have by silencing the crowd. When we played well and did things we were supposed to do, we could make those gyms seem mighty quiet.

Being punctual: If I say I'll meet you at 4:30 and I show up late, I'm saying that my time is more important than yours. That is selfish and arrogant. The players knew I usually arrived early to team meetings and practices, and I expected everyone to be there and ready to go. Phil Ford has kept his watch set ten minutes fast to this day because of it.

Praising: In practice it was extremely important to praise the unselfish play. For that matter we praised not only the unselfish play, but effort and execution. All parents, coaches, and teachers should praise behavior or action they wish to see repeated.

Positive reinforcement is crucial to building a team. I used to watch the young people play in our basketball camp, searching for someone who wasn't chasing the ball on offense, but was instead setting screens to free his teammates. I would blow my whistle on him and say, "Did you guys see

David set that screen?" When play resumed, everybody would be setting screens, and the problem then became that everyone was setting screens.

Sometimes I wrote a note on my practice plan to remind myself to find something to praise in a player who was struggling. I would wait until he did something worthy of praise, and then I would stop practice and draw attention to him. But first he had to do something to give me reason to praise him. I didn't do it falsely.

I believe the value of praise is diluted if not handled properly. A study came out of Columbia University a number of years ago in which they experimented with a group of ninth-graders who had failed an algebra test. They took a group of sixteen students and told eight of them they had received a C on the examination. The other eight were told they had failed. They immediately gave the students the same test again. Four or five of them who had been told they received a C *actually* improved to a C, while the others did not improve that much.

But the problem with that, to me, is that we are praising when praise has not been earned, and the benefits are bound to be short term. I wonder how much work ethic and self-esteem can be built when you are given phony praise. Sooner or later the player comes to realize it is phony, and a few years after graduation he may look back and believe he was conned, which detracts from the dignity of the player and the player-coach relationship.

I believed in being critical as well as in praising, and I raised my voice when I saw an action I didn't wish to see repeated. But in correcting a player, it was extremely important to talk about the act and not the person. For instance, I would not tell the player he was a "selfish person" if he was chasing the ball to hunt his shot. But I might say, "That appears to be a selfish thing, to shoot when you should be moving intelligently without the ball."

If a player persisted in a type of behavior, and punishment was warranted, I believed in doing it at once. We might tell the team to run a sprint, or we would excuse the player from practice and tell him he had let his teammates down. Once a player was excused from practice, he was required to see me sometime before the next practice, since he was temporarily off the team.

Planning practice: I used to draw up our practice plans in the evenings after watching tape of the previous day's practice or game. It would take me about an hour and a half to plan each practice. I was meticulous about it, because practice was the most important time I spent with our players. Our philosophy, our rituals, our strategy all came together in practice. At our staff meetings, I asked for input from our assistants, and if one of them felt we hadn't done something well in practice the previous day, I would make the changes in my plan to include that. We also determined in advance where the coaches would be positioned in practice each afternoon and what they would work on. But I very definitely ran practice, and I believed in having one voice heard at practice and on the bench in games during time-outs. I always told the assistants to throw out suggestions to me, which they did, and I accepted some and discarded some.

I prepared a master plan of practice in August, which included the times and dates that I wanted to put each part of our plan into place. We also had a weekly practice plan of things we wanted to accomplish in each seven-day cycle. The weekly plan was very flexible and subject to change, depending on how we were playing at the time.

If I had my career to do over again, I would have held more staff meetings, and I would have delegated more. That's good for the assistants too. So instead of sitting at home planning practices by myself, or looking at game tape at one o'clock in the morning, I would do it more in the office with assistants.

Importance of preseason practices: Each October 15, the official first day of practice, was a special day for me. The six-week stretch between October 15 and the opening game was my favorite time of the year because it was a time of real teaching. I could break bad habits or build new ones. I even stopped smoking and began an exercise program on that date. Each October 15, I knew I would be home for six straight weeks. But then I would blow all the good habits once December arrived and the season started. I'd quit exercising. But I'm happy to say I did not resume smoking.

Those six weeks were when we laid the foundation for our team. It was when chemistry and unselfishness were built and strategy was implemented. Once those six weeks were over we could truthfully say, "Now we're ready to play." Still, we had to continue to improve.

Coaching one game at a time: After each game one of my assistants handed me a scouting report of our next opponent. Each of the three assistants was assigned the job of scouting certain opponents, whom he then studied for the next week. But I refused to look ahead. For instance, if we played Clemson on Wednesday and Duke on Saturday, I paid no attention to Duke until Wednesday night after the Clemson game. Looking past an opponent in this sport, especially in a league as competitive as the ACC, was an invitation to defeat. We respected each of our opponents. After all, each gave basketball scholarships, just as we did, and each worked hard to be successful.

After the game I would go home or back to the hotel and take the scouting report of the next opponent with me, as well as a tape of the game we had just played. I gave the game a quick look, knowing that it would be graded possession by possession in a five-hour study session the next morning. I then turned my attention to our next game, read the scouting report, and prepared our practice plan.

Doling out scouting information: We didn't give our players extensive information about an opponent, because we wanted them to concentrate on our own execution and the way *we* played. We had a stubborn streak. We never believed in "taking what they gave us." Instead, we took what we wanted.

The opponent never wants to give you very much. There is a reason they're giving it to you—because they want to win. We waited a little longer and took what we wanted. I once got on Serge Zwikker, our seven-foot center, in a '97 NCAA tournament game when he launched an outside shot. "But coach, I was open, I was wide open," he said.

"Serge, there's a reason you were wide open," I said.

If our upcoming opponent ran the old UCLA cut, we would have a defense in our repertoire to combat that, and in practice that day we would work on that defense. But we were more concerned with ourselves than our opponent, because we believed our principles would make it hard for the opponent to run what they wanted against us. One reason we incorporated changing defenses was that we wanted the opponent to worry about us. Our pressure defense and our Scramble were designed to take teams out of what they liked to run.

Basketball is a tournament sport in which you only have one day to prepare (we had twenty-four hours between games in the NCAA tournament—it's now at least thirty-six hours—and we played on consecutive days in the ACC tourney). Our goal was simple—to take away what the opponent did best—and our players gained confidence knowing that we had answers to the opponent's offense.

Throwing in some junk: Bob Knight, the brilliant coach at Indiana, and I had discussions about the advantages of doing one thing on defense and doing it extremely well, as opposed to changing up. Indiana usually stays with one defense, and they execute well. Our goal at North Carolina was to be good at pressure-man defense, but we also had some junk thrown in to give the opponent something to worry about, something they would have to spend practice time on. Maybe our pressure defense suffered by working on other defenses.

Bill Guthridge and Gene Keady, the fine coach at Purdue, were roommates one summer at Kansas State. We played Gene's team in Alaska in

1986 and again in Dallas in 1987, so I had Bill ask him what was the toughest thing about preparing to play our team. Coaches learn that way. Gene said that we had hurt his team so much with the Scramble defense in 1986 that he kept his players over Christmas to practice against it in preparation for our game against them in Dallas the following year. Gene told Bill, "We practiced so much against your double team that I think it was a mistake, because we made our players apprehensive about it."

Giving opponents something to worry about should have played to our advantage during the ACC and the NCAA tournaments, and I think it did.

The go-to Guy: I got so tired of hearing the phrase *go-to guy*. If you thought he was your go-to guy, you could bet the other team did too, and was going to do everything in its power to take the ball out of his hands with the game on the line. I thought every man on the team should be a go-to guy at any period of the game, early or late. If not, that player shouldn't be playing. Obviously you wanted your best shooter to take the last shot or to get fouled. But you also wanted options that involved every player on the court. Just about all great teams have a starter who is content to only get about six shots a game, but who, if you leave him open, can knock them down.

Competition in practice for playing time: If one of our players was doing the job and was trying hard, it was difficult to dislodge him from his starting position once he had won it. Others did it differently with success. When Tex Winter was head coach at Kansas State and Bill Guthridge was his assistant, they changed starting lineups just about every game. Bob Knight changed his lineup constantly, not by sitting great players, but by interchanging them with others. Maybe it gives players hope to have a substitution pattern like that. It does keep practice interesting and it surely worked out for Kansas State, Indiana, and others.

At North Carolina, though, our goal in choosing a lineup was to reward defense. The top seven players at this level of play are going to be able to score, but until they showed us they were solid on defense, they wouldn't play. The foundation of our entire philosophy started on defense, and we tried to sell that as a motivating force.

Our players certainly had a chance to move up and win starting jobs. We changed lineups over the years. It was tough to do, but we sometimes did it. The toughest for me probably involved Ed Stahl, who started for us for two years before I benched him and named Tommy LaGarde the starter during Tommy's sophomore year. The last example would have been 1994 when freshman Rasheed Wallace became a starter in February in place of senior Kevin Salvadori.

I never penciled in a starting lineup until just before the season started, because you never knew how hard someone might work and improve over the summer. One example was Darrell Elston, a young man who came to Chapel Hill from Tipton, Indiana, in 1970. Darrell was more heavily recruited for football, but he was determined to play basketball. Coach John Lotz saw enough potential to persuade me to offer him a scholarship, but at the end of his sophomore season he was the thirteenth man on a fourteen-man squad. I called him in for a talk. I told him we loved having him on the team and he was welcome to stay, but I suggested that, in his best interest, he might consider transferring to play more. "Quite honestly, I don't see you getting much playing time here," I said. Darrell went home to think about it and then called to tell me he had decided to stick it out.

That summer he worked eight hours a day on his game. On October 15, the first day of practice, Elston was a different player. In fact, he was so improved he became a starter for his final two seasons, made All-ACC as a senior, and played pro basketball in the ABA. He inspired my unofficial "Darrell Elston rule": Never pencil in a lineup over the summer.

Competitive drills: I think this is very important in teaching. If we had a drill and the players knew what to do and it had become a habit, then we would make it competitive. We never made the drill competitive until the players completely understood what to do. The first focus was to be sure the players understood what we wanted, and repeated it.

But when everyone had it down, we would split into squads and compete to "win" the drills. What's more, we made sure something was at stake. The losers had to run sprints.

Being critical: We did not want our players to criticize a teammate for making a mistake. We felt that was so important. But it's so true in our society that the tolerance level toward others is extremely low. A big part of playing as a team was the understanding that players support each other. You could say: "He who is without sin may cast the first stone."

The Blue Team: The best move we ever made to bring a team together was to go to the Blue Team in 1969. The Blues were usually made up of players eight through twelve on our team. The Blue Team entered the game for two minutes during in the first half, and would make four, five, or six passes, and played hard on defense. It was tremendous for team morale and it made our practices so much better. Those five substitutes knew they were going to play in the game, so you can imagine what a positive effect it had on them in practice.

The best Blue Teams had two or three walk-ons, or seniors who weren't playing much. They understood what we were after and enjoyed trying to do it, and they weren't trying to impress the coach or earn more playing time. No matter if the Blue Team was winning or losing; they still came out of the game after two minutes. They knew this and gave everything they had while they were in there. Sometimes the opponent would try to take advantage of our Blues and would rush on offense and take bad shots. Opponents thought they could press them, but it usually didn't work because the Blues were so good at moving the ball around.

But we began to question the need for the Blue Team in the 1977 season, and had our last Blue Team as we knew it in 1981. We were at Michigan State in December and had a nice lead in the first half, as a high school prospect named Earvin "Magic" Johnson watched from the stands and later visited our locker room. There were four freshmen on the Blue Team that year, and they were obviously trying to impress the coach. My gosh, you've never seen such bad shots! We won the game, 81–58, but it was not a good night for the Blues.

Maybe the Blue Team will come back one day. It is not as easy as you might think, though, to find the correct personnel for a team like that. It takes special people—unselfish, team-oriented hustlers.

One of my coaching mistakes: I never scrimmaged enough as a coach. Each year I would tell my assistants to remind me in January and February to scrimmage more.

We wanted to make sure that we worked on our delay game at the end of practice, and every other day we tried to put players in overtime situations. I wanted to get our execution of those situations down to the point of habit.

We covered all situations that might occur during a game and how we wanted to react. For instance, if the score was tied with twenty-five seconds left in the game, and we gained possession of the basketball, I very rarely would take a time-out, because I felt a time-out would allow the defense to set up something. We hoped we knew which play to run at that point offensively. We wanted a very good shot, or to be fouled with at least three seconds remaining to give us a chance for an offensive rebound. If I had done a good job in teaching, we should not need a time-out. The aim was to come away with at worst a tie ball game. But more often than not we came out with a win, via a good shot, a foul, or an offensive rebound. We also practiced a soft zone press called prevent-defense after we went ahead with three seconds left to prevent our opponent from scoring.

We went over these situations so as to be prepared when they arose in actual games. Another scenario: If we had one foul shot with a second to go and we were two points behind, we knew we would play our "Archie" and do some stunting on the foul line for a missed free throw. The word *Archie* came from shooting the ball extremely high so that our rebounders had more of an opportunity to screen and get in position for the rebound. That happened twice over the years, and we did get the offensive rebound, but we failed to make the shot, so I can't say we were successful.

The problem with scrimmaging is that players would revert back to old habits if we didn't go through part-method teaching. Different coaches use different methods of teaching, learning, and improving. We'd have a ten-minute scrimmage almost every day, or two five-minute sessions. But I knew coaches who scrimmaged throughout practice, and that method of teaching is not all bad. I just decided to show our players what we wanted, five on five, then we broke it down into small components, and after developing good habits we came back to it as a whole in gamelike conditions.

The way we played over the years at North Carolina was a product of our practices. We built our togetherness, our consistent effort, and our execution in practice.

Running: We didn't run after every practice. It was good to cancel running every now and then as a reward for a good effort. But when practice was poor I might say, "We didn't get much accomplished today, so let's do some serious running. That way we'll get something done."

We used to save all of our running for after practice. But sometimes that meant that the running wouldn't occur until an hour after the players had lost a drill, by which time they had forgotten what they had done wrong. Also, the ones who lost and had running to do were more worried about the last five minutes of practice than what we were working on at the time. We changed that so the punishment was immediate. On days when we had competitive drills, the losers did the running immediately after the drill while the drill was still fresh in their minds. The winners got to stand and watch.

Recruits watching practice: Because we did work so hard, we wanted recruits to see our practices firsthand. We may have scared off some highly ranked prospects, but we wanted to scare them off. If a prospect didn't want to work hard, we needed to know that before we signed him, not after. We didn't want a recruit to be surprised once he got here. We tried to tell each one of them exactly what it would be like.

The "tired signal": Nobody can play forty minutes at full speed the way we wanted to at North Carolina. Even with today's TV time-outs, it can't be done. I told players they could raise a fist when they were tired and we would substitute for them, and they could put themselves back in the game once they were rested, although I would say for whom. On time in the 1973 season, Ed Stahl gave me the "tired signal." I substituted Mitch Kupchak for Ed. After about four minutes I asked Ed, "Aren't you rested yet?" He said, "Mitch was playing so well, I didn't want to replace him." I replied, "Ed, I wasn't going to put you in for Mitch! Let me make that decision." It surely demonstrated an unselfish attitude.

Since 1968, when one of our players came out of the game, I wanted him to sit in the first chair next to Coach Guthridge. That way, he could tell coach when he was rested and ready to return, and I would send him back in. On the other hand, if the player was angry when he came out, sitting next to Bill in the first chair helped him to control his emotions. (Frank McGuire told me never to give a towel to a player when he came out of a game, because he might throw it.) Another reason I wanted him in that chair was so that he would be close by and I could lean over and talk to him.

Why the "tired signal"? Over the years I saw players refuse to tell the coach they were tired because they were afraid they wouldn't get back in the game. That happened sometimes at Kansas when I played there. At Carolina, if we saw a player show a lack of effort, we made him sit for a few minutes assuming he was tired. That encouraged the players to use the "tired signal."

Robert McAdoo liked our tired signal so much that he wanted to use it in the pros. During his rookie season, he told his coach in Buffalo, Jack Ramsey, about it. Jack said sure, use it. Mac got tired in his first game, gave the "tired signal," and came out. Jack coached by kneeling near the scorer's table several paces from the bench. After sitting for a couple of minutes, Mac approached Jack and said, "Coach, I'm ready to go back in." Jack waved him off and told him to sit down. He had forgotten the deal. It was the last time Mac gave the "tired signal" in the NBA.

Senior benefits: Our players do enjoy being seniors on our basketball team. We do expect all the seniors, including walk-on seniors, to be leaders, which is why all are considered captains until the permanent captain is chosen by the team after the season.

Michael Jordan, J. R. Reid, and James Worthy have said one of the problems of turning pro after the junior year was missing their senior year as the team leader along with some privileges accorded to our seniors, including:

- Pictures of seniors on the cover of our media guide.
- Each senior is individually featured on the schedule card.

• Each senior is honored before his last home game, which we started as a ritual when I became head coach.

• Each senior starts his last home game and plays at least the first two minutes. Every other year that is the Duke game. Some people are worried when the walk-on who hasn't played much all season starts an important game. All but one time the nonrecruited walk-on has done well. This is an example of something more important to me than winning. Therefore, every squad member starts at least one game.

• Seniors make decisions on where to eat and other things off the court, including rules.

Seniors' team rules: Our rules were almost always made by seniors, and I enforced them. There was one player who was late for curfew on the night before an important NCAA tournament game. The seniors had set the curfew, so I felt they should be included in deciding what, if any, disciplinary action was warranted. I went to our two seniors and I said, "I think we should send him home, but it's your last team and I'll let you overrule me. You decide what to do. Get back to me within an hour." I wasn't sure what they would do since the player who had violated curfew was a good friend of theirs as well as an excellent player. But two minutes later there was a knock on my door. "Get him out of here," they said. "He shouldn't play in this game." It was a big game, but we won without him. He understood the decision and accepted his punishment, and came back to play one of the best games of his entire career in the next round.

Some years the seniors passed tough rules, and other years they had no specific rules at all. The curfew rules got ridiculously elaborate, like this one: *Two* nights before the game they had to be in by 1 A.M. I ended up saying, "You don't *have* to stay up until one. It's okay to go to bed earlier than that."

One February afternoon in 1974, the seniors on the team asked to see me in my office after practice. They had something important to talk to me about. "Can we see you after we get dressed?" they asked.

After their showers, Bobby Jones, Ray Hite, John O'Donnell, and Darrell Elston came upstairs to the office. They were a responsible group of leaders. I was genuinely concerned that we had a major problem, one that had somehow escaped my attention.

"What's up, gang?" I said.

"Coach, we've got a real problem."

A lot of things go through your head when you hear those words.

They said, "During the water break, some of the young guys are taking more water and using all the cups. Some of the other guys can't get their drink before practice resumes. We're running out of cups before everyone can get a drink."

We established a pecking order: seniors would go first, then juniors, then sophomores, and freshmen would go last.

After that meeting I thought, *If this is a team problem, how lucky can a coach get?*

When I began coaching I didn't think of the things that were so important in our program as being rituals. The revelation came when I heard my friend Dr. Anthony Campolo—spokesman for the poor, pastor, and professor of sociology at Eastern College, Pennsylvania—speak on the subject. Families have rituals, so do religions, and I realized that the program at the University of North Carolina did too.

Rituals are tools in building family life, church life, teamwork, and even company life. They are tiny, repetitive gestures with which you build togetherness. In the 1960s and 1970s, we were unwittingly constructing a series of rituals meant to foster loyalty in the small family-society that was Carolina basketball. Church communion is a ritual, a family dinner is a ritual. Tony believed that simply going through the motions of a ritual helps in bonding, and so do I. In fact, I would encourage all coaches to have team rituals, because they help promote closeness and unselfishness.

Some of ours:

• **Pointing to the passer:** It began when John Wooden and I attended a Fellowship of Christian Athletes conference in Colorado in the mid-sixties. On that trip, Wooden told me he wanted the receiver of a pass to say a quick thank-you to the passer or wink at him. I agreed, but I wanted an even more overt gesture, because I felt that while spectators always knew who scored, they were rarely aware of the passer. So the next season, we asked the player who scored to point to the passer in acknowledging the unselfish act of passing the ball to him. Everyone likes to be appreciated.

In those early years we made it a rule in practices, games, and even in our basketball camps that the man who scored must acknowledge the passer. Even I would jump up on the sideline jabbing a finger at the passer. Then, in studying our game tapes, I noticed that our assistants and bench players were doing the same thing. We looked like the Rockettes. Soon, even the spectators in the stands at Carmichael were doing it too.

In 1972, the ritual underwent a permutation when a young man named Bobby Jones joined our team. A lot of times you hear players described as "gangly," but Bobby, at six nine, really was, and to this day he's still in excellent physical condition. Bill Guthridge had found Bobby when he went to scout his brother, Kirby. Bobby was just a high school sophomore, but Bill could see he was a diamond in the rough. He had speed, was a quick jumper, and had lateral quickness too. He had great soft hands and could catch any ball that came his way. Jones became one of the most complete players ever to pass through Chapel Hill, and he would go on to become one of the great defensive players in the history of the NBA with the Denver Nuggets and the Philadelphia 76ers. In 1999, Scottie Pippen tied Bobby Jones and Michael Jordan for most number of times named to the All-NBA defensive team, as voted by the league's coaches (nine).

During that '72 season, Bobby started a new pointing-to-the-passer ritual when, in the heat of a game, he took a great pass but missed a fast-break layup. He still turned around and thanked the passer. We called that the Bobby Jones rule. If you got a great pass and missed, you still thanked the passer. Then we went even further: If a player received a great pass and was fouled on the layup and got two free throws, he should still point to the passer. We called this a "coach's assist" in our statistics since it isn't recognized as an official assist by the NCAA. I believe a player should be credited with a full assist if the pass recipient was fouled on a layup. The passer had made a great pass, which had forced the defender to foul to stop the layup.

Moreover, I thought it would be fun if the scorer not only turned to thank the passer, but then pointed at the screener who helped him become open for the shot. The only problem with that could be that the scorer, so busy pointing, might not get back on defense.

• **Standing for a teammate:** We told our players that if the president of the United States entered the room, we'd stand out of respect. To our way of thinking, a teammate was more important than anybody. So when a player came out of the game, his teammates showed their appreciation by standing and applauding. That did wonders to promote unselfishness. We didn't make our players cheer for a basket or an otherwise good play, but we did demand that they applaud a teammate when he left the court. That was not optional. The coaches also stand to applaud, even if the player hasn't played well.

• **Helping him up:** If one of our players drew a charge in a game or dived on the court in pursuit of a loose ball, our other players would rush over and help him up. Why? Because he did it for the rest of us. George Karl, who also played for us in the 1970s, actually went on the floor too often. I feared for his safety. He would dive after balls he didn't have a chance to get. He was too valuable to us to lose to injury. In practice, our coaches will run to help pick up the defender who drew a charge.

• **Sprinting to the bench:** On substitutions and during time-outs, we wanted our players to sprint to the bench, just as they sprinted to form a circle around me at the sound of the whistle to open practice. We worked hard to be in the best shape possible, and I wasn't against sending a message to the opponent either. Hopefully they thought, *Gee, those North Carolina players never get tired.* Also, we would have more time to talk at a time-out.

• **Stacking hands:** Before taking the court prior to tip-off or after time-outs, we stacked hands. Later, our players would leave the bench after a time-out, form their own huddle, stack hands again, and maybe add a word like "good defense."

• **Routines for foul shooting:** We also insisted an individual player could have his own individual ritual, but he should do the same thing every time. If that meant taking two dribbles before a foul shot, then take two dribbles *every* time. It became a routine and put his mind on the performance of the ritual rather than on what the consequences of a missed shot might be. You see professional golfers performing their own rituals before every shot and every putt. They call it their preshot routine. Let the mind focus on the routine instead of worrying about the results. Before practice, we often had our players go to the side of the court to shoot a ball at the wall. We wanted them to focus on spin and shooting form without worrying about whether they were making the shot.

If practice was the foundation of our program, recruiting was the floor. We applied the same principles to recruiting that we did to team building.

My friend Al McGuire says there is something unnatural about a grown man trying to make small talk with a teenager whom he just met, and I agree. Recruiting is a peculiar and sometimes unsavory business, and I followed my own methods in bringing prospects to North Carolina. I wasn't a salesman, I didn't like talking on the phone, and I didn't feel comfortable with unwarranted flattery. We absolutely refused to make promises about playing time. I would simply say, "Here's what we have to offer. I hope you choose it."

It once was said that at Carolina we didn't recruit, we selected. But truth was that I wanted the player to select *us*. Roy Williams, the outstanding Kansas head coach, had a good comment. Roy said, "It's true that Coach Smith selects. But he also happens to select the same people that Duke selects, and that I select, and that the leading programs in the country select. Getting the ones you select is a different story."

I did have two great assets: our university and our winning basketball program in which players improved. Later on, when graduation rates were made public, that fact helped us also. Most young men make a "basketball decision" rather than deciding which school would be better for them academically. We have a great chance to persuade an athlete who is an excellent student to visit our school, as do Duke and Virginia. Still, some ill-prepared academic students can be great prospects in basketball, and they will end up playing in Division 1.

However, very seldom do we sign a young man who doesn't have at least one parent visit with him in Chapel Hill. The recruiting visit is important, and this is the point where the university campus and the college town help so much. Also, we have already sent the prospect the list of twenty-three five-star universities that participate in Division 1 basketball (not including the eight Ivy League teams, which don't provide athletic scholarships).

Our own players spend time with the prospect on the visit, which is a plus for us. We tell our players to be honest in answering his questions and try to determine if he will fit in well. Many of our players brag about how many prospects they help us sign. They even keep score. One player hosted five different prospects, and he and I were pleased he was four wins, one loss.

The fact that our teams have been successful and are on television often helps as well. A good indication of the interest in Carolina athletics is the fact we have always been in the top two of the Collegiate Licensing Company's list in paraphernalia sales. You see Carolina shirts, hats, and uniforms all over the country. In 1998, we were second to Florida State, with $75 million in sales for $2.7 million in royalty revenue.

Still, recruiting could be a complicated and demoralizing business, and it was at its worst in the 1970s. We tried to simplify our process as much as possible in order to stay above it, which is my advice to anyone in the business of collegiate athletics. First of all, you look for the best players, and then you check to see what their academic records are to ascertain that they can gain admission and graduate. Next, you ask a player, "What's your goal in college?" If they say their goal is to get an education and become a better player, we've got a good chance that everything will work out. We had the opportunity to recruit two young current NBA players, but backed away when they told us they only intended to stay in college one year. If they say they want to average 30 points as a freshman, you should probably walk away.

The best way to err in recruiting is to accommodate a player who doesn't suit your philosophy or to offer him inducements. It's a fallacy that cheating can help a program win, that there is something called a "quick fix." Illegal recruiting undermines your chemistry. You've created a young man who expects a handout and refuses to pass the ball to a teammate, and meanwhile you've ruined your sleep with the fear of getting caught. What satisfaction would winning bring if you broke the rule to accomplish it? Seems to me you would have a lot of empty victories.

There is no certainty that you got the best player either. We saw it all the time: great high school players who didn't pan out in college or the pros, and overlooked young men who became greats. I agreed with Terry Holland, the former Virginia coach who once said, "Even if I could pick the five I wanted every year, there's no guarantee I'd win a championship."

The best argument against improper inducements I ever heard was the case of Al Wood, whom we recruited in the spring of 1977 out of Gray, Georgia. Two other schools really came at Al hard, offering him all sorts of extras, which were of course illegal, ranging from cash to an automobile. We learned of this after Al signed with Carolina. Al's high school principal, Mr. Curtis, could see what was going on, and he called Al in for a talk. "Okay, let's say you get a new car at this particular school," he said. "The car will be old in four years and won't mean anything. You'll get some money that you're not supposed to have, but you know you'll spend it. You'll be at a school that's not as good as Carolina is and that doesn't play nearly as good of a schedule. You won't improve much as a player, and you won't get national exposure."

The principal, who was also Al's coach, made it absolutely clear to Al why he should do the right thing. I'm not saying Al wouldn't have made the same decision on his own, but it impressed me that he received such sound advice from his high school coach and principal. It was a case of an educator standing up for the right thing. The end result was that Al came to Carolina with little fanfare, and it was even more satisfying to me when Al was the first senior chosen in the 1981 NBA draft. By the time he was a senior he was such a leader for us that he sometimes corrected his teammates in practice before I could.

Mitch Kupchak received similarly good advice when we recruited him out of Brentwood, New York, in 1972. His high school coach Stan Kellner summed up the entire process. "If they're promising you something, imagine what they're promising other kids just like you," he said. From then on, Mitch looked at every coach with skepticism. When his decision came down to Duke and Carolina his coach asked to see the film of the Carolina-Duke freshman game.

It's a shame our society has gotten to the point where people say, "How can you win by doing it the right way?" As if you *have* to do it the wrong way to win, when the truth is that in the long run, cheating makes it harder to have a winning *program,* although you could win some games.

One thing I never, ever did was promise a player he would start. Early on I was recruiting a young man from the New York City area, when he abruptly told me we had no chance with him. He said, "Don't come visit, because I'm going to Tennessee. They promised I would start as a sophomore." So he went to Tennessee and started the first four games as a sophomore. He started—and after five minutes they would take him out. They kept their word, all right. For exactly five minutes. From then on, I used that story when prospects would ask me about guaranteeing them playing time.

No one knows absolutely for sure if a player is going to develop, and some McDonald's High School All-Americans never started in college. For instance, in our league, Clemson had two McDonald's All-Americans we tried to recruit who didn't start there as juniors or seniors. We had a Mc-Donald's All-American who helped as a reserve. Duke and N.C. State have also been in this situation. In many respects, the decorated high school player comes to college disadvantaged. He doesn't work as hard, nor does he have realistic expectations of his NBA potential. Many times this young man transfers to another school if he isn't an immediate star.

I'll tell you something else. If a young man is willing to play a little defense, he'll do fine. Example: In 1986, the best high school player in the country was Lloyd Daniels, the New York City playground wonder. I went to the Five-Star camp in which Daniels was playing, and I noticed this heavy-legged and kind of skinny kid who was somehow able to stay with Daniels defensively. I turned to a man sitting next to me and said, "Would you mind telling me who that is guarding Daniels?" He said, "That's our guy." It was Rick Fox. The man I had spoken to was Pete Smith, an assistant high school coach from Warsaw, Indiana, where Rick played. Rick committed to us in the fall of his senior year. Some of the press that covered our recruiting that year said Carolina was losing its edge because we signed Fox instead of more prominent players, but when Rick had such a tremendous impact for us from 1986 to 1990, and then was a first-round draft choice who has had a satisfying career with the Boston Celtics and the Los Angeles Lakers, our judgment looked pretty good.

To me, another fallacy in recruiting was to promise a player how much he would score. One prospect told me that the coach from another school assured him, "If you come here, you'll be our leading scorer." A couple of their players even said, "We'll give you the ball. You're going to be our key guy."

My question is, what did all of the other players on that team think? I told the player if that's what he wanted, he should go to that school, because he wouldn't get that kind of treatment at Carolina. He came to Chapel Hill anyway and helped us win a championship.

The more honest we were with a prospect, the fewer attitude problems and misunderstandings we would have with him later. Harry Gotkin, Frank McGuire's old friend and scout, once promised a recruit that if he came to Carolina, he'd get to go to California on a road trip. When the recruit arrived he asked me, "When are we going to California to play?" I told him we didn't have a California game on the schedule. He protested that Mr. Gotkin had told him we were supposed to play out on the coast. So I called Harry and asked him why he did that.

He said, "When they get to Chapel Hill, they'll be happy."

In the days when coaches were allowed to buy recruits meals and extend favors, even the most decent young man could become slightly mercenary. Larry Brown and I recruited a tremendous young man named Geoff Petrie, who eventually went to Princeton, and after a fine-playing professional career later became chief executive for the Sacramento Kings. The first time we took Petrie to dinner in the spring of 1966, his junior year, I asked him what he wanted to eat. "Whatever, a hamburger would be fine," he said. I had to talk him into eating a steak. That, of course, was before he became a sought-after recruit.

The next fall we took Petrie to dinner again. This time he said, "I'll have a double shrimp cocktail and a filet mignon, medium rare."

When alumni and fans dabbled in recruiting, it became potentially dangerous. That's why I was always so private about our recruiting. My rule was that our staff wasn't to talk to anyone about whom we were recruiting. Often, my wife didn't even know the names of the young men on our list. I did a call-in radio show for eighteen years, and I frustrated hundreds of callers by refusing to answer their recruiting questions. I didn't want some overzealous alumnus out there putting money in the pocket of one of our prospects, and I thought the best way to guard against that was to keep it as private as possible. But increasingly, recruiting became a sport in and of itself, and now every school's recruiting list is common knowledge.

It was our philosophy not to recruit junior college players or transfers from other four-year schools. I felt that bringing in a JC player was not fair to the sophomores who had worked hard to become contributors to the team. It was like denying them a promotion they were in line for, as it would be with transfers from four-year schools. We made a famous exception with

Bob McAdoo in 1971 shortly after Tom McMillen reneged on his commitment to us. I rationalized the six-nine McAdoo because we had known him since he was in high school in Greensboro, and because he had barely missed qualifying for Carolina academically. McAdoo was bright, but the courses he had taken weren't quite what we needed, so he went off to Vincennes Junior College in Indiana for two years and turned into a JC All-American and a nationally recruited player. In high school McAdoo had tied for the state high-jump title with another of our recruits, Bobby Jones, and he had a magical shooting touch. McAdoo's mother was a schoolteacher and liked what Carolina stood for. She called me and said, "Everybody is recruiting my son except for North Carolina. I like the way your team looks. I saw a picture of the team with their pretty blue blazers, and they always look so nice."

So we recruited McAdoo, and it was a natural fit for both of us. I explained to him how elaborate the team's bonding had become, and that he would be sort of like an adopted child at first, but he was an immediate success for us, both as a person and as a player. He made All-American, and helped us to get to the Final Four in 1972 after playing on the '71 Pan Am Games team. After only one season at Carolina, McAdoo became our first player to leave early for the NBA. The Buffalo Braves made him wealthy, and Robert made the correct decision with my complete blessing. In all good conscience, I couldn't advise him to turn down the kind of money he was being offered, which was a significant amount. By way of comparison, I was making $18,000 a year at the time. I heartily approved for a lot of reasons, which I will go into in a later chapter. Even though I only coached McAdoo for a single season, he is as loyal as any of our former players. One year when he was playing in Italy he called me and asked for a tape of ours. "Can you send me the seventy-two highlights?" he said. "These guys don't know how to play as a team."

I tried to be as candid as possible with our prospects. When I say I was a bad recruiter, I mean I didn't tell them what they wanted to hear. I experienced only a handful of instances in which a recruit or his family brazenly sought illegal inducements. I'll give you three instances.

In one home, Bill, Roy, and I sat in the young man's living room while his family said, "You got him." I replied, "Great." They looked back at me and said, "The ball's in your court." I told them I didn't understand what they meant. They kept saying it, "The ball's in your court." It dawned on me that it was my cue to tell them what extra things we would do for them. Shortly afterwards I got up and left, and within two or three days we were out of the running for that player.

On another occasion, a young man's mother made a frank overture to me. "My son's going to fill your arena," she said. The implication was that he deserved something in return, that he was entitled to some recompense. I said as politely as I could, "Our arena is already filled. And if it wasn't, we wouldn't be trying to fill it that way." I told her we were offering her son a straight-up scholarship, nothing more. She said, "I certainly understand where you're coming from, and thank you for visiting."

Another mother said to Eddie Fogler and me: "You know, my son is six eleven and he has to have specially made clothes. And he can't sit in that little car out there." We left immediately.

On a recruiting trip, Roy and I went into one of the poorest neighborhoods I had ever been in as a head coach. It was obvious to us this prospect's family was desperately in need of money although they did not appear to be searching for a deal. However, I thought they could be tempted, since his mom was supporting all the children by herself. Looking at the surroundings I told the young man and his mother, "Look, if you're going to cheat, don't just go for a car. Get big money. However, you will be happier if you come to Carolina 'legally.' " We heard later he had accepted $50,000 from another school. Not long afterwards, coach Roy Williams received a letter from the young man. "Dear Coach," the prospect wrote. "I am going to ——, for reasons that are known to you."

But there were some good recruiting stories too. In 1974, we became embroiled in the recruiting of Phil Ford, the best young point guard in the country, and the son of teaching parents from Rocky Mount. Phil personified Carolina basketball as much as any player ever. He was sensational with the ball—smart, dedicated, and great in the clutch. He grew into one of the staunchest friends and aides we ever had. When the rules were enforced and hand checking was called, Phil was all but impossible to stop one on one.

Phil could do it all—shoot, drive, handle the ball, and play defense—but his intelligence was even more impressive than his physical skills. By his junior year, we became so much in sync that often when I would stand and signal a play from the bench, Phil would already have called it. I learned to just sit and let Phil handle it. In the Four Corners, I would fold my arms and cross my legs, because the game was over. He was National Player of the Year in 1978, an Olympic gold medalist in 1976, an All-American, and the NBA Rookie of the Year in 1979, and he has none of those awards displayed.

Before all that, however, he was an adolescent in the center of a recruiting war. Everybody wanted Phil, and he heard some powerfully persuasive arguments. Maryland's Lefty Driesell promised to start him as a freshman and said the ball would be in his hands for four straight years. North Carolina State was the defending NCAA champion, and head coach Norm Sloan tantalized him with the prospect of playing alongside the Wolfpack's David Thompson, the two-time All-American who was regarded as one of the best players the league had ever known.

But I had something to offer too: the University of North Carolina. Phil still laughs about how hard I lobbied his mother, Mabel, on the education he would receive in Chapel Hill. She was not a basketball fan, and when she heard I was coming to visit them in their home, she said, "Isn't it nice that North Carolina is sending one of their deans to our house?" His mother and father both had master's degrees and both were schoolteachers.

Everyone was promising Phil the world, but when the subject of playing time came up, I told him there would be no promises at Carolina. He would have to earn it. After I left, Mr. Ford told Phil, "You should consider that a positive. It means next year he won't be out there promising your job to some other hotshot recruit."

Phil says he could tell his parents favored Carolina because when other coaches came to the house his mother would fix an ordinary, everyday meal. But when I showed up, he said, the table looked like Thanksgiving. Eddie Fogler would stay at Phil's house but in a better room than Eddie Biedenbach, N.C. State's assistant. Our Walter Davis, Mitch Kupchak, and Mickey Bell were great student hosts for Phil when he visited. Along with Eddie Fogler, I give credit to our players for recruiting Phil. To schools offering illegal inducements, Mr. Ford said: "You can have my son for a nickel, if that's where he wants to go to school. If he doesn't, there's not enough money in the world."

Of course, we were right to want Phil as badly as we did, but not just for the obvious reasons. Recruiting couldn't tell you what was inside of a young man's heart, whether he had the drive to match his physical talent. Phil had as much as anyone I've seen. Every year on the first day of practice we made the players do a timed mile run to check their conditioning. When Phil was a freshman, we went over to this old cinder track at a prep school nearby. Phil came down the line running just slightly behind his time. He accelerated and then accelerated again. As he raced toward the finish line, he suddenly *dived,* headfirst. He launched himself across the line and hit the cinder track in a full roll. When he stood up, he was raw and bleeding. But he had made his time. I couldn't believe it. I thought, *This guy wants it.*

I didn't bother to go over and see about Phil, although our trainer Marc Davis did. I just hit the button on my stopwatch and turned to my assistants,

Bill Guthridge and Eddie Fogler, who were openmouthed. "We've got our-selves a player," I said.

That same toughness surfaced when Phil was playing against Clemson in the 1976 ACC tourney. An elbow accidentally hit Phil in the mouth, knock-ing his front tooth out. He picked up the tooth, took a pass and dribbled over to our bench with the clock running, and handed the tooth to our trainer, John Lacey. He now has a false tooth there.

One recruiting story is interesting to me, since a group of Jersey City guys still remain my friends today. I met them while recruiting Mike O'Koren in 1975–76.

Mike had narrowed his choice to Duke, Notre Dame, and Carolina. His brother Ronald didn't like Notre Dame, and his high school coach was push-ing Duke, since his former teammate at Hudson Catholic, Jim Spanarkel, was a freshman at Duke. I think his mom, Rose, liked Eddie, Bill, and me (his father was dead), but I wasn't sure of some older buddies who had pro-tected Mike in the neighborhood.

When Mike chose to sign with us, he invited us to a neighborhood party put on by these friends—Eddie Ford, Gibby Lewis, and Ron Steinmitz. When I arrived, these three began a Jersey "routing," as they called their ver-sion of a roast, which involves one needle after another. It was something for which my Kansas background had never prepared me. I ended up laughing most of the night. I also earned three new, loyal friends who blast anyone who ever says a negative thing about Carolina basketball. They are special.

When it came to recruiting, some Carolina fans said to me, "Oh, we'll be happy as long as you keep bringing in fine young men to represent the uni-versity." But I never wanted to test them by going 7–20. The fact was, play-ers made the program. We looked for people with talent, but who were also compatible with our work ethic to improve and our philosophy of sharing the ball. The result, ironically, was that we had more than our share of All-Americans and future pros. The last recruit I got truly upset over losing was Tom McMillen. And years later I did mind losing Shaquille O'Neal to LSU and Grant Hill to Duke.

But by then I had learned that if somebody said, "You're losing them," it meant we never had them in the first place.

8

Highs and Lows

On March 2, 1974, Phil Ford was still a high schooler who sat in his Rocky Mount living room watching Carolina play Duke on television. As the game wound down, Phil got up from his chair. He couldn't stand to watch any more. Carolina was trailing by 8 points with just seventeen seconds to go, and he didn't want to see us lose. Phil went outside to wash the family car. A few minutes later he came back in to find his father still sitting in front of the television and the game still going on.

"What's happening?" he asked his father, confused.

"Carolina tied the score and we're in overtime," Phil Sr. said, incredulously.

It was part of the Carolina philosophy that we were never out of a game, and what happened that day was an example of our philosophy at work. When you gave effort for its own sake, the most amazing things could happen. What our players did against Duke in those last seventeen seconds has been acclaimed as perhaps the greatest comeback in the history of college basketball, the one TV announcers often refer to when a team is behind late in a game.

Duke was already celebrating what appeared to be a certain victory. It would have been a sweet one, too. They had suffered a searing loss to us earlier in the season, 73–71, when Bobby Jones stole an inbounds pass at midcourt with just seconds to play. He dribbled forty-five feet for a layup at the buzzer to win the game for Carolina. As Jones laid the ball in, he just kept on running into the dressing room.

But now some fans were filing out of Carmichael Auditorium, already bemoaning the loss. It was over. I still thought we had a chance, but even I knew it would take a virtual miracle. There seemed to be absolutely no doubt about the outcome. Eight points was a pretty big mountain, especially since there was no 3-point shot in those days. It was desperate catch-up.

Our philosophy in all games, I hope, was to take it one possession at a time. We had practiced late-game situations over and over. We had rehearsed and simulated every single day. This is what happened:

John Kuester launched a shot from the corner and missed. But Bobby Jones got the rebound and was fouled. We took a time-out. In the huddle I told the team, "Okay, when Bobby makes these two free throws, let's get right into our Twenty-four defense. Don't allow them to get the ball inbounds. In the *unlikely* event that Bobby should miss, foul the rebounder immediately if we can't get the offensive rebound."

Jones made his free throws, cutting Duke's lead to 6. Our pressure defense created a turnover. Duke's Bob Fleisher tried to inbound the ball and couldn't find an opening. Finally, he tried a desperation play. He bounced the ball through the legs of our Ed Stahl.

Walter Davis intercepted it. He fed Kuester for a layup, to roars, and we took another time-out.

Now Duke led by only 4. Suddenly, the flow of spectators stopped at the doors. People began to file back in.

I smiled as our players came to the bench. "Hey, we have them thinking down there that they could lose this game," I said. "Let's play the Twenty-four defense again. If they get it inbounds, foul immediately."

Again, Duke couldn't inbounds it.

The ball went off the leg of Duke guard Tate Armstrong and trickled out of bounds. Carmichael was now in a state of pandemonium, with spectators rushing back to their seats.

Carolina ball. We ran a play designed to free Davis on the right baseline. He got an open shot—and he missed. But Bobby Jones rebounded and scored and called a quick time-out to stop the clock.

Duke's lead was now 2, with six seconds left. "If they get the ball inbounds, foul immediately," I repeated.

This time, Duke got the ball inbounds. We fouled instantly. Four seconds left. Pete Kramer went to the free-throw line to shoot one-and-one. Unfortunately for us, he was one of the best free-throw shooters in the ACC.

He missed the front end.

Stahl got the rebound for us. Immediately, we took our last time-out. Our players sprinted to the bench, while Duke appeared stunned. The crowd noise was now deafening. In our huddle, I could barely make myself heard. Everyone in the arena was on their feet. I drew the players close to me and screamed my instructions.

Thinking that Duke would expect us to go to Bobby Jones on a deep pass, I decided to use Bobby as a decoy. The plan called for sophomore Mitch Kupchak to inbounds the ball because he had a knack for making long throws. He would fake to Jones and then look for Walter Davis, a freshman who was setting a back screen for Jones. Walter was quiet and bashful, but he was smooth and graceful in his play, which earned him the nickname "Sweet D." He also became one of the best pure shooters I ever saw.

Kupchak, who couldn't move on the baseline, reared back and pretended to hurl the ball toward Jones. Three Duke players immediately converged on Jones, going to our goal. Meanwhile, Davis had received a screen from Kuester and sprinted to the sideline. The idea was for Kupchak to find Davis on the sideline, at a spot even with the top of our key. That play was open, a perfect setup for a twenty-footer. But Davis was a freshman, and in the excitement moved to the sideline but farther from the basket.

Kupchak hit him with a perfect pass. Davis took three long dribbles and launched a shot from thirty-two feet.

It banked in.

The game was tied, and we were going to overtime. The crowd erupted, and so did our bench. Walter just stood straight and still in the spot from which he had shot, showing no emotion whatsoever. It took a moment for it to sink in. Then suddenly, he threw his hands over his head and ran to the bench, where he was mobbed. Later, he admitted, "I didn't mean to bank it." But it was the first of many clutch shots he would hit throughout his career, an eventual five-time NBA All-Star.

Bill Guthridge was supposed to catch a plane that afternoon for Arkansas, where he was being interviewed for a head coaching job that evening with their athletic director, Frank Broyles. I turned to Bill. "You go ahead and catch your plane," I said. "We should win now." Bill slipped out of Carmichael unnoticed to meet the Arkansas jet.

I didn't tell our team what I told Bill. Our bench was still in the throes of celebrating, and I decided things were a little too festive. Our players were congratulating each other right and left. "Hey," I snapped. "You haven't won anything yet. We have a tie score with five minutes to play. Pay attention." In fact, we fell behind by 4 points in the overtime, but we rallied again to win, 96–92. As the buzzer sounded, the crowd flooded onto the floor.

We finished the season 22–6 and 9–3 in the ACC, tied for second place. Guthridge turned down the Arkansas job and remained on the UNC bench. N.C. State, led by the brilliant David Thompson, went on to win the national championship after defeating Maryland and Tom McMillen and Len Elmore in the ACC tournament, 103–100, in overtime, to make the NCAA tourney. We went to the NIT. And, of course, Phil Ford signed with Carolina. Five of our six losses were to N.C. State and Maryland.

The next day at practice I handed Walter Davis a ball. I told a manager to put three seconds on the clock and I posed Walter in the same spot. I told him to make that shot again.

He shot an air ball.

But a few months later, in the middle of our summer basketball camp, I asked Walter to try again. I handed him a ball in front of all those campers. He threw up the same shot and made it. A swisher.

The year 1976 was a special and memorable one in my life. Not only was our Carolina team an ACC champion and in the Top Ten national ranking, I had the opportunity to coach the U.S. Olympic basketball team in Montreal. The most important thing in my life was my marriage in May to Linnea Weblemoe. Linnea had graduated from Whittier College with a degree in chemistry in 1967 and had worked in the medical field for several years before entering the University of North Carolina Medical School in 1972. We were married shortly after her graduation and just prior to the Olympic team's practice. Our wedding was the day before the start of the board meeting of the National Association of Basketball Coaches in Las Vegas, so Linnea's honeymoon consisted of this NABC meeting and watching our Olympic team play its exhibition schedule, culminating in the trip to Montreal for the Olympics.

Linnea, my parents, my sister, and my son received tickets to many Olympic events, including the spectacular opening ceremonies, and enjoyed every minute of it. Linnea, who has a keen sense of humor, comes from a family in which all four grandparents were Scandinavian. She tells the story that she married me because my name is Smith, which was a welcome change after hearing people mispronounce Weblemoe for much of her life.

We have two great daughters: Kristen Caroline was born on March 14, 1979, and Kelly Marie was born on February 23, 1981. My parents thought they were through with grandchildren, but they were rejuvenated when Kristen and Kelly came into their lives. I certainly was, too. Kristen's and Kelly's relationship with brother Scott and sisters Sharon and Sandy has enriched the lives of the five of them, and makes me feel like a very lucky father. Kristen is a student at Carolina, and Kelly is at the University of Pennsylvania.

A committee of basketball people, which included Henry Iba, Red Auerbach, Pete Newell, Wayne Embry, and Dave Gavitt had selected me to be the 1976 United States Olympic basketball coach at a meeting in early 1975. It was a great honor. I felt, however, that a different coach should be selected for each Olympiad so others could share in this great experience. This was my feeling, and still is, even though Mr. Iba did an outstanding job of coaching our Olympians in 1964, 1968, and 1972.

While the committee named the head coach, I was allowed to name my own assistants. I chose two great ones in Bill Guthridge, my excellent assistant at Carolina, and John Thompson, the terrific coach of Georgetown, who was, and is, a great motivator.

We had to build a team in a short period of time. Our Carolina philosophy wouldn't help us much here. At Carolina, we never talked to our players about winning; with the Olympians, it was all about winning. We had one goal and one goal only: to win the gold medal. In the 1972 Munich Games, the United States had lost the gold in basketball for the first time ever, on a series of horrendous officiating calls, to the Soviet Union. The U.S. team, which was coached by Hank Iba and included our Bobby Jones, refused to accept their silver medals. Because of the controversial ending to those Games, there was heightened interest in the United States to win back the gold, which added to the pressure on the players and coaches.

The team that went to Montreal for the 1976 Games would play international teams much older and more experienced and under a set of international rules that permitted extremely physical play. Also, basketball was becoming a truly global game, and other teams were catching up with the United States. Professionals were not eligible to play for us, which meant we would be the youngest team in the tournament. To exacerbate matters, a few of the best collegiate seniors declined to try out for the Olympic team for various reasons. This group included Robert Parrish, Leon Douglas, John Lucas, and others who were named on various All-America teams. All

Mom and Dad returned to their Topeka home in 1982 after they had been to New Orleans to see our team win the national championship. Their neighbors decorated their front door, which made for a happy homecoming.

The Steering Committee, chaired by the late Skipper Bowles (third from the left in the front row), breaks ground for the construction of the Smith Center on campus, April 1982. Chancellor Chris Fordham is shown to the right of Skipper. The building was constructed entirely with private funds, which is the way it should have been done.

Mom and Dad (at age eighty-five) made the trip from Topeka to Springfield, Massachusetts, for my induction into the Basketball Hall of Fame. From the time I started playing athletics as a child, they were very supportive of my participation.

The 1982 inductees into the Basketball Hall of Fame in Springfield get together before the ceremony. From left, the great Bill Bradley, who showcased his many talents as a college basketball player at Princeton and in the NBA for the New York Knicks; Dave DeBusschere, a star for the Knicks; Jack Twyman, an NBA standout for Cincinnati; along with yours truly.

A surprise picture birthday present for Jo-Ann Davis on a trip. Left to right: Skipper Bowles, Linnea Smith, me, a friend of the Davises, university benefactor Walter Davis, Des Bowles, Chancellor Fordham, and his wife, Barbara.

One of the most unsung players we ever had at Carolina is Sam Perkins. He was a great player as well as a tremendous young man. He's shown here leaving the floor in Carmichael Auditorium after we beat Duke in Sam's last home game. Sam's 1984 Carolina team, which finished 28–3, was one of the best ever in college basketball, in my opinion.

Two of our best—Phil Ford and Michael Jordan—returned to Chapel Hill for a game in 1986. Phil's NBA career was over by then and he was in the banking business. Michael, in his still-early NBA playing days, was recovering from an injury that had sidelined him. Our former players returned to Chapel Hill as often as they could, and we were always thrilled to see them.

My son Scott's wedding day. He's pictured in the middle with his bride, Kelly Haynor Smith. The children in the front row, from the left, are Drew and Megen Kepley, and Kelly and Kristen Smith. Back row, from the left, Sharon and Tim Kepley, Kelly and Scott, me, Linnea, and Sandy Smith.

Another one of our great teams—the 1987 team that finished 32–4 and 14–0 in the ACC—participates in the ritual of huddling and stacking hands before the start of play. That team made it to the Final Eight before losing 79–75 to one of Syracuse's best teams.

© Sally Sather

While my assistants were encouraged to offer advice to me during games, and they did, I addressed the team during our time-outs. Roy Williams and I are seen in this huddle, and with their backs to the camera are players Jeff Lebo, Kevin Madden, Rick Fox, and Steve Bucknall. What a lucky man I was to coach so many great young men.

© Hugh Morton

Coaches on our bench, from the left: Bill Guthridge, me, Phil Ford, Randy Wiel, and Dick Harp. The player in the picture is Kevin Madden.

The great Jack Nicklaus and I teamed up for a round of golf at one of the courses he designed—Elk River, in the mountains near Banner Elk, North Carolina. I don't like to brag, but between the two of us we have won twenty major golf championships.

Daughters Kristen and Kelly are beautiful in their handsome dresses, which were a gift from Spanish National Basketball Coach Antonio Diaz Miguel, who is not only a terrific coach, but also a superb host.

Our players are a happy group, as they should have been, after they played brilliantly to beat Duke, 96–74, in the 1991 ACC championship game in the Charlotte Coliseum. Duke eventually won the NCAA Championship and we played in the Final Four.

© Hugh Morton

Spanish National Coach Antonio Diaz Miguel (facing the camera) talks with Bill Guthridge and me before our game in the Canary Islands in December 1991. The man to the left is another Spanish coach, Joaquin Costa.

© Jim Hawkins

Bill Guthridge, Phil Ford, Randy Wiel, and I contemplate the action in one of our games at the Smith Center. Bill is now head coach at North Carolina, Randy's head coach at Middle Tennessee State, and Phil is an assistant to Coach Guthridge.

Our team believed in thanking the passer by pointing at him. It was an important part of our program because we always strived to recognize unselfish play as well as extraordinary effort. Here I, assistant coach Dave Hanners, and player Eric Montross thank one of our guys for a good pass.

With former chancellor Bill Aycock, who selected me as Carolina's head coach thirty years before this picture was taken.

© Bob Donnan

© Hugh Morton

Our assembly before practice (when we would discuss our Thought of the Day and our Emphasis of the Day) in the New Orleans Superdome the day before we played Kansas in the 1993 Final Four.

Part of our group at the Doug Moe Invitational, this one held at the Country Club of North Carolina in Pinehurst. Among those in the picture are Michael Jordan, Doug Moe, Bob Galloway, Kevin Lougherty, George Irvine, Larry Brown, Kevin O'Conner, television commentator Bill Raftery, NBA associate commissioner Rod Thorn, Del Harris, and Bob Bass. (If a defendant walked into a courtroom and saw us sitting as his jury, he'd probably petition the court for a change of venue.)

My family and my sister Joan's family at our annual beach vacation in 1995 at my friend Maurice Koury's beach home. As you can see, we draw quite a crowd when we get together like this.

Our present office staff surrounding Michael in the office kitchen: Linda Woods, Angela Lee, Kay Thomas, and Ruth Kirkendall.

Vince Carter, the NBA Rookie of the Year for 1999, thanks one of his teammates for a good pass as he watches the action from the bench.

Chatting with good friend Bill Miller before one of our games. We kid Bill about being the "Lou Gehrig" of Carolina basketball. Going into the 1999–2000 season, he had seen 555 straight Carolina games, home and away.

Getting some strategy tips from Brent Musburger (left) and Dick Vitale. They were in the Smith Center to work one of our games for ABC Television. Brent covered our national championship win in 1982. Dick's enthusiasm on ESPN (since 1979) helped ignite the interest in college basketball.

In 1997, after we beat Middle Tennessee State on February 1 to begin a sixteen-game winning streak that took us to the Final Four, we gathered for dinner, honoring my former assistant and player, and now head coach of Middle Tennessee State, Randy Wiel. I'm pictured in the front with my brilliant administrative assistant, Linda Woods. From left in the second row: assistant coach Dave Hanners; assistant coach Phil Ford; assistant coach Pat Sullivan.

Bill Guthridge, Phil Ford, Dave Hanners, and I have our eyes on the action in my last year of coaching in 1997.

We were a happy group after winning the ACC championship in 1997. These players came a long way: We began 0–3 in the ACC and were 3–5 after the first half of the conference season. They didn't lose again until the NCAA Final Four, which snapped a sixteen-game winning streak. I must admit, it was a good way for the "old coach" to go out.

There wasn't much I enjoyed about the media countdown en route to our breaking Adolph Rupp's record for coaching wins. I must admit, though, that on the day the record fell—March 15, 1997, in the NCAA tournament against Colorado—I was thrilled to see so many of my former players after the game. In the stands in Winston-Salem for the game, from the left: George Karl, Sam Perkins, Randy Wiel, Mitch Kupchak, and Bobby Jones.

One of our family rituals was the summer beach vacation at the Kourys' home. This was in the summer of 1997, and these are my five children, from left: Scott, Kelly, Kristen, Sandy, and Sharon. As you can see, we're all in uniform.

At the beach with my grandchildren in 1997. Megen Kepley is at the left holding her cousin Brian Smith. I'm holding grandson Luke Combs, and Drew Kepley holds his cousin Morgan Smith.

My family, along with my sister Joan's.

I was given an ESPY Award for Courage in February 1998. I didn't think at the time that I deserved it, and still don't, but I was flattered to be so honored. Senator Bill Bradley, at my left, presented me with the award. Then when I went onstage to receive it, I was surprised and happy to see some of my former players there. From the left, they are Walter Davis, James Worthy, Brad Daugherty, Charles Scott, and Billy Cunningham. Doug Moe was there, next to Davis, but is not in the picture.

The 1998 National Coach of the Year in college basketball, Bill Guthridge, with his wife, Leesie, on the occasion of the team banquet for the 1998 ACC champs and NCAA Final Four participants.

© CBS TV

I worked the 1998 tournament for CBS Television as an in-studio analyst. I'm shown here with CBS veterans Greg Gumbel (left) and Clark Kellogg, who took great care of this "rookie."

Linnea and I were invited to a state dinner at the White House in June 1998 in honor of President Kim of South Korea, whose son was studying in the United States and was a Carolina basketball fan. Linnea is greeted by Hillary Rodham Clinton, while I exchange greetings with another knowledgeable fan of college basketball, President Clinton.

Official White House Photo

Linnea stands outside the Queen's Bedroom in the White House. It served as our quarters when we went to the state dinner in June 1998.

At Pebble Beach preparing to tee off late in the summer of 1998. On the left in the floppy hat is Buck Adams, one of my closest friends, as well as my golf mentor and frequent playing companion. Tommy Kearns (in the light-colored jacket), who was North Carolina's starting point guard on the 1957 NCAA champions, and Brokie Lineweaver completed our foursome. Sadly, Buck was dead ten days later. I miss him terribly.

I was given the University Award
in January 1999, a great honor I
will cherish. Two of the special
speakers are with me here—
Michael Jordan and Charles Scott.
What a backcourt.

Daughters Kristen (left) and Kelly
together on our back porch in 1999.
How lucky can a father be?

basketball people knew the Americans would have trouble bringing a gold medal back from Montreal.

It was great to have a familiar face beside me on the bench in the person of Bill Guthridge. Having worked with me at North Carolina, Bill could anticipate what I wanted done, and his organizational skills would prove to be invaluable for us. I had first met John Thompson in 1970 when I recruited Donald Washington, a young man for whom John and his wife, Gwen, were serving as legal guardians. Donald was a gifted young man who had lost his parents, and John helped him through his senior year at St. Anthony's High School in Washington, D.C., where John was head coach.

I made an official recruiting visit to the Thompson home, which was the beginning of my close friendship with John. I was extremely impressed that most of the questions he asked me were about academics. "What courses is Bill Chamberlain taking?" he asked. Fortunately, I knew. John told me later I was the only coach to pass the test. Donald eventually came to Carolina, but it was his wife, Gwen, who suggested to John that I should be invited back in the recruiting process. Unfortunately, Donald played only seven games in his sophomore year as a starter before breaking his foot. John and I talked regularly about Donald, as parent and coach. But then our conversations grew broader, and we began talking late at night about all sorts of things. I knew he was a terrific basketball coach, so when the Georgetown job opened up I enthusiastically recommended him, along with many others. We shared a lot of the same basketball philosophy. When I was named Olympic coach I immediately thought of him as one of my assistants. He remains one of my closest friends.

We conducted trials for six days and appraised sixty candidates. Bill, John, and I didn't select the players; the selection committee did. I had a single vote. I was allowed to advise the committee on the type of players I was looking for, but that was no guarantee I would get the players I wanted. In fact, I lost several arguments. Three players I wanted were not named to the team, while seven players made it from the Atlantic Coast Conference. I would not have picked all of them, but some in the media still criticized me for having seven from my own conference. I had no problem with the selection committee having this authority. If the members took their time to be there, they should be more than a rubber stamp.

We worked out the candidates in grueling two-a-days for three hours at a stretch on the campus of N.C. State in Raleigh. With just six weeks to form a team, we certainly didn't need any inflated egos. We needed players that were unselfish and good defenders. Bill, John, and I weeded through the players looking for telltale weaknesses. We purposely set up subtle tests to see which players were cooperative, such as ordering them to run, not walk, to the fountains for their water breaks. One player was discarded when he took twenty-seven shots in a scrimmage, most of which were blanks. Another was rejected because he didn't have a shred of defensive commitment.

We ran them hard so we could tell who really wanted it. We demanded they run a mile in under six minutes during the first day of tryouts. One player I thought would be on the team was Marquette's Bo Ellis. But on his second lap of the mile run, Ellis veered off the track and kept on running, straight off the North Carolina State campus to the local inn.

I wouldn't see Bo Ellis again until the 1977 NCAA championship game—and then I saw too much of him. He surely demonstrated his ability that day.

When the selection committee announced the Olympians, four North Carolina players were on the team: Phil Ford, Mitch Kupchak, Tommy La-Garde, and Walter Davis. These four selections excited me very much but also created a bit of controversy, since some people alleged I was showing favoritism. They remarked that the American flag was red, white, and Carolina blue. But there were legitimate reasons for their selection. LaGarde and Kupchak had been selected to the Pan-Am team in 1975. They gave us badly needed big men, since few had tried out. Not only was Walter Davis one of the fastest men in camp, he also had a great week in tryouts. Phil Ford was inarguably one of the best players in the country. Phil didn't play particularly well in the trials until the last big scrimmage. I wanted to tell the committee, "If Ford doesn't make this team, you need to look for a new coach." But that wasn't necessary. Each merited his selection. As a result of the collegiate no-shows at tryout, the pool of big men was depleted, and La-Garde and Kupchak, each six ten, were vital. Red Auerbach and Al McGuire had told some media that center would be our weakness and we probably wouldn't win the gold.

Kupchak was a thoughtful, loquacious senior with the heart and constitution of a warrior. It worried us when Mitch said something hurt "only a little." That usually meant he was ready for traction. Day in and day out he had played with a back ailment that would have put ordinary souls in the hospital, but he was relentless, a competitor who never took a play off. He didn't know what it was *not* to have pain. But he didn't call it pain, just a minor ache. Nevertheless, he had led the ACC in rebounding the previous year. He had been unable to play on the Pan-Am team the previous year because he finally had elective back surgery between his junior and senior years. He had a great senior year at Carolina, leading us to a 26–4 record and the ACC regular-season championship with eleven wins and one loss, plus being selected All-American.

The four Carolina players blended well with the eight others, including two selections from Indiana, Scott May and Quinn Buckner. Coach Bob Knight's Indiana team was coming off an undefeated NCAA championship season. I liked the idea of having Knight's players, who were disciplined and well grounded in fundamentals. Adrian Dantley from Notre Dame, Ernie Grunfeld from Tennessee, Phil Hubbard from Michigan, and three other players from the ACC—Steve Shepherd from Maryland, Kenny Carr from N.C. State, and Tate Armstrong from Duke—completed the team.

Once the team was selected, we settled into training camp in Chapel Hill and played an exhibition schedule. Prior to that, Bill Guthridge went to London to scout the Olympic-qualifying tournament. He suggested upon returning that we use international referees to call our exhibition games so our players could grow accustomed to the physical style of play they would face.

We put the players through our version of boot camp. It was our way of bonding them quickly. The work habits of the North Carolina and Indiana players helped set the tone for the whole team. It helped, too, that we were possibly underdogs going to Montreal. Even our fellow coaches said publicly that they weren't sure we could do it with such a young team. During tryouts, one player who didn't make his mile time of five minutes forty-five seconds and knew he had to run again to make the team came by my room and asked, "What do you mean I have to run a mile in five minutes forty-five seconds?" I told him that he didn't *have* to do it, but added: "You just won't be on the team, that's all. Otherwise, we'll see you at five o'clock and you'll run it again." The player said he was going to call his coach. I told him to go ahead, certain that his coach would agree with me. He called his coach, and we never heard another complaint from the player.

Ordinarily, a coach asks his players what their goals are and works to develop them over the long term. We didn't have time for that in putting this team together. We would live together for two months and then go our separate ways. All of us knew that our only objective was to win the gold medal. Each player had a role, and each was asked to sacrifice for the good of the team. We didn't have much size, so Adrian Dantley and Phil Hubbard would have to play inside, out of their usual positions. Dantley showed he was ready to go by losing fifteen pounds before reporting to trials. It gave him more quickness than I had seen from him.

However, another young man had a different mind-set. He was playing selfishly with little regard for the team and without commitment on defense. In front of the other players I told him, "The rules say I can't take more than twelve players to Montreal, but they don't say I can't go with eleven. If you don't get going, you won't be making the trip." The player did a complete turnabout and was a positive force in Montreal.

I love the Olympic spirit as it pertains to basketball. There is something about it that discourages self-absorption. Officials in Montreal had stat sheets after the Games, but we didn't know how to read them, nor did we care. Everything was discussed in terms of nations and teams rather than individuals. There was no recognition for high scorers, only the medal. I appreciate that sensibility.

One of the positives about being a national coach was that I was invited to clinics in many countries and was able to meet basketball coaches from around the world. Sandro Gamba and Ettore Messina, who both served as national coaches of Italy, came to Chapel Hill to watch our team practice. Two national coaches of Greece, Panagiotis Giannakis and Efthimis Kioumourtzoglou, have seen us practice in Chapel Hill. In fact, Efthimis spent a year in Chapel Hill earning his master's degree.

Of all the international coaches I was so fortunate to meet, my closest friend from that group is Antonio Diaz Miguel, who is now in the Naismith Basketball Hall of Fame. He coached the Spanish national team for nearly thirty years. Starting in 1974, after I met him in Madrid, he visited four schools in the United States each January. Along with his assistant, Jose Luis Cortez, Antonio came to see Lou Carnesecca of St. John's, John Wooden at UCLA, Bob Knight at Indiana, and then to Chapel Hill to see us. This continued until he resigned as Spanish national coach in the mid-1990s. At Carolina, we watched tapes together and included them in our meetings. Antonio was largely responsible for expanding the game in Spain, and a big breakthrough came in the mid-1980s when the king of Spain held up a scheduled soccer game so that the nation could watch the basketball team play the Soviet Union on television.

I got to know Antonio especially well in 1976 when he brought his Spanish team to Chapel Hill in preparation for the Olympics. His team would practice in the morning by themselves but would scrimmage against us in the evening. This was great work in preparing for the Olympics. In addition to being a terrific basketball coach, Antonio is a well-known designer. Bob Knight and I own two gorgeous leather overcoats designed by him. There are only four in existence. The other two are owned by Antonio and King Juan Carlos.

Once our United States team left Chapel Hill and arrived in Montreal, we lived in a cinder-block dormitory in the Olympic Village. Bill and John were roommates, and they spent time going around trading and shopping for Olympic pins. We met one of the favorites, Italy, in the first round. The average age of their players was twenty-seven. We won by 20 points after leading by 30. Our bench was so enthusiastic that we were warned a technical foul would be called against us for cheering our teammates. I stayed to scout our next opponent, Puerto Rico, and sent our players back to the village. I didn't believe in letting our players watch the next opponent. I wanted them to focus on the scouting report of their coaches rather than coming up with their own evaluations based on what they saw in one game.

I didn't know there were television sets all over the village that showed closed-circuit coverage of the Games. Our entire team watched Puerto Rico lose by 30 to Yugoslavia. Puerto Rico looked terrible in the game, and our players became overconfident. Against Puerto Rico the next day we barely won, 95–94. The Puerto Ricans shot 64 percent from the floor and were virtually unstoppable, thanks to their two guards. Neftali Rivera was Puerto Rican by birth but got his game by way of Manhattan, where he was a playground star. The other guard was Butch Lee, who was also born in Puerto Rico and played in New York. He won National Player of the Year at Marquette in 1978. We were lucky to come away with a win.

There was just one bit of controversy with our team, and it was over the sneakers. In the Diplomat Hotel, Puma had a huge store set up, and Olympic athletes would go by and get things free. However, the U.S. Olympic Committee made a deal with Converse for the basketball teams (women's and men's) to wear its shoes. In our opening-round game, one of the players wore Adidas, which he preferred. I hadn't noticed, but afterwards a U.S. official pulled me aside and said, "Don't you know Converse paid for our team to wear their shoes?" I told him I would speak to the player, which I did, warning him that the U.S. Olympic Committee wouldn't allow him to play if he wore the wrong shoes again.

We were undefeated in Pool A after beating Yugoslavia and Czechoslovakia, earning us the right to play host Canada, while Yugoslavia met the Soviet Union. Many wanted to see a rematch of the grudge game between the United States and the Soviet Union four years earlier, but it was not to be. Yugoslavia defeated the USSR by 5 points to reach the final. We played superbly to beat Canada and reach the gold medal game.

We had only a day to get ready. I credit John Thompson, who gave a powerful talk to the players after we finished watching film. He spoke to their emotions, aroused their patriotism, and talked about how fortunate we all were. We had reached the gold medal game despite all the naysayers, and we wouldn't have wanted anyone there in our place. "Finish it off right," John admonished.

When I arrived at the locker room before the game, Coach Thompson and Coach Guthridge came up to me and said, "We have a problem." John gestured into the locker room and said, "Two guys in there have Pumas on." As I went into the locker room, I realized two of our players were indeed lacing up Pumas instead of Converse. Should I order them to change shoes and spoil the concentration right before tip-off in the gold medal game, or let it go? It didn't take me long to decide. "We are only going to be together for forty more minutes," I said to the coaches. "It's not worth the fight to tell them they have to change." For one of the rare times in my life, I ignored a disciplinary matter. Had this happened with one of my Carolina teams, it would have been a different story. Again, the goals were different: coaching your college team long term versus coaching the U.S. team short term.

We jumped to an 8–0 lead, then built it to 44–22 just fourteen minutes into the game. The Yugoslavs threw elbows, and Adrian Dantley took seven stitches over his eye in the second half. Still, the Yugoslavs never came closer than 10. We won, 95–74.

I will never forget Buckner dribbling and dancing away the last ten seconds to the delight of his teammates and coaching staff.

John, Bill, and I stood off to the side at the award ceremonies and watched our young men mount the podium to receive the gold. Since coaches were not considered competitors, we did not join the ceremony, which I thought was totally appropriate. College basketball could learn from that ideal. Our reward was to hear "The Star-Spangled Banner" played honoring these twelve young men who were gold medal winners. We had done what few thought we could: regained the gold with a team of collegiate underclassmen. I felt the victory was very much in the old spirit of the Olympics, because the young men on the team were thrilled to be there. They had a freshness every day, and they weren't all sure they would get opportunities to play as pros. Looking at their faces, I knew they were just as proud as they could be. Going in, we promised that we would play together as a team. And that's what we did.

Before I knew it, the Olympics were over and it was time to go back to work on behalf of Carolina basketball. The prospect of coaching a gold medal team and national championship team in the same year was a tantalizing one.

When we were healthy, I thought we had perhaps the best team in the country in 1976–77. But as is so evident, the best team doesn't always win in college basketball. Especially not in the roulette wheel of NCAA tournament play.

Our Carolina team that season was a widely divergent group anchored by the leadership of four seniors. John Kuester was that selfless guard every team needs, a great defensive player who might only get six shots a game but who would make four of them. Walter Davis was our marksman. Tommy LaGarde was a quick jumper, a big man of six ten who was pleasantly different and could run like the wind. Phil Ford as a junior was defining himself as perhaps the finest point guard the league had ever seen. Then there was Mike O'Koren, a precocious six-foot-six New Jersey freshman with an expressive face and a natural sense of humor. When a member of the press asked what sort of background he came from, he said, "I'm from the upper lower class."

We went 13–1 before we suffered three losses in four games, including a 20-point blowout against Clemson. But I believed in the team and wanted them to keep their confidence. After the Clemson game, I said, "No practice tomorrow. On Friday I'll tell you how we're going to win a championship." I was certain this team would make the breakthrough. One thing had changed in the conference that made it easier to gain entry to the NCAA tournament. In 1975 the NCAA began issuing at-large bids, so winning the ACC tournament was no longer the only route to winning a national championship. Also, South Carolina had left the conference, replaced by Georgia Tech.

Unfortunately, we weren't healthy from February 9 or maybe it was just bad luck. First, Tommy LaGarde tore knee ligaments and was lost for the season. Just before he went down, we were awesome in beating a good Maryland team, 97–70. It was one of the best games a team of mine ever played. Somehow three reserve freshmen filled in for him: six-nine Rich Yonakor, six-nine Steve Krafcisin, and the six-ten Jeff Wolf, a trio I laughingly referred to as "Yonwolfsin."

Next, Walter Davis broke a finger on his right hand so badly during the ACC tournament that his screams in the locker room made our players weep. He had to undergo surgery to repair it. Then Phil Ford hyperextended his elbow on the last play of the game against Notre Dame in the NCAA regional semifinals. He made the winning free throws in the dying seconds, as we beat one of the Fighting Irish's best teams, 79–77. To top it off, we did it on St. Patrick's Day. With Ford still ailing, we somehow found a way to beat Kentucky, 79–72, in the NCAA East final at College Park, Maryland.

We arrived in Atlanta for the Final Four looking like a bunch of casualties. LaGarde's knee was in a cast, Davis had a splint on his shooting hand, and Ford's elbow was in a sling and packed in ice. He couldn't shoot anything beyond fifteen feet. As an indication of how vital those players were to us, all three wound up being first-round NBA draft choices.

Still, we thought we had every chance of winning a championship. For once we didn't have to face the prospect of losing to UCLA. John Wooden had retired in 1975 after winning ten NCAA titles in twelve years, opening up the field for everyone else. It was our first trip to a Final Four in five years, and I couldn't believe the growth of the event. Tickets to the Atlanta Omni were impossible to get except at scalpers' prices. There were TV cameras everywhere, and you had to have a pass to do anything, including get on an elevator. We were to meet UNLV in one semifinal. UNLV, coached by Jerry Tarkanian, was a fast run-and-gun team that featured a future pro in Reggie Theus, and many felt the Rebels were the nation's best team that year. Our bandage brigade relied heavily on Mike O'Koren for scoring, but despite his 20 points, many of which came on backdoor layups, we trailed the Runnin Rebels by 6 at the half. But in the second half we mixed up tempo with our Four Corners. Ford, operating out of the Four Corners with his bad elbow, had 12 points and ten assists. We eked out an 84–83 win in which O'Koren had 31 points. After the game a writer asked him if that was his best game. O'Koren replied, "So far."

In the other semifinal was Marquette, coached for the last time by Al McGuire, who had announced his retirement in December. Marquette played a roller-coaster game against Cinderella UNC-Charlotte, and won in the last seconds on a shot by Jerome Whitehead.

We were in the championship against Marquette, a team that massaged the ball offensively while laying back in a tough zone defense. They had bulk and discipline. Whitehead, Bo Ellis, and Bernard Toone packed in the frontcourt, a lineup of six nine, six ten, and six seven, respectively, while Butch Lee and Jimmy Boylan ran the backcourt.

The Warriors came in on a gigantic wave of emotion, given that McGuire was planning to retire afterwards. They led us, 39–27, at halftime. It seemed as though everything dropped for them, while we had to labor for anything offensively. We were in familiar territory. We had trailed in virtually every game of importance from February on. We had trailed Purdue, Notre Dame, and UNLV in the tournament, and won each of those games. Coach Guthridge called all of our NCAA games before Marquette as "Huggies." They were all wins which brought about a lot of hugging and enthusiasm following the game. At halftime I told our team that if we kept applying defensive pressure, they were bound to grow tired and would cool off.

In the second half, we rallied. O'Koren scored the first four baskets, and then two big shots by Walter Davis tied the score, 43–43, with fourteen minutes to go. We went to Four Corners after the teams exchanged baskets. Some critics have questioned the decision ever since. But they didn't question it when we used it to beat Notre Dame and Kentucky to get to the Final Four.

You don't change your coaching just because you're in a championship game. The Four Corners is what had gotten us there in the first place. It had been our stopper all year. In fact, we nicknamed it the "Goose Gossage" after the famed relief pitcher because it was so effective at preserving a lead. Spreading out had put a lot of big games out of reach. When you were up by 6 and you spread out, that was going to be the final margin if the other team didn't do something drastic. Also, I wanted to get Marquette's big men away from the basket instead of letting them sit back in a zone. The Four Corners could force them to come out.

We were breathing hard from the 12-point comeback, so I sat down O'Koren and Kuester for a rest. I replaced them with Bruce Buckley and Tom Zaliagiris, a decision that looked pretty good when Zaliagiris came off the bench to steal the ball from Marquette's Jimmy Boylan and converted it into a layup. Marquette tied the game, 45–45, on a jumper by Toone. By now O'Koren was waiting at the scorers' table to check back in at the next whistle.

But the whistle didn't come. McGuire signaled Marquette to stay passive. The Warriors wouldn't come out and play us, and O'Koren couldn't get back in the game. My assistant, Eddie Fogler, said, "How about a time-out?" I shook my head. I didn't want to take a time-out to give Marquette a chance to talk about how to defend our Four Corners. Al was standing up and hollering instructions to his players, and I felt it would have been a mistake to give him a free time-out at that point.

Finally, the Four Corners created an opportunity: Bruce Buckley broke loose and Ford hit him with a pass for what should have been a layup—but the size I was so concerned about finally told. Bo Ellis—the man who ran himself off the Olympic team—rose up and made a great block of Buckley's shot.

Marquette replied by retaking the lead and never lost it again. We lost the game, 67–59, to a Marquette team that played at its highest level.

I've never liked to play the "What if?" game. There are no answers. What if I hadn't gone to the Four Corners? What if I had taken a time-out to get O'Koren back into the game? What if we had a healthy outside shooter?

What if Phil Ford hadn't hurt his elbow? Ford said later he had wide-open jumpers from the corner but couldn't get the ball to the basket. Marquette won the game; that's the only sure answer.

After that game, we had to contend with critics who questioned our most basic philosophy. They said that we were too conservative to win a national championship. Frank Barrows, a respected writer for *The Charlotte Observer,* wrote an exhaustive analysis of the program, in which he charged that we overemphasized consistency, which prevented us from rising to the great heights necessary to make a successful tournament run. It was said that we would never win a title as long as we were so programmatic.

I disagreed with the analysis. Of course I wanted to win a championship, but a title was more important to outsiders than it was to me. They overlooked our consistency, which was an achievement in its own right. Getting to the Final Four consistently was harder than winning one national championship and then having your program disappear. More than thirty coaches had won national championships, but only three coaches had reached the Final Four four or more times. Which mountain was harder to climb, I asked myself, the one that thirty people had climbed, or the one that only three had climbed?

A championship was indeed the one thing we lacked. At the highest level we weren't winning the big game. But we had won an awful lot of big games to *get* there. We had to believe that if we remained true to ourselves and our philosophy, if we continued to give effort, the championship might come one day.

9

A So-called Monkey off
Our Backs

I don't think anyone in basketball believes that the NCAA tournament always produces the best team as champion. In our system of "one loss and you're done," anything can happen—and that is precisely what has created the huge interest in the event. People come to the arenas thinking the mighty could fall, and they often do. Basketball is a sport in which, as Coach Clair Bee once said, "One point's worth a million, and one second equals a lifetime," and that statement was most true in the NCAA tournament.

Back in 1977, after we lost to Marquette in the NCAA championship game, a few people thought we had to win a title to be successful. But we didn't have to win a championship to feel we were doing a good job of coaching. Actually, I was thrilled for our players to reach the final game and took it as a compliment that those few people thought we should win a championship. Between 1959 and 1977 Carolina was never ranked number one in the weekly polls, and yet we managed to make five trips to the Final Four in an eleven-year stretch. We hardly had reason for complaint.

I didn't believe we were the best team in the country, except maybe in 1977 when healthy. Rather, we were a Top Ten team that gave itself chances to win a championship, often against long odds. In an era so dominated by UCLA—with its ten titles, seven in a row between 1966 and 1975—the only other programs that managed to win a single title were N.C. State, Marquette, and Indiana. The difficulty of winning the whole thing was compounded by the fact that, until 1975, we had to win the ACC tournament to even get into the national tourney. For instance, the Final Four in 1989 in Seattle were Illinois, Duke, Seton Hall, and Michigan. None of these teams won its conference championship.

So the peculiar truth of the matter is that, entering Carolina's 1978 season, I was content with what we had accomplished. We had a good record in the NCAA tournament. In order to win the NCAAs, you have to be healthy, you have to be very good, and you have to be very, very lucky. You also can't control whom you play in the tournament. Larry Brown told me that when his Kansas team won the national championship in 1988, they never played the higher-seeded team that they expected to play. Lower-seeded teams beat higher seeds so often in the NCAA tournament that we shouldn't call most of them upsets.

It was and is a tournament in which Princeton could beat UCLA, Richmond could beat Syracuse. Practically every team of note has lost to somebody in a so-called upset. Even the rules in college basketball, unlike those in the NBA, are designed to help the underdog. We have a thirty-five-second shot clock as opposed to the twenty-four-second clock in the pros; we allow zone defenses; we play forty minutes rather than forty-eight; and our 3-point arc is close enough to the basket to play a significant role in the outcome of a game, also an ally of the underdog.

If college basketball really wanted to decide the best team, we would name regular-season champions according to the last poll, as they do in college football, or we would play a series, like the NBA. Imagine the interest if the 1998 Chicago Bulls had been forced to play in a "win one game or go home" tournament. Think of how unjust it would have been, and how much harder it would have been for the Bulls to win a championship that way, rather than in a best-of-five- or a best-of-seven-game play-off series, from which the best team has a better probability of emerging. Still, the NCAA tournament was what gave college basketball that little touch of madness— it wasn't the most fair method of determining a champion, but it was the most interesting one.

There were some years when I didn't think we'd make it to the Final Four, and we did. Some years we were knocked out when I thought we were the better team. But each time, I felt, "Life goes on." In fact, the program was full of accomplishments and young men we should have been proud of, whether they were ranked number one, four, or fifteen.

In the 1970s and 1980s our conference was generally acknowledged as the deepest and best in the country, with several national championship contenders, and we took turns knocking each other off. Carolina, which had dominated the region since 1966, now found itself challenged on its front doorstep with the resurgence of the N.C. State program under Norm Sloan. National contenders would also emerge at Maryland and Virginia, in addition to Duke. Each school in the league considered us its archrival, and at the ACC tournament, fans made their sentiments clear with something they laughingly called the ABC Club. It meant they rooted for "Anybody But Carolina." A common derisive crowd chant at ACC tournaments was "Carolina refs, Carolina refs. . . ."

When David Thompson and Tom Burleson chose to go to N.C. State in the early '70s, it solidified State as an ACC and national contender. We had wanted both of those players, and generally, the pull to Chapel Hill was strong for high school students from within the state. We had suffered the occasional loss, such as the six-ten Randy Denton as well as Kenny Dennard and Jeff Capel to Duke. But the signing of Thompson in 1972 coupled with some close losses to the Wolfpack over the next couple of years did not sit well with our fans. In that era, N.C. State was our top rival.

Regional loyalties were split between the two schools, situated just thirty miles apart in Chapel Hill and Raleigh, and there were arguments even within families. That kind of competition is always difficult for the coaches, but while I competed with Norm Sloan, I respected him too. Ironically, Sloan's son entered Carolina on a Morehead Scholarship in the late '70s and lived in a dorm next to fraternity row. Everyone was aware that Norm's wife, Joan, had a beautiful voice and sang the national anthem before every home game he coached at State. I'm told that each morning when Norm's son walked to class, one fraternity's brothers would sing, "Ohh say can you see . . ." Apparently the heckling bothered him enough, as it would anyone, that he gave up his scholarship and left campus. But he did return as a postgraduate in our dental school.

Around this same time, I began getting letters from an anonymous N.C. State fan with a Fayetteville, North Carolina, postmark. The mail was always addressed to "Coach Nose" in Chapel Hill. What bugged me most was not the profanity-laced tirades inside the envelope, but the fact that the post office actually delivered the letter to me without a name or address!

That was the emotional backdrop against which Carolina and N.C. State played for the ACC championship in 1975. But now there was an added motivational factor: That year the NCAA changed its rules to allow *two* teams from a conference into the national tournament. No longer would the ACC tournament be the sole deciding factor in gaining admission; now the league champion would qualify, and so would an "at-large" team. Since Maryland had won the regular season, the Terrapins were a lock for the at-large berth. Carolina and State, tied for second place in the regular season, would be playing in the tournament championship to decide not just the ACC title, but the second conference rep to the NCAAs.

Our fans were spoiling for a victory over State and its great player David Thompson. We had failed to beat the Wolfpack in Thompson's sophomore year, when they went 23–0 but were on NCAA probation and forbidden to go to the tourney because of Thompson's recruitment. Then in Thompson's junior year State won the NCAA championship. Those two years of losing close games to State were difficult on our Carolina fans, but our 1975 team, with Phil Ford starting as a freshman, made a break-through with a big win over State in February. We survived overtime games against Wake Forest and Clemson to reach the championship and then upset the Wolfpack in the ACC final, 70–66. Ford was named MVP of the tournament.

State was so crushed that the team voted not to go to the NIT. Meanwhile, we moved into the NCAA tournament on a high, and reached the Sweet Six-teen with a defeat of New Mexico State. But our run finally ended when Syracuse beat us by 2 points in the regional semifinals in Providence, Rhode Island. Still, we finished in the top ten of the polls. But to show how fast things could turn, three seasons later Duke replaced N.C. State as our big rival in the minds of our fans. Bill Foster coached Duke to the '78 national championship game, while we won the regular-season ACC championship, but lost to a Top Twenty team, San Francisco, in the subregionals.

Two more examples of good Carolina teams knocked out early came in 1979 and 1980. In '79 we weren't ranked in any preseason polls but were number three in the final poll. We defeated Duke, ranked number one in pre-season, for the ACC championship—only to have our season prematurely ended when we met Pennsylvania in the second round of the NCAA tourna-ment and lost, 72–71. Penn would go on to represent the East in the Final Four, the last Ivy League team to advance that far.

In 1980 we had to play Texas A&M, the Southwest Conference cham-pion, in just the second round, and we had to do it in Denton, Texas. It didn't help any that our terrific freshman James Worthy had broken his ankle in January so badly that he needed two steel pins placed in the bone, and missed the second half of the season. Still, we had high hopes. A special group of seniors—Mike O'Koren, Jeff Wolf, Dave Colescott, Rich Yonakor, and John Virgil—had engineered an upset of top-ranked Duke by 15 points at Duke in January, and then topped the Blue Devils by 25 in the final game of the regular season.

We lost to Texas A&M in double overtime. In the next game, the Aggies suffered a double-overtime loss of their own against Louisville, the eventual NCAA champion. That was the kind of rough treatment a team could expect in the NCAA tournament.

Our 1981 team was an interesting mix. Al Wood was our senior leader, Worthy was back for his sophomore season, Jimmy Black was our junior point guard, and we started another senior, Mike Pepper. (Interestingly, Pepper hadn't come in as a prominent recruit, but he turned into a great contributor. When we signed him, Howard Garfinkel, who ran a prestigious basketball camp and who was an excellent judge of talent, said, "Pepper will look good in the team picture.") Jim Braddock was a sophomore, and Matt Doherty and Sam Perkins were freshmen. We were pleased to get Worthy back, although he would have trouble with the pins in his ankle all year, and we even had to hold him out of the last regular-season game at Duke. But James really came on in the postseason and played by far his best basketball of the year. Virginia had won the regular-season ACC title with its sensational sophomore Ralph Sampson, but we won the tournament with back-to-back 1-point victories. We defeated Wake Forest, 58–57, when Mike Pepper hit a jumper with eight seconds to go, followed by Maryland, 61–60, when Al Wood scored 4 points in the final two minutes.

After opening NCAA tournament play with a victory over Pitt, we were shipped out west to play Utah on its home court—a team picked to go all the way to the Final Four. We won, and that earned us a regional championship meeting with Kansas State, a game in which freshman Doherty recorded 16 points, 5 rebounds, and 3 assists as we prevailed, 82–68. With the victory, we were back in the Final Four. In the national semifinals in Philadelphia we faced Ralph Sampson and Virginia, a team that had beaten us twice in regular-season meetings. We pulled off the upset: Our sagging-man defense contained Sampson, while Al Wood delivered a virtuoso offensive performance, with 39 points, a semifinal record that still stands.

Two days later in the national championship game we met Indiana, a team led by Isiah Thomas and whose excellent coach, Bob Knight, had them playing so well they hadn't experienced a close game in the tournament. The

Hoosiers led us by just 1 point at halftime, 27–26. Isiah Thomas was great and ended up being the MVP of the Final Four. We had beaten Indiana in the regular season, 65–56, at Chapel Hill and the year before at Indiana on Dave Colescott's foul shots. We had visions of doing it again. But Worthy, who was having a great game, was called for three fouls, and I had to sit him in the first half. We weren't a deep team, and that situation was exacerbated by Worthy's sub Pete Budko's sprained ankle. Eddie Fogler, one of my assistants, to this day refers to those fouls against Worthy as "phantom fouls." Still, the Hoosiers were better than we were that night, and they won, 63–50.

Our players went home disappointed and hungry. We honestly felt that if we dedicated ourselves, we had another chance at a championship the next year.

Really, our first title was shaped years before the moment itself finally came. The confluence of events began with the arrival in Chapel Hill of some wonderful prospects. I remember when a gangly eighth-grader from Gastonia, North Carolina, showed up at our summer camp. James Worthy was one of a very few young men I ever looked at as a high schooler and felt certain was going to be a college star and pro player. It was a long wait, watching him grow up. I used to joke about Worthy, "We were hoping he would go hardship and leave high school after his junior year so he could come in and help us out." He had incredible quickness for a man of six eight, and even in high school, a great feel for the game. He was an excellent passer and could finish plays. What's more, he came from a solid home, with parents, Gladys and Ervin, who were special to all of us. Our assistants, Eddie Fogler and Bill Guthridge, used to compete over whose turn it was to call "the Big E," which was our nickname for James's father. I have seen tapes of Mr. Worthy's church sermons, and so I know he can be serious on occasion.

Even as a fifteen-year-old, James was big for his size. At first I tried to be reserved in my appraisals of him, because I had seen a ten-year-old at our camp one year who was so talented we couldn't believe it, but by the time he got to college he struggled to make our junior varsity. But James was a different matter, I quickly realized. Our camp gyms were set up by age groups, and our former player Doug Moe was in charge of coaching James's gym. At noon on Monday, Doug came to me and said, "Get him out of here. He ruins all the competition." James was so good it just wasn't fair to play him against the other eighth-graders. We sent him up one level to the next older age group. That didn't work either. Finally, we tried him two levels up. That did it. We put him against the tenth-graders and it was a fair fight.

Every year James came back to our camp until finally it was time for him to visit colleges on his official recruiting visits. He chose six, including the University of Hawaii. Mr. Worthy put his foot down. He said, "You can take four trips and they better be schools you're interested in." James narrowed his choices to Kentucky, Carolina, UCLA, and Michigan State. When he got to East Lansing, Michigan, he called home. By then James had spent so much time around me he could mimic my voice perfectly. Ervin answered the phone and heard a perfect imitation of Dean Smith: "Has anybody heard from James up there at Michigan State?" James said into the phone. "We got word he might sign up there." After talking to "me" for a couple of minutes, "the Big E" caught on and burst out laughing.

Sam Perkins was a six-foot-nine left-hander from Brooklyn raised by his grandmother Martha, a devout Jehovah's Witness. She was very strict, so Sam only left the apartment to go to school or to ride his bicycle around the neighborhood. At Tilden High School he would play some basketball in his gym classes, but he never went out for the team. Then in the summer between his sophomore and junior years some friends talked him into playing in a school yard tourney. One of the spectators that day was a local case-worker in social services named Herb Crossman, who was such a basketball nut that he used to watch the neighborhood tournaments. It was hard to miss Sam's obvious height, but Herb also noticed that he had quickness, excellent hands, and an even temperament. Nothing seemed to bother him. Herb began working out with Sam and discovered that he also had a bright mind and was a good listener.

The next fall, Herb was offered a job in the Schenectady-Albany area, and he accepted it. His wife was pregnant with their first child, and they wanted to get out of the city. But Herb hated to leave Sam, so he went to Martha with a proposal. He wanted to take Sam with him and serve as his legal guardian while Sam finished high school at an excellent school in the Albany area, Shaker. Martha was reluctant, but Herb convinced her that Shaker had a terrific academic reputation. Sam could get a first-rate education and leave the city behind for suburbia. Herb did mention that they had a basketball team, "in passing," but Martha wasn't impressed by sports.

By the time Sam arrived at Carolina, he had arms that seemed to unfold forever. Once, we measured his reach: When he stood flat-footed on the floor and held his arms up, his reaching height was nine feet four. The only Carolina players who compared to that were Eric Montross (nine five), Warren Martin (nine six), and Brendan Haywood (nine six). Sam could not only hold his own with seven-footers, he had an incalculable knack for playing on winning teams, as he would prove at Carolina, and later in the pros when he reached the play-offs in all but two of sixteen seasons (and counting). He chose us over Syracuse, Houston, UCLA, and Notre Dame. In fact, Herb told me that Notre Dame coach Digger Phelps told Sam he was crazy if it wasn't N.C. or Notre Dame. I quickly bragged on Digger and the South Bend campus.

Sam had absolutely no ego about playing time. In fact, when he was a freshman he told me after a month of practices that senior Pete Budko should start ahead of him and that he just hoped to come off the bench to contribute. Sam went on to become MVP of the ACC tournament that year, and an All-American for three straight years. Every season I scheduled several thirty- to forty-minute talks with each player individually. I always told my secretary to leave an hour and a half for Sam, because I knew we would talk about everything, not just basketball. He was a great pleasure to coach, and every one of his NBA coaches has told me the same thing. Bob Knight truly enjoyed coaching Sam on the 1984 Olympic team as well.

It's a myth that we didn't know what we had in Michael Jordan. We knew we had a great prospect. And we knew enough to try to keep it a secret when we were recruiting him. But it's also true that we didn't suspect to what lofty heights he would lift the game or what a capacity he had to push himself.

When Michael was seventeen, he was a slender six-three and had played only one season of high school varsity. As a sophomore at Laney High in Wilmington, North Carolina, Michael had been cut from the varsity and played with the B team. In February 1979 Bill Guthridge got a call from Mike Brown, who was the athletic director for New Hanover County schools. Mike wanted to tell us about this kid who was a junior at Laney, who had suddenly shot up to six three. Mike thought he had a chance to be a Division 1 player. "There's this junior down here at Laney that's starting to really come on," he said. Mike told us he was a good athlete, a good student, and he thought we'd want to take a look at him.

Bill Guthridge went down to check him out, and when he got back the next morning I asked him, "What do you think?" In Bill's estimation, this Jordan kid had exceptional quickness, great hands, and he tried hard for a high school player (but then, no high schooler has ever really worked hard). But Bill added something.

"He's unmilked."

That was his term for it, and what it meant was, while Michael had some obvious natural talents that couldn't be coached, there was also a lot left to teach. "I think he'll be an ACC player, so let's put him on the list, and we'll start writing him," Bill advised. We decided to keep an eye on him and watch his development.

That summer we were smart enough to invite Michael to our basketball camp. Our camp had become prestigious, and most of the top prospects came from all over the state. Roy Williams and Eddie Fogler hadn't laid eyes on Michael before then, and neither had I. That first day Michael separated himself from the rest of the campers.

The campers had free time to play pickup while everyone registered. Roy and Eddie were in charge of running the games in Carmichael, in groups of thirty. They ushered more than four hundred kids in and out of the gym over the course of the afternoon. Somewhere in all that, Michael jumped right out at them. After Michael's group was finished with their session, Roy pulled him aside and asked if he wanted to stay for a second session. Michael nodded and went back on the court. After it was over, Michael was supposed to leave. But he snuck back onto the court for a *third* session. He just kept showing up. At the end of the day, Roy and Eddie came into the office and told me what happened. "Wow, this guy came back and stayed there," Roy said. I asked which one. Roy said, "Mike Jordan, the kid from Wilmington."

Every morning during camp I would make my rounds, winding up at Carmichael by noon, where I would watch the older players, who were rising seniors. That next morning, I made it a point to seek out Michael and give him a long look. It was my very first sighting of him. I know I'm supposed to say he was surrounded by a golden light, but the truth is, he wasn't. The only thoughts I had were that we were going to recruit him, and that he had quickness and competed hard in every drill and scrimmage. I knew that Coach Frank Fuqua, who taught defense to the campers for over thirty years, was excited about Michael's defensive potential. Also it was obvious that Michael had great "hops," as they say. He could jump. But we don't pick a prospect based on jumping. If we did, we could save a lot of time by going to track meets and recruiting the high jumpers.

By the end of camp, however, I was impressed enough by Michael that I'd had lunch with him a couple of times, which was unusual for me unless the player in question was among our top recruits. When Michael's parents, Deloris and James (she always called him Ray), came to pick up their son, we met with them and told them we'd like to be among the schools they considered. Roy and Eddie suggested to Mr. and Mrs. Jordan that they send

Michael on to a prestigious camp for national prospects, called the Five-Star, which was held every summer in Pittsburgh. It was the only camp at that time in which kids could play against prospects from other states, and some of the best high school and college coaches across the country participated. It was run by Howard Garfinkel, who was a superb appraiser of talent.

Roy and Eddie had already called "Garf" about placing Michael in the camp. I said, "It would be better for us if we didn't send him up there for everybody else to see." But Roy and Eddie felt we'd get a clearer idea of how good Michael was from watching him against top competition. Michael went to Pittsburgh—and became MVP of the camp. He turned a lot of heads. When we went up to check on him, Garf raved about him. Michael was such a secret that he hadn't made any of the prospective high school All-America lists, but Howard promptly announced that he considered him one of the top ten best prospects in the country. We were still trying to act as though Michael was a nice regional player. But now word was out.

Michael narrowed the schools he would consider to South Carolina, North Carolina State, North Carolina, and Maryland. It wasn't until after the process that I heard he really liked UCLA, but they never recruited him, fortunately. Bill Foster, who had just left Duke to become head coach at South Carolina, was persuasive, and he took the Jordan family to the South Carolina governor's house. Also there was always Lefty Driesell to contend with at Maryland. Mr. Jordan told me that in his recruiting pitch Lefty said, "Maryland's almost as close to you as North Carolina now that they have that new cut-through bridge." Lefty tried to get Mr. Jordan to believe that the new Chesapeake toll road would make it easy for them to drive to Maryland. Mr. Jordan said, "He must think I'm a fool. I've driven to New York many times, and I know how far Maryland is."

The Jordans went with Michael on all of his visits, which tells you about the strength of that family and what interested, involved parents they were. We always encouraged parents to come with a recruit, because if a parent was willing to go to that trouble and expense, it meant they were serious about North Carolina. It was the best possible sign to us. In fact, I can remember only two instances in which a recruit later signed with us when at least one parent or legal guardian didn't come with him. (A few years later, Shaquille O'Neal had what I thought was a great visit to Chapel Hill until it dawned on me that he had come alone, without his mother and father. Still, he gave me a handshake at the airport and assured me he was "90 percent certain" he was coming to Carolina. A few days later he announced for LSU.)

That fall I went to see Michael at home in Wilmington. Bill Guthridge and Eddie Fogler came with me, and as usual, my friend Eddie Smith offered us his private plane. Linnea joined us with our daughter Kristen, who was just six months old, so that afterwards we could all head to the beach for the weekend. (Eddie's pilot, Jerry Burnham, often flew me to see high school players in games or practices and would keep me company in those school-boy gyms. On one trip we went to Hickory, North Carolina, to see James Worthy, whom I had been recruiting for years by then. Jerry watched the game for a few minutes and then pointed to James. "I think he could help our team," he said, seriously. I smiled. No kidding.) I also took my son Scott to the game, and in keeping with our philosophy of not talking about our re-cruiting with anyone, I told him not to tell anyone in his Carolina fraternity that he was going to see Worthy play. As I dropped him off after the game, one of his fraternity brothers asked: "Hey, Scott, how did Worthy play?"

The Jordan home was spacious and comfortable, with a big backyard and a new room that Mr. Jordan had added on. We all took chairs, but Michael chose to sit on the floor with a basketball in his hands. He just sat there, palming and stroking the ball. I said, "You like that ball, don't you?" at which he smiled and said, "I sure do!" Michael and his parents asked us a lot of questions, most of which had to do with academics, and we could tell they had done their homework. We could also tell they felt warmly toward us when Michael didn't want them to show us his room upstairs, but they did anyway.

Roy and Eddie stayed in touch with the Jordans during Michael's senior year and became good friends with the family. One day Roy mentioned to Mr. Jordan that he liked to chop wood for the exercise, and said he'd like to get a woodstove for his house. Mr. Jordan said he would take care of it. A few weeks later, he hand-delivered a woodstove to Roy's house. It was a hobby of Mr. Jordan's to make woodstoves by hand, and he loved to give them to his friends as gifts. Roy was stunned and said he couldn't accept it without paying for it. Mr. Jordan said, "I'm tired, and if I have to carry this back out and take it all the way back to Wilmington, I'm going to be angry." He wouldn't let Roy pay him a dime. From then on, whenever Roy moved, Mr. Jordan would make him a new woodstove for his new house. Eventually, when Roy went to Kansas as a head coach, he had to sell his house, leaving the woodstove in it. A prospective buyer asked him what brand of wood-stove it was. "It's a Jordan," Roy said.

By the time Michael signed with us in November of his senior year, his reputation had grown and so had his game. I flew to Dudley, North Carolina, to watch him play against Southern Wayne on the road. He responded well, against a good team. Michael's teammate six-eight Leroy Smith went to UNC-Charlotte on scholarship. I was surprised his team didn't make a run at the state championship but in a tourney, one loss and you are out. After the season, Michael starred in the prestigious McDonald's all-star game, and lost the MVP award to Adrian Branch, who had a higher profile and who was Maryland bound. Michael would have some of his greatest moments against the Terps, and there was no doubt in my mind he was sending a message to Branch. It was the last time he would ever be overshadowed by Branch. Michael narrowly won the award for ACC Freshman of the Year, with Branch a close second.

An interesting footnote to that spring before he enrolled is that Michael had an opportunity to go to Germany to play in the Albert Schweitzer Games. He turned it down, because he didn't want to miss any of his math classes. He loved math and he loved the teacher and he didn't want to miss it. Which showed something, I thought at the time. He called me up and asked what he should do. I said, "If you can afford to miss class, go ahead. It might be a good experience to travel to Europe." Well, he didn't go because he didn't want to miss classes and risk messing up his grade.

That fall we got reports from our upperclassmen who played in pickup games with him. We heard he was a little wild, that he was fast and quick, and that he could help us. There were some reports that he could be cocky and talk a little, but it was harmless stuff, mostly bluster. I think he was a little scared when he came here. He told me in one of our early freshman meetings that some of his buddies at Laney High School said, "You'll never play there. You won't get off the bench. Why don't you stay here at UNC-Wilmington?" I think at first he believed a lot of that. These days everyone has pro ball on their minds. But the truth is that when Michael Jordan was a college freshman, the pro game was on the back burner for him. I never heard him bring it up.

The first time I noticed something truly unusual about Michael was actually during a defensive drill. When practice began we had to teach all the freshmen the rudiments of our defensive philosophy. Defense was what we spent most of our time on in preseason practices, and on this day we stressed denying the man one pass away in our pressure defense. We were teaching a particular technique in defending backdoor plays. In high school Michael had been taught to turn and defend facing the ball, but I wanted him to learn to look over his shoulder and to see both man and ball. I remember stopping him during the drill and showing him what I wanted. I walked him through it. "This is the way I want you to do it," I said. "It'll take you awhile to make that change, but we think there are good reasons for it." Which I then explained to him.

The next day when the same drill came up, Michael defended it correctly, doing exactly what I had shown him the day before. It took most freshmen weeks to break an old habit. He had mastered the new technique in the space of twenty-four hours. After practice I told the staff, "I can't believe this. Jordan's already got it down. Maybe he stayed up all night and worked on it, but he had it right today. We're talking about a quick learner here."

Michael had primarily played near the basket in high school, but now we tried to make him a guard. In our offensive station during practice, we had a simple drill: Catch the ball, look inside, fake a pass in one direction, cross over, and explode to the goal. He did that too, got it down right away. When we put a man on him one on one, his combination of quickness and execution left the defender out of position. What's more, he appeared to *enjoy* practice.

As practices wore on, it was evident that Michael was going to play—a lot. The question became whether we would make him a starter with the four players who were returning from the team that had lost the 1981 NCAA championship game to Indiana. After the annual Blue-White scrimmage, we had a decision to make. Should we go ahead and start him in the backcourt with Jimmy Black, the adroit point guard who had led us to the NCAA final the previous year? The alternative was to start Jim Braddock, a junior who was a better outside shooter and ball handler. Our players knew they would not be named starters unless they had demonstrated skill and execution defensively. Usually, talented freshmen had trouble on defense. At that time in my career I had already started three freshmen in season openers: Phil Ford, James Worthy, and Mike O'Koren. I can't think of another perennial Top Twenty team that started as many freshmen as we did.

Sports Illustrated made us their preseason number-one pick, based on our returning talent, and wanted to put our starting five on the cover of their season-preview issue. I agreed that they could photograph James Worthy, Sam Perkins, Jimmy Black, and Matt Doherty. But I declined to add a fifth player. The cover was scheduled to be shot early in October, long before Jordan was even being considered as a starter. He still had much to show me on defense before he moved into contention to start, and I told him so. The editors of *Sports Illustrated* suspected Jordan would be a starter and pleaded with me to let him pose with the others. They pointed out how peculiar a basketball cover with four players, as opposed to five, would look. But I declined.

First of all, we had a rule forbidding freshmen to be interviewed by the media before they had played their first regular-season game. The rule was designed to ensure that sportswriters would write about the players who had already played here. The temptation was to write about the new faces—but that could create a rift between our returning players and the freshmen. In our program, freshmen learned that there was a hierarchy in which they earned their way upward. They didn't star on national magazine covers before they had so much as played a game.

The *Sports Illustrated* people persisted. An editor named Larry Keith, whom I knew during his undergraduate days at Carolina, called me and said, "But I heard Jordan's going to start." There was still a very real possibility Jimmy Braddock would be our starter, and I certainly didn't intend to let *SI* pick my starting lineup.

We had two preseason Blue-White scrimmages. Afterwards I always had a meeting with each player. I called it the "Where You Stand" meeting, and in it I told each player where he stood on earning playing time as we prepared to enter the season. In Michael's case, I told him, "Michael, defensively, if I find that you can really be a factor, then and only then would you be considered as a starter." After that he really came on. He showed that he knew our principles defensively better than most freshmen. About two days before the opener against Kansas, I made the decision. He would start.

But I surprised him with it. He didn't know until we were in the locker room at the Charlotte Coliseum shortly before the game and I wrote his name in chalk on the board. He was excited, but he knew just because he would start in the opener didn't mean it was engraved in stone.

Michael wasn't an instant "star"; rather, he was an important part of a potentially great team. The 1982 season was actually an up-and-down one for him, which is what you'd expect for any freshman. One of the areas that needed work was his outside shot. The problem was that he had such huge hands, which actually made it harder to shoot. It was like my trying to shoot a volleyball. The result was that a lot of teams played zone against us, with the aim of stopping Worthy and Perkins inside, while giving our other three open shots. But I told our perimeter people, "We first look inside [to Worthy and Perkins]. Our opponents *want* us to take the quick outside shots." They listened and had the discipline to wait for what we wanted, and the result was that as a team we shot 53.7 percent—with Perkins shooting 57.8 percent and Worthy 57.3, getting most of their points inside or some on offensive rebounds.

Jordan shot 53.4 percent, while Doherty and Black were over 51 percent. Michael did take the most shots, with 358 to Worthy's 354 and Perkins's 301. Those figures indicated just how patient and unselfish our players were in their shot selection. Of course, we always looked for easy fast-break baskets from our pressure defense. However, with no shot clock, our opponents often resorted to ball control. Also, since Perkins and Worthy could both put the ball on the floor, we could go to our delay game with a lead. In some games the margin was large enough that we could substitute early. Those factors are demonstrated by the fact that we averaged only 67 points a game for the year, which is the lowest of any team I ever coached. Our opponents averaged 55. (But I was never interested in the number of points per game, as long as we had more than the other team.) By going inside, this team also created a lot of shots from the foul line, making 477 to our opponents' 263 in thirty-four games.

Against Kentucky in the Meadowlands the day after Christmas, a big game in which we were ranked number one and they were number two, we faced one of those packed-in zones. The Wildcats gave us nothing but jumpers, and Michael had a very inconsistent first half shooting, going 3 for 8. I kept him on the floor in the second half, and he wound up 8 of 13 for 19 points in thirty-five minutes. Worthy had 26, Perkins had 21, and we won, 82–69. Phil Ford, who was with the Kansas City Kings, called me up and marveled at my patience with Michael. "I got to wondering, when you kept him in there, if maybe his high school coach had something on you," Phil kidded me.

Michael was fortunate to be surrounded by a superb cast. Worthy was now a junior on his way to National Player of the Year honors, and Perkins made first team All-America as a sophomore. Two players have been overlooked on that team, senior point guard Black, who defended well and ran our team, and sophomore forward Doherty, a selfless and vastly underrated player whose sole objective was for our team to win. Each of our starters had basketball savvy; they were smart, unselfish, and liked to play defense.

We started the regular season number one, and we ended it that way. We stayed healthy too, with the exception of a sprained ankle and a bout with the flu that briefly sidelined Sam. One of our two losses occurred when Sam couldn't play against Wake Forest at Chapel Hill. A bad throat infection that put Michael in the infirmary for five days shortly before the ACC tournament scared us, but he recovered just in time.

The second-best team in the country was either Georgetown, Houston, or Virginia with Ralph Sampson, who would go on to be the three-time National Player of the Year. We met the Cavaliers in the ACC championship game. Virginia gave us our other loss at Charlottesville three weeks earlier. The ACC tournament wasn't as important as it used to be, because an NCAA bid was no longer at stake, but it was still prestigious and it was important to *us*. This particular team wanted to win everything. Also, if we won, we would be assigned to play the NCAA East regionals just down the road in Raleigh.

It was the game that became notorious for spawning the shot clock for college basketball. We led, 44–43, with 7:34 to play when I signaled the Four Corners. Virginia was sitting back in a zone with the seven-foot-four Sampson camped underneath the basket. I thought we had a good chance of dictating the end of the game from the Four Corners because it might lure Sampson out. But when we held the ball, Virginia refused to come out and force the issue. Nearly five minutes went by before either team made a move, which didn't sit too well with television producers.

Finally, with twenty-eight seconds remaining, Virginia accumulated enough fouls to send Doherty to the line. Doherty made the first one but missed the second, and Virginia got the rebound. We still had fouls to give before Virginia would go to the free-throw line, and we used that to our advantage, slowing them down and making it tough to score. With three seconds left, Black knocked the ball off of a Virginia player's knee, and we regained possession. Virginia fouled Doherty again, and this time he sank two from the free-throw line to give us the lead, 47–43. Virginia scored a meaningless basket as time expired.

Afterwards both teams were heavily criticized for the way the game was played in the last seven minutes, and there were all sorts of conversations about the need for a shot clock. I received literally hundreds of hostile letters from Virginia fans, including one from a Lutheran pastor in Charlottesville, blasting me for my decision to try to pull Sampson from underneath the basket. The media cried out for a shot clock. Actually, I had been pushing for a thirty-second clock, coupled with the 3-point line, for several years. The weaker Division 1 teams, which tended to use ball control to give themselves a chance to win, needed a feasible 3-point shot if we were going to have a shot clock. In our annual ACC coaches' meeting in May 1982, Coach Guthridge suggested that we should play all of our conference games in the upcoming season with a thirty-second clock and a 3-point circle—which we did.

We moved on to the 1982 NCAA tournament to meet James Madison, which had upset Ohio State in the first round but was still considered a Cinderella team. I dreaded games like that. I would much rather have played Ohio State than James Madison, which was so ably coached by Lou Campanelli and had two solid seniors in their lineup who had wanted to come to Carolina. Games such as Carolina–James Madison make the NCAA tournament special. The seeding system used today makes the NCAAs fairer than they have ever been. The David-and-Goliath nature of early-round games was preferable to the old days in the NCAA tournament, when there was no seeding system and television often decided matchups. In 1976, to accommodate TV, we were paired against SEC champion Alabama in the *first round* in Dayton, and we lost. We ranked number four in the country, and they were number six. It was ludicrously unfair to make two such contenders meet in the opening round.

Shortly before we played James Madison, CBS announcer Brent Musberger said, "North Carolina should have no problem." With nothing to lose, James Madison played a terrific game of ball control against us, and we won just barely, 52–50. That's the beauty of our game. We had been number one all season, and yet we came within 3 points of being knocked out in the second round by a team that would have had trouble winning a single game against us in a best-of-seven series. It points out a major difference between college basketball and the NBA.

After two more victories that were more comfortable, over Alabama and Villanova, we had a berth in the Final Four in New Orleans. Worthy was the MVP of the regional, but Black was a critical factor for us. He had seven assists against Alabama, and 25 points in two games on 10 of 12 shooting. After we defeated Villanova, 70–60, in Reynolds Coliseum in Raleigh, an interesting thing happened. Our team refused to cut the nets down.

Maintenance workers brought out ladders and scissors, and the press and photographers positioned themselves under the basket to record the moment. But our players declined, abandoning tradition. I was already in the dressing room so I didn't know until later what they had done, or rather, what they hadn't. In the postgame press conference, a reporter asked Worthy why they hadn't taken the nets down.

"The nets we want are hanging in the Superdome in New Orleans," he said.

It was a mission statement. We went on to New Orleans, where we were to meet Houston, and this time a TV remark worked in our favor. Steve Grote, another CBS commentator, said on the air, "It's a shame that Louisville and

Georgetown have to play in the semifinals, because they're the two best teams left in the field." Houston was led by All-American guard Rob Williams, but as I scouted them, the players who stood out to me even more were Clyde Drexler, whom no one had heard much about yet, and a big young man off the bench named Akeem Olajuwon, who blocked shots as well as any player you'd like to see. But Perkins was too much for Houston, with 25 points and 10 rebounds, while Jimmy Black was once again his invaluable self, holding Williams to 2 points and 0–8 shooting from the field. We won, 68–63, and one play stands out most in my mind. It was a drive out of the Four Corners that resulted in a thunderous dunk by James Worthy over Larry Micheaux, right in front of our bench. Also, we shot a scarcely believable 76 percent in the second half.

That set up a meeting with Georgetown and my friend John Thompson. The big news became my relationship with John and the fact that we would be on opposing benches with a national championship at stake. The press relentlessly pursued the story, but John handled it beautifully for both of us. He said our friendship was a private matter, and our feelings should stay between the two of us. To dwell on it publicly, he said, would devalue our close relationship. I admired his response and was grateful for it. I've stuck to the policy ever since and certainly don't intend to break it now. The other news was that we had another chance to win a national championship, the so-called monkey on my back. I didn't think I had one back there, but apparently the press kept writing about it. Jimmy Black had said, "We want to get the monkey off Coach's back." While I appreciated the sentiment, I didn't want our players to put added pressure on themselves. I wanted each of our teams to win championships, but again, we had already won so many crucial games just to *get* there. After all, this was our seventh Final Four in fifteen years in which we had to win the ACC tournament to qualify for seven of those years.

We had just a very short workout on the Sunday before the game. With such a short turnaround, we had to hope that our principles could stand up to a very stern test from Georgetown. A team's preparation is more mental and emotional than it is strategic. On the day of the championship I passed James Worthy's brother, Danny, in the hotel hallway on our way to the pregame meal. "What about your brother?" I asked. "Is he ready to play?" Danny didn't hesitate. He said, "I've never seen him so zeroed in. I'll be shocked if he doesn't have a great game." I had the same feeling. We were about to see the genesis of the nickname "Big Game James." Worthy knew what second place was, and he didn't want to experience it again. He still burned over the '81 loss to Indiana. In fact, he was still burning over a loss in high school. His Gastonia Ashbrook team had beaten crosstown rival Huss High, starring a guard named Eric "Sleepy" Floyd, three times in the regular season only to be upset by them in the state finals. Sleepy Floyd was now a starting guard for Georgetown, and I knew James couldn't wait to take the court against him.

The team was quiet and reflective at the pregame meal. I never could tell if our players were ready to play based on their pregame attitude. There were days when I thought we were too loud at pregame, and we performed beautifully on the court. There were days when we were quiet and withdrawn, and we played awful. And vice versa. I had heard a lot of coaches say, "I could tell we were ready to play." I wished I knew what their secret was.

Worthy said later he was nervous before the start of the game. He came out for warm-ups a full hour before tip-off. In fact, most of the players were a little tight, which I've always thought was a good sign. It usually disappears in the first few minutes.

It was one of those rare gems of a championship, in my opinion among the most well played in NCAA history. Both teams played up to their abilities and to the importance of the occasion, bringing their best performances on the championship night. Georgetown was led by the formidable Patrick Ewing, and Coach Thompson's pressing defense was extremely hard to play against. We had our All-Americans in Worthy and Perkins, and a remarkably disciplined supporting cast led by Black and Doherty. We shot 53.2 percent for the game, and Georgetown 52.9—that's how close it was and how well we both played. What's more, we were maintaining the same high standard defensively. One thing was apparent right away. The team that won would have to play at their best for all forty minutes.

Georgetown came straight at us. Ewing rose in the air swatting at everything we put up and was called for goaltending five times in our first nine shots. It was deliberate strategy. Thompson had told him before the game, "Don't let anything go in; try to block it." It worked to a certain extent, but Worthy, as his brother promised, was having perhaps the best game of his entire career. By the game's end he would have hit thirteen of seventeen field goals, for 28 points. At halftime we trailed, 32–31, and Worthy had 18 of our points. I was fairly pleased with our ballhandling and shot selection, although I told the team we had to do a better job on Floyd. Ewing had hit some tough shots against Perkins. I praised our team's poise against Georgetown's intense pressing defense, particularly Black.

Shortly before the second half, Thompson and I met at the scorer's table and had a funny exchange. Ewing was known as a deliberate free-throw shooter, and sometimes he flirted with violating the ten-second time limit. I could see that the officials were counting each time he stood at the line. I didn't want them to call that kind of technicality in a game of this magnitude, so I called the head referee, Hank Nichols, over, and John joined us. "Listen, don't call Ewing for ten seconds," I said. John started laughing. "You're planting seeds," he said. I turned to Hank and I said, "I mean this, Hank. Don't call it." I really was sincere. I thought it would be the worst call in the world in a championship game.

Back on the floor for the second half, neither team could get a comfortable lead. Meanwhile, a player no one had expected to be a deciding factor was quietly working his way toward having a great game. Young Michael Jordan was delivering the single best performance of his freshman season, hauling down rebounds and playing great defense. Michael had become more consistent as the season progressed, but this was his most complete game of the year. After the game he would grade out as our best defensive player for the first time all season. He also wound up with nine rebounds, which was remarkable for a guard playing against Georgetown's front line led by Ewing.

With 3:28 remaining and Carolina leading by just one point, 59–58, Michael made a great play. He received a pass in front of our bench, around the extended foul line, and suddenly drove to his left. Ewing swooped in on him. I was certain Ewing would either block his layup or foul him. Instead, somehow Michael's left-handed layup touched high off the glass. It fell gently through the net. Score: Carolina, 61, Georgetown, 58.

But Georgetown scored the next 4 points. Ewing made a little jumper that rolled around the rim before it fell in to make it 61–60, Carolina still leading. After we missed a free throw, Sleepy Floyd responded with a jumper from the lane that ticked on the front of the iron, caught a good bounce, and dropped. Georgetown led, 62–61. The crowd of more than sixty-one thousand stood as one and roared with excitement. But interestingly enough, in those football arenas you don't hear as much of the crowd noise at courtside as you do in a smaller arena.

At first I was going to let our players just play without a time-out, as we normally would, since we should always know what to run, based on our practices for just such a contingency. But Georgetown put on a passive press, and our players hesitated. Eddie Fogler said, "Coach, they don't look comfortable. Do you want a time-out?" I thought he was right, so we took the time-out with thirty-two seconds left.

Our players came to the bench, trailing by 1 point. When they took their seats in front of me, I smiled at them. "We're in great shape," I said.

I didn't sense or feel any tension from them, although Michael said later he was so nervous the roof of his mouth was dry. I told them I expected John Thompson to have the Hoyas in a zone, and if that was the case, "We're going to run Two." If it was man-to-man, "Run B-Three for James."

Our Number Two zone offense was a continuity scheme in which the first option was to go to Worthy down low, or pass to Sam or Matt coming to the high-post area. Or if the Hoyas "ganged" their defense in the paint to stop our inside plan, Black could always pass crosscourt against the zone to Michael. If Georgetown was in a man defense, our B-3 called for Worthy to come out to the top of the key and then receive a back screen by Black. Worthy would reverse to the goal hard for a backdoor, and then buttonhook when the pass went to Black after he had finished screening. If Worthy was fronted, Perkins would come to the foul line for the pass, and either shoot or pass to Worthy, "sealing" his man for the layup. I heard talk later that Worthy wasn't our first option on the play, but that was completely wrong. Worthy was our first option, and why not?

"Line up to get the ball inbounds, take the first great shot, and pound the boards," I said. "If they get the rebound, foul the rebounder. Now, when we score we will be in our Thirty-two defense."

I reminded our players that we had been over this very sequence, 1 point down with thirty-two seconds to play, frequently in practice. Then I repeated the game plan once more before we broke the huddle.

Finally, I said, "I'd rather be us than Georgetown at this point. Wouldn't you?" They nodded in unison.

John Thompson was a big James Worthy fan, and I figured he wouldn't let Worthy beat them. He would make it as difficult as possible for us to get the ball to James. I had a hunch we could wind up with Michael as the shooter if the Hoyas were in a zone. What reassured me about the play was that if Michael was our best option, at least we had great board coverage, with Perkins, Worthy, and Doherty ready to rebound. As the players broke the huddle, I said to Michael, "If it comes to you, Michael, knock it in."

The inbounds pass went to Black, and Georgetown was indeed in a zone. But we didn't move as quickly into our Number Two zone offense as I wanted. (You could certainly say that Jimmy was calm!) The Hoyas did cover Worthy, and Jimmy made a good fake before he passed it crosscourt to a wide-open Michael on the left wing.

Michael's shot looked good as soon as it left his hand. I saw that it had perfect spin through the air. Michael told someone later that he shut his eyes after the release and that he never even saw what happened to it. The ball snapped neatly through the net, with sixteen seconds to go.

As it turned out, Sam Perkins was all alone under the backboard while two Hoyas tried to box out Worthy. If the shot had missed to the far side, Sam would have been in perfect position to get the rebound and the put-back, and might well have been the hero for us.

As Michael's shot slipped through the net, the arena erupted. Interestingly enough, you can see on replays that despite the pressure situation and the pandemonium in the arena, our bench was very composed. Our coaching staff practically sat with our chins in our hands. As for me, all I was thinking at that moment was about what we needed to do next, which was get into our Thirty-two defense. The Thirty-two defense was like the old "run and jump," and it was conceived to make it hard for an opponent to run a play.

We led, 63–62. Coach Thompson was smart not to call a time-out. Instead, his well-coached players pushed the ball upcourt before our defense could get set. We would have done the same. There was plenty of time left. But Jordan made a great defensive play by jumping into the passing lane at precisely the second that Fred Brown was going to pass to Sleepy Floyd. Off balance, Brown tried to redirect the ball.

He threw it right to Worthy, who had somewhat overrun the play going for a steal, and was slow in getting back.

I think Brown made the mistake because Carolina was in white jerseys, and Georgetown, as a number-one seed, had worn white in all of its tournament games. James's white jersey must have looked like that of an ally. James plucked the ball from the air and made a smart play, dribbling downcourt and killing a few more seconds off the clock, instead of dribbling straight to the basket. Georgetown finally fouled him with two seconds to play. *Now* our bench went crazy. Players and managers were jumping up and down all over the sideline, but I was mad. They were acting as if the game was over, and it wasn't, I told them sharply. We still had to finish it.

Coach Thompson used his last time-out to make James think about the foul shots. James had been jumping up and down with Perkins, thinking the game was won. During the time-out, I told James to concentrate on his routine and make both free throws. I also told our team that Georgetown was out of time-outs, so we wanted three players to get back at midcourt.

James missed the first foul shot. It suddenly occurred to me that I should have told him to miss the second one on purpose if he missed the first one.

Georgetown would have trouble getting the rebound and getting the ball up-court for a shot in the last two seconds. But if he made the second shot, Georgetown could set up a Hail Mary on the inbounds pass, and anything could happen.

Fortunately, James missed the second. Georgetown rebounded, and slung the ball up the court to Floyd. They would get off one last shot—but it was a desperate fifty-footer by Floyd. It wasn't close. But not until the buzzer sounded did I stop worrying.

I immediately went looking for John Thompson. We met at the scorer's table, and I hugged my good friend. "You did a great job tonight," I said. "It was the best team we played all year, and it was our best game." (Later, Thompson said to the media, "The student wanted to show the teacher." He really wasn't a student of mine. He was and still is a great coach.)

Then I went looking for my team. The first player I found was Jimmy Black, who had tears streaming down his face. I swept him into a hug and told him he was great. Jimmy had played such a superb game—he had not lost the ball a single time against Georgetown's relentless press. Before the game I would have been happy to settle for four turnovers against their press. It was a crucial contribution and an unsung performance.

Next, I went to the postgame press conference. All week I had been constantly reminded by the press that this was our seventh trip to the Final Four without winning an NCAA championship. But I could honestly say that this would have been the first time I would have left the Final Four disappointed if we had not won. In our six previous trips, we had never been ranked number one. I thought we were the best team in college basketball in 1982, even though we were a young one. We were solid defensively, difficult to stop on offense, and a good rebounding team. Also we were mentally tough.

Even so, we could have lost in the first round to James Madison, or just as easily been defeated by Georgetown. That is the nature of our great game.

Carolina and Georgetown had both played well enough to be champions. It amazed me how much 1 point, a single point, could mean to fans, press, alumni, spectators, players, and coaches. It meant *too* much. Even in the midst of the celebration, I couldn't let go of the thought. A single point shouldn't determine who was called a loser and who was painted a winner, who enjoyed such public adoration and who went into mourning. The teams were too close, too talented, too equally hardworking to be greeted so separately and disparately by public opinion.

Don't mistake me: I was thrilled for our team to win the title. I knew how committed our players had been since the loss to Indiana the previous year, and how determined they were to redress the loss. I was deeply grateful to them and overjoyed that I would never have to answer another question about not winning a national championship. That so-called monkey was off my back. But honestly, I felt very much as I had when we made our first Final Four. I was proud of our team and relieved that we had stayed healthy, since we weren't very deep. And I could not shake my sympathy for the Georgetown Hoyas, who did not deserve to feel as if they had lost something.

Each of us should be happy for the other, I thought. After all, there are more than three hundred teams playing Division 1 college basketball, and we were the only two left playing. Ordinarily I didn't like coaching against a friend, but in this instance I appreciated it. It meant that each of us had had a great season. I would feel the same in later years in losing to Roy Williams's Kansas team in 1991, and in defeating them in the 1993 Final Four.

It amazed me then, and still does, that a team finishing number two in the United States gets so little respect. I call it the Buffalo Bills syndrome. Buffalo went to four straight Super Bowls, an achievement for which they should have been congratulated. After all, they did for four straight years what the other thirteen AFC teams had tried and failed to do. But each time Buffalo lost, people called them a failure. I'll never understand that. American society seems to require a number one or nothing at all. That is not only an unrealistic mind-set, but a fairly unintelligent one. Think about it. Think about how many big games Buffalo had to win in order to reach four Super Bowls.

When we returned to Chapel Hill the next day, twenty-five thousand people poured into Kenan Stadium for a celebratory rally. I didn't go, nor would I ever go to one. I felt those things should be for players, not coaches. Instead, I took my small daughter Kristen for a walk. It was a gorgeous spring day, and we strolled slowly through the neighborhood.

I never was bothered by the talk about our not winning a national championship as much as other people were. Family and players and friends minded on my behalf, I know. But I knew how good and how lucky you had to be to get to a Final Four. I knew just how many *other* games we had won over the years that were also important. Some people say the regular season doesn't mean anything. Well, I don't see people turning in their tickets when Kentucky plays Louisville in December.

We beat Georgetown that night by 1 point. That 1 point should not change perceptions of me. It certainly didn't determine how good or bad I was as a coach or as a person.

In Kenan Stadium that day after we won the championship, the crowd chanted to James Worthy, "One more year! One more year!" I wanted James back too, but I wondered if it would truly be best for him. He had an opportunity to leave college early to play in the NBA and would shortly have to make a decision about his future.

The first pick in the NBA draft would go to either the San Diego Clippers or the Los Angeles Lakers, to be decided by a coin flip. I made some calls, trying to gauge James's chances of being one of the first three players chosen. I talked with Jerry West, the Lakers' general manager, who said, "I'll promise you I'll take him." Jerry is as honest as can be, and whatever he says, you can count on. He also told me roughly what the Lakers would offer James if he came out of school. Next, I learned that the Clippers would take him as the first choice if they won the coin flip. So James was a sure first pick. In each case, I asked for a ballpark figure. I was told that James was certain to make $500,000 a year for five years: $2.5 million. Guaranteed. That might sound small by today's standards, but in 1982 it was a big contract.

James and his parents and I met in Greensboro in April to discuss his status. James was undecided when he arrived. But I didn't see how he had a choice. We talked, and I told the Worthys what I had learned, and gave them my advice. It certainly adds perspective when a college athlete suffers a serious injury as James did during his freshman season when he broke his ankle. I simply gave the Worthys the information I had, along with what I felt were the pluses and minuses of turning pro versus staying.

We would still be a young team, despite the loss of seniors Jimmy Black and Chris Brust to graduation. With James back as a senior and his classmate Jim Braddock at point, Perkins and Doherty as juniors, and Jordan as a sophomore, we could win it all again. On the other hand, James would have no insurance on the ankle and he would be drafted number one by either San Diego or Los Angeles, and still graduate. That made it an easy choice, in my mind. James loved going to school in Chapel Hill, but his father agreed with me: He should turn pro. That's what they decided to do.

I'll never forget NBA draft day. James didn't go to New York since he was in summer school, so the two of us borrowed the Lotz family's living room to watch the draft on TV. Even though the Lakers had won the coin flip and

Jerry West assured us he would draft James number one, we both were nervous. The announcement came: "The Los Angeles Lakers select . . ." After the word *select* there was a pause. And then we heard: "James Worthy." We leaped off the couch and yelled.

People ask why I am a supporter of early entry into the professional drafts for certain undergraduates. If the undergraduate is sure to be drafted in the Top Five, which means he should be financially secure for the rest of his life, and if playing in the NBA is indeed his goal, he should go. In American society, each person has a right to be employed, including young men who are good enough to play pro basketball.

There was no hue and cry when Gene Hoffman, a talented Carolina student, left our basketball program. He came to me after his sophomore season and said he would be leaving school to start a computer business with three other UNC students. They came up with a plan that would enable people to block out advertising while surfing the Internet. That brilliant idea was hugely successful, and it made Gene and his partners wealthy. From that start, they branched out with additional ideas, which were also successful. Had Gene been a player in our program, many would have recommended that he stay in school and finish his four years. There were no protests when Gene left UNC early, no newspaper stories detailing his reasons, no pep rallies with students chanting, "Two more years, two more years!"

That's because Gene was our first team *manager* to leave early for the "pros." He was also featured in *Forbes* magazine during the summer of 1999.

The public outcry against turning pro early seems to be reserved for basketball players only. When Davis Love III and Ray Floyd leave Chapel Hill early to join the pro golf tour, or ten different Stanford tennis players do the same, no one seems upset. The reason, I suspect, is that fans are afraid basketball players turning pro early will affect the fortunes of their team. The local *News & Observer* wrote beautiful stories about high school senior Josh Hamilton, who had signed a baseball contract as the number-one pick in the major-league draft. No one suggested he should go to college next year!

What I mind is that the debate is cast in moral terms, that players who stay for four years are considered good guys, and those who leave early, somehow bad. Actually, all nine of our players who went pro early loved Chapel Hill and college life. Six of those nine returned during the summers to earn their degrees. We have high hopes that the others will do likewise.

Most young people enter college to get a degree that will allow them to pursue a vocation in which they have a high degree of interest, and perhaps even a passion. Our players were no different. At Carolina, we had two players with reasonable chances of playing in the NBA who turned it down because they wanted to do something else. The six-ten Rusty Clark and six-three Steve Hale each instructed me to tell NBA scouts they had no interest in pro basketball because, in both cases, they had already been accepted to medical school and were anxious to get on with becoming doctors. But practically all of the other pro-potential players I coached would postpone medical school or law school to play in the NBA for a few years. That didn't mean they didn't value a degree. They all knew a degree was necessary in order to find a job that would be meaningful to them. But basketball was a meaningful job to them too.

My first experience with this situation was in 1972, when Robert McAdoo elected to give up his eligibility after one year at Carolina so that he could be drafted number two by the NBA's Buffalo Braves. We sat down and talked about his goal of getting a degree, and the result was that, on his behalf, I asked his agent to insert into his contract a bonus clause of $50,000 if he came back and got his degree. That would be about $250,000 in today's dollars.

It's said that the NBA wants to do more to encourage players to stay in school. Yes, the NBA *wants* players to stay in school, but not for entirely altruistic reasons. The longer a college player's career, the more free marketing the NBA enjoys, and the greater the star power of the athlete when he does turn pro. But the main reason the NBA wants players to remain in college is that many underclassmen simply aren't ready for the league. In drafting, NBA teams can be more certain of a collegiate senior than, say, a freshman who won't improve sitting on an NBA team's bench. The NBA perhaps needs a farm system, as in baseball, which it could use for development of players who aren't interested in going to college (maybe the Continental Basketball Association would serve the purpose). If a young player does well, his parent club could then bring him up to the NBA. A college player might stay in school if he knew he was going to play for a CBA salary. But those players who will command NBA first-round-draft-choice money will probably choose to come out, no matter what.

There should be nothing wrong with the fact that a student leaves college early to pursue his passion or chief vocation. There was no controversy, no moral objection, when John McEnroe left Stanford after his junior year to play the tennis tour, or when Tiger Woods did the same after his sophomore year to join the PGA tour. It was the logical progression in their careers to turn pro; they had done as much as they could in their sport at the collegiate level, and to stay in school only meant risking injury and jeopardizing their ability to negotiate their optimum livelihood. McEnroe promptly won Wimbledon and Woods, the Masters. It was very difficult for me to tell a young man not to accept millions of dollars in professional contracts just to stay in college one or two more years, if he could be drafted as a lottery pick.

The task of evaluating a young player's precise worth would grow increasingly complex over the years, given the brewing labor struggle between team owners and the NBA Players Association. In 1995 the owners and players association agreed to a set rookie pay scale over three years before a player could seek a contract as a free agent, in an effort to control spiraling salaries. But it created more of a problem than the one it was designed to fix. Owners needed protection from themselves in giving rookies long-range (six- or seven-year) guaranteed contracts for huge dollars. They agreed to the set scale because, even though it was for big dollars, if someone turned out to be a bust at least it wouldn't go on for seven years. But the purpose was defeated when young players like Kevin Garnett in Minnesota and our Rasheed Wallace in Portland, after proving themselves in only their first two years in the league, were promptly signed by their clubs for an additional six years. Minnesota, eager to lock up Garnett, made him a deal for a reported $115 million, while Portland signed Wallace for $68 million. The eventual result was that the owners called for a lockout. After the labor dispute that shortened the '99 season, a new collective-bargaining agreement was reached. Rookies now have a set pay scale of four years before they can seek free-agent contracts. The problem now is that underclassmen who think they will be drafted in the first round choose to "start the time clock" to free-agent status.

For some reason when it comes to collegiate team sports like basketball and football, we try to exert moral pressure on the players to stay in school. We tell them that they should sacrifice their own best interests, that they owe it to their teammates and the university not to run out on them. Actually, an NCAA scholarship is good for only one year at a time, so the player is not breaking an agreement with the school if he chooses not to return.

In discussing with our players whether to turn pro, I did not tell them to give up their *education,* just their eligibility. There was a big difference. The nine Carolina players who left school early did not forgo degrees. James Worthy, Michael Jordan, J. R. Reid, Antawn Jamison, and Jerry Stackhouse (who left after his sophomore season) all came back to earn their diplomas. Vince Carter and Jeff McInnis will have theirs by the summer of 2000, if not before, and Rasheed Wallace a year after.

One fact people lose sight of is that only fifteen or twenty players leave the collegiate game early for the pros each year—out of four thousand Division 1 players. The skill of those few players may be gone, but there are lots of great players left, and college rules give each team a chance to win. Schools like Carolina will always have the bands, the enthusiasm, the great games with last-second shots. The spectacle of college basketball isn't hurt, and the NCAA tournament will continue to be one of the most anticipated sporting events of the year even if ten or twelve leave school early to play professionally.

The first time I felt there was something truly unprecedented about Michael Jordan as a player was in the summer between his freshman and sophomore years. I have never seen that kind of improvement in anyone, ever. We had asked him to work on a few things, such as his left-handed dribble and his outside shot. He had become pretty consistent from fifteen to eighteen feet, and we wanted him to build that out, especially since by then we knew the ACC was going to the 3-point shot and to a shot clock. But we weren't prepared for the exponential leap he made in his game.

Again, it was unforeseen. Despite his shot against Georgetown, no publication listed Michael as a preseason All-American. He was just a sophomore with a still-emerging reputation. But for one thing, he had gotten taller. He arrived at Chapel Hill standing six three and a half, and now he was six six. (In fact, I think he continued to grow even when he left college. Every time I see him, he looks bigger.)

He was faster. On his timed run, he clocked a 4.55 in the forty-yard dash as a freshman, but he ran it in 4.39 as a sophomore. He was more mature physically, he could shoot consistently, and his savvy was better. In preseason pickup games, I'm told, he more than held his own with our NBA alumni who came back to Chapel Hill to work out, guys such as Al Wood, Dudley Bradley, Phil Ford, Mitch Kupchak, and Walter Davis. His confidence grew, and he said later it had done wonders for him to make that shot against Georgetown.

One afternoon in practice, Billy Cunningham came by to observe. In 1982 Billy was the head coach of the Philadelphia 76ers, and he knew ability when he saw it. After practice Billy said, "He's going to be the greatest player who ever came out of here." I blanched at the remark. We've had a lot of great players at Carolina, and I was trying to protect Michael from being overpraised.

Once practice started, Michael dominated in our competitive drills, in which the losing side would have to run sprints. Sometimes I would stack a five-on-five game against him, putting many of our strongest players on one side, and still his team would win. One afternoon he whispered to one of our assistants, "My side's not going to run all fall." He ran a few times, but not many.

The start of the 1983 season was another lesson in the unpredictable pendulum swings of college basketball. Even though Worthy and Black were gone, we had All-American Perkins and Jordan, as well as Matt Doherty, Buzz Peterson, Jimmy Braddock, and Warren Martin returning. Plus, we had a fine incoming class in Brad Daugherty, a baby-faced teenage center, and guards Curtis Hunter and Steve Hale. With Worthy gone, we didn't have time to bring anyone along slowly, and I thrust Daugherty into a starting role after a few games. When Brad began practices on October 15, he was still just sixteen years old. As a sophomore he had been the manager on his high school team in Black Mountain, North Carolina, but grew into a great prospect as a senior. If Worthy had stayed for his final year, we were thinking of "redshirting" Brad so he would have a season to mature physically.

Then injuries struck. Michael broke his hand and played in a hard cast for the first four games. We opened 3–3 against a tough schedule, losing on the road to Missouri, Tulsa, and St. John's. But once we became healthy we went on an eighteen-game winning streak and became number one in the nation.

On February 10 we met second-ranked Virginia and Ralph Sampson, who was by now a senior. At first, it looked as if we were on our way to a resounding loss. We trailed by 16 points with less than ten minutes to play, and we were still down, 63–53, with 4:12 left on the clock. But then our players staged a remarkable comeback.

Jimmy Braddock hit a 3-pointer, and Matt Doherty hit two free throws to pull us to within 5. When Sam Perkins sank both ends of a one-and-one with 2:54 remaining, we trailed by just 3 points, 63–60. Virginia went to a stall. We were forced to foul, sending Sampson to the line. He missed the front end of his one-and-one. We got the rebound. Braddock tried another 3, and missed—but Jordan rose in the air for the put-back. Now it was a 1-point game.

Jordan went to work. As Rick Carlisle brought the ball upcourt for Virginia, Jordan swiped it away and raced to the opposite end for a slam dunk, and a 64–63 lead for Carolina. By now Carmichael was in a state of frenzy. Carlisle brought the ball up again and tried to get off a game winner, but it missed. Jordan went up so high he won the rebound battle with Sampson to assure the victory.

We tied Virginia for the first place in the conference, and eventually beat them twice. But in the end, it wasn't our year. We advanced all the way to the Final Eight in the NCAA tournament before losing a close game to Georgia in the NCAA regional finals at Syracuse in an upset. We finished 28–8, ranked number eight in the final poll. We returned home from Syracuse that same evening.

At 10 P.M. that Sunday night, Michael Jordan was in Carmichael Auditorium shooting by himself, I'm told. I was recruiting in Dave Popson's house in Ashley, Pennsylvania.

Jordan finished second in the voting to Sampson as National Player of the Year. He did it without any preseason attention, which was absolutely remarkable. At the start of the year he hadn't even been listed among Converse's Top 100 players in the country. He was better every season he played, except perhaps for the one in which he played baseball. The fact is, if baseball had not experienced a strike, and Michael had continued to improve his hitting, he might have never come back to the NBA.

Once again the question of a player turning pro came up, but this time with a surprising result. It was the spring of Sam Perkins's junior year, and I made calls to the NBA teams with the first eight picks. I also talked with Herb Crossman, Sam's guardian, who wanted Sam to graduate in four years. Most of the team executives I talked with thought Sam would be a good pro, but only one of them, Jack McClosky in Detroit, promised me that Sam would be selected with his eighth pick if he was available. I called Sam into my office and told him I didn't think he should turn pro, since I couldn't promise that he'd do better than eighth pick.

"Pro?" Sam said. "I wasn't even thinking about going pro!"

With both Perkins and Jordan returning as All-Americans, most publications listed us as number one in preseason. But Michael was feeling some pressure because he had been runner-up as Player of the Year in the voting, and now he felt he should do even better. When we went out to the Stanford Invitational, he did not even make the All-Tournament team. Against Stanford he played only seven minutes in the game because of foul trouble. Then he didn't make the All-Tournament team at the Holiday Classic in New York either. Still, we won both tournaments, and Sam Perkins was twice the MVP. After we returned to Chapel Hill from New York, Michael and I had a long talk. He was just so gung-ho, trying so hard to meet other people's expectations and to win Player of the Year awards. I said, "So what if you don't? Don't worry about other people's expectations." And from then on it was full steam ahead. Michael and Sam Perkins were great players, and they were joined by Matt Doherty, the still-developing Daugherty, Steve Hale, a player so tough he once put himself back into a game after suffering a punctured lung, and a colorful new addition in guard Kenny Smith of New York, who became yet another freshman to start his first game at Carolina.

In December we went to Syracuse, where Kenny went up against a more publicized freshman point guard from New York, Pearl Washington. I was concerned about who would guard Washington, so before the game I asked Kenny if he thought our double-teaming Scramble defense would be effective. Kenny said, "Please, Coach, it will bother him just like it does me in practice." We played the game before thirty-two thousand, but we took a sizable first-half lead that silenced their fans. Kenny was 5 for 5 on field goals with three assists, while Pearl threw the ball away three times in the first half under defensive pressure. We went on to win easily. It was one of the best games a team of mine ever played.

We won twenty-one straight games, and Michael and Sam were both listed as Player of the Year candidates while working well together. In a victory over Maryland, Michael's slam dunk for the final 2 points became a classic piece of highlight footage. I didn't see it live, as I was already hurrying to half-court to shake hands with Lefty Driesell. After the game Michael asked me, "Was that dunk too showy?" I told him I hadn't seen it. But I have seen it since and I *do* like it.

We were 17–0 when Kenny Smith broke his wrist, hit from behind and knocked to the floor on a layup against LSU. Steve Hale, who had seen considerable time off the bench, moved into Kenny's starting slot at point and did an admirable job. Steve was a little better than Kenny defensively, and a good all-around athlete, although he didn't quite have Kenny's speed with the ball. We were 25–1 going into our last regular-season game against Duke at home.

Over the next three weeks I made two major mistakes. Our doctors told me Kenny could play with a cast on his broken left wrist. We had won six straight games since our lone loss to Arkansas, but I thought Kenny could help us to give Steve some rest, and we badly wanted to finish league play at 14–0, although we had already clinched the title. Kenny was so anxious to play that, to listen to him, he didn't even need a cast. So I let Kenny come off the bench against Duke. Generally, a player's first game back after an injury could create a team chemistry problem since the team had become used to the existing substitution rotation. Our guards, Hale and Peterson, were now comfortable with their roles, while Kenny couldn't dribble with his left hand due to the cast. Still, I gave him some playing time. The result was that Hale and Peterson were thrown off balance, and we struggled. Matt Doherty had to hit a jumper at the buzzer to force overtime. Finally, we won in the second overtime, 96–83.

My second mistake was to give the team three days off because I wanted our players to enjoy spring break. We reassembled March 7 to practice for the ACC tournament in Greensboro, which would begin on March 9. We were 26–1 and ranked number one—exactly where we had been a year ago. My thinking was that we would come back refreshed and focused on the NCAAs, rather than on the ACC tourney. The result was a pair of losses. First we lost to Duke, 77–75, in the ACC tournament.

After beating Temple in the second round of the NCAA tourney, we met Bob Knight's well-prepared Indiana team. They controlled the tempo on offense (there was no shot clock) and defensively gave open jump shots to anyone on our team *except* Jordan and Perkins. We were down by 12 with 5:35 to play, but we managed to close to within 2 points with 2:07 left. But Indiana was shooting 65 percent for the game, in part thanks to Steve Alford's 9-for-13 shooting and 27 points. We never could get closer, and lost, 72–68. Virginia, the ACC's fifth place (tie) team, then upset Indiana to go to the Final Four.

I felt absolutely awful for our players and blamed myself, as I should have. Our team had finished number one in the final regular season polls, and offensively they had averaged 80 points a game while shooting 54.3 percent from the field, and 78 percent from the foul line (making 551 to our opponents' 308). And we were an excellent defensive and rebounding team. We might not have won the NCAA tournament, but we would have played better if I had not tried to bring Kenny back with his wrist in a cast, or given the team three days off for spring vacation. In the Final Four, the ACC was represented by Virginia, which lost to Houston and Akeem Olajuwon in a close game. In the championship game, my friend John Thompson and his Georgetown Hoyas beat Houston for the title. But as in 1982, I felt that we would have been the best team if the title were decided by an NBA-type series rather than a one-game finale. It was tempting to wonder what that team could have done under NBA rules, with forty-eight minutes of play, a twenty-four-second shot clock, and no packed-in zones.

Jordan won all of the National Player of the Year honors, so we couldn't have held him back too much, as some critics who went strictly by the numbers later suggested. Michael averaged 20 points a game as a sophomore and 19.6 as a junior, but any good pro scout knows that he had better check the field goal and free-throw percentages and any other number ahead of points scored. Any good pro scout also knew that Michael would be a great pro defender. The key statistic in Michael's junior season was not how many points he averaged, but the fact that he shot 55.1 percent on 448 shots. A couple of even more telling statistics were that Perkins shot 59 percent (while getting fouled 181 times and making 85.6 percent of his free throws), and eighteen-year-old Brad Daugherty shot 61 percent. Michael shared the ball with a couple of very effective players inside. Grant Hill's career average at Duke over four years was 15 points, as he shared the ball with players such as Christian Laettner, Cherokee Parks, and Bobby Hurley. Most pros who see extensive playing time will average more in the NBA than they did in college.

Michael never brought up the subject of going pro early. I simply told his father we should talk a couple of weeks after the season. Billy Cunningham had told me that Michael would be one of the first three players chosen if he came out. "Chicago needs a hero," Billy told me. "They'll draft him three." After Michael's sophomore year, when he came in second for Player of the Year, Billy had predicted, "He'd be just perfect for the pro game—no zones, the up-and-down play." The more I listened to Billy, the more convinced I became that he was right. Ironically, Billy's 76ers were drafting number five, and they were interested in Perkins, if he was available. But he ended up drafting Charles Barkley, since Sam was selected number four by Dallas.

I started asking around to get a feel for where Michael might go. The first pick in the NBA draft would belong to either Houston or Portland, to be decided by a coin flip. The third pick would go to Chicago. I called Rod Thorn, who at the time was Chicago's general manager and a friend of Billy's. He said there was no doubt in his mind that if Jordan was available, he would choose him number three overall. I called Bill Fitch in Houston, who said, "Let me check and I'll get back to you, honestly." He called me back and said, "If we win the coin flip, we're taking Olajuwon. If we lose the flip, we'll take Jordan." Next I called Stu Inman at Portland. He said, "We've done a lot of studying and we need a big guy. If we win the flip, we're taking Olajuwon and if we lose the flip, we're going to take Sam Bowie."

Armed with that information, I asked the Jordans to meet with me in my office. "If Michael enters the draft, we know he'll be picked either number two or number three, and he'll live in Houston or Chicago," I said. In either case, they were good cities for him. I informed them what sort of money would be offered, which was similar to what James Worthy had gotten from the Lakers: $2.5 million over five years, guaranteed. "It shouldn't be any less, it could be more, but this is the minimum," I said.

In that initial talk between the four of us, it was obvious that Mrs. Jordan, Deloris, really wanted Michael to get his degree, along with his sister Rosalind, before he went pro. Mr. Jordan very definitely wanted him to come out. Michael and I weren't sure; I was neutral, and he was undecided. Meanwhile, Eddie, Roy, and Bill wrote down all of the reasons he should stay. They didn't want him to go. But I kept thinking of Cunningham saying, "Chicago needs a hero." Other than Bears running back Walter Payton, they didn't have one.

I said, "Michael, the decision is yours. I'm comfortable either way."

I certainly could have talked him out of it, there's no doubt in my mind. He was wavering. "I want to be able to give my speech at the senior banquet," he said. He was genuinely undecided. I said, "The three of you get together and make your decision, and we'll have a press conference in the morning." That night they talked, and the next morning we met a half hour before the scheduled press conference. They had decided for Michael to go pro. "It's a good decision," I said, and I meant it.

The next step was to choose an agent. We had a short list of three or four firms that had done well with our other players, a policy I recommend to other coaches.

I felt it was my job to give a player as much information as possible about his prospects in the NBA, and to shepherd him through the process of choosing representation, because agents weren't always reliable. Agents act as if they can get somebody drafted, when the truth is they never can, just as no one could *make* me give a scholarship to a player. We learned about agents over the years through experience as we watched our former players such as Larry Brown and Doug Moe negotiate in the pros. There were times when I wished they had had more help handling their money.

Back in 1972 we had three players who were prospective pros in Bob McAdoo, Dennis Wuycik, and Bill Chamberlain. Since we didn't yet have a system in place for screening and selecting agents, I personally met with several who were vying to represent our players. However, I did depend on my lawyer, Travis Porter, to sit in on the presentations to the player and his family. One agent came to my office and told me that if I delivered a player to him, he would take 10 percent of their salary in commission and send 5 percent of it to me. Naturally I told him to leave the office. Later I told the story to a New York newspaper. The paper quoted him as saying that he had never met me, nor had he ever been to Chapel Hill.

We finally came up with a system that minimized the risks of players falling into dishonest hands, I felt. Each May we would ask a handful of prospective agents and attorneys to come to Chapel Hill for interviews. In a conference room, we would gather a panel made up of the player, his parents or guardians, myself, and some loyal friends and advisers to the program, among them former deans of our business schools. They were invariably formidable and tough-minded men like Paul Rizzo, the former IBM vice chairman, and Paul Fulton, the president of Sara Lee Inc., and Jack Evans, our present faculty representative of athletes, sat in for several years. Former dean of the law school, Ken Broun, and our former-player-turned-attorney Richard Vinroot often sat in, along with Angela Lee, who worked in our office and has a law degree, and Bob Eubanks, former chairman of the UNC board of trustees and a sharp financial analyst. An annual presence was Bill Miller, an accountant from Charlotte, who has sat in on every agent interview since 1985, and who is very tough in asking the agents questions. Bill has handled all financial matters for me, Roy Williams, Bill Guthridge, Eddie Fogler, and Phil Ford over the years, and he is so meticulous in looking over financial records on behalf of our players that he will call up the financial manager and tell him he is overpaying on a bond by one eighth of a percent.

Two or three lawyers representing a firm would sit at a conference table and make a presentation, and then we would subject them to thorough questioning. The interview would last an hour and a half. After the interview, we would inform the group that there was not to be contact with our player again. The player and his advisers would tell me which agents he'd like to talk to again by telephone.

Once the agent passed muster and was chosen to represent a player, I would make one thing very clear. "If you do a good job with him, and if he's happy, you will be invited back here again," I said. That would be the carrot. But then came the warning. "Don't mess up," I would say. "Or not only will you not come back here, but I'll tell every coaching friend I know that you haven't done right by our guys."

One firm that had impressed me in the seventies was Dell, Craighill, Fentress, and Benton, which had been founded by a group of friends from the University of Virginia Law School, and whose associates had been close to Robert Kennedy in the 1960s. They served as agents to Arthur Ashe and

Stan Smith, but in the 1970s they began adding basketball players to their client list, and in 1972 Dennis Wuycik was one of them. They also helped George Karl when he became a free agent in 1973. One thing that helped their cause was that Frank Craighill had been a Morehead scholar at Carolina before he went on to law school. I also liked the fact that they billed by the hour, at a rate of $100, like most law firms, rather than charging commission.

However, when I received a copy of the bill to Bobby Jones for 270 hours for negotiating a contract with the Denver Nuggets, I hit the ceiling. There were four lawyers involved, each being paid $100 an hour. That resulted in a $27,000 bill. I called immediately and told them Bobby would not pay that much. It should have been an easy negotiation, since Bobby had been drafted third by Houston in the NBA. For the future, we told them we expected to know in advance what the costs would be. We settled on a 2 percent fee for salary when Bobby received it, and they earned more for endorsement contracts they negotiated on Bobby's behalf.

But by the time Michael Jordan, Sam Perkins, and Matt Doherty were ready to go to the pros, the firm had undergone a "divorce." Frank Craighill and Lee Fentress split off to form their representation company, Advantage, while Donald Dell and Ray Benton formed ProServ Inc. They divided their clients based on which lawyers had worked most closely with the players. Phil Ford, James Worthy, and Mike O'Koren were assigned to ProServ, while Bobby Jones went to Advantage.

We invited both groups in to meet with our players in 1984, as well as Larry Fleisher and Bill Madden, who also represented some of our former players. Each year I tried to invite a new group in because I did want our players to go with different agencies. I thought it was more healthy to let the agencies compete against each other. I didn't tell our players whom to go with, but I hoped it worked out that we had some variety.

At the end of the interview process, Michael and his parents chose Donald Dell and ProServ, while Sam and his guardian chose Lee Fentress and Advantage. Both were reputable organizations with good track records. ProServ's Donald Dell had two young assistants, Bill Strickland and David Falk. Donald did all the talking and would head up the negotiations for Michael with Chicago. David Falk sat in on the negotiations and would help with marketing and matters such as his sneaker endorsements. A few years later, Falk and Strickland would split from Dell and form their own company. But back then, Falk was a disciple of Dell's.

After Michael's decision to go to the NBA, I had asked Donald to call Rod Thorn to talk possible contract figures if Chicago drafted him. I did say he might not be chosen by the Jordans, but to make this one call. After Dell was in fact chosen, there was one thing I wanted him to do: arrange an attendance clause. Michael was a huge draw, an Olympic gold medal winner, and the National Player of the Year, while Chicago had averaged just 6,182 fans per game the previous year. I told Dell, "Be sure you get an attendance clause in his contract." I was certain Michael would significantly boost ticket sales in that arena, and I thought he should earn a bonus for it. I was still thinking back to what Billy said: "Chicago needs a hero."

The contract that Dell and Falk handed Michael to sign didn't have an attendance clause, and it gave the seventh option year to the Bulls instead of to Michael, which was unheard of. What's more, the amount was too low in my opinion. Later Dell wrote me a letter, explaining that guards just didn't command the same amount of money that big men did, and compared Michael's contract to that of Sidney Moncrief in Milwaukee. I said, "He's a player. Don't worry about positions." Bob Knight, who had coached Michael on the Olympic team that summer, felt exactly the same way. He told his acquaintances in the NBA, "Draft him as a player." He understood Michael wasn't a conventional guard. Before Michael signed with the Bulls, I went to see him play in an Olympic team exhibition game in Greensboro, where I sat with then-owner Jonathan Kovler. He kept saying, "Michael's a guard." But then Michael retrieved a great rebound. I couldn't resist saying, "I don't know of a guard who could do that."

I told Michael, "Don't sign the contract." But Donald and David came back and said, "Well, they wouldn't give us that kind of money." The result was that for years Michael was among the most significantly underpaid men in the league, even through his second contract. In my estimation, he made what he was worth only during the final two years in Chicago. Michael's presence in Chicago indeed created a ticket bonanza. In his rookie season the arena went from being two-thirds empty to sold out—an increase of more than twelve thousand a game. He would have made big money had the attendance clause been included.

I was always interested in the contracts of our players, and I always hoped they weren't underpaid compared with other league salaries. Still, when any of them signed a contract, I felt they should live up to it. In Michael's case, once he signed he believed as I did about contracts. He simply went about his job.

The second thing that upset me was their commission on Michael's shoe deal, which has been hailed as a breakthrough and a model of its kind. In conversations with the attorneys during the interviews, I told them, "My five-year-old, Kristen, could get Michael three hundred thousand dollars a year on a sneaker contract." It was obvious that was the bottom floor for signing Michael to a sneaker deal, and I suggested that whomever Michael chose to represent him was not entitled to the usual 10 percent advertising commission on that amount. It was the very least Michael would command, no matter who drew up the contract, because Converse, Adidas, and Nike were all preparing for a bidding war. The commission on the shoe deal, the Jordans and I decided, was going to be either 10 percent on anything above $300,000 per year, or 5 percent of the total deal when it was paid. It would be the Jordans' choice after they saw the contract. Donald Dell and David Falk agreed to this when Michael chose them to represent him.

But while I was in Europe giving a basketball clinic, David called Mr. Jordan suggesting a third option regarding the shoe commission. David explained that he thought it would be about the same for the Jordans, while at the same time better for ProServ. He assured Mr. Jordan that I wouldn't mind this third alternative. However, he made that statement without ever speaking to me. Michael signed the deal.

I called the Jordans from Europe and asked which shoe company he had chosen. Michael told me excitedly that Nike had great new ideas and he had gone with them. "Which one of those two options for the shoe commission did you choose?" I asked. He replied, "David and Donald had a third option." "What?" I exclaimed. "Let me talk to your dad." I knew I was upset and didn't want to dampen Michael's enthusiasm. "What's this about a third option?" I asked Mr. Jordan. He explained that ProServ had told him it was essentially the same deal, but that it would mean more money for ProServ without at all hurting Michael. "It doesn't sound like the same deal to me," I said. "Me either," said Mr. Jordan. I haven't checked the figures since, but at the time I didn't see an added benefit to the Jordans. More than two years later, David apologized to me in a Charlotte coffee shop for not talking it over with me first.

He also apologized for speaking with Brad Daugherty the day before the NBA draft of 1986. Brad was choosing between ProServ and Advantage, but neither group was to speak with him by phone or in person until he had made his decision. I found out David had broken our rule. During a phone conversation while Brad was in New York, Brad mentioned to me that he had had a good breakfast with David Falk in the hotel and that he had also seen him on the bus from the hotel to the draft. Brad did end up rejecting Falk and choosing Advantage instead.

I never told a player not to go with David Falk or Donald Dell, with two exceptions: (1) when David contacted Brad after we asked him not to, and (2) when David called Jerry Stackhouse directly instead of going through our Agent Day process. As long as Michael was pleased with Donald and David, they were certainly welcome to talk with our seniors. I tell our players they may choose anyone whom we invite to Agent Day. I don't even suggest an agent when asked. The decision is made by the player and his family.

It's said that David Falk made Michael Jordan a lot of money over the years. I know that is true. But Michael Jordan created David Falk more than David Falk created Michael Jordan.

Michael kept his emotional connection to Carolina through the years, which overjoyed all of us. I loved it that he wore his Carolina shorts underneath his Bulls uniform. In his second season with the Bulls he was trying to recover from a foot injury, and the Bulls wanted him to stay up there and rehab. But Michael insisted that he wanted to be in Chapel Hill, and he came back and recuperated a whole winter here, in time to rejoin them for the latter part of the season.

That same year, I was changing planes in the old Atlanta airport with some time to spare when I realized a Bulls game was on TV. They were playing the Celtics, and Michael was having a great game. I stood in the middle of an aisle and watched as he poured the points in. He hit 30 and then 40. A crowd started to gather, and shouts went up as Michael hit 50 points. I stood there, my neck craned toward the screen, going crazy with everyone else, as the game went into overtime.

I looked at my watch, worrying about my flight, which was two gates away. Michael finished with 61 points. I saw his final total, ran for my gate, and made the plane.

Michael warned me that he was going to retire that first time when he walked away from the game in 1993 to play baseball. He felt such an obligation to always be at the very top of his game, night in and night out, and he was aware that fans on the road expected him to be at his best. The demands on him were constant and unrelenting. James Jordan had told me, "I think this is going to be his last year." I suspected he had a case of burnout, and I thought it was a smart decision for him to retire if he felt this way. I told him so before the season began. Also, we agreed it would be interesting for him to give baseball a shot. During that 1993 basketball season he told me privately he was working on his hitting at an indoor batting cage.

Michael played all kinds of mind games with himself trying to stay fresh. One day he called me from Sacramento and said he was really worn out. I said, "How are you going to get up for this game?" Michael said, "I'm going to pretend the guy guarding me thinks I'm too old, and I'm going to have to show him."

I had always promised Michael I would come see him play at least one game in Chicago. One afternoon in 1993 when he was in the midst of the play-offs against the Knicks, he called. "You better get up here," he said.

"So the retirement's still on?" I asked.

"I haven't wavered for a moment," he said. "But I'll still wait until the fall to be sure."

I was up there the very next day. My friend Paul Fulton is a Carolina alumnus and a huge fan of Michael Jordan and the Bulls, and as president of the Sara Lee Company he had season tickets for the Bulls games. He said to be sure to arrive in time to see the player introductions. I got there early, in time to see Michael beforehand in the dressing room, where he sat in a special room arranging all of the free game tickets he gave away. I had a bite to eat with his dad and visited with his mother. I reached my seat in the old Chicago Stadium arena just as the lights went out. Then a spotlight came on, the music blared, and an announcer introduced the first four starters. Then he screamed, "And now, from North Carolina . . ." I couldn't hear the rest because the noise in the arena was so loud, but I'm certain he said, "Michael Jordan."

I honestly believed Michael would make it in baseball because of the rapid improvement I had seen in his basketball when he was at North Carolina. I have been told that he had improved as a hitter throughout the first summer, and I'm certain he would have worked at it. Who knows, if there hadn't been a baseball strike? Of course, it helps to know that he returned to the NBA late in 1994–95 to win three more titles before retiring again in '98.

To me it is the defining characteristic of Michael Jordan's career that he steadily improved every year he played the game. Recently I asked Michael when exactly he felt he became such a "pure" shooter. He replied, "In about my fourth year in the NBA." In fact, I would go so far as to say that the best he ever played was in his last season in the NBA. Even on the day he retired I didn't see any erosion in his skills, his leadership, his savvy, or even his quickness defensively.

Michael was extremely gifted athletically and is perhaps the most competitive person I know. (This is also why I want to be his partner in golf.) But it frustrates me that his unstinting work ethic is overshadowed by his many other accomplishments. His development was very grounded in principles; it wasn't otherwordly, much as he could make it look so. You could trace his growth quite clearly. He is a human being first, and the fact that he is so determined to get better—in everything he does—is the great lesson to be learned from him. Nobody I know worked harder at his craft than Michael Jordan.

I always told our players this quote, which I heard from a great Methodist pastor, Dr. Ernest Fitzgerald: "If you do what you can, with what you have, where you are, then you can't be a failure." Michael just did it best.

10

Keeping Our Perspective

Interest in college basketball skyrocketed beginning in the late 1970s, thanks in large part to more games being shown on television. With our North Carolina teams on television so often, we would be representing our entire university. I think our players responded admirably in that regard.

Increasingly, college basketball was a game played out on national television, with huge sums at stake in the form of steadily spiraling rights fees. In 1995, CBS would pay *$1.725 billion* for the rights to televise the NCAA tournament over eight years, the richest deal in the history of sports television up to that point. (The new contract will be even more!) In contrast, when my 1953 Kansas team played Indiana for the national championship, the local television station, WDAF-TV, agreed to show the game on *delayed* telecast after the conclusion of a boxing match between Bobby Dykes and Pierre Longlois. But while TV brought about more interest and more coverage, it could also cloud priorities. Everyone wanted to appear on TV, and with the appearance of the ESPN cable network in 1979, more games than ever could be broadcast nationally. Some schools would agree to any starting time just to be involved. But the good news was that it was a game greatly suited for TV. Alumni across the country could watch their favorite teams; viewing the game brought families together, ten-year-olds side by side with grandparents in the living room; and it was a lot better for children than violent programming. I still get letters from people telling me how much the family bonded watching North Carolina basketball on television.

North Carolina was on TV constantly. When Carolina made it to the Final Four, applications to the university rose dramatically; we would have as many as nineteen thousand prospective students vying for three thousand places in a freshman class in the late 1980s and 1990s, and a great majority of these were in the top tenth percentile academically. (Carolina had long been ranked in the top twenty-five of universities nationally, and it was an early member of the select American Association of Universities.) Through basketball we had a national fan base, experiencing the kind of widespread popularity enjoyed by a couple of other schools, such as UCLA in its heyday and the perennial power Notre Dame in football.

The basketball program was truly "the front porch" of the university, as Chancellor Ferebee Taylor once explained. Chancellor Taylor had been a Rhodes scholar following his undergraduate days at Carolina and a corporate lawyer in New York before returning to Chapel Hill as chancellor from 1972 to 1980. He liked to say the most important part of the "house" was the education of the students, but he understood the value of athletics in their rightful place (and he continues to be a good friend). What he meant by the phrase *the front porch* was that, quite often, our basketball team—as well as the cheerleaders and band—were the most visible aspect of the university, right down to our faces. Even the football team could hide behind their helmets. So we tried to do it right.

I asked myself certain questions: As a public figure, what were my obligations when it came to taking stands on social issues? The same as any faculty member: to say what I believed. Should a collegiate coach endorse products in advertising? I chose not to, since I felt it might separate me from faculty. But these were not always simple questions.

I tried to tell myself that I was a teacher as well as a coach of a Division 1 program. But the jobs differed in one important respect: A teacher didn't have as many people watching the examination and grading his students in their living rooms. There were a couple million assistant coaches out there watching us, anxious to critique our performance and our comportment. There was no better example of that than my announcement in 1997 that I was retiring. I was shocked to find that my press conference was carried live on ESPN. I couldn't help mentioning that I felt our society's values were mixed up. When a Nobel Prize–winning professor retired, there was a simple announcement in the newspaper. It was a Kierkegaardian "switching of price tags."

In 1981 Carolina began an extraordinary streak of thirteen straight seasons in which we reached the Sweet Sixteen or better in the NCAA tournament, and in the process received as much coverage as any team in the country. But our players won sixty-five NCAA tournament games and thirteen ACC tournament championships, and won outright or shared seventeen regular-season ACC titles. They did all of this while representing the university in an exemplary fashion on the court in front of those vast audiences.

Nothing typified the college basketball boom more than the building of the Smith Center, which opened in 1986. Chancellor Taylor had put the fund-raising for it on hold in 1978 until the funding for the new library was complete. It was a great decision, since the "house" needed some work. By the time the basketball arena was completed, it held 21,572 seats and cost about $34 million. But I said to the administration, "You know, we don't really need this." I thought we were doing just fine in Carmichael, which seated ten thousand at the time, and that the money and effort could go instead to a burn center for the university hospital or something other than "the front porch." From a business standpoint, I've always believed that when you *can't* get a ticket, that's the best situation for a program. Nor did I buy the theory that we needed a state-of-the-art facility to recruit. I don't think a facility necessarily sells a prospect. If you're winning and improving players' skills, and they graduate, those things, coupled with our beautiful campus and college town, are the things that sell. Still, it was difficult to believe that even in the early seventies, in the nine-thousand-seat Greensboro coliseum, the crowds for some single games against Penn State, Northwestern, and Nebraska numbered less than four thousand fans. Times had changed.

Although I wasn't pushing for a new arena, I was enlisted to help in fund-raising, since all of the money to build it would come from private sources, with no taxpayer or state help, which made sense. What finally sold me on the project was the fact that the increased capacity would mean more students could get into the games, as well as alumni. Also, I had great respect for Skipper Bowles, the legendary Carolina political fund-raiser who was chairing the project. Skipper was the father of Erskine Bowles, President Clinton's former chief of staff. Skipper said to me, "You've got to go out with me on the dog-and-pony show." We went off on a tour of forty stops throughout the state, but I don't know how much help I was. Skipper was expert at persuading a crowd to open up their checkbooks. But I wasn't as ambitious. I would say, "You know, we don't really need this arena. There are a lot more important things on which to spend your money: the church, the university, to fight poverty." Which was true. Then I would add, "But if you're giving to the university and there's some left over, maybe you could go in this direction." The strange thing was, the more I said we didn't need a new arena, the more they seemed to want one.

On one stop we went into the home of a wealthy alum and made our presentation.

"What do you think I should give?" the man asked.

I wasn't comfortable answering the question, and after stammering for a few seconds, I said: "What about ten thousand dollars?"

Skipper excused us and took me outside the office for a few minutes for a good talk. We reentered the room, and Skipper asked the man to ask the question again. Then Skipper took over, and when all was said and done the man gave $250,000, which guaranteed him buying good seats as long as he continued to give to the Educational Foundation annually.

From that point on, Skipper said he would do the talking when the question of the amount of the pledge came up. He was a generous man himself who did not mind asking others for money to support what he considered to be worthwhile causes.

Some basketball people say it's harder to win in a big building than it is in a bandbox where the home crowd is close to the court and more of a factor. Still, our players have won in the Smith Center at almost the identical rate that they won in smaller Carmichael. Our program has remained pretty much a fixture in the nation's Top Ten. In 1984–85 we were ignored by the experts in the preseason, not picked to do much of anything with the loss of Jordan, Perkins, and Doherty. Instead, we went 27–9, tied for the ACC regular-season title, and finished number eight in the country.

It was the season in which Kenny Smith and Brad Daugherty came into their own. But in the first round of NCAA play, we lost Steve Hale, a young man who was among the most self-sacrificing players we ever had, to an injury. Hale was an immensely popular figure, a left-hander with longish brown hair that flew like a horse's mane when he ran. Basketball was fourth on his list of priorities after religion, family, and studies, but on the court he played as if his life depended on it. He was as tough and competitive as they came, in addition to being a brilliant student.

Hale was racing for a layup en route to an NCAA tournament victory over Middle Tennessee State when he was shoved in the back and took a vicious fall. Typically, he got up and prepared to shoot his free throws, even though we could see a lump the size of a cantaloupe on his shoulder. We removed him from the game before he could shoot the free throw, and two days later he underwent serious shoulder surgery. Great victories over a well-coached

Notre Dame at South Bend (Digger Phelps, the coach, had joked that it wasn't a home game since we used the home team bench) and Auburn in Birmingham then got us to the regional final before we succumbed to the eventual national champion, Villanova, 56–44.

In 1985–86, for the second straight year, we lost to the eventual NCAA champion, this time Louisville, in the round of sixteen.

The year had begun with great promise as we won our first twenty-one games and were ranked number one in the country. We defeated Reggie Miller's UCLA team, 107–70, in what was supposed to be the inaugural game for the new arena. But it wasn't completed yet, so we played in Carmichael instead. Brad Daugherty was twelve of twelve for us. Still number one, on January 18 we finally *did* inaugurate the Smith Center by toppling number-three Duke, 95–92. Hale scored 28 points, many of them on backdoor cuts, over a Duke team that would lose to Louisville in the national finals. In a wheelchair, Skipper Bowles would throw up the ceremonial opening jump ball. But on February 20, Hale dived for a loose ball against Maryland and took a knee in his chest, collapsing his lung. He put himself back in the game in the overtime period.

Hale returned from that injury just in time for the postseason, but we weren't as sharp as we needed to be. We got past Utah in Ogden, Utah, and Alabama-Birmingham before we lost to Louisville in the Sweet Sixteen. With the conclusion of our season, three valued friends and memorable personalities departed: Hale, fittingly, went on to medical school; Brad Daugherty became the NBA's number-one draft pick; and Eddie Fogler took the head coaching job at Wichita State, leaving our bench after fifteen years as a coach and four as a player.

But the 1987 Carolina team was one of the best in history. That team beat thirty-two teams against a great schedule, ranked number two in the final poll, and went 14–0 in the ACC, only to suffer a severe disappointment in the NCAA tournament. We stayed healthy except for our All-American senior point guard, Kenny Smith, who had knee problems at midseason. Kenny missed a home game against Georgia Tech with his sore knee, but we won by 37 in what may have been one of the best pressure defense performances of Carolina teams. Then he was barely cleared to play at Clemson, and had 41 points on fourteen of nineteen shooting. But afterwards doctors decided he needed arthroscopic surgery, and he sat out a 2-point loss at Notre Dame when we were number one in the poll in early February. Just one week later, he returned for a win at N.C. State, 96–79. It was a triumph of modern medicine and our doctor, Tim Taft.

Our ACC freshman of the year was J. R. Reid of Virginia Beach, but it was a senior-dominated team. Smith would surpass Phil Ford as our all-time assist leader and earn one National Player of the Year award, while Joe Wolf made All-ACC and would be the number-seventeen pick in the first round of the NBA draft. Their fellow seniors Dave Popson and Curtis Hunter were crucial contributors as well. Sophomore guard Jeff Lebo, a great perimeter shooter from Carlisle, Pennsylvania, with floppy hair and cleft chin, was third among our five double-figure scorers and had a great year playing alongside Kenny. Another freshman, willowy six-ten Californian Scott Williams, played in all thirty-six games and provided frontcourt depth.

Our 32–4 mark tied the school record for victories. Our season ended in the regional finals, where we faced the team that would be runner-up for the national championship, Syracuse, which featured three future NBA familiars in Derrick Coleman, Ronnie Seikaly, and Sherman Douglas. We made a great comeback and had a chance to tie the score with less than a minute to play, but lost, 79–75.

I was distraught for our seniors, truly down. We had been contenders for the championship all year, and we were good enough to win. Our only losses were by 5 at UCLA, by 2 at Notre Dame, by 1 in the ACC final to N.C. State (a team we had beaten by 17 twice in the regular season), and by 4 to Syracuse. All four losses by 5 points or less.

But anyone searching for perspective on the game of basketball didn't have to look far the following fall. On October 15, 1987, the worst few days I ever experienced as a coach began with a 4 A.M. phone call. The call was a nightmare that was real. That fall, Scott Williams's mother, Rita, had confided in me that her marriage to Scott's father, Al Williams, was over, and that she was frightened of what Al might do. I talked to her on October 7 from the Los Angeles airport, and she told me that she had moved in with her sister and that Al threatened her life. She said she felt better since she had switched cars, and that she had done all she could legally to protect herself from him, seeking help from the police. She added that she had made a recent trip with three girlfriends to Palm Springs and had had a great time.

Eddie Fogler, Bill Guthridge, and I had enjoyed two trips to the Williams home when we were recruiting Scott in the fall of his senior year in high school in Hacienda Heights, California. The family was extremely hospitable and intelligent about the recruiting process. Scott was a model student, a thoughtful person, and a prized recruit, so it was no wonder that everyone from Dodgers manager Tommy LaSorda to Bill Cosby was calling him to push their favorite school. But the entire family made education their first priority; Rita's parents both had master's degrees, and Al, a personable man, was happy in his managerial work for Sears. Rita went to a lot of trouble over coffee and dessert. Off the porch was a beautiful swimming pool with a waterfall. Everything appeared to be perfect.

But on that October 15 morning, I woke to a ringing telephone to hear the voice of Rita's brother, Corvan, on the other end of the line telling me that Al had shot and killed Rita, and then had turned the gun on himself in a murder-suicide. Looking back, it was my feeling that Al had chosen the opening day of basketball practice to commit this tragic act because he knew Scott would be in constant touch with his basketball family.

After I hung up the phone, Linnea, who knew Rita, sat with me and we talked and grieved. At 6 A.M. I finally called Bill Guthridge and told him the dreadful news. "I need company when I go over to the dorm to tell Scott," I said.

We decided not to wake Scott yet because we knew it would be the last sleep he would get for some time. We checked his schedule and found he had a 9 A.M. class. Finally, at 8 A.M. we met at the office and drove over to his dormitory, Granville Towers. Scott was getting dressed to go to class.

"Well, your dad did it," I said.

Then I told him what his uncle had told me.

Scott finished dressing and said he needed to take a walk. He left the dorm and walked around for about fifteen minutes or so while Bill and I stood outside waiting for him. When he returned, we helped him prepare to go to California for the funeral. Linnea and I flew out to Los Angeles the day before the service to see what help we could be.

Finally, Scott returned to school. I had the uneasy feeling he wasn't dealing with his grief. It would take him years, if ever, to come to terms with what had happened, according to professionals in the field of violent trauma and sudden loss.

It used to be that October 15 was a good day for me. It represented the official start of fall practices and a new season. But never again would I feel the same way about that date. It was surely a difficult time for all of us associated with the Carolina program. Somehow we struggled through it, as did Scott and his family.

All who know Scott are delighted with him today as an intelligent, caring, well-adjusted young man who is happily married and continues as an NBA player, for Milwaukee, having completed nine seasons. While with the Chicago Bulls he was part of three NBA championships and his current NBA contract extends until 2002.

.   .   .

As we returned to practice and prepared for the 1987–88 season, we had just one senior returning, Ranzino Smith, a homegrown guard from Chapel Hill. We had lost four significant players to graduation, and no one expected us to do much under the circumstances.

But we served notice that we were a team to be reckoned with when we met top-ranked Syracuse, with Seikaly, Coleman, and Douglas, in the Hall of Fame Tip-Off Classic in Springfield, Massachusetts, on November 21. We accomplished a memorable upset, despite the fact that we entered the game under duress; earlier I'd suspended sophomore J. R. Reid and senior Steve Bucknall, two of our key players, for one game as punishment for their parts in an off-campus problem with an N.C. State fan. We were young to begin with, but without Reid and Bucknall the team we'd have to put on the court against powerful Syracuse would be seriously inexperienced. It meant that Rick Fox, our freshman from the Bahamas by way of Warsaw, Indiana, would have to take the court for his first starting assignment against the number-one team in the nation, and so would his fellow redshirt freshman Pete Chilcutt.

We seemed out of sync against the Orangemen, who led us by 14 points with 15:39 left. Then we mounted another one of our furious comebacks, in part thanks to the crucial contribution of Fox, who scored 15 points on seven of eight shooting, and to the play of guards Jeff Lebo and Ranzino Smith.

We cut the deficit to 85–83 with just a few seconds to go, with one last possession. We worked the ball to Chilcutt, who hit a turnaround jumper as the horn sounded, to send the game into overtime. We eventually won, 96–93. That kick-started a season in which we eventually went 27–7 and were first in the ACC regular season (we played the usual eleven games at home, plus two with home crowds in Greensboro, and had a number of tough road games, including victories at UCLA and Illinois). J. R. Reid became a consensus All-American, and Jeff Lebo and Ranzino Smith developed reputations as marksmen, Lebo shooting 46.4 percent from 3-point range, and Smith 41 percent. And Scott Williams averaged 13 points and was a key on defense, which was remarkable under the circumstances.

In the second round of the NCAA tournament in Salt Lake City, we faced a dangerous opponent in Loyola-Marymount, coached by Paul Westhead. That team played at a furious pace. They put up a shot every six or seven seconds, and on defense they overplayed all receivers, switching on all screens, forcing one-on-one play without defensive help, which tends to bring about quick shots. It was a style that was unique to college ball, and there was no way to prepare for it in one day—which was the same problem we tried to give to our opponents.

Before practice I explained to the players that Loyola-Marymount's style of play meant that both teams would probably score 100 points (we averaged 82 for the year). Doug Moe, head coach of the Denver Nuggets, who was in town for a night game against the Utah Jazz, came by our practice and was surprised we spent so much time drilling on our backdoor plays. We also practiced getting back and picking up on five-on-five defense.

We had a drill to prepare for Loyola's style. One of our players would score a layup to start the drill, and our second team was instructed to sprint the ball to the other end of the court without even taking it out of bounds. Anyone on the second team would shoot within eight seconds, and we practiced boxing out for the rebound. We repeated it over and over. It was the closest we could come to approximating the play of Loyola-Marymount. Doug watched for a while and remarked that if the Nuggets, who were leading the NBA in scoring, were to play Loyola, there would be 300 points scored.

I told our players we wouldn't shoot any jumpers in this game—unless Jeff Lebo or Ranzino Smith had an open 3-pointer. Rather, we wanted post-up shots from J. R. Reid, Scott Williams, and Pete Chilcutt, as well as layups from our backdoor cuts. The result: We shot 81 percent from the floor, an NCAA tournament record. Loyola-Marymount was as well drilled in its system as we feared, with the late Hank Gathers leading the way, but we won, 127–97. I was glad we wouldn't have to play against them again. Our streak of reaching the NCAA Sweet Sixteen remained intact. After beating Michigan, we lost to Arizona in the Super Eight.

Our chief rivalries in the ACC ran in cycles, although we were usually the top target of the other teams in the league. We considered it a compliment to be in that position, and our players responded to that challenge consistently well. In 1978, Duke had replaced N.C. State as the team many of our fans most liked us to beat. Coach Bill Foster took his Duke team to the 1978 NCAA championship game, losing to Kentucky, which indicated Duke was back to the level of Coach Bubas's days in the 1960s.

Consistency is not easy to maintain in our conference, where there were so many good teams. Remarkably, all nine ACC schools have been in the NCAA Final Eight since 1980. The arrival of Ralph Sampson, who was seven three and as athletic as most gifted small forwards, catapulted Virginia into the national limelight. We had some sensational games with Virginia in that four-year period from 1979–80 to 1983. Terry Holland did an excellent job coaching his players. Virginia made it to the Final Four in 1984 after Sampson graduated and was the number-one NBA draft pick. At the end of

Sampson's four-year career in Charlottesville, I was surprised when Rick Brewer, our sports information director, informed me that we had won six of ten meetings against Virginia in that time period. All the games were close. Of course, the dynamic Lefty Driesell had some terrific teams at Maryland during this time. So, we had more than a full plate at North Carolina trying to fend off these strong programs.

It grew even more intense prior to the 1981 season. Three new coaches came into the league at the same time—the media called them the "Young Lions." Jim Valvano arrived at N.C. State, Bobby Cremins at Georgia Tech, and Mike Krzyzewski at Duke. While I was impressed with all of the coaches against whom I competed in the ACC, it wasn't easy to build friendships in such a competitive environment. The fans of the various schools made it hard because they wanted to win so badly. Also, when your teams play against each other two or three times a year, and you often recruit the same players, building a mutually respectful relationship takes some doing. Norm Sloan, the former coach at N.C. State, and I were late learning that, but we did, and I consider him a friend today.

Ann Holland, Terry's wife, helped us bridge this gap in 1981 when she organized a dinner for the basketball coaches and their wives to be held at the ACC spring meetings. This helped us get to know each other better away from the packed arenas, and I think it did make things better in our conference.

In the spring of 1981, Linnea and I arrived at this dinner a few minutes late. After general introductions, there wasn't a table available near the group, so Linnea and I seated ourselves at a table about fifteen feet away. Seeing us isolated in this way, Jim and Pam Valvano graciously came over to join us. We enjoyed our conversation with them. Linnea particularly liked each of the coaches' wives and would look forward to seeing them at the conference meeting annually. We added up the number of children of the families at that first dinner. The coaches had four boys and twenty-one girls. Linnea had just given birth to Kelly in February, so we had the newest child.

These dinners became more relaxed as the years passed. We named Bobby Cremins as the unofficial program chairman to decide which subjects we should discuss. Bobby came up with some interesting ones, just let me say that. Still, there was plenty of competitive interplay in our coaches' meetings. The morning after this initial dinner, I excused myself to go to the restroom. Later, Bobby asked: "What do they have against you?" Apparently while I was away, one coach had said: "We've got to figure a way to get that guy." Bobby, when he coached at Appalachian State, used to come to Chapel Hill to look at basketball tapes with Eddie Fogler. We liked

Bobby, he liked us, and he didn't understand why another league coach wanted to plot against us. Ann's dinner helped us overcome such petty jealousies.

When Tommy LaGarde, one of our former players, was married in 1983, he had his wedding reception at a Raleigh Country Club community where Jim and Pam lived. Before going to the reception, Linnea and I decided to go by and surprise the Valvanos. They were delighted to see us, and we sat around and talked for about an hour. In fact, Linnea and I were late getting to the reception because we enjoyed our visit so much.

Even if we eliminated recruiting, and instead pulled together a team from the student body with open tryouts, there would still be a rivalry between Duke and Carolina. Or N.C. State and Carolina. Or Wake Forest and Carolina. In the last few years the Duke rivalry has been the most intense.

Under Mike Krzyzewski's leadership Duke again became the school our students would most like to defeat. Bob Knight was Mike's college coach at West Point, and Mike served as one of his assistant coaches at Indiana. Mike was coaching at Army in 1980, and had done a good job there, though he learned, as did Bob Spear earlier at Air Force, that winning at the service academies is hard. Even though West Point was coming off a losing season, Bob Knight called me in the spring of 1980 to tell me that Mike had his choice of two Division 1 jobs—Duke or Iowa State. I remember Bob saying he thought the Iowa State job might be better since the Big Eight wasn't as strong in basketball as the ACC. We both agreed, though, that Duke would be easier to sell to recruits. Bob said he had to call Tom Butters again—Duke's athletics director at the time—to continue his campaign for Mike. Bob had other of his former players and assistant coaches doing great coaching jobs at the time. Certainly, a résumé that includes time learning under Bob Knight would be a huge positive for anyone interested in hiring a coach.

Duke has long had an excellent basketball tradition. Vic Bubas took multiple teams to the Final Four when he coached there. Bill Foster's 1978 Duke team was beaten in the NCAA championship game. Now, Duke is a solid national contender each year with Mike in charge.

He brought the background of Knight's pressure defense, a great work ethic, leadership skills, and a fantastic ability to sell young players on Duke University for their college experience. His teams have won four official ACC basketball championships, seven regular-season titles, and two national championships, with a remarkable eight trips to the Final Four. As a head coach of international teams, Mike's 1990 U.S.A. team won the bronze medal in Argentina in the FIBA World Championship and the silver medal in the Goodwill Games in Seattle. He was also head coach of the U.S.A. team in the World University Games in 1987, which won a silver medal.

Carolina-Duke emerged as the top college basketball rivalry of the 1990s. To the credit of our players, Carolina had won fourteen games to Duke's seven in the decade until Duke won three times in 1999. I was amazed to learn it was only the third time that Duke had swept us in seasonal competition since 1964, while we swept them fourteen times during the same time frame.

I was always hearing how creative the Duke students were. But I didn't think it was creative when I heard them chant, as our players were being introduced, "Antawn sucks," or "Vince sucks," and so forth. Also, back in 1969, they named Carolina players on their All-Ugly team, and in 1980 they named an All-Acne team with a Carolina player the captain. But in 1989, at a time when competition between the two programs was becoming especially heated, I felt they crossed the line.

Over the '89 regular season, Carolina and Duke split road meetings: We upset the undefeated and top-ranked Blue Devils at Cameron Indoor Stadium in January, 91–71, while in the final game of the season they beat us at home, 88–86. During the game at Duke, the students decided to be cute, or what they thought was cute, by raising a sign that said, "J.R. Can't Reid" and chanted it as well.

In the press conference the week of the ACC tourney, I indicated that I felt the sign was a racial slur; they were suggesting that J.R. couldn't read because he was black. (There was a white backcourt player at Brigham Young University in the '90s named Reid, but he never would have heard such a chant.) I felt that such stereotyping, even in jest, breeds racism, and so in reply I made what I thought was a perfectly reasonable comment: I said that Reid and Scott Williams had a combined score on the SATs higher than that of Duke's Danny Ferry and Christian Laettner, both of whom were white. We had tried hard to recruit Ferry and Laettner, and both had visited our campus, so I knew their scores, which were good.

The signs prompted me to speak up about a subject that had always bothered me. I felt the SATs were culturally biased, and somebody needed to say something on that subject. My point was that J.R. and Scott grew up in lovely suburban homes and had well-educated parents and access to good school systems, which were determining factors in how they performed on standardized tests. I didn't set out to stir up a controversy. I just felt something needed to be said. The reason I used the combined scores of the two black players and the two white ones was so that no one could accuse me of picking on one player, and because all four had grown up in white suburban cultures.

But Duke fans responded with outrage, accusing me of violating the privacy of the players by discussing their scores, and suggesting I was being mean-spirited. But I didn't say what the scores were or reveal any specific information. I could have been saying that Reid and Williams's scores averaged 1500 to Ferry and Laettner's combined 1490 average. Any school in the country would have been proud to have all of them.

My timing wasn't ideal. It incited Duke's team on the eve of the ACC tournament, and we met them in the championship game. The result was a game that has been generally acknowledged as one of the fiercest in conference history. Duke had swept us in three meetings in 1988, the only year since 1966 that we hadn't beaten them at least once, and if they were to win two of three meetings in '89, it would have been a dangerous trend. Duke, meanwhile, was seething over my comments about Ferry and Laettner.

Our team was made up of superb backcourt leaders in our seniors Lebo and Bucknall; a pair of juniors in the frontcourt, Reid and Williams; as well as sophomore Fox. From the outset, the game was marked by physical confrontations underneath the basket between Reid and Ferry. The game seesawed back and forth as both teams turned the ball over under pressure (we gave up 24, the Blue Devils 18, by the game's end). We jumped out to a 20–8 lead, but Duke pulled to within 4 at the half.

In the second half, we were tied five different times. The crucial play came with 1:46 remaining, the game tied at 66–66. Bucknall drove the lane against Duke's David Henderson, scored, and drew a foul. The 3-point play proved the difference, as we held on to win, 77–74. Four of our players—Lebo, Reid, Bucknall, and Fox—were named to the All-Tournament team.

We were elated. But the elation was short-lived; when we returned home to Chapel Hill that Sunday evening, we learned that we had inexplicably been denied a preferable assignment in the NCAA tournament. Duke got it instead. There should have been a very tangible reward for winning the ACC championship; both teams had assumed that the winner of the game would earn a preferential assignment from the NCAA and have the right to stay in the East regional. (Duke, Virginia, and Carolina had tied for second place in the ACC behind N.C. State, but we had victories outside the conference over Georgia, Indiana, Stanford, Arizona, Missouri, UCLA, DePaul, and Vanderbilt, all teams that made it into the postseason tournament.)

Nevertheless, Duke was given the second seed and assigned to the NCAA East, with a relatively easy draw to get to Seattle for the Final Four. We were shipped back to Atlanta as the number-two seed in the Southeast region, where we would have to play UCLA in the second round. We got by the

Bruins, 88–81, after trailing for most of the game. That earned us a meeting with Michigan in the Sweet Sixteen in Lexington, Kentucky, before a pro-Wolverine crowd. Meanwhile, Duke won over South Carolina State and West Virginia to earn a trip to the Meadowlands to play Minnesota. When a member of the press asked me how I felt about our matchup with number-three seed Michigan, I said bluntly, "I'd rather play number-eleven seed Minnesota."

It would be the third straight year we had to play the Wolverines, a difficult task, since we had knocked them out of the NCAA tournament the previous two years. Their seniors, led by Glen Rice, hadn't forgotten. They got 34 points from Glen Rice, including an important 3-point off-balance rainbow with two minutes remaining. Our Reid and Lebo played superbly and the rest of the team played one of its best games all season. Still, Michigan won, 92–87. Our season ended with a 29–8 record, while Michigan went on to become the eventual national champions. But there was some consolation: For the ninth straight year, we had won at least twenty-seven games, and finished at number four in the final national poll.

Afterwards, J.R. decided to go early to the NBA draft and was the number-five pick, which made the decision a good one for him. His mom, dad, J.R., and I had a long meeting in Chapel Hill, and it was a toss-up as to whether he should go pro. He returned for his degree over two summers. Lebo and Bucknall graduated. The result was that the next year we were given our lowest seeding in the NCAA tournament in fifteen years. We were assigned the number-eight spot in the Midwest Regional in Austin, Texas, which meant we would play number-nine Southwest Missouri State, coached by Charlie Spoonhour, one of the teams no one wants to meet in postseason. They had almost upset Kansas and UNLV in the last two NCAA tourneys with ball-control offense and solid defense. We won a tough game, 83–70.

But all it did was earn us a meeting with number-one-ranked Oklahoma two days later. Not often did North Carolina find itself an underdog, but in this game we were. Still, executing beautifully, we slowed down the Sooners' run-and-gun offense, to lead by 2 at intermission, and by as many as 7 in the second half. Oklahoma went ahead by a point, 74–73, with fifty-five seconds left. But with the shot clock about to expire, Fox, our leading scorer along with Williams, hit a 3-pointer from twenty-five feet away to restore the lead to Carolina.

With eight seconds left the score was tied, 77–77. We took a time-out as a rebound went out of bounds off an Oklahoma player. As the team sprinted to the bench, I thought about using Fox as a decoy to set up our sophomore marksman, Hubert Davis. We had a play to create an open jump shot against either zone or man defense, called Forty-four Sideline. Under the circumstances, the game tied with eight seconds left, we would be looking to shoot with about three seconds on the clock. That way if it missed there would be time for a tip-in, an offensive rebound, or a foul.

In the huddle I reviewed the time situation and the Forty-four Sideline play. Rick would catch the inbounds pass from point guard King Rice at the extended foul line, fake a shot, and drive to the free-throw line. If he were wide open, he could shoot. The two post men would be screening each other for rebound position. Rick would draw most of the defenders. Hubert would float down from the top while Rick drove the middle, using a rear screen, from King coming up from out of bounds. Rick would pass to Hubert, who would make a seventeen-foot shot and win the game.

But as our players stood to leave the bench, Hubert looked hesitant to me. He said, "What place on the floor should I try to shoot the ball?" I quickly called the other four players back. "Rick, you run Hubert's spot," I said. "Hubert, you be the decoy, dribble to the middle, and find Rick! You know what to do on that!" Then I smiled. "Rick, remember, we only need two to win, not a three-point shot."

It worked out better than I'd hoped. All of the Oklahoma perimeter people moved to Hubert, and Rick was so wide open, King didn't have anyone to screen. When the big guys moved into their screening action, the defense never saw the pass. Rick took the pass, saw an opening to the goal, made a beautiful six-footer off the glass, and we celebrated as time ran out. (Hubert and I are sure he would have scored if I hadn't switched them, but we'll never know. Hubert made big shots for us and for the New York Knicks later.)

We had preserved our streak and would go to our tenth straight Sweet Sixteen, this one in Texas against Arkansas. However, in practice the following Tuesday we lost our savvy power forward and third-leading scorer, Kevin Madden, to a serious knee injury. Arkansas was probably better anyway, and ended our season.

As the decade drew to a close and another one began, we brought to Carolina a new future in the form of five highly recruited freshmen. One, Cliff Rozier, would tranfer to Louisville after his freshman year, but the other four, Brian Reese, Eric Montross, Pat Sullivan, and Derrick Phelps, would give us some big seasons ahead.

·   ·   ·

There were certain issues I chose to take a stand on as interest in the game grew and it became increasingly commercialized in the '80s and '90s. I could have supplemented my income with endorsements, but I chose not to. Other professors did not have endorsements, and neither should the basketball coach. Also, I refused to promote alcohol products on the air in my weekly radio and TV shows. I was pleased that Carolina did not (and does not) use any advertising in the basketball arena or football stadium. To my knowledge, Carolina and Notre Dame are the only schools that do not allow signage in their buildings or stadiums.

With such immense interest in college basketball, I wanted our players to continue to be ordinary students—who just happened to be on the university's basketball team. Still, it was impossible to ignore the fact that some of them were becoming national figures, thanks to their winning and the TV exposure.

Carolina did not allow athletic dorms when I arrived as head coach, and it still doesn't. I can remember football coach Jim Tatum and Frank McGuire encouraging players from out of state to join fraternities, because they felt being in a small, close group would prevent homesickness. But some of them could not afford fraternity life. When I became head coach I made a rule that our players could live anywhere on campus, but I did not want them isolated in apartments off campus. They ate with their fellow students and other athletes at the then–newly built Chase Dining Hall, and so most of them chose a dorm nearby, Avery or Ehringhaus. Still, they generally wanted to be with their teammates, and most chose to room with fellow players, although an occasional exception would choose a nonplayer. Then, in 1967, Bill Dooley arrived from Georgia as our new head football coach. Georgia had an athletic dorm, and I can understand why Dooley was in favor of them because he could control his players' study-hall schedules, eating habits, and discipline. Football is dealing with one hundred student-athletes, while in basketball it is generally twelve. The university allowed him to put all of his players in Ehringhaus, although it still housed more nonathletes than athletes, and a dining hall was installed for all scholarship athletes, men and women alike.

At about the same time a new dorm called Granville Towers was built one block from campus. The new dorm was privately owned but under university supervision, and it housed and fed fifteen hundred students in a complex of three high-rise buildings. I asked that our basketball players be allowed to stay in Granville, if they chose, because it offered unlimited access to food and drink, which was important for athletes like Steve Previs, who would drink six or seven glasses of orange juice for breakfast. Granville was so large that our players, who numbered just a dozen among fifteen hundred, naturally associated with all kinds of different students. They might room with another basketball player, but they might not. It was up to them. However, I also told them they were free to choose any other dorm on campus if they preferred.

Granville was set up in small two-bedroom, one-bath suites, with two students to a room. It also had a common dining hall, and a swimming pool and basketball court outside. It was almost like a small college in itself. Our players dominated the softball intramural competition and even won the Hill Championship one year.

One thing that upset me so much about the 1972 decision by the NCAA to make freshmen eligible was that it undermined the assimilation of athletes into the student body. The great thing about ineligibility was that it threw freshmen into the midst of campus life and forced them to spend a year as average college undergrads. I'll give you an example. The scholarship members of our 1966–67 freshman team were Jim Delany, Eddie Fogler, Charles Scott, and Al Armour, but they spent a season playing freshman basketball with eleven walk-ons. There were only three or four scholarship players on any given freshman team, while the the rest were culled from the student body. It meant that a future NBA player often became best friends with nonscholarship students—future lawyers, doctors, teachers, and businesspeople—and developed lifelong relationships with these fellow members of their team. Our 1966–67 freshman team had a thirty-year reunion in 1996 in Chapel Hill during a spring weekend, and only two members could not be there, although of course they wanted to come. Of those nonscholarship players, there were three doctors, a dentist, two lawyers, and a number of businessmen. Only Eddie Fogler became a coach.

That's why we decided to keep our jayvee team alive in 1973 when freshmen were ruled eligible. Mitch Kupchak played with the varsity that season, but two other scholarship freshmen played with the jayvee. I saw the jayvee as a symbol, a bridge to the student body, because it gave a nonrecruited student a chance to put North Carolina on his chest and play for our team. What's more, we always tried to promote one or two hardworking players from the jayvee to the varsity and give them a scholarship. One year we had as many as sixty-six players try out for the jayvee team.

Most schools, save for the Ivy Leagues and Kansas, have abolished the jayvee, citing costs. But the last time I checked, the tab for our jayvee team was $5,400. I think it's a small price to pay for a good policy. For $5,400 a year, they wore our old uniforms, had paid officiating, and got to take one road trip. Eighteen students had a wonderful experience and were thrilled to be out there, playing the preliminary game to our twelve varsity home games. What's more, it has been a great training ground for our assistant coaches. Larry Brown, Bill Guthridge, Eddie Fogler, Randy Wiel, Dave Hanners, and Phil Ford have all done stints coaching the jayvee, and over the years won some noteworthy victories over junior colleges and prep schools with Division 1 scholarship recruits on the roster. It was a great way for them to experiment with some of our ideas, while building pride and making students feel part of the Carolina basketball program. Actually, the jayvee team usually ran the same offense and defense as the varsity.

In fact, in my one year as freshman coach (in 1959, when I was Frank McGuire's only assistant) I became very attached to my players. It was extremely hard to cut young men from that squad. I got it down to nineteen players after a week and I couldn't cut anymore. Frank said, "I told you, cut them quickly. Otherwise you get to know them." Phil Ford is the current coach of the jayvee and has the same problem. He usually keeps eighteen players and finds a way to let most of them play. It was a sign that the student body felt close to our team when even the job of student manager became a coveted one. Coach Guthridge was in charge of student managers for years, and the job was so desirable that he began "trying out" students for the positions. The jayvee now has eighteen student managers and eighteen players. All eighteen managers hope to make the short list of four varsity student managers.

I always thought it was a marvelous thing when a jayvee player was promoted to the varsity and made genuine contributions to the team. A young man named Mickey Bell played freshman basketball and became a very important defensive stopper for us in the mid-1970s, and even guarded David Thompson. Bill Chambers, a member of our 1972 team, gave us crucial minutes against Florida State in the Final Four. Pearce Landry of Greensboro was good enough to become a sixth man on our varsity in 1995. Landry should have been recruited by the ACC schools out of high school, but he somehow slipped through the cracks and spent two years on the jayvee before he made the varsity. He typified the hustle mentality of the jayvee plus exceptional athletic ability and basketball savvy.

I've just chosen those four examples arbitrarily, and I wish I could name *all* of the nonscholarship players who contributed to our success, but there were so many of them over thirty-six years that it would be a chapter in this book. However, all lettermen are listed in the Appendix. Some of those nonscholarship players actually started more than one game for Carolina, and every senior started his last home game, which was always an important ACC matchup. Those who actually became full-time starters for us were Charlie Shaffer (1963, 1964), Bill Brown (1965), John Yokley (1966), with Ralph Fletcher (1968) and Ged Doughton (1979) being part-time starters.

But despite our best efforts, it was becoming increasingly difficult for our players to maintain the aura of ordinary undergraduates. Their fellow students wanted autographs for little brother back home. After we won the 1982 championship, for the first time ever I allowed our juniors and seniors to move off campus and into apartments—because I felt they were entitled to some privacy. When word got out which dorm the players were staying in, people would come to town and there would be autograph sessions going on all the time. As juniors, Michael Jordan and Buzz Peterson liked Granville so much they chose to stay there for the convenience of meals and weekly maid service. They came close to renting a basement apartment in the home of Howard and Lil Lee.

I tried to get across to our coaches and the players that we should never behave as though we were privileged, no matter how much others wanted to treat us that way. I didn't want our players cutting in line to register ahead of others, or slipping in front of the line at the movies. These were small things, and yet they weren't. I talked to the staff, to myself, and to the players about remembering that we were just a part of the UNC community.

It was important to demonstrate that academics was always our first priority. The coaches in our program had a great relationship with the faculty. We built up a trust over the years because the faculty knew that we recruited with the aim of making sure our players could do the work at the university. I could tell how supportive the faculty was of our team based on the number of tickets they bought at the faculty rate. For several years there has been a waiting list for faculty members who wanted to buy tickets.

Ironically, one of the benefits of our success was that we could afford to charter flights back from late-night road games so our players wouldn't miss more classes than they absolutely had to. In 1981, for instance, we chartered a 727 to fly our players back to Chapel Hill from an NCAA subregional game in El Paso. That was expensive, but our only other choice would have been to stay out West, which would have meant our players missed an entire week of class. We had won on a Sunday night and had to be in Salt Lake City for a Wednesday-noon NCAA press conference. (We gave the band and the cheerleaders a lift so they wouldn't miss class either.)

Each year the NCAA mandated those day-before-the-game press conferences, which meant teams had to travel on Tuesday or Wednesday, even though they would not play until Thursday or Friday night. Each year, we missed more class time during the NCAA regionals than we did the rest of the season. I could be impatient in those press conferences, but I also understood it was a valuable experience for our players. In 1993 someone asked George Lynch if he was nervous about playing in the Final Four. He said, "My most nervous moments were riding with Coach Smith to the press conference."

In 1995 we played a road game at Notre Dame with a 9 P.M. tip-off because of television scheduling. We chartered in to South Bend and left for home right after the game, renting the Denver Nuggets' 737, managing to get home even though we ran into a snowstorm in South Bend, with drifts all over the place. The next morning, a professor called me and said, "What in the world? I just saw this guy playing on television at Notre Dame at eleven at night, and next thing I know he's in my nine A.M. class. That's impressive."

The freshman class that enrolled in the fall of 1990 was considered our best in some time. Eric Montross was a close-shaven, heavily muscled seven-footer from Indiana whose high school coach, Jack Keefer, had worked our camp for the previous nine years. Pat Sullivan was a six-seven frontcourt player from Bogota, New Jersey, who had grown up hero-worshipping and mentored by an older New Jersey player transplanted to Carolina, Mike O'Koren. Derrick Phelps was a Queens-bred guard who came to Carolina following the path of fellow New Yorker Kenny Smith. Brian Reese was an explosive player from the Bronx who had followed Carolina basketball since he started playing the game. Phelps and Reese played in summer leagues on the same team and even took their recruiting visits together to Chapel Hill. The fifth member of the class was Clifford Rozier, an excellent six-eight prospect who would leave after the season because he felt there was too much discipline in the program. But Clifford and his mother are still in contact with me by telephone.

We had a nice amalgam of upperclassmen in seniors King Rice, Pete Chilcutt, and Rick Fox, junior Hubert Davis (who is the nephew of Walter Davis), and George Lynch, a versatile sophomore with a high-wattage smile. The freshmen gave us as much depth as we ever had, although we used them off the bench as subs.

The result was a return to the Final Four. We ran up a 29–6 record against a schedule that included Kentucky, Connecticut, Alabama, Purdue, and

Stanford, all NCAA tournament teams, plus a great win over Notre Dame in the Meadowlands by 35. We won a league-record twelfth ACC tournament title—second was N.C. State, with six—when we blew out Duke, 96–74, in the title game. In a way, that loss may have fired up the Blue Devils, who went on to win the NCAA championship.

NCAA tournament victories over Northeastern, Villanova, Eastern Michigan, and Temple got us a berth in the Final Four at the Hoosier Dome in Indianapolis, where we met Kansas, coached by Roy Williams, who had left our staff in 1988 to become the Jayhawks' head coach. Kansas had beaten number-one regional seed Indiana, among others, to be there. There was a certain paradox at work: We were playing against my alma mater, Kansas, which was coached by Roy, a North Carolina alumnus. It was funny to watch both teams call their offenses and defenses, since we used the same terminology. When one team had the ball and called out, "B-One," "B-Two," or "B-Three," the other team knew exactly what offense to expect. Defensively, if we heard "Twenty-four" or "Twenty-three" we knew how they would set up. We were eliminated by our well-schooled opponent, 79–73.

In 1991–92, observers supposed we would struggle to find new leaders after the departure of point guard King Rice, and the loss of Fox and Chilcutt to the pros. But we shaped up as a team that could not be counted out of a game—in part thanks to the example of senior Hubert Davis of Lake Braddock, Virginia. Hubert had come to our summer camp for seven straight years beginning at age ten. When he was six, he had been taken by his father to the Montreal Olympics to see his uncle Walter Davis play, and he rode back to his home outside of Washington, D.C., with Walter, Mitch Kupchak, and Phil Ford. So you might say he was thoroughly indoctrinated in Carolina basketball.

I would watch Hubert at our camps, and later at Garfinkel's Five-Star camp during the summer before his senior year in high school in Lake Braddock. He was also a highly regarded receiver in football his senior year, named All-Metro in the Washington, D.C., area. I decided he could be an ACC player, although I doubted whether he would ever start for us, since he didn't appear very quick. I told his dad, Hubert Sr., that I would give him a scholarship, but if he wanted to play all four years he should join coach John Kuester at George Washington, where he would be a key recruit. I also told Hubert Sr. I still wanted to be close friends with him and Walter and the rest of the family, and if I didn't play Hubert very much I was concerned that they would be mad at me. Hubert Sr. told me that his son would accept any amount of playing time, he just wanted to be part of the team and then go on to law school.

It showed how much I knew. Hubert became an All-ACC selection, the first-round draft pick of the New York Knicks, and continues to be one of the top percentage 3-point shooters in the NBA. Like his uncle he is a pure shooter.

An inconsistent young team built a 23–10 record. We beat Purdue by 23 at home and Seton Hall at the Meadowlands by 29, and yet twice lost to an N.C. State team that would finish seventh in the ACC. Perhaps the high points of the season were an upset of top-ranked Duke and a remarkable 22-point comeback against Wake Forest. The latter was the biggest deficit a Carolina team rallied from in school history. We trailed by 20 with 14:49 to go, and were still down by 11 with 6:17 remaining. But Pat Sullivan tied the game at 78 with two free throws with sixteen seconds left, and Brian Reese performed the final heroics, with a twelve-foot jumper at the buzzer. Despite the ups and downs, we still reached the Sweet Sixteen for the twelfth consecutive year by beating a strong Alabama team that featured Latrell Sprewell and Robert Horry.

But all of those dramas would seem like just a prelude to 1993, when our players turned comebacks into regular occurrences. We were deep and experienced: Ten of our fourteen players were either juniors or seniors, which I've always said is crucial for a great college team. The class that had come in as freshmen in 1990 were in their third season, and senior George Lynch had become a magnificent player and leader; he was en route to being named the MVP of our season, and he would finish his career as one of just two players in ACC history to compile at least 1,500 points, 1,000 rebounds, 200 steals, and 200 assists in a career. In addition we had Donald Williams, a six-three sophomore with touch and an active style I liked; senior Henrik Rödl, a vastly underrated basketball player and terrific defender from Heusenstamm, Germany; and two big men off the bench, the seven-one Texan Matt Wenstrom and six-ten Kevin Salvadori, to spell Montross and Lynch.

By the end of January, we had run up a 9–1 record, and our only loss had come to Michigan in the Rainbow Classic in Hawaii, by a point, 79–78, when Jalen Rose batted in a missed shot by teammate Jimmy King at the buzzer. The game had the intensity of an NCAA tournament game. Both teams left the floor that night knowing that their effort couldn't be faulted, and that a better basketball game might not be played all season. The press decided that Carolina and Michigan could very well meet again in March.

But it looked as though we were in for a very public defeat when Florida State came to Chapel Hill on January 27, 1993, in a nationally televised meeting with ACC title implications. At stake was first-place standing in the league: We came in with a 5–0 mark, while the Seminoles were 5–1 and on a five-game winning streak. A victory on our home court would put Florida State in position to challenge for the regular season conference championship, although Duke, with Grant Hill, Bobby Hurley, and Cherokee Parks returning from the NCAA championship team, was also in the mix.

We had a couple of reasons to look forward to the meeting. A year earlier, Florida State guard Sam Cassell had labeled our crowd "a wine-and-cheese crowd." Also, it would be an interesting collision of talent and a good measuring stick for our team. Florida State was one of the most athletic teams the league had ever seen, with a host of future NBA first-round picks in seniors Cassell, Charlie Ward, and Doug Edwards, and sophomore Bob Sura. They also had a quick big man whom I highly regarded, the six-eight Rodney Dobard.

ESPN, sensing that the game had national and not just regional ramifications, convinced Florida State head coach Pat Kennedy to allow a camera and microphone to be installed in his pregame locker room. (We turned down frequent requests to do the same over the years. It was my belief that our locker room was for our players and our coaches and no one else—not the media and not the chancellor. Had the president of the United States asked, he would have been denied admission too.) We learned later that before the game, the Seminoles' Kennedy killed time in the locker room by leafing through our media guide, and he stopped to read the section on Carolina's all-time greatest comebacks. In a program known for comebacks, the game we were about to play would rank among the best of them.

At the start, Florida State played better than we did. They had quickness and they had a plan. Defensively, they played a sagging zone, which meant that sometimes they had five men inside a fifteen-foot area. Our seven-foot center, Montross, picked up three quick fouls and had to spend the better part of the first half on the bench, while Matt Wenstrom played admirably in his place (8 points and three rebounds in the first half). But Florida State was playing extremely well, while we were missing the wide-open shots they invited us to take. Dobard was killing us, on his way to hitting eight of twelve field goals for 17 points, with seven rebounds and six blocked shots. As a team the Seminoles got thirteen offensive rebounds. In the last ninety seconds before intermission, we had a major lapse and gave up 7 straight points to trail, 45–28, at the break.

Florida State was a confident team in the halftime locker room—as we found out by sheer accident a few days later. It seemed that ESPN's technicians forgot to turn off the camera and microphones after Kennedy's pregame speech. What went on in the Seminoles locker room was recorded, although not broadcast. Cassell, the talented guard who had labeled our fans the wine-and-cheese crowd, was strutting. "I can't believe that Dean Smith thinks Donald Williams can check me," he said. "I can't believe Dean Smith thinks Henrik Rödl can check me." Actually, Cassell hadn't hurt us. He had just 7 points, compared to 11 for Sura and 10 apiece for Edwards and Dobard.

While Cassell was spreading his own brand of inspiration, Kennedy was telling his players, "With this big of a lead, we don't need to score but so many points to win the game."

Frankly, we weren't having nearly as much fun in our locker room. I was upset that we weren't holding our box-outs. I understood that it was difficult to turn down open seventeen-foot shots, but we needed to be more patient and look inside first. In the first half we had shot just 32 percent.

Things were no better to begin the second half. Florida State built its lead up to 21 with 11:33 left, and they still led by 20 when Henrik Rödl, who always seemed to play a key role in our comebacks, hit a 3-pointer with 9:21 to go. I jumped up and called a time-out. As the team came to the bench, I said, "This is going to be fun!"

With the time-out, I was sending a message to both sides. I wanted to let our players believe that our comeback had just begun. Also, I wanted to plant a seed with Florida State. I wanted them to think, *Uh-oh, here they come,* and to consider the very real possibility that they could still lose the game. But I doubt that they thought they had a problem, up by 17 with under ten minutes to play.

In the huddle, I talked to our players about what we had to do: Put the pressure on defensively, and box out—refuse to allow FSU any offensive boards or second shots. I said, "There's plenty of time left. One possession at a time. At the next time-out, let's be down only twelve points." I gave our players a short-term goal, something to shoot for. We didn't want to get too far ahead of ourselves.

Our plan hit a snag when Edwards scored on a follow-up for the Seminoles (despite a great box-out by us) to push the lead back up to 19. There would be other disheartening moments over the next eight minutes that could have caused us to think, *We can't get it done tonight.* But our players weren't trained to think that way.

We ran off 15 straight points, and the noise built steadily in the arena with every unanswered basket. George Lynch hit a 3-pointer to cut it to 73–57 with 8:51 to go. Derrick Phelps, who I thought was the best defensive guard in the college game that year, drew a charge from FSU's point guard, Ward, a player I liked and respected, with 8:43 left. Then Donald Williams hit a 3 that made it 73–60 with 8:38 remaining, and Florida State took a time-out. The arena was rocking, and Florida State's time-out told me they were concerned. Our players gathered around. "We have a long way to go," I said. "But isn't this fun? There's a lot of time left, so be patient and get the shot *we* want. Keep up the defensive pressure and box out!"

Florida State missed its next shot.

Rödl sank another 3; 73–63, with 8:06 left.

Rödl stole a Cassell pass out of our Scramble defense and threw it to Phelps, who scored with 7:42 on the clock. Now the deficit was 8, down to single digits. Florida State took its second time-out.

It was so loud in the building that I had to scream in order for our players to hear me. The bench was in such a state that I had to calm them down. "Are you having fun?" I asked. "Are we going to stop, or are you going to finish it? We want Twenty-four defense into Thirty-two. It's not complete yet," I said.

Back on the court, Edwards fouled Montross, pushing him to the floor. Pat Kennedy, trying to halt our momentum, had been flirting with a technical foul, and now he got one. On the ensuing possession, Donald Williams hit a leaner from ten feet to make it 73–69 with 6:52 left.

In two minutes and thirty-two seconds, our players had cut a 21-point lead down to 4, and they had done it against one of the nation's best teams, who would be in the Final Eight. The feat bordered on the miraculous. ESPN's announcing team, Mike Patrick and Dick Vitale, struggled to find words to describe it. "In my fourteen years at ESPN this is by far the biggest turnaround I have witnessed involving teams this good," Vitale said.

But it was far from over. In yet another discouraging sequence, we missed three straight point-blank layups. Rödl fouled Cassell, who sank two free throws. It was a 4-point turnaround. Instead of cutting the lead to 2, as any of those layups would have done, we trailed by 6; 75–69, with 5:21 left.

But we hung in there, clawing out points and making critical defensive stops. On one possession, we switched to a point zone in a successful attempt to lure the Seminoles into a quick shot and a miss. Phelps and Reese made three key free throws between them, and our defense trapped Edwards on the sideline, forcing him to call his team's last time-out with 2:56 left. I literally had to shout above the crowd. "You've done great, and there is a lot of time left to do the job," I yelled. "They will go to Edwards, or give the ball to Cassell. Help off Ward on Cassell. Offensively, go to a quickie for Montross!"

Out of the time-out, Cassell did drive and put up an off-balance shot. We helped off Edwards—and Edwards scored on a follow, another huge play that could have broken us. But our guys weren't about to stop now.

A neat jump hook by Montross brought us to within 1; 77–76, with 1:59 left.

What we did next made all of the highlights. We were once again in our Scramble defense. Rödl and Phelps trapped Ward at midcourt. With no time-outs left, the best Ward could do was try to get the ball to Sura off to his left. But George Lynch, who had a great knack for being around the ball, read Ward's mind, stole the pass, and raced unhindered down the court for a slam dunk. That gave us our first lead since the opening three minutes of the game, 78–77.

After Florida State missed and we rebounded, I signaled for our Four Corners. We gave the ball to Donald Williams, and with the shot clock running down he took Cassell to the basket, drawing a foul with 37.7 seconds left. Donald made both foul shots, and we led 80–77. Next, I put our team in our X defense, which was a switching-man pressure designed to protect against the 3-point shot. I told the team, "No fouls, no three-pointers, no layups."

On Florida State's next possession, in a switch on the screen at the ball, our seven-foot Kevin Salvadori ended up on the quick Cassell, while our six-three Donald Williams switched over to cover the six-eight Edwards, creating two potential mismatches. But Donald did precisely what he was taught to do. In that tense moment he made the correct judgment, and ran at Cassell for what we call a "switchback." That forced Cassell to pass to Edwards. Meanwhile, Salvadori made the switch *back* to Edwards. It took the ball out of Cassell's hands and put it in the hands of Edwards, who certainly wasn't one of their best outside shooters. Edwards chose to try from 3-point range. He missed. We got the rebound, and Donald Williams was fouled. He made two free throws with a few seconds left, and we won by 5, 82–77.

We had outscored the Seminoles 31–6 over the final 9:24.

It was a huge win over a team that would later advance to the Final Eight of the NCAA tournament. In the Florida State locker room, we heard later, the Seminoles were in a state of disbelief. They played great for thirty-one minutes—and then we played great.

We would meet the Seminoles once more in 1993, on February 27 in Tallahassee. Our players refused to be intimidated by the capacity crowd, and won convincingly, 86–76. "If you guys keep this up," I told them at halftime, "I'll lead the singing of 'Amen' in the locker room." And fortunately, I did!

The victory proved our team liked big games on the road, an important quality for a tournament-bound team.

The Florida State comeback proved to be a critical building block for our team, and a valuable experience, because in the NCAA tournament we would have to recover from double-digit deficits on three different occasions. In the East regional semifinal, we trailed Arkansas 25–14 in the first half before going on to an 80–74 victory in a game that wasn't decided until the last fifteen seconds. I laughingly gave some credit for the win to North Carolina alumnus Walter Dellinger, a member of the class of '63, who was a Duke law professor who was serving as President Clinton's associate counsel on constitutional issues. Shortly before the game, Dellinger wrote this memo to Clinton attorney Bruce Lindsey:

"Re: Implicit Article II Requirement of President Neutrality:

"As the principal constitutional counsel to the President, I was alarmed to learn that the President was considering attending in person the sporting event to be held tonight in New Jersey, and that this decision was being made wholly without any serious constitutional analysis."

The memo continued at some length, outlining the various legal arguments against President Clinton making an appearance at the game, and particularly cautioning him against delivering any "pep talks" in the Razorbacks' locker room.

The memo concluded, "Since 'sports' now occupies the central role in American life that was the preserve of 'ports' in 1787, a reasoned elaboration of the underlying evolving jurisprudential principle of Article I, Section 9, Clause 6 would clearly mandate Presidential Neutrality in this larger context."

The following day, after Carolina had beaten Arkansas by 6 points, President Clinton replied to Walter in a handwritten note, a copy of which I have: "Walter, it was only your opinion which kept me from the game—I would have been worth 7 points. Thus you altered the course of history, eroded confidence in the power of the Presidency, and delayed justice for another year. And you call yourself a defender and promoter of the Constitution? Congratulations, Bill."

Forty-eight hours later, we fell behind Cincinnati and Nick Van Exel in the regional final, 29–14, before we recovered. With 0.8 seconds remaining the ball belonged to Carolina under our own goal, and the score was tied. I took a time-out to draw up something other than throwing the ball high to Montross, because Cincinnati had a big front line in the game and would be expecting just such a play. I quickly decided to use Montross as a decoy screener and Donald Williams as a second option for a jump shot. I explained the play: It would begin with three in a line facing the ball, with Phelps inbounding. Donald Williams would be away from the ball and sprint to the foul line extended on Phelps's side, which would empty the weak side.

Reese, the last of the three, would step to the corner and wheel back to get the lob right in front of the basket. Lynch, behind Montross, would move to the ball on a fake from Phelps. Montross would yell for the ball, while being sure to screen Reese's man if they switched. Montross could be open.

As they left the bench, I reminded Brian to catch and shoot the ball quickly. "Very little time," I said. As it turned out, all went according to plan—except for one thing. Brian caught the ball about four feet in front of the basket. But he tried to dunk by crouching before jumping. The dunk rattled out of the basket as the horn blew to end regulation. We would go to an extra period. In my opinion, Reese's dunk would not have counted even if it had gone in, because of the time he took to gather himself for the jump.

"All right," I said, as the players came to the bench. "We haven't had overtime yet this year. We need the practice." We went on to a 75–68 victory that earned us a trip to the Final Four in New Orleans. I learned afterwards that Reese's dunk *would* have counted had it gone in. I was just as happy it didn't (now!) because it would have caused some controversy over the clock.

The '93 Final Four field was flatly one of the strongest ever: Michigan, Carolina, and Kentucky all advanced as number-one seeds from their region, while Kansas came to New Orleans as a number-two seed, having upset top-seeded Indiana in their region. By now the Final Four had grown to such gargantuan proportions that more often than not it was held in Super Bowl stadiums, not arenas, and you needed a pass to get anywhere. We defeated the Jayhawks in a game that was closer than the final score, 78–68, while Michigan beat Kentucky in the other semifinal.

That meant the championship game would be a rematch with the Wolverines—and a reprise of that 1-point game that was decided at the buzzer in Hawaii. We knew just how good the Wolverines were. They had the entire package you look for in a champion: size, skills, athleticism, experience, and sound coaching by Steve Fisher. The Wolverines' splendid "Fab Five" recruiting class of two years earlier was made up of Jalen Rose, Chris Webber, and Juwan Howard, all of whom have done well in the NBA, plus Jimmy King and Ray Jackson. But what made them exceptionally dangerous in my mind was the fact that they had been runners-up for the NCAA title the previous year. In 1992 a Michigan team primarily made up of freshmen had lost to Duke in the final. There was no hungrier opponent than one that had lost a championship a year earlier—we had proven that in 1982.

Michigan had been thinking about a title all season long. But so had we. On the day that our preseason officially opened, each player had found a photograph of the Louisiana Superdome in his locker, with the words "North Carolina—1993 NCAA Champions" superimposed at the top.

I had the idea of using a picture to motivate the team after listening to a speech by Jerry Bell, a professor in our business school. I had known Jerry for some time, but in 1992 he was in charge of choosing faculty to appear at an annual World University conference held by the Young Presidents Organization in St. Moritz, Switzerland. Jerry asked me to deliver a speech entitled "Is Coaching Management?" to the CEOs, and in addition to speak on athletics in general and give a basketball clinic to the youngsters who would be there with their parents. I accepted, as it was a great opportunity to take my family to Europe, and I would be able to listen in on the other enlightening sessions on leadership. Linnea and I spent time with Al Hunt of *The Wall Street Journal* and his wife, Judy Woodruff of CNN. Al and I were on a panel with former chancellor of Germany Helmut Schmidt, who was very interesting.

Linnea, Kristen, Kelly, and I had tied this trip with a basketball clinic in Sardinia, an island off the coast of Italy. Ettore Messina, the Italian national coach, had arranged the clinic. Kristen and Kelly, who were thirteen and eleven respectively at the time, always enjoyed these trips to Europe. At St. Moritz they even had a separate camp for the young people during the day.

Just recently, Kristen complained that I always have a basketball clinic to do in our travels as opposed to a complete vacation. I told her Linnea and I had decided it was a great way to really see foreign countries, since the local coaches gave us a sense of the mores of the country and could guide us to the best places to see. Also I enjoy giving basketball clinics to coaches, and this way the four of us are together.

"Okay, good answer," Kristen replied.

I have continued giving basketball clinics for Nike since I retired as coach. Phil Knight, Nike's CEO, has been generous to our athletic department and to many Carolina coaches, including myself. Nike gives the Carolina athletic program a considerable amount of money and equipment, in exchange for which our twenty-eight men's and women's teams wear Nike shoes and apparel. The basketball program entered into this arrangement in 1993, but I insisted that the entire Carolina athletic department be included.

A new five-year contract between Nike and the Carolina athletic department was signed in the summer of 1997. I consider this income advertising revenue, no different from Coca-Cola paying for advertising in game programs and on coaches' television and radio shows. This revenue does our athletic program a great deal of good. I would like to see the money go to the athletic department directly, as other advertising revenue does, rather than to each program and coaching staff individually. The athletic department would then decide what to pay coaches out of that, as Carolina's and most other schools' athletic departments do with revenue from coaches' television and radio shows. I used my share of Nike's money to help our entire staff, and to create and sustain the Dean E. Smith Foundation, Inc., which distributes gifts to charities, gives scholarships, and supports traditionally underfunded academic departments, such as the school of education, the Black Cultural Center, and the school of social work. We also help the Childhood Trust, of the UNC Department of Psychiatry, which works to prevent child abuse.

At St. Moritz, Jerry Bell had given me an audiotape of a former participant in the conference. He said he had lost weight by looking at a picture of himself every day. In the picture, an in-shape body had been superimposed over his real one. Looking at it helped him to eat properly and exercise to make the picture come true. That's when I had the idea of doing something similar for our team.

I had seen a picture of our 1982 championship game, a distant overview of the arena with a caption that read "Congratulations UNC National Champions." We simply doctored the caption to read "1993 National Champions" and faded Georgetown's name from the scoreboard. Ever since, we have manufactured pictures of each Final Four arena and given them to our players, but it doesn't always work. We went to the Final Four in 1995, 1997, and 1998. Maybe we forgot to put the word *champions* on the pictures.

Sometimes NCAA finals are error-ridden affairs, with both teams pressured and nervous. But Michigan and Carolina took the floor of the Superdome as if they were oblivious of the fact that it was a championship game in front of a sellout crowd of 64,151, with millions more watching at home. In my opinion, both teams played even better than they had in Hawaii.

The only sign of tension came when our starter at the two guard spot, Donald Williams, gave the "tired" sign early and came to the bench. Tired players not only made mental errors, they had a tendency to rest on defense, and that was the one thing you didn't ever want in any kind of game. A player resting on the court would have been disruptive to our entire scheme, given how much we emphasized team defense.

When Williams came to the bench, he said apologetically, "I'm not tired so much as I am nervous." I sent in our senior Henrik Rödl, who was really the equivalent of a starter at guard along with Williams and Phelps. Then I turned to Williams on the bench. "That's okay," I said. "It's a good sign. If you're nervous early, you won't be nervous late." I really believed this. Nerves at the beginning meant you were ready to play. Just like a pitcher in the first inning of a baseball game, basketball players always calm down after the first few minutes of a game. It was good to get over the nerves at the outset.

One thing that concerned me going into the game was that Michigan had not made a single 3-point shot in the semifinals against Kentucky—and this was a team that could shoot the 3. Their main strength was inside, where their big front line, led by the six-ten Webber and the six-nine Howard, could score and pound the offensive glass, but they could also strike from outside, and I worried that they were due to hit some 3's. We alternated a point zone to try to contain Webber and Howard inside with our staple man-to-man, along with the periodic Scramble. Even Rose threw the ball away a couple of times against a double-team in the Scramble.

I was right about the 3's. Rob Pelinka, one of their best perimeter players, hit two tough ones, and Jalen Rose drained another as they went on a 19–4 run, to take a 23–13 lead in the first half. But we responded to Michigan's run with one of our own. A 12–2 spurt tied the game at 25–25 with 7:49 to go. From there, the lead swung back and forth before we built a 42–36 lead at intermission.

I felt good in the dressing room at halftime. Our players were focused and playing well—and so was Michigan. It was almost ideal for a championship. But I also knew both teams could play a little better. I bragged on our team defense, which had forced the Wolverines into ten turnovers, three of them from the ball handler Rose, whom we had trapped occasionally. I told our players we had done a good job on Webber, but he was the one they would be looking to in the second half. Webber had gotten 27 points against us in Hawaii, and we didn't want a repeat. Lynch was putting pressure on Howard, preventing him from making their high-low pass to Webber.

Offensively, I congratulated our players for taking care of the ball. We had given up only three turnovers, and generally put up good shots. The only thing I could wish for was that we would shoot a little better, but I never discussed missed shots or free throws with our players. We had some good looks in the first half, but Michigan was also a great team on defense, which contributed to some poor shooting.

We knew we were twenty minutes away from a national championship. I kept my remarks simple. "Don't worry about the score," I instructed them as usual. "Let's just play well on each possession, get good shots, and limit them to one shot. If we do that, we may be a very happy team in an hour." That was basically my whole message, in addition to pointing out mistakes to correct on defense. Then we went back onto the court for the final half of the '93 season. Later, I heard that George Lynch talked to his teammates all the way back to the court, and it is a long walk in the Superdome.

Both teams came out playing with the same poise and determination they had shown in the first half. We managed to hang on to a slim lead for the next eleven and a half minutes, as both sides played with intensity and concentration. I knew it had been a long time with no stoppage of play for a TV time-out—a factor that would become crucial in the late going. The casual spectator might be surprised to learn coaches pay close attention to TV breaks. But it was just such a nuance that could make the difference between two teams as close as Michigan and Carolina.

What happened with the TV time-outs was this. It was the NCAA's policy to take time-outs at the first dead-ball stoppages after the sixteen-, twelve-, eight-, and four-minute marks of each half. (I should point out that a dead ball is defined as the clock stopping. If it stops for a foul shot, there is no TV time-out unless the player makes the shot and the ball is dead.) But if a team called a time-out, it replaced the TV time-out coming up. With 15:55 remaining in the game, there was a dead-ball stoppage, and CBS called a time-out. We knew the second commercial break was scheduled for the first dead ball after the twelve-minute mark.

But CBS had to change its plans when we surprised Michigan with full-court pressure, led by George Lynch, with 15:16 to go. The Wolverines tried to inbound and couldn't. *They were forced to take one of their three time-outs.*

CBS went right back to commercial. Most people watching at home probably didn't think anything of it at the time. But it mattered, because Michigan would be without a time-out later when it most needed one.

By rule, CBS no longer could take commercials slotted for the twelve-minute mark. Now the next CBS break wouldn't come until the eight-minute mark, or as soon thereafter as game action permitted.

But the game action *didn't* permit. The teams sprinted up and down the floor at such a furious pace that there was no convenient place for a break. With 8:35 left, Webber broke loose for a slam dunk to give Michigan its first lead of the second half, 60–58.

When Howard scored with 6:59 to go, Michigan hung on to a 62–61 margin, and the action continued without a dead ball.

By now I was concerned about our stamina. We had played for a full 8:34 stretch without a rest, an interminable amount of time by today's basketball standards. George Lynch, our senior leader, gave the "tired signal" and came to the bench.

Then four more Tarheels gave the "tired signal."

There was 6:50 left in the game, we trailed by a point, and four of our players were holding up fists. I gestured to four relief players, who jogged from our bench to the scorer's table and waited to check in. There was a TV time-out coming at the next horn—but judging by the action thus far, who knew when that might be? I looked at the clock and back at our players. They were exhausted and knew they should come out if they wanted to help the team. We couldn't wait.

When we got the ball, I signaled time-out, stopping the game.

I wanted a fresh team on the floor. It seemed all but certain this game was going down to the wire, and we needed to be rested for the finish. So we stayed with our "tired signal" rule, even though it meant that after the time-out we would send just one regular starter, Montross, back to the court.

Subs in: Eric Montross, Henrik Rödl, Pat Sullivan, Scott Cherry. Players out: Donald Williams, Derrick Phelps, Brian Reese, Kevin Salvadori. (George Lynch had taken himself out of the game a minute earlier.)

When we broke from the huddle, Phelps, Lynch, Williams, and Reese sat on the bench, gratefully catching their breath. I thought we could buy a couple of possessions with this group. Michigan wasn't applying much full pressure, and I had confidence that we could run our semi-delay: Four perimeter players would look inside to our single post, Montross. It was the right thing, I felt.

But few others did. Back in Chicago, Michael Jordan sat watching the game with some of his Bulls teammates. As we returned to the floor after the time-out, Michael stared at the TV screen aghast. Later that spring he told me how he had reacted. "What is Coach doing?" he yelled at the screen.

There were other factors that influenced my thinking. I was concerned about Derrick Phelps, who had a lingering back strain he had suffered in the ACC tournament. The injury was so painful he had sat out the conference championship game and was still feeling the effects of it. He had come out for long stretches of the game against Kansas. Midway through the second half against Michigan, it began to tighten up, and I had to pull him. Now he sat at the end of the bench, trying to stretch. I turned to his friend Brian Reese. "Do you think your buddy will be able to play hurt?" I asked.

"He's ready," Reese said.

I surveyed the rest of our bench. Lynch was exhausted, and that wasn't good. George was a fierce competitor and as trustworthy a leader as any coach could want. He had put heart and soul into our quest for a national championship—he would finish the season with three consecutive triple-doubles—but in the process he had exhausted himself physically and emotionally. George was not especially intimidating at six foot seven, but he routinely played like a much bigger man. He had ten rebounds in that win over Arkansas in the East regionals at the Meadowlands in New Jersey. In the East regional finals, after trailing Cincinnati by 29–14 at halftime, George had fourteen rebounds to help us trim the deficit and force overtime. In the semifinals against Kansas, he had *ten more* rebounds. His performance was even more meritorious when you considered that on every possession he was going up against men taller and heavier than he was. He also played defense with fire in his belly.

We needed him on the court, obviously. But if we expected him to help us at the end, we had to give him a rest. He couldn't possibly have much left.

As the four nonstarters took the court with 6:50 to play, they moved the ball crisply, but had difficulty finding an opening in the Michigan defense. We moved well without the ball, and the shot clock ticked down to ten seconds. I yelled at Cherry, who was right in front of me with the ball and appeared to have a crease to the basket from the left wing, to go at his man. "Take him!" I shouted. I thought Scott had a good chance to drive and get fouled. Scott started his move, but then checked it and dished the ball off. One more pass and the ball went to Rödl, who had to force up a tough shot from the corner just before the clock ran out. The ball didn't touch the rim, and we were called for a shot clock violation.

Michigan's ball. I wasn't too unhappy, because we'd shown good passing and player movement, although we would have preferred a strong drive to the basket or a good shot. Still, a clock violation was better than throwing the ball away and giving Michigan a fast-break opportunity. But when we didn't get a good shot off, up in the television booth CBS commentator Billy Packer criticized my decision to sit four starters. "This was a very calculated move and I wonder why North Carolina sat all of their scorers down with that time-out," he said. ". . . Dean Smith was looking for one possession out of them, but I think that was a calculated move that didn't work, and really didn't have the odds in favor of it working." I respect Billy, who was a former assistant coach at Wake Forest, and I know why he said it.

In thirty-six years of coaching North Carolina basketball, I never made a single decision based on what I thought the critics would say afterwards. Nor did I ever worry about it. First of all, it would rob you of all effectiveness (unless it was something from which you could learn). My profession was coaching, and I studied it daily. I lived this life. I should never tell someone in another field how to do his job. A basketball or a football coach understands his personnel and knows best what he can get from his team in the same way that an engineer knows how to build a bridge. But by its nature the job is a very public one, and you put yourself in a position to be criticized. Decisions have to be made quickly and under extreme pressure. There are risks to be taken and educated guesses to be made.

By now I was accustomed to being second-guessed. Back in the days before the shot clock, when we sometimes held the ball at the end of the game, decisions were especially hard to make. Every time we went to the Four Corners, I knew there would be a price. If we lost, critics invariably said it was because I had gone to the Four Corners.

One well-known coach once advised me never to do anything bold or unusual on the bench, because coaches would always be criticized for it. (Obviously I didn't heed his advice.) Dick Crum, the North Carolina football coach for ten years during the 1980s, once told a fan who called in on a radio show to criticize him, "Every man knows how to do two things—how to charcoal a steak and coach a football team."

So it never crossed my mind to worry about the consequences when I made those substitutions against Michigan. I was too engrossed in the game action to think of anything but how best to serve our team at that moment. I never thought about what sportswriters might write about me until afterwards, when a reporter asked, "Can you imagine the criticism you would have gotten if it hadn't worked?" It wasn't important to me. Sure, I wanted our reserves to get a good shot off, but it was one possession in a frantic game with a lot of action.

But there was a larger reason I didn't think twice about putting four reserves into the national championship game. The "tired signal" was there for a good reason. Our players were being unselfish and trying to help the team by taking themselves out of the game at that juncture. What kind of message would that send to our players to change our rules now? It would be telling them that we didn't have the courage to do the things in the NCAA tournament that we practiced daily and in regular-season games. We preached that every game was important, and we tried to attach the same significance to each. Why? Because a team has to win a number of important games to get to the championship game itself. You can't play for a title without winning the games that come before.

I always believed that any player on our team should be good enough to play for one or two possessions in any game, and I thought it was important for a coach to show confidence in his entire team, not just his starters. I honestly thought that group off the bench would score against Michigan. Even though some of them didn't play a lot, they had worked hard in practice and showed they were capable of scoring against good competition like our starters in practice.

But after they failed to get a shot off that touched the rim, the horn sounded to stop the clock with 6:06 left. Michigan had the ball—and still led by one.

Players in at 6:06: Williams and Phelps. Players out: Rödl and Cherry. (Lynch still hadn't told me he was ready.) In the Olympics, Scott May was out on the tired signal, and Yugoslavia (first game) switched a zone. I said to Scott, "Are you sure you're tired?" I should have said this to Lynch!

Michigan's Rose hit a 3-pointer. Now it was 65–61 with 5:24 to play.

"I really think Dean Smith needed to get those scoring starters back in the game and gut it out for the last five minutes. He had no scoring on the floor," Packer told the CBS viewing audience.

We worked the shot clock on our next possession, making sure we got what we wanted. It was a jumper off the left baseline by Williams from about twelve feet, off a great screen by Sullivan, that swished. We followed that with a great defensive play when Phelps knocked the ball away from Rose, but we gave it right back when we threw the ball away trying to hit Phelps on the fast break. At that stop in play, there was 4:31 left on the clock. I sent a rested Lynch and Reese back into the game.

But Michigan was a championship-caliber team, and Jimmy King hit a jumper to put the Wolverines up, 67–63, with 4:14 remaining. Billy Packer, recalling an important trend, informed his viewers that the Wolverines had a 30–0 record when leading with five minutes or less in the game. They were in that position now.

But if Michigan had history on its side, we knew 4:14 was plenty of time to turn things in our favor, especially given the pace of the game so far. I don't know if the Wolverines were tired at this point. I can't speak for them.

I only know what happened, and that it was obvious our players were fresh and ready to play in the last four minutes.

3:50 to play: Williams hits a 3-pointer from the right wing to cut Michigan's lead to 67–66.

3:20 to play: Lynch blocks a jump shot from King. Montross retrieves the ball, throws it to Reese, who in turn hits Phelps on the break for a layup— and a 68–67 lead for North Carolina.

On Michigan's next possession, King shot an air ball. Perhaps he was tired, perhaps not. We wanted to go inside to Montross, but Michigan played great interior defense and closed him off. Still, Lynch wiggled his way into the lane, took a pass, and managed to put up a shot over the outstretched arm of Howard, Michigan's best shot blocker. The ball fell in with two seconds left on the shot clock. Carolina led, 70–67, with 2:28 remaining.

The two defenses took over for the next 1:25, with neither team able to score. But we had the ball against Michigan's pressure with over a minute to play when Lynch made a terrific pass to Montross inside for a dunk.

1:03 left: North Carolina 72, Michigan 67.

But it was still far from over—hadn't our own players proven that to other teams time and again with those comebacks? With forty-eight seconds left, Michigan's Jackson, his foot on the 3-point line, sent up an arc that dropped through the net, trimming our lead to 3 points.

And that's when Michigan took its final time-out.

Back on the floor after the break, we turned the ball over when one of our players inadvertently stepped out of bounds with the ball. Michigan had the ball with forty-five seconds remaining and a chance to tie.

Rose missed a 3-pointer—but Webber got the rebound and scored on the follow.

36 seconds left: North Carolina 72, Michigan 71.

Michigan fouled Pat Sullivan with twenty seconds to play. On the way to our foul line, I said to Derrick Phelps, "We have three fouls to give. Tell the others." I watched with relief as Derrick told his teammates; I didn't want to have to call time-out and give Michigan a breather. Pat sank the front end of a one on one to give us a 2-point margin. But after he released the ball and stepped into the lane, Michigan's Rose bumped him, hard. "I'll hit you even harder on the next one," Rose promised. Sullivan ignored him. His next free throw was right on line, but ticked off the back of the rim.

Webber rebounded, turned to his left, obviously intending to pass the ball to Rose, Michigan's best ball handler, who was poised near the sideline right by our bench. But just as Webber started to throw it, Lynch jumped into the passing lane. Webber, startled, checked his throw and walked. He took two full steps in open court for everyone to see! But for some reason the official, looking right at the play, didn't blow his whistle as he should have to reward George's defensive play. He simply stared at Webber and didn't call it. Someday I'm going to ask that official why he didn't, since it was so obvious to everyone else in the building. Billy Packer said loudly on the air, "He walked!"

Webber, having gotten away with the travel, realized time was running out. He needed to get to the other end of the court in a hurry, as he had no outlets, thanks to George and the others.

We were in a position where we could commit a nonshooting foul against the Wolverines, give them the ball out of bounds, trap them and commit another nonshooting foul, make them take it out of bounds, and foul them still again. With eighteen seconds on the clock, there wasn't a great deal of time.

Lynch and Phelps harassed Webber and funneled him into the corner in front of his own bench. Then they closed in—and trapped him. Webber was now hemmed in by two of the best defenders in college basketball. He had nowhere to go. In the heat of the moment, the Wolverines had fanned out to run the fast break and left nobody for him to deal the ball to. Webber looked around frantically.

I expected Lynch or Phelps to foul, because we had told them to. But they never even had time to. Webber was so tightly wrapped up, with nowhere to go, that he did what most players do in that situation. He quickly picked up the ball and called time-out.

Except his team didn't have one.

Webber had taken the time-out quickly, without thinking. He simply stopped his dribble and signaled. When Webber called a time-out his team didn't have, he committed a technical foul. It was automatic: Carolina got two free throws and the ball. It would have been better for Webber if that referee had whistled him on his walk. Michigan would have lost possession, but that was all. Instead, Donald Williams went to the line and sank both foul shots, making the score 77–71 for Carolina with eight seconds left.

Rose threw up a long-distance prayer from the left side that missed. Lynch got the rebound, and the game was over. Fittingly, it ended with the ball in the hands of a player who had done as much as anyone to decide the outcome.

After we got back to Chapel Hill, I wrote Webber a letter congratulating him on the great game he had played, and telling him not to feel bad about the time-out. It did not cost his team the game. We won the game over the course of forty minutes. Michigan didn't lose it in two seconds. Some people blamed the eventual outcome on him, which was unfair not just to him but also to our players, who made such a heroic effort over the last few minutes.

Lynch was a perfect example. After giving himself a three-minute rest, all Lynch did in the last 4:30 of the game was block a shot by Jimmy King, make a shot in the lane over Howard, throw a great pass to Montross for a dunk, step in front of Webber to create a travel that wasn't called, and team with Phelps to trap Webber and force the excessive time-out. It was as complete a performance as you could ask for from a player down the stretch.

Would Lynch have finished as brilliantly without his rest? Would Williams have been fresh enough to score 9 points in the last 4:45 without a break? Would North Carolina as a team have outscored Michigan 14–4 over the last 4:12 if we had not exercised our "tired signal" rule, pulling our scorers and going with reserves off the bench for a possession?

We'll never know.

11

I May Be Wrong, But!

T he lyrics of an old song say "I may be wrong, but I think you're wonderful." If you are reading this book, I guess I could call you "wonderful," and I doubt if I would be wrong! But it's the words *I may be wrong*
in those lyrics that suggest the spirit with which I share some of my beliefs
and understandings about faith, God, and life. I may be wrong, but this is
what I believe for now.

One of the things I like about basketball is that we start the game 0–0, all
even. There is no advantage for being rich, no disadvantage for being poor;
the white player and black player line up all even for the center jump to start
the game. No one is granted an advantage, nor is anyone penalized, because
of his skin color. The athletes are not asked to state their religious beliefs.
Foreign players compete under the same rules as the Americans. Just before
tip-off, our little village known as college basketball is color-blind, anti-
discriminatory, nonelitist, and just about as fair as humans can make something.

Wouldn't it be terrific if society operated under the same set of guidelines
as basketball? Coach John Thompson said that basketball has done more to
bridge the gap between races than anything else in our society. At the very
least, it seems to me, basketball should teach us this lesson: that people of all
races and nationalities, coming from totally different backgrounds and hold-

ing various political views as well as different religious beliefs, can excel when given an honest and equal chance.

In my thirty-six years as head basketball coach at North Carolina, I guarded my privacy tightly, to the point that I was occasionally criticized for it. I always attempted to tell reporters requesting interviews that I would be happy to talk with them about our players and our team, but not about myself. Some writers would begin an interview asking about our players, then subtly try to shift the focus to my personal beliefs and me. I resisted. I wasn't a recluse, nor did I fear where their personal questions might lead. I just wasn't comfortable using the podium provided me as head basketball coach at North Carolina to talk about myself, and I certainly had no desire or hidden agenda to tell others how to live their lives, how to behave, or what to believe. Except on a few occasions (such as taking a public stand calling for a verifiable nuclear freeze, signing a petition against the death penalty, and working with Bob Seymour and others at Binkley Church to attempt to break down racial barriers in our town and state), I declined invitations to endorse products and political candidates, even though I had some strong opinions on my candidates. It wasn't that I felt disenfranchised as a basketball coach, but I also wasn't Ruler of the Universe. I tried to be careful which torches I carried, as well as judicious in the comments I did make. I understand it was illogical and wrong for the basketball coach at North Carolina to receive more public attention than the university's chancellor and the professors on campus, but nevertheless, that is the reality of our society. I took my responsibility as a university employee seriously.

So, undertaking this chapter was the most challenging thing in the entire process of writing this book. For instance, I disagree with the so-called Moral Majority and Christian Coalition on many issues, but I support their right to believe what they choose and to try to win others over to their point of view. (It does bother me that the talk of prayer in public schools has been made such an issue, when Jesus tells us to go into a closet to pray.) Where we part ways is in the intolerance I contend they demonstrate toward those who disagree with them. I don't want to fall into the same trap here.

I once was told never to look down on a human being or look up to a human being either, for we all are on the same level before God our Creator. I do not pretend to have the "right" answers for everyone, so if you disagree with what I have come to believe, I certainly honor your right to do so. I may be wrong. And since each human being is unique and we come from different circumstances throughout this world, I respect your right to disagree. My pastor, Jim Pike at Binkley Church in Chapel Hill, has taught a helpful adage that speaks to me: "When we disagree, we agree to disagree without being disagreeable!"

At least part of many disagreements can be traced to the need to be right. Former Princeton coach Pete Carril was called to the platform to be inducted into the Basketball Hall of Fame in Springfield, Massachusetts, a year ago. He quickly thanked everyone for the honor, but then began a short talk about how "you don't have to be right all the time." Also, the noted sociologist, author, and speaker Tony Campolo writes, in discussing lessons he learned while working in Ireland to try to bring about peace between the Protestants and the Catholics, "The whole time I was in Northern Ireland, I heard nothing but talk of 'rights,' but it occurred to me that being Christian is not about demanding their rights as much as it is people called by God to live out the responsibilities of love. . . . When Protestant and Catholic fundamentalists stop demanding their legal rights at the expense of one another and begin to sacrifice their privileges in order to show love, they will be on their way to acting like Christians."

I genuinely believe in one of our Thoughts of the Day used by our team: "Never judge your neighbor until you have walked in his moccasins for two full moons" (except basketball referees—ha!). I try to keep that thought prominent in my mind.

Our 1994 Carolina team played Liberty University, founded by Dr. Jerry Falwell of the Moral Majority, in the opening round of the NCAA tournament. Dr. Falwell said before the game that he was confident his team could do well against us, even though we were ranked number one in the nation, and he asked God to lead his team to victory. It was almost as if he were saying that his team had some extra weapons they could throw at us. When a writer asked me to comment on Falwell's plea to the Almighty, I merely said, "I think God loves all humans the same."

I do have some very strong beliefs that serve as a beacon in my life. It doesn't mean that I have all the answers or have cornered the market on wisdom and understanding. Our upbringing, our life experiences, our reading and listening to tapes, and our further exploration of new ideas shape our beliefs much in the way a rock is altered after years of sitting beneath a mountain waterfall. But just as the water keeps falling and pounding new creases into the rock, life also evolves, shaping our beliefs in different ways. So this is what I believe *now*.

God hears his or her named called on the athletic stage frequently these days. I don't think any human being receives special favors over another—

not athletes, not generals, not politicians, not nations. It is common these days to see athletes pointing to the sky and uttering a prayer after completing a pass or scoring a basket. In June 1999, after a crucial NBA play-off game, I heard a gifted athlete thank God for the win and for his outstanding performance. A suggestion that God has given a victory has always bothered me. You do not often hear the losing team members claim, "God didn't want us to win, I guess." Perhaps that professional athlete really wanted to say, "I prayed to God for a clear head and to do my best and gave thanks for the privilege of playing the game." In her book *Beyond Our Selves,* Catherine Marshall spoke of Christians who may call on God as a "Celestial Bellhop" to grant their wishes. I may be wrong, but I do not see God that way. It reminds me of a sermon on prayer of Dr. O. Dean Martin, the former pastor of Trinity Methodist Church in Gainesville, Florida, in which he said, "God answers prayer in four ways: yes, no, wait, or you gotta be kidding."

Many nice letters came following the '93 NCAA championship game with words of congratulation on our win. One came from a pastor in Ohio who was cheering for Carolina. He wrote to tell us that God had answered his prayers throughout the game for us to win. I may be wrong, but the idea that God cheers for one team to win over another is not my idea of God.

Tony Campolo tells a similar story of the time he competed in a Philadelphia high school hundred-yard-dash competition. Three close friends were running, each representing different schools. Even when they worked out together, one would win, the other friend would finish second, and Tony would finish third every time. When the big track meet was over and the outcome was the same, the winner told the sports reporter he wanted to thank God for his winning run that day. The friend who came in second turned to the third-place Tony and said, "What does God have against us, Tony?"

An athlete who has a centered faith may perform better because his lifestyle may help him overcome anxieties experienced by other players, and he may be better rested and more focused as a result of his faith. But, in my opinion, constant practice helps performance the most. I remember in the late '60s we had a player who, though he would cross himself before every foul shot, still was shooting only 60 percent. My friend Monsignor Newman came by the office one day to say with a chuckle in his voice, "Tell Dick to quit crossing himself before a foul shot. He is making the church look bad." In my day superstitions, which one could say are a form of prayer, were baseball players' way of asking for help. I remember a pitcher who would not step on the baseline walking to and from the dugout. A hitter I knew had a superstition of touching his hat twice before getting in the batter's box. If he were a .300 hitter, he was still going to be a .300 hitter regardless of his superstition, in my opinion.

If Christianity promised to be a magic wand to provide everything one wishes, such as perfect health for individual and family, perfect performance, a problem-free life, then one would choose Christianity immediately, for the wrong reasons. Who would not choose it?

I understand that a basic belief shared by many religions is that God creates each human being to have freedom of choice. If I choose to smoke three packs of cigarettes a day, then one day I should not blame God if I have lung cancer. If some drunken driver crosses the middle lane and strikes my child's car, killing her, I do not think it is God's will when the wrong choice was made by the driver to drink and drive. If some athlete intercepts a crucial pass, that athlete has made a choice to practice and use his talent. I do not believe that tragedy is God's will, as so many people say. Perhaps it would make it easier to accept the death of a young child in an accident, but never for a moment could I believe that it was God's will. Fortunately, God did not make us robots he could move in any direction. I know my golden retriever does not have freedom of choice if I throw a ball. His choice will always be to go get it. We humans do have freedom of choice. We may choose God's spirit to be with us or not choose God's spirit to be with us. That is each individual's choice.

As a father of five children, I would not care which one of my children would win in a tennis match against the other. I would want them to enjoy participating in tennis; both would be winners. I would love them both, even if one of them were behaving better than the other. If one said to me, "Please help me win," I would probably laugh. Perhaps our Creator may look at competition that way, since each human has God's unconditional love. Certainly, the Creator has far greater love for a human than any human parent can give. In the Bible, the apostle Paul wrote to the church in Rome, "If God is for us, who can be against us? . . . there is nothing . . . that can ever separate us from love of God." I would add: not even losing the game! When one loses the hundred-yard dash or the championship game, it is not because "God is against us." When one wins, it is not because "God is for us" either. I believe the Creator sees all humans as winners.

I remain convinced that there can be values learned through participation in athletics, but our society's complete emphasis on winning, rather than participation, is a problem. Doing one's best deserves more applause and appreciation than it receives in America these days. Listen, I fell short here too.

I strove mightily to feel good after games in which we played well but lost. Sadly, most of the time it was easier for me to feel good after winning, even when we had played poorly.

I had suggested the title of this chapter be "You Must Be Living Right." If you play golf, as I try to do, you know that sometimes you hit the ball into the trees. If you are lucky, sometimes a ball may hit a tree and pop back out onto the fairway. If this happens when I am playing with Roy Williams, the Kansas coach, he will invariably say, "You must be living right!" When I am playing golf with Frank McGuire's and my friend Dr. Lou Vine, he would most likely say, "Clean living does it." My friend Bob Eubanks generally will say, "You lucky dog." And he, in my opinion, is the one who is correct. I should add that when the ball gets a bad bounce, I do not remember ever hearing anyone say, "You must be living wrong." But bad bounces do happen. So when Roy or Lou says, "You must be living right," or "Clean living does it," I always seem to reply with a quote from the Bible, "It rains on the just and the unjust." I do not tend to add the quote attributed to Jesus of Nazareth, who once said, "In this life you will have tribulations!"

So I may be wrong, but I believe we humans are not exempt from the common lot in which many tragedies occur. Natural disasters such as earthquakes or tornadoes can take lives of good people and bad, and it certainly wasn't God's will that someone was killed. Sometimes, some good things can happen after a horrible tragedy, but that isn't why the tragedy occurred. I believe it is theologically without basis to suggest that God is the source of any kind of suffering or any other problem as a result of our sin. God is not a vindictive God, but a loving one who provides freedom of choice to each of us. We won't have bad luck if we ignore God—or good luck, for that matter, if we try to make good choices. It is enough for me to know we are all loved, forgiven, and accepted as we are. Our Creator also provided the spirit in each person to guide us if we choose. For all of this we should be grateful. I believe the Christian faith is motivated by gratitude, which we can repay with ethical action to others. With the Spirit's guidance, we will be at peace in this world. I do attend worship services each Sunday if I am in town. I know some friends who say the church is full of hypocrites. They are right, but there are many hypocrites outside the church as well. I am a hypocrite, if you go by the proper definition that describes "one who does not consistently live out what one believes." For instance, I know if I swing too hard trying to hit the golf ball, it seldom is a long, accurate drive. I know I will be more successful if I make a smooth, effortless swing, yet I will still overswing with bad results. I also make dumb decisions instead of listening to the Spirit. When I give up my decision making to the power inside me, I am generally satisfied that I've made a good decision.

Some people say Christianity is for the weak, that we use it as a crutch. I agree that I am in that mold. As Søren Kierkegaard says, "a person comes to God from a point of need." However, a Jesuit priest, Father John Powell, indicates in his book *Unconditional Love* that we humans are conditioned to be weak. Powell quotes Dr. Alfred Adler, a noted psychiatrist who worked with Freud and yet became a critic of Freud's, as saying, "The helplessness of the infant gives rise to universal feelings of inferiority."

Apparently, our Creator has created this vacuum inside, as St. Augustine dubs it, that keeps us from contentment until we choose God's spirit to fill the vacuum. St. Augustine said, "Our hearts are restless until we find rest in Him." We in America attempt to fill this vacuum with power, money, prestige, or even through entertainment so we won't recognize our discontent. Apparently, Kierkegaard thought the same way about the Danish culture over one hundred years ago.

Anytime I begin to think I am a good person, all I need to do is read First Corinthians, chapter 13, substituting my own name in place of the word *love*. For instance, where it says, "love is patient, love is kind," I read, "Dean is patient, Dean is kind"; "Dean is not envious or boastful or arrogant or rude"; "Dean does not insist on his own way"; "Dean is not irritable or resentful." And all of a sudden I know I have some work to do and must depend on the grace of God. Of course, I am taught that God is love, so I substitute, "God is patient, God is kind." He (or She) is the only one who can score 100 percent, in my opinion. At devotional time, for fun, we would have each of my children substitute their name as well.

When I joined Sharon and Sandy for a ritual before putting them to bed, and later Kristen and Kelly, we also might read the story of the prodigal son (Luke 15). As you may remember, the younger son takes his share of the inheritance and squanders it, coming home stone broke. The father in the story, whom Jesus compares to God when he tells it, could have rejected him completely for throwing his life away. Instead, the father greets him when he is far off and throws a party on his behalf. The older son, who stayed behind, wasn't happy with the attention the younger son was receiving for all the bad decisions he made. So one night when reading, I would substitute Sandy's name as the son who left home and Sharon's name for the older son. A week later I would reverse the names, with Sharon leaving home and Sandy being the older brother. Interestingly enough, they each soon wanted to become the younger brother (as did Kristen and Kelly) who, after messing up his life, was welcomed home by the father. That son was forgiven and very, very grateful. He would be more likely to do what the father wanted, simply out of gratitude! Again, I believe the Christian faith is motivated by gratitude, not a fear of Hell or seeking Heaven. It doesn't appear sound to me to be motivated to be good to others here on this Earth by the reward of Heaven; that's selfish. I would hope that we would be good to others out of gratitude for God's love, acceptance, forgiveness, and the gift of the Creator's spirit.

How can we do something to repay God? As I "pick and choose" through the New Testament, there are two parables that have helped me try to respond in gratitude for God's gifts. Obviously, I am not talking about material things when I mention God's gifts.

How we can respond to God's forgiveness is clearly shown in a parable that Jesus told in Matthew 18:23–34, which I will paraphrase. The king forgave his servant's debt of $50,000 after the servant begged for forgiveness. Later the forgiven servant refused to forgive the debt of a friend to whom he had loaned a mere $5. When the king learned of the forgiven servant's lack of mercy just after the king had shown mercy to him, he withdrew his offer and demanded payment of the entire $50,000. The obvious point is, God expects us to forgive other humans if we are to be forgiven by Him.

Another parable that clearly illustrates how we can do something for God is found in Matthew 25:31–40. It says that if we feed the hungry, give shelter to those who do not have it, visit the sick and those in prisons, and otherwise do something for the disadvantaged of this world, it is as if we had done it to God. "Truly I tell you, just as you did it to one of the least of these who are members of my family, you did it to me." Maybe it was that scripture that inspired us to take the UNC basketball teams to visit prisoners, including death row inmates, at the state prison in Raleigh. Over the years, I have visited there with my players several times. November 1998 was particularly memorable, because a prisoner named John Noland, who had become an ardent Carolina fan through our visits, was executed. My pastor, Jim Pike, who was his spiritual adviser, told us how much our visits had meant in his eight years on death row. He never missed hearing a UNC ballgame on the radio. I called John on the telephone some hours before his execution and was moved by the deep gratitude and confident Christian faith of him and his family. My call to him and my visit to Governor Hunt, a former member of Binkley Church, to plead for clemency were featured stories on the local news. I learned later that as the lethal injection was administered, John smiled at his family and began to sing, "Amazing Grace, how sweet the sound that saved a wretch like me." Not only his family, but the family of the victims and some of the guards, tearfully joined in singing with John as his earthly life ended. My pastor told me that at 1 A.M., outside the gates of the prison, where people were gathered in a vigil of faith against the death penalty, awaiting the 2 A.M. execution, he saw a lonesome man in favor of the death penalty defiantly holding a sign that read, "Dean Smith loves killers." I do not condone any violence against any of God's children, and that is why I am opposed to the death penalty. That sign seemed a kind of confirmation. Actually, it was every person in this state of North Carolina, including me, who killed this man, since we set the laws.

These two parables I mentioned have been helpful to me, in addition to other writing from the Bible. As a book by Robert McAfee Brown entitled *The Bible Speaks to You* explains, it would be difficult to believe that every word of the Bible is literally true, but it can still speak to people as they read it, even now. Although I have trouble believing every word in the Bible, as it was written by human beings, and do not take it all literally or give every passage equal weight, the Bible is a book about who God is. It is not a textbook or a rule book. Some of my friends tell me I pick and choose certain stories that fit what I want. I suppose I just did this with the parables that spoke to me.

I may be wrong, but I tend to agree with the theologian-preacher Barbara Brown Taylor, an Episcopal priest and professor at Piedmont College and author of several books, when she discusses "Holy Scripture and Otherness of God." One of the journals to which I have subscribed, along with the *Christian Century,* is called *Context.* It is published by Dr. Martin Marty of the University of Chicago Divinity School. He quotes Taylor in a recent issue on this subject, and she says it well for me: "The more widely I read the Bible, the less I understood people who held it up as a primer on family values. I could not find one single healthy family in it, unless I counted Mary, Joseph, and Jesus, but even they were a blended family who suffered periods of estrangement. Moses and Paul were murderers, Jacob was a swindler, King David was an adulterer, and Judith used sex to lure Holofernes to his death. Is this really a book we want our children to read? Contrary to popular opinion, the Bible is not about God-fearing men and women who made the world a better place. Instead, it is a book about real people, which is to say, people who lie, cheat, and kill just about as often as they love, heal, and give birth. On the whole I believe it is much safer to approach the Bible as a book about a moral God than as a book about moral human beings and even then it may be necessary to adjust one's working definition of moral. . . . Our arrogance is stunning, but so is God's loving kindness. We may challenge scripture all we like. We will inevitably dismiss great chunks of it, but it will not go away. And, although there are human fingerprints all over it, it remains God's excellent tool for reminding us that we are not God—just God's beloved people, sustained by God's word." (From *Circuit Rider,* January/February 1999.)

I have covered my early years growing up in a Christian home with frequent trips to church on Sundays. I attended youth camps at Baptist-affiliated Ottawa University under the charismatic leadership of Roger Frederickson, who had a great influence on young people. Later my family belonged to the First Baptist Church of Topeka, Kansas, and we attended some of the conferences at the National American Baptist Conference Center at Green Lake, Wisconsin.

Following junior high, I prayed to get into an adult-league baseball game, and I also added to the prayer that I would be a medical missionary if the prayer were granted. That "Celestial Bellhop" mentality was prevalent in my thinking at that time. I was put in the game, so I felt guilty for a number of years, knowing that I wanted to teach and coach. After experiencing the usual distractions and semirebellion in high school and college relating to the Spirit, I did discover that every good vocation can be a "Christian vocation" equal to any vocation for which the church is the employer.

Although I did not always attend worship service in college, I did find inspiration and meaning when I heard Dr. Dale Turner speak at the Congregational Church there. Dale was also my professor in a religion course as a freshman and truly had a gift of speaking, whether in the classroom or the pulpit. Not only was the church in Lawrence, Kansas, always packed, I understand his new church continued to be well attended at the University Congregational Church in Seattle, Washington. I have stayed in touch with Dale over the years; I have even bought many of his books to give to friends, including former players. Many of his columns written for the *Seattle Times* have been published as well. I was one of those who endorsed his latest book, along with a member of the University Congregational Church, Bill Gates.

I probably headed back toward a search for meaning in my life as an Air Force lieutenant in Germany in 1954–55. There was no television there, so I began to do more reading. Of course, there was the base movie theater with frequent changes of movies. After seeing *Magnificent Obsession,* starring Rock Hudson, I was so impressed that I checked out the book by Lloyd C. Douglas. The story was about a doctor who did good deeds for people, usually providing financial assistance—with one stipulation. They could not tell anyone else about the transaction, nor could they pay him back. Douglas had been a pastor of a Congregational church, so he simply was writing about a real-life situation inspired by the Sermon on the Mount. Dr. Douglas also wrote biblical stories as fiction, such as *The Robe,* a *New York Times* best-seller, and *The Big Fisherman.* I read them all and was touched by what was said in these books.

I found myself beginning to reflect back on the spiritual part of my up-bringing. I am a firm believer in religious education for youth, whatever the religion or denomination. Just as my parents exposed Joan and me to Christian education as children, so did we expose our children. We gave them this background, this instruction, but they could make their own decisions as adults. A Carolina professor once told me he wanted his young children to decide on their own whether or not to go to church and church school with their parents. That brought to mind the wisdom of Dr. O. Dean Martin, to whom John Lotz introduced me via tapes of his sermons, which were in-spiring. I was privileged to have dinner with him on several occasions before his death from a brain tumor at age fifty-two. Dr. Martin said it was dumb to leave religious education to chance, whether the religion is Christianity, Ju-daism, Islam, or something else. I agree: Children are going to drive cars one day, and you don't leave it up to them to learn on their own. You put them in driver's education. More seriously, you don't give them a choice about at-tending grade school or not. You know it's important, so it's mandatory.

As I look back, I am grateful to my parents for the family devotions, al-though not regular, for making me go to church at a young age, and most im-portant, for showing Joan and me the value of the spiritual part of life.

My search for understanding in life has been enriched by listening to many tapes, particularly those of Dr. O. Dean Martin and Dr. Tony Campolo. Also, I've learned by reading books by the theologian Dr. Robert McAfee Brown, who also edited the Layman's Theological Library, which I studied back in 1966. Certainly, Søren Kierkegaard has been most interesting to me, as has Father Powell, and Dr. Elton Trueblood, a prolific writer whom I met in Earl-ham College, in Richmond, Indiana, in 1968. Del Harris, the ex–Los Angeles Laker coach who was coach at Earlham College, had invited me to do a clinic in Richmond. I said that if he could arrange a visit with Dr. Trueblood, I would come. Dr. Trueblood allowed me to come into his home, and we had a good visit in his library. Later, it turned out, he did follow basketball and Car-olina to some degree. One time when he was in the Chapel Hill area, he called, and we had lunch. I have also been inspired by the Jewish theologians Martin Buber and Victor Frankel. Frankel was a prisoner in the Nazi concentration camps during World War II. He noted that some people in the camps gave up quickly and others didn't. Those who hung on were those who could see hope in the midst of horror. He said something like, "The last of the human freedoms is that one can choose one's attitude in any circumstance. One can choose one's own way. Sometimes you cannot change the circumstances of your life, but you can always choose the attitudes you take toward them."

The Binkley Church, obviously, has helped me over these past forty years. Dr. Robert Seymour was our first pastor and led the congregation from April 1959 (when my family and his family joined the church) until 1989. He and his wife, Pearl, the organist and a huge Carolina basketball fan, carried out leadership roles not only in the church but in the Chapel Hill/ Carrboro community as well. They have been awarded every honor for service to the community that Chapel Hill has. It would take another book to fully cover the influence the Seymours have had on many people, including the Smiths. Each of my children has been baptized at Binkley, and it has been a real church family. Being a university community, many of our members are associated with the university, but still we have a great cross section of "town and gown."

Dr. Linda Jordan replaced Dr. Seymour as pastor. When Linda resigned, Jim Pike came in from the Wilmette Community Church in Wilmette, Illinois. Coincidentally, Jim's father was the head football coach and assistant basketball coach at Garfield High School in Terre Haute, Indiana, where he coached my old teammate at Kansas, All-American Clyde Lovellette.

When we joined the brand-new Binkley Baptist Church, there were twenty-five members. Today it has approximately five hundred members. Being a part of the growth of the congregation has been a part of my own growth and understanding of the Spirit's love for all human beings. To give an idea of the impact it has had on my understanding, I will share some words recently written by my pastor, Jim Pike, on our fortieth anniversary: "Binkley Baptist Church is a welcoming and affirming congregation. From the beginning, Binkley has stood against the prevailing culture. This church began 40 years ago as a congregation committed to Civil Rights and determined to make a Christ-like difference in a racially segregated world. So, today, regardless of the economic status, race, age, political affiliation, national origin, or sexual orientation, all are welcome in this place. We practice the inclusive love of God and Grace of Jesus Christ which excludes no one in God's human family. At Binkley, we joyfully claim in full membership in this congregation persons who may be gay or lesbian and are grateful for their presence, leadership and love in our community of faith."

Biblical writers do not include any statements by Jesus dealing with homosexuality. However, he does talk about divorced persons, of whom I am one. Certainly, divorced people are loved and accepted by others, as they should be. So it is difficult to understand where the homophobia comes from. I surely hope it doesn't come from a Christian church that affirms each and every person as a child of God. I am not even sure if homosexual behavior could be called a sin, since I can't believe that a choice is involved. I have been attracted to women and can't believe there would be a choice between a woman and a man to be with. I may be wrong, but I do believe we are born with our sexual orientation. There are clinics to try to turn sexual orientation around. However, I have been told that it would be equally difficult to turn heterosexuals into homosexuals through therapy. Perhaps those who are against homosexuals could read First Corinthians, chapter 13, on love. Dr. Robert McAfee Brown has another book out now, *Speaking of Christianity,* in which he indicates that only about 31 percent of the population in the United States has been married only once, and to members of the opposite sex. What do we do with the other 69 percent, many of whom are single or divorced, other than simply let them live on the same level as all of us do before God?

I may be wrong, but I think the primary focus of the Christian faith is love. In one of John's epistles in the Bible, I remember reading, "those who say I love God and hate other humans are liars. . . . For those who do not love their brother or sister whom they have seen cannot love God whom they have not seen." I John 4:7 also says something to the effect that "anyone who loves, knows God." This is not just thinking in terms of the nuclear family, but the whole human race as God's family. We are all brothers and sisters in the human family. It is like we are all aboard the big ship Earth, and we surely want to keep the ship in good condition for the future. This is where environmentalists have a very good point.

Although Binkley has many people from different denominations, including Roman Catholics, I have been a lifelong Baptist. I value the principles of Baptist freedom for theological thought, biblical understanding, and interpretation. A Baptist, historically at least, is not only free, but is responsible for reading the scripture and interpreting the Bible for himself or herself. One hopes this is done in the context of the church community. According to Baptist principles, every church is autonomous and free to determine its understanding of God's leading and its interpretation of scripture. And all individuals in the Baptist setting are free to disagree with one another, even with the pastor, but cannot require others to accept their views of scripture.

That freedom appeals to me. It is a key factor in my personal search for understanding. I may be wrong, but I am free to seek and to study and interpret issues of biblical faith as best I understand it, as I am led by the Holy Spirit.

Today there are some groups calling themselves Christian, such as the Christian Coalition and what used to be the Moral Majority, who seem to have a punitive attitude rather than a loving one toward their neighbor and toward the social issues of our day. Last year I received a survey for Christian voters to complete and return. I have no idea how my name was on their list, since it was mailed by the Christian Coalition. I don't correspond with them. One question was, "Do you consider yourself conservative, liberal, moderate, or other?" I checked the square next to "other" and then wrote in "Christian." Many of them are pro–death penalty, antiwelfare, antiabortion, pro–military buildup, antigay and -lesbian, and pro–assault weapons. In a way, such Christianity has given Jesus a bad name, for if we say Jesus loves you and me, then why aren't we more tolerant? Why aren't we more compassionate to people in need? Why aren't we more loving of enemies? Why aren't we concerned about the growing gap between the rich and the poor? Love of God means addressing the needs of our neighbors, in my opinion, as well as acceptance and tolerance for differences. I may be wrong, but I agree with Robert Reich, former secretary of labor, who said, "America is richer now than it has ever been, almost a third wealthier than it was just fifteen years ago. It is, in fact, the richest nation in the history of the world. Yet despite all this affluence there remain basic things—things that other, less wealthy nations accomplish, like giving all children a decent education and providing all citizens with adequate health care—that America can't seem to afford to do. It's not that these basic goals are anathema to us; it's just that every time we approach the point where they seem attainable, we decide that we can't afford them quite yet." You can't hate your neighbor who is different or who is poor and say you love God. That is a lie. I may be wrong, but I think being grateful to God leads to ethical decisions that surely include education for all children, reasonable options for health care, and openness toward those who seem different. One of my personal ideas in this regard is to suggest that our government pass along whatever money comes from inheritance taxes to a fund to help the poor.

Tennessee author and civil rights leader Dr. Will Campbell spoke at Binkley in April 1999. Will escorted black children to school in Little Rock during the turmoil of 1957 and was the solitary white man who labored with Martin Luther King to found the Southern Christian Leadership Conference. Dr. Campbell said that the theology of certitude is a problem; one guy said

God told him to tell me how to live and if I don't do it his way I am doomed. It is almost like saying, "My God can beat up your God!" Basically, I believe we need to accept others as God accepts us without condemning everyone who has a different way of looking at things (this includes me!). Campbell also spoke of racism as "alive and well in America" a quarter of a century since the marches and demonstrations that marked his early years. "Racism lives, for example, in the workplace and in jails and prisons bursting at the seams with mostly African-American inmates. Affirmative action has not evened things up. Just look at who the CEO's are and how they're chosen. Plus, racism is not ended when a black male is eight times more apt to be convicted than a white. . . . There have been a lot of changes for which we are grateful, but there's a lot of things that have not changed enough."

Our Binkley church is very much what I would call a church "headquarters," where we gain strength from each other to go out to be the "Church in the World." The Church of the Savior in Washington, D.C., was a very good role model for our church. I have been to their church headquarters on Massachusetts Avenue in D.C. Many of our members are in politics and many are involved in nonprofit organizations bringing about social change. In 1996 our church commissioned four members who were elected to political office, including Congressman David Price. Although our church hasn't become the true "Koinonia Group," which Dr. Elton Trueblood describes in his book *Incendiary Fellowship,* we do believe that because of God's love and acceptance for us we must respond to our fellow humans in need of love and acceptance. The institutional church is certainly not perfect. We go there knowing how members still make the same mistakes as other people, but we see it as a kind of hospital, a healing place with other sinners who hope to learn and do better in caring for others. It is a different place, though, as far as tolerance and caring go, which seems to me to be very Christian, or perhaps I should say Christlike. I have often said, "I am sure glad I am not in charge of the Universe!" My church sees the issues of the world as spiritual concerns and understands that all people of the world are people about whom God cares and, therefore, about whom we need to care. Binkley takes up issues of poverty, homelessness, racial justice, peace, women's rights, the end of the nuclear arms race, materialism, abolition of the death penalty, and full inclusion into the community of faith of all people, including persons who just happen to be gay or lesbian, or mentally ill. The end of domestic abuse and violence and concern for the environment are among the important issues for Christians and other religions to address. I think of Christianity not as a shot giving us immunization from the suffering of the real world, but as a shot in the arm that strengthens us for making a difference for good in the real world.

Dr. O. Dean Martin told me this story about the fundamentalist university student who spoke to him confidentially about his friend Sarah. "Sarah is Jewish and doesn't believe in Jesus," he said. "Will she go to hell when she dies?" Dean asked her, "Would that make you happy?" "Oh, no!" replied the student. "Maybe God will be as nice as you," Dean answered.

What about life after death? No human being knows for certain, but what we read in the Bible certainly gives hope that there is something special for some. I personally believe there is something special for all humans who pass this life. Like an interruption to what we are doing in this world, we move into something much better.

Dr. Elton Trueblood, in his book *A Place to Stand,* has an entire chapter on "Life Everlasting." As a respected professor of philosophy, he quickly points to Plato and Socrates and what they believed four hundred years before the Christian era.

Socrates is supposed to have said these words a short time before his execution: "And now, O my judges, I desire to prove to you that the real philosopher has reason to be of good cheer when he is about to die, and after that death he may hope to obtain the greatest good in the other world." Socrates was called a "Christian before Christ."

I'm guessing everyone hears his or her Spirit. Socrates did, and "knew" something was ahead. I have no proof, but an afterlife surely makes sense. "Little man" cannot think like the Creator of the Universe! The title of J. B. Phillips's book *Your God Is Too Small* is another way of saying the same thing.

I like Dr. Trueblood's statement in his book about the belief in life after death: "The rationality of the belief depends not upon absolute proof, which we have learned not to expect anywhere, but rather upon a balance of alternates. The reasonableness of continued life exceeds the reasonableness of the finality of physical death." There is a reason for the hope that is in us. I believe in a loving God who wouldn't hurt one of his children.

My search for understanding has led me to be grateful for the Holy Spirit in each of us to help guide us. I may be wrong, but I believe that Spirit is available for each human being throughout the world, whether they be Jewish, Christian, Buddhist, Hindu, Muslim, or of another religious faith, and that God's love is inclusive of all. This Spirit has been called the Creator's Spirit, the Holy Ghost, the human spirit, the Higher Power, the conscience, the Counselor, the Comforter, and other names. Most human beings, if not all, do feel the power of something inside them attempting to help in decision making. Every so often I feel that my Spirit sees or feels the Holy Spirit in another person; yes, even in my enemy.

In the past several years, I have had two close friends who have suffered from the disease of alcoholism and are finding new strength through Alcoholics Anonymous meetings and their twelve steps toward sobriety. As a result, I studied AA's twelve-step program and found it to be similar to the steps outlined by the Christian Oxford Group founded in England. In fact, in the last few years church groups have wisely adopted the twelve-step program, changing the first step from powerlessness over the disease of alcoholism to powerlessness over the "sin disease," a separation from God.

I did attend an AA meeting with one of my friends and was extremely impressed with the openness and acceptance for each speaker as he or she told how it used to be and how it had all changed. It is hard to imagine standing up in our church or any church and speaking of all the bad things we have done and still feeling fully loved and accepted, as people are in AA. Perhaps the "anonymous" part could make it easier. Most AA members seem to be finding a truly new life day to day, because they have made the decision to turn over their decision process to what many in AA call the Higher Power. On one tape, I listened to a man named Charlie, who was explaining the twelve steps and quipping, "My decisions were all so bad; why wouldn't I try something else? Besides, now I know where my car is parked after going out on Saturday night!" At the end of the tape, he remarked how lucky all of them were. Because of the twelve-step program, they no longer have the many resentments most of us carry with us, but have turned their resentments over to this Higher Power. As part of the program, they write down their many resentments against persons and institutions. They learn that their resentments only hurt themselves. Charlie said, "I resented my business partner so much that each morning I would have a drink with my coffee and make up ways of revenge. All the time that SOB was lying on the beach in California and wasn't thinking one second about me. I wasn't hurting him, but I was hurting myself." Charlie and his business partner are now neighbors and best friends.

I predict that the institutional church will be more like a twelve-step meeting in the future. In church, as in one of these meetings, people find peace and contentment in turning their life over to the Higher Power, or what I might call the Holy Spirit. People in recovery look at themselves as limited human beings who make mistakes and are lovable and forgiven. That's not a bad way for any of us to look at ourselves.

If we do listen to the Holy Spirit, we probably will come closer to living the way we were created to live, and so enjoy the true good life, rather than practice a so-called good life founded on materialism. A year or two ago, I received the tape of a sermon by Len Strobel, associate pastor at the famous Willow Creek Church in Barrington, Illinois. The title of the sermon was "What Would Jesus Tell Michael Jordan?" The title appears to be arrogant. It is as if Reverend Strobel would know what Jesus might say to anyone. However, the sermon isn't really about Michael Jordan, but it is about materialism and Christianity. The pastor has a way of making it very clear that although money does offer some of the same things as Christianity, it is basically fool's gold, as opposed to the real thing. Money fails to deliver contentment or inner peace. Reverend Strobel makes the point, and I agree, that Michael Jordan gains a different and deeper kind of satisfaction from his many gifts to charity, which include a million-dollar contribution to the Carolina School of Social Work, than from his athletic exploits.

A sermon of Dr. Martin's entitled "The Bluetick Hound" makes this point in a parable about a bluetick hound chasing his car every day. When the man finally decides to stop his car, the dog has no idea what to do once he has reached his goal. The bluetick hound illustrates the way it is with so many who have chased after money and success. Jim Pike recalls reading an interview with O. J. Simpson long before his infamous trial. In the interview O. J. Simpson said, "I sit in my house in Buffalo and sometimes I get so lonely it is unbelievable. Life has been good to me. I've got a great wife, good kids, money, my own health . . . and I am lonely and bored. I often wondered why so many rich people commit suicide. Money sure isn't a cure-all." It is too bad that only the rich know for sure that money cannot bring happiness and contentment.

That is the way I see it. There is always the chance that I may be wrong, but this is what I believe for now. Perhaps I can sum up my understanding of God and human beings this way: "What do you call the guy who finishes last in his medical school class? Doctor!" So I would like to add, "What do you call the worst human beings you know? Human beings loved by the Creator!"

12

Winding Down,
Looking Ahead

It's difficult for me to speak impartially when the subject is college basketball. Our game, played the right way, is the most beautiful sport of
them all. We're the perfect game for television. The big ball is easily followed by the camera and the eyes of the viewers. The raging emotion of the
sport—the highs and the lows—is written on the faces of the players. There
are no protective face guards, no helmets to shield their feelings. Fans see
this and identify with their favorite team in a way that isn't possible in any
other team sport.

Our game is unique and has so much intrigue that I don't agree with those
who fret because some of our players leave college basketball early in order
to play in the NBA. We've gone through that since 1972 at North Carolina,
involving some excellent players, and we survived it. There are plenty of
good players to go around. And I'm not just talking about enough good players for Carolina, Kansas, Duke, Kentucky, UCLA, and Indiana either, although, with their success, they do have some recruiting advantages. Still,
it's necessary for those schools to make good recruiting decisions. At North
Carolina we played several players in big NCAA tournament games who
weren't offered Division 1 scholarships. While most male youngsters from
my generation dreamed of playing major league baseball, basketball is
clearly the game of choice now. College basketball will always have stars.

Instead of dwelling on those who leave early, we should spend our time talking about the ones who are still playing. After all, there are approximately four thousand players in Division 1 basketball. Fewer than twenty underclassmen are drafted each year. Why so much attention on the ones who leave?

With all due respect to the NBA, in many ways its game can't match the college game. They are two entirely different games, with different rules. The biggest difference might be the quality of the rivalries, some of which date back to the turn of the century. Rivalries such as Carolina-Duke, Indiana-Purdue, Kansas-Missouri, and Kentucky-Louisville are hard to match. College basketball has a pageantry that is unique, and it all adds up to sights and sounds that television loves. The NBA is terrific in its own way, but I just don't see it as a threat to our game, as some argue.

But just because college basketball is healthy and popular doesn't mean we don't have problems. We do, and they need to be addressed. Billy Packer likes to say that he's often wrong but never in doubt. With that in mind, let me take a crack at what I see as some of our game's pressing concerns.

Excessively rough play: Basketball was meant to be a game of finesse, speed, quickness, and agility. I'm afraid we've come near the point where we've made weight lifting almost as important to college basketball as jumping, running, moving the feet, ballhandling, and shooting.

In my opinion, we should reverse this unfortunate trend before it hurts our game more than it has already. How did this rough play evolve? Maybe some of it trickled down from the NBA game to ours. Some of the post play in professional basketball resembles Saturday-night wrestling. I watched an NBA play-off game last spring between Utah and Portland in which a Utah player locked arms with a Portland player, then pulled his opponent's arm toward him and flopped, as if he were the victim. Thank goodness Joey Crawford, a veteran official, saw the fakery for what it was and called the foul on the Utah player. But plays such as that, even when they're detected, are harmful to the sport. High school and college coaches see it, often hear a commentator talk about the player's savvy in making such an illegal move, and then choose to teach it themselves. To the NBA's credit, it realizes its game is too rough and is moving in a direction to clean it up.

While I'm quick to point out that television is one of the main reasons college basketball became so popular, it might also have played a role in making the game as rough as it is. Commentators and producers don't like to see trek after trek to the foul line, so they sometimes come down hard on officials who call fouls. No official wants to be criticized on television. He can be sure that he won't be criticized if he doesn't call fouls away from the ball—and this is where most of the rough, illegal play exists: away from the ball. My good friend Bill Raftery, who does a splendid job commentating on college basketball on CBS and ESPN, likes to refer to fouls as "nickel-and-dimers." Bill and I disagree here. After all, it might be a "nickel-and-dimer" if a defender flicks the elbow of a shooter, but that's all it takes, a little flick, to send the shot astray. These little tricks that some players use—and are sometimes coached to use—to get away with fouls are a pet peeve of mine. We had a player in the ACC who was unbelievable with his feet. People who were guarded by him fell like ducks in a shooting gallery. His trick was to get his feet entangled with his opponent's and trip him. He was good at it, I'll give him that. A Georgia Tech fan sent me a tape of the player doing it or I wouldn't have noticed (it wasn't a Georgia Tech player), and when you looked for it, it was easy to see what he was doing. I'm sorry to say he usually got away with it.

It's my feeling that we must stop players from committing fouls (and coaches from encouraging them) under the assumption the officials won't call all of them. I know of a West Coast team in the 1970s that felt if they fouled on every possession, the result would be what the coach called excellent defense. The coach bragged about it. His reasoning was that only so many of the fouls would be called. Unfortunately, he was right. Somehow, there's a prevailing notion on the part of fans that fouls called on each team should be about equal, even though one team might be taught to do its best not to foul while the other has fouling as a cornerstone of its defensive philosophy. The best officials won't be swayed if one team has many more fouls than the opponent, but others might. Officials shouldn't even know the number of fouls against a team except to know when to shoot the bonus.

Most veteran coaches I know are alarmed with the roughness of the game today. Two of the greatest names in basketball history—John Wooden and Bill Bradley—not long ago were asked what they see as current trends in basketball, and what worries them most about the game's future. They each said they are alarmed at how much the officials let go in today's game.

Now, no one is suggesting that we want to turn college basketball into a foul-shooting contest. Far from it. But if the officials were instructed by their supervisors to call the fouls, the game would clean up. Also, the supervisors would have to penalize the officials who don't. It would also become more exciting for fans, because these great athletes would be allowed to demonstrate their skills. There's one thing that every basketball player in the United States—from church league to the NBA—shares, and that's a desire to stay in the game. They're not going to continue to foul if they know the officials are going to call them, thereby dispatching them to the bench for excessive fouls.

What can be done to clean up the game? Here are some suggestions:

• Reduce the number of fouls needed for disqualification in high school and college basketball from five to four. We once had a rule in college and high school basketball that a player would be disqualified after four fouls. Fewer college players are fouling out of games in the 1990s than in the 1970s. I think it would help our game now to return to the old way, although I don't expect many to agree.

A way to ruin the game would be to increase the number of fouls allowed. Back in the 1960s, John Nucatola, a Hall of Fame official, served with me on the Basketball Rules Committee. He convinced the committee to conduct an experiment in high school basketball in New York City in which a player would be granted unlimited fouls. I was present for one of those games. Any foul after the fifth personal on a player was treated as a technical foul—free throws and possession of the ball. This particular game featured two star players—Jim McMillan, of Jefferson High in Brooklyn, who was recruited by us and would play at Columbia University, and Solly McMillen, of Erasmus High, who went to DePaul. Talk about a trek to the foul line! As I recall it, Jim McMillan had eight fouls in that game and Solly had twelve or thirteen. It was a mess. The coaches wanted their best players to stay in the game, even at such a high cost. The parade to the foul line resulted in a high school game that took over two hours to play.

• Call intentional fouls against players who grab jerseys or who interlock their arms and fake being fouled. The ACC player who made an art out of tripping opponents should have been called with some intentional fouls, as a deterrent. These so-called cute tricks really bother me. Sadly, it is extremely hard for teams to lose games with this type of play, and some coaches feel forced to teach this rough stuff.

• Widen the three-second lane to make it conform to international standards. The fight for low-post position is ferocious in today's game because most college players will score or get fouled when they catch the ball that close to the basket. If the lane is widened, the defensive player may be more willing to let the post man catch the ball, because it would be harder to score, and we might not have so much wrestling for position.

• Call fouls away from the ball. I recall when I used to argue at our ACC meetings to have three officials rather than two calling our games. Norm Sloan and Lefty Driesell opposed me, arguing that we had a hard enough time finding two good officials to work a game, so finding a third one who was competent would be a real challenge. We did go to three officials, and we did get better full-court coverage, so that fouls away from the ball were more often detected and called. Still, even with three officials, too many fouls are uncalled. Certainly, an official must watch the ball, but with three officials there is no excuse not to see the illegal screening or offensive pushing away from the ball. And if it is seen, it should be called! At least one official is assigned coverage of illegal activity off the ball, but very few fouls away from the ball are called in a game, and this is where the illegal activity is happening. It should be emphasized that when we allow the game to get as rough as it's become, we make the officials *too important.* They begin to pick and choose what to call, which is not fair to them, and certainly not fair to the players.

Full-time officials for college basketball: To get the college game called consistently and correctly, maybe we need to go to full-time officials as the NBA has. Such a system would give supervisors control over their officials. If officials didn't call the game the way it was meant to be called, the supervisors could dismiss them, and the officials would be out of their full-time job. Most of the men officiating Division 1 basketball have full-time jobs outside of refereeing. I can hear the outcry against this now: It would cost too much money; it would harm the amateur status of the college game and make us too much like the pros; the best officials in college basketball would not give up their chief professions to referee full-time.

On the other hand, if we had full-time officials, that would be the job they worked at twelve months a year. They would attend clinics and small study sessions on a regular basis, watch tapes with their supervisors, be instructed on the rules on a year-round basis. They would devote forty hours a week to basketball officiating. If they continued to make mistakes, they could be subject to fines or the eventual loss of their position. Officiating basketball is about as close to an impossible job as a person could have. Given the difficulty of it, devoting full time to the profession would provide us with better officiating. I don't see how anyone could argue with that. The new TV contract for the NCAA tournament is being discussed now. In all probability, the money will be substantially increased, so Division 1 basketball could afford full-time people.

NCAA: College basketball, even with our problems, is a special game. The NCAA men's basketball tournament creates so much interest, and with it revenue, that it finances about 85 percent of the NCAA's annual budget. When we signed our latest contract with CBS to show the men's tournament, we insisted that the network also telecast the women's Final Four. The women's Final Four was helped tremendously by getting that exposure, and now its tournament is shown on ESPN. We could do even more to help the women's game if we followed the plan of Terry Holland, the excellent former coach and now athletics director at Virginia. Terry says we shouldn't be marketing men's and women's basketball at the same time so that they compete for viewers and ticket sales. He suggests moving the women's schedule to September, October, and November, with the national tournament to take place before Christmas. I think it would create tremendous interest in women's basketball. A true basketball fan would enjoy watching basketball in September, and as we know, television can create interest in going to the game.

The 1972 NCAA convention—known as the "cost-saving convention"—resulted in changes to college athletics that in my opinion have been harmful to student-athletes. This was the convention that, among other things, made freshmen eligible for varsity competition, took school-bought blazers away from players, many of whom couldn't afford to own a sport coat, and abolished the $15-a-month portion of the full scholarship that had for decades given players their so-called laundry money. The convention was all about saving money, and the best interests of the student-athletes were trampled. Shortly thereafter, another awful decision was made. The NCAA abolished the four-year scholarship and made each grant for one year. In other words, the governing body for college athletics made it legal for colleges to renege on agreements made with student-athletes during recruitment.

How should we go about undoing some of the harm caused by these changes in NCAA bylaws?

• All athletic scholarships should be for four years, not one. Just last spring a prominent Southeastern Conference university saw its football coach in effect "fire" six of his players. How an institution of higher learning could stand by and allow this to happen is beyond me. That the NCAA could pass legislation that encourages this type of behavior is disgraceful. What kind of message are we sending to young people when we show them by our actions that universities can treat student-athletes this way? Some have suggested that basketball players who leave school early for the NBA are somehow not living up to their scholarship agreement. The truth is, their scholarship was only year-by-year, and the players who decide to leave early for the pros certainly aren't breaking any contract.

• To help basketball players with financial need, as determined by the Pell Grant process that is already in place, we should give those on full scholarship $2,000 a school year in money earned from NCAA men's basketball tournament television revenues. Some of these students don't have the money to go out for a pizza with their friends or to go to a movie. We need to do more for these needy student-athletes to make them feel as if they're a real part of the student body. The present scholarship does not provide the full cost of attendance, which some academic scholarships do. This additional money would match that of the best academic grants. The NCAA recently said that student-athletes on scholarship could work during the school year. This is a good rule for nonrevenue sports that have many athletes on partial scholarships, but dangerous, because it opens the door for boosters to offer jobs to football and basketball players. This would be a mistake. We know full well that many such jobs would be phantom jobs, in which the athlete is paid for doing very little work. We should learn from experience; this has been a problem since the 1930s. This additional $2,000 stipend that I'm suggesting would prohibit football or basketball players from holding a job during the school year. After all, the demands of schoolwork, practice time, games, travel, and dealing with the media don't leave players from those two sports enough time to have jobs during the school year.

• Football, with its eighty-five scholarships, should be excluded from gender equity considerations under Title IX. Please don't get me wrong. I'm all for women's athletics, and Title IX has forced many universities to offer women a chance to compete in athletics. It was, and is, the right thing to do. But there is no women's sport that gobbles up eighty-five scholarships, as football does. By keeping football in the equation, many universities are having to drop sports that have been important to men on campus for generations. It was sad that when Providence lost in the NCAA baseball play-offs last May the defeat not only ended its season but was the last game ever for Providence baseball. It was dropped for financial reasons. I think it's bad that some colleges can have a women's golf team but not one for the men, for example. Sports are helpful in the development of all college students. It is too bad that golf is the only game that is played by the honor system, where you call the penalty on yourself.

• If we took a poll of chancellors and university presidents, most of them would say that the most serious problems on campus are alcohol related. Alcohol is the leading cause of death on college campuses and for all persons under twenty-five. Most of the rapes and assaults on campuses across the United States are alcohol related.

We all know this, yet we encourage the sale of beer. We do it by allowing the beer companies to place ads on the telecasts of men's basketball and football games. I've debated this issue since 1986. I wish I could say I'm winning. I'm not. However, some progress is being made. North Carolina and Wisconsin are two universities on record as not accepting beer advertising in university-related activities that the schools control. There are no beer commercials in the radio broadcasts of our sporting events, no beer ads in our game programs, and no beer ads in arenas. Since Carolina and Wisconsin took this stand, twenty other universities across the country have adopted similar policies. I call that progress.

It's important to understand that North Carolina does not have institutional control over the advertising sold in our ACC television package for football and men's basketball. We have a vote, but we're only one of nine members. We have been promised by the ACC that it will revisit this business of allowing beer commercials on league football and basketball telecasts before the next contract is signed. We have had some other minor victories. On ACC basketball telecasts, the announcers used to "throw" to a commercial by saying: "We'll be back after this from our good friends at Budweiser." It wasn't enough that we allowed Budweiser to advertise on our basketball telecasts; we also introduced them as "our good friends." Now the announcers just say they'll be back "after this from Budweiser." The beer ads are still there, and the ACC continues to collect the money. But at least they are not "our good friends" anymore, at least not publicly.

We need to understand that children start following athletics at the age of nine or ten. These beer ads are highly appealing to them. When beer companies say their ads aren't directed at young people, I find it hard to believe. Do you think the kids don't like the lizards on the Budweiser spots? How about the frog that would get his tongue stuck to a beer can? Beer companies are in business to make a profit, and these television commercials are designed to help them sell beer. Over twenty years ago, when the legal drinking age in North Carolina was eighteen, it's little wonder that when my son, at age eighteen, went to the beach the first thing he wanted was a beer. The commercials showing volleyball, pretty girls, the beach, and the beer all appealed to him. He thought it was the thing to do. He'd been fed the message for years, and our universities serve as the willing vehicle.

There's another glaring truth about many of the beer spots: They highlight outright dishonesty, stealing, and lying. The man sitting in the back of the limousine lies about his name to get a beer. The pretty girl befriends a boy on the beach and covers him with sand so she can steal his beer. The beer ads always feature pretty women and handsome men, and happiness seems to come from drinking. That's the message.

Bubba Smith, the former NFL football star, was featured in Miller Lite commercials in the days of the "tastes great, less filling" debate. He quit the role when he spoke at a junior high school and learned that's what he was becoming known for in the minds of the students—as a salesman for beer. Beer lobbyists are careful not to tell us that the ethanol content in a can of beer is the same as in a shot of liquor. In North Carolina, we can buy beer at any corner convenience store, but have to go to a liquor store to buy liquor. Ask yourself this question: If aspirin were the leading cause of death on college campuses, do you think chancellors, presidents, and trustees would allow aspirin commercials on basketball and football telecasts? They wouldn't, not for a minute.

Virtually every high school in America has at some time suffered the tragedy of alcohol-related deaths. Young people die in automobile accidents because of drinking and driving. Young girls are raped in alcohol-related assaults. College students under the influence of alcohol fall to their death before they reach age twenty-one. Congress made a good decision many years ago when it disallowed tobacco advertising on radio and television. And in print ads now the tobacco companies are forced to display in large type the dangers of their product. If Congress can do the right thing in the case of cigarettes and chewing tobacco, why are the politicians so reluctant to treat beer advertising, whose product kills thousands of young people each year, just as firmly? It's a blemish on our society, and it's a shame that we allow it to go on. It is also puzzling to me that the liquor companies are not winning the right to advertise on TV if beer ads are allowed.

Surgeon General David Satcher recently said, "Alcohol abuse kills and injures more of our young people and costs our society more than all the illegal drugs put together. The misuse of alcohol is a major problem among college students."

When I testified in 1993 before a joint Senate-House committee that was studying the effects of advertising by companies that produce alcoholic beverages, Senator John Danforth of Missouri, a Yale Divinity School graduate, asked me if I thought tobacco use was "inherently wrong." I told him I was a former smoker and I guessed it was. I wasn't as prepared as I should have been; I wish I had debated him more. After all, a smoker does harm only to him- or herself, and might die of lung cancer at age sixty, instead of living to seventy-two. But alcohol abuse is an overwhelming menace to our society.

Look at the number of broken homes caused by alcoholics, the number of women who have been battered and raped in alcohol-related incidents, the number of people killed and maimed on our highways each year by drunken drivers, the loss of production in our workforce because of alcohol-related problems. We really have to struggle to rationalize that beer advertising is harmless. The evidence points the other way.

There's been some publicity about my wife, Dr. Linnea Smith, and her work to call foul on some truly unsporting practices. Unfortunately, much of that publicity is inaccurate: It's either misinformation spread by the commercial sex industry or misrepresentation published in unauthorized biographies of me. I'd like to set the record straight.

We in sports can be the trailblazers when it comes to social justice issues. I'm lucky to work in a field that transcends barriers, opens doors for people based on nothing more than their amazing athletic abilities rather than the conditions of their birth, like skin color. Sports is blind in that respect, thankfully. And yet it has some blind spots in other respects.

For instance, the *Playboy* All-America list is an annual event that named me its inaugural basketball Coach of the Year in 1976. Linnea and I went to that first *Playboy* awards weekend, an all-expense-paid gala at Lake Geneva, Wisconsin. Like most of you, we were influenced by today's culture; we didn't want to seem like prudes. So we went and were feted and I was photographed with basketball players who were also on an all-expense-paid trip for the magazine.

But after we came home, Linnea did some research. She got more information and decided not to play ball with *Playboy* again. After looking at research material, so did some of our players. It was hard for Linnea to do the research and a hard decision to go public with it, but she chose to do that when faced with the facts.

Some may wonder why a stand against *Playboy*, when it is mild in comparison to the ever-escalating explicit and dehumanizing pornography available today. *Playboy* is the prototype of commercial sex magazines and is perceived by many to be mainstream and legitimate. It is the so-called men's magazine that most consistently uses college sports and athletes to further legitimize its publication and attract young readers. Because the magazine is perceived by many as being legitimate, and because of its widespread distribution, it is more insidious, and the potential for negative impact may be greater.

Also, *Playboy* is a nonsports publication with an unorthodox (and arbitrary, at best) selection process, so really, how much validity can its All-

American Team truly have? Plus, it's a preseason designation, not a post-season merit-based award. Again, where's the validity except using popular collegiate athletes as a marketing tool for the magazine?

And last, it's not a real award like an Associated Press All-American: If you turn this down, your name is simply taken off the list and the "award" goes to the next person . . . who agrees to travel to a place and be photographed for the magazine.

Most important of all, Linnea pointed out that it seemed that the message of *Playboy* was to make sport of women. How could we support this? How could we, as members of a community that believes in raising people up, close our eyes to a practice that seemed to be aimed at holding certain people down? Linnea and I are pleased with Kenny Smith, J. R. Reid, Eric Montross, and a few other players from Carolina and other schools across the nation who have declined *Playboy*'s invitation through the years. These athletes have minds of their own and, after careful consideration, chose not to participate. Certainly those who chose to be on the *Playboy* All-American Team had that choice also. I laughed when Tommy Amaker, a good friend and former Duke player and assistant, said he accepted the award in 1986 since "it was the only train at my station."

Also, coaches John Thompson, Roy Williams, Bob Knight, Tom Osborne, and other college football and basketball coaches have declined *Playboy*'s invitation to be its Coach of the Year after seeing Linnea's research results.

After a few years of research and discussion, Linnea formally took her concerns about *Playboy* and a list of recommendations for consideration to the NCAA. With the support of some influential coaches, long-standing NCAA director Walter Byers, in a letter to me and his top-level staff, made a statement about the lack of value of preseason awards such as *Playboy*'s except for the commercial promotional value to the magazine and not the college players. The paper also called into question the validity of awards such as *Playboy*'s which have no sanctioned merit-based selection process.

But the story doesn't end there. In 1993, the prestigious Knight Commission on Intercollegiate Athletics made its final report to those of us in sports. It counseled that we place a premium on fairness, equality, competition, and recognition of merit for *all* student-athletes, both men and women. The Knight Commission called it "keeping the faith." Linnea took the message to heart and took on what she considered the discriminatory practices of *Sports Illustrated*. She asked the tough question: How can a magazine that publicly supports what the Knight Commission stands for publish an annual swimsuit issue? Thanks to those in the ongoing national grassroots campaign with whom Linnea and others joined ranks, there was an enormous turnover in advertisers. They were also concerned about the unsportsmanlike image the magazine portrayed with that issue, which also reflects poorly on the magazine's own standards for serious sports journalism. A wave of public support moved *SI* to create a separate sports-free men's magazine to feature swimsuits, to offer a swimsuit issue–free subscription rate for those interested in sports and sporting news, and most important of all, to remove images of children from the swimsuit issue. We applaud *Sports Illustrated* for its efforts.

But trust me, not all of Linnea's efforts have paid off. She's had her share of spectacular failures. After years of fashion show luncheons, the National Association of Basketball Coaches, at the Final Four in 1986, decided to schedule a meaty program for the wives. Linnea jumped at the chance to promote her cause to the group. To her dismay, many in the audience walked out during the explicit slide presentation. Only two out of the hundreds attending signed up for more information. The bottom line: The timing, venue, and expectations were all wrong. The issue was controversial. But it was still important for people in sports to hear the message.

Through the years, Linnea has been just one of the messengers speaking out against discrimination against women and exploitation of children. A researcher, educator, lecturer, consultant, and author, she has developed educational materials and conducted workshops about pornography as a public health and safety problem as well as a social justice and civil rights issue.

So, the naked truth about my wife, sex, and centerfolds? It all comes down to this: Sports is all about breaking down barriers. But not just the barriers of speed and scores, championships and personal bests. It's also about breaking down stereotypes and the barriers that limit opportunities and a fair playing field for all. Sports are the embodiment of good health, fair competition, mutual respect, cooperation, and character development. Linnea's work is the work of sports, to lift up *all* people.

Our game of college basketball has grown to the point where a good argument could be made that there's too much interest in the sport these days. It has become enormous. I am absolutely convinced that I could have been just as happy in my career coaching at a Division 3 school—no athletic scholarships, no TV coverage, no big buildings, no huge crowds. To form a team we'd post a message on the bulletin board: BASKETBALL TRYOUTS TODAY. ALL INTERESTED SHOULD BE IN THE GYM NO LATER THAN 3 P.M., PREPARED TO PRACTICE.

Of course, it was a far different stage at North Carolina. We competed under bright lights with concentrated media scrutiny. But the day Chancellor Aycock hired me to be head coach in 1960, he didn't say, "Win x many games or else." He said: "Give the university a basketball team of which it can be proud." We tried to do that.

Still, while Chapel Hill is a wonderful place to coach basketball, the position at Carolina involves much more than coaching the players in practice and games, which I never tired of. It involves speaking, public appearances, media requests for interviews, having television and radio shows, as well as responding to all types of requests from worthy organizations. Even saying no takes up much time. I was always fired up to coach, but eventually the other parts of the job began to take a toll, though my staff tried their best to shield me from them.

Beginning in the early 1990s, I almost always felt at the conclusion of each season that I would retire from coaching. By the time April rolled around, I was drained. I think most coaches are. I tried to be careful not to make career decisions when I was in that state.

That was wise, because in June the juices would start flowing again. By August, as I began to plan our strategy for the next season, I would take basketball tapes of our team with me to the beach for our family vacation. When the press asked me over the years about my retirement plans, I told them the truth, which was that I didn't have my life blueprinted, but the first time October 15, the first day of practice, rolled around and I wasn't excited and enthusiastic about my job, I would retire.

Although I didn't discuss it with anyone, it's accurate to say I considered retiring after our 1991 season. We went to the Final Four, were ACC champions, and had a 29–6 record. We lost three outstanding seniors in Rick Fox, Pete Chilcutt, and King Rice, but we had some excellent young players returning. The program was in good shape. By July, however, the excitement was back for me. I was ready to coach again.

While I considered retirement each spring during the 1990s, there were things that absolutely had to be in place before I would leave. Since our program wasn't in the greatest shape when I took it over in 1961, I was always determined to leave my successor what could be a good team for a couple of years. I would not even consider compromising that, as long as my health was good and my enthusiasm was high. My goal was to leave the next coach good players and a strong program.

Some people thought I might leave after we won the 1993 national championship. Some of my friends, while they didn't want me to retire, thought leaving after winning the NCAAs would be the perfect way to exit. As it happened, it never entered my mind.

I certainly couldn't even consider leaving after the 1995 season, when we went to the Final Four. It was a special year, and at its end Jerry Stackhouse and Rasheed Wallace decided to leave their college basketball eligibility behind after their sophomore seasons and go early to the NBA. They should have: Both of them went in the top four of the draft, and Rasheed is a well-paid star for Portland, as is Jerry for Detroit. Jerry has his college degree, which is a remarkable achievement considering he left at the end of his sophomore year. We're still hoping that Rasheed will finish his college work too, and there are some good signs that he intends to do just that. They're both wonderful young men. Rasheed, because he played with such emotion, sometimes got a bum rap, but he was a genuine pleasure to coach. There were published reports after he decided to go to the NBA two years early that I was happy to have him out of Chapel Hill, but that was an absolute fabrication; I was happy for their good fortune, but disappointed I would no longer be their coach. Rasheed and Jerry were intelligent, respectful of their coaches and teammates, and unselfish players. Rasheed is now doing many things for needy people in his hometown of Philadelphia, and Jerry is helping the disadvantaged in the Kinston, North Carolina, area, his hometown.

I knew our team would have to work extremely hard to get back to the NCAA tournament the following season, 1995–96, after losing Rasheed and Jerry. Our only experienced players returning were both guards— Dante Calabria and Jeff McInnis. Our top six in 1995 were Stackhouse, Wallace, Donald Williams, Calabria, McInnis, and Pearce Landry. Landry came to Carolina as a walk-on and played two years on our junior varsity, which was a mistake on my part. He was good enough to have been a scholarship player from day one. Seven-foot Serge Zwikker got some valuable experience when Rasheed hurt his ankle in the 1995 ACC tournament. We had three freshmen coming in for the 1996 team—Antawn Jamison, Vince Carter, and Ademola Okulaja. We were excited about the future of those young players, along with Serge on the front line, but we had our work cut out for us. The three freshmen were in our top seven all year, along with Calabria, McInnis, Zwikker, and Shammond Williams. We managed to finish 21–11, with a 10–6 record in the ACC, and we made the NCAA tournament. We lost some very close games that year—in overtime to Georgia Tech, by 2 to Villanova in Maui, by 2 to Texas in Austin, by 3 to Georgia Tech, by 3 to N.C. State, by 6 to Maryland, by 2 to Clemson, by 4 to Florida State. You can see how close that young team came to having a sensational season.

Quite frankly, by this time it was taking me longer to rewind after each season. Retirement was on my mind, but now something else entered the equation to complicate matters in a way that I struggled to understand. As I was reminded constantly by the media, I was closing in on the late Adolph Rupp's record of 876 wins by a college coach. While I wanted each of our teams to win all of their games, catching Rupp in the win column was a record that meant nothing to me. I just wanted the talk of it to go away. A few years earlier, I became so frustrated by it that I mentioned to North Carolina sportswriters Ronald Green and Irwin Smallwood, who were in Chapel Hill to join me in a round of golf, that the record was so meaningless that I would quit the game before breaking it. It was an off-the-cuff comment that would not go away. People kept reminding me of it.

It certainly wouldn't have bothered me to walk away a game short of Rupp's record. It was never my goal to break it. In fact, I don't think they should even keep coaching records. The records belong to the players. That's why I really did enjoy the moment in the 1976 Olympics when the gold medals were presented to the U.S. team, on the platform with a spotlight on them, as John Thompson, Bill Guthridge, and I were off to the side with tears in our eyes. I think it would suffice for the record book to read something like this: "North Carolina's 1997 team finished 28–7 and made the Final Four. That team was coached by Dean Smith." Don't add up the records for all my teams. Just the record for *that* team.

That's the way I always looked at my thirty-six North Carolina teams— one team at a time. I didn't keep a running record of how many games we had won or lost over my career. In fact, one of the things I enjoyed most about coaching college basketball was that we had a new team each and every year. Players left, young ones came in. Each year there was new chemistry, and there were new challenges. I was lucky to be a college coach. I think this emphasis on past records and traditions sometimes kept players from receiving the credit they deserved. The tradition of winning can be quite a burden on young people. I told our players not to worry about what the 1969 or 1982 teams did. "This is your team," I would say, "and enjoy it and do the best you can. Don't worry about measuring up to the past or about what others say about you."

Inevitably, I suppose, talk of my possibly breaking Rupp's record mushroomed. I was genuinely ready to step down before it happened, but my former players certainly didn't want that to happen. My assistants, Bill Guthridge, Phil Ford, and Dave Hanners, as well as my former assistants, Roy Williams, Eddie Fogler, Randy Wiel, John Lotz, and Larry Brown, were adamant about my staying on the job until we surpassed Coach Rupp's record for wins, as long as I was healthy. Former players, such as Charlie Shaffer, Larry Miller, and Dick Grubar also campaigned for me to stay on the job. I received scores of letters and calls from former players who thought the record would serve as a compliment and true achievement for each young man who had played for me. When it was put in that light—as a record of achievement for North Carolina's players—it took on a different meaning for me. My friends convinced me that retiring just to keep from breaking the record would be the wrong thing to do, and I agreed with that. Still, if the enthusiasm was missing, or if I didn't feel the excitement to coach, I would not have stayed on for the sake of the record.

Going into the 1996–97 season, I didn't know what to expect after Calabria graduated and McInnis went pro. We were extremely young: Our top six consisted of one senior, one junior, three sophomores, and a freshman, Ed Cota. We got off to an impressive beginning, although we went into the first game against Arizona with question marks. For one, I had hoped to return to our favorite way of playing defense—pressing, trapping, and causing havoc for the opponent. We tried that against Arizona with poor results. That defense, as much as I preferred it, was not best suited for this young team. So after spending the summer mapping strategy that included pressure defense, and after spending all of preseason on it, I felt we had to return to the more conservative man defense that we had used in 1996. We threw in some point zone with Zwikker in the game.

It isn't a bad defense, but it's also not "North Carolina defense." During the transition to the new defense, our team responded with nine straight wins, including a win over UMass in the Meadowlands and a 69–60 win at Princeton, a place that most top programs refuse to visit. It's easy to understand why. Princeton is hard to beat anywhere, but in their campus gymnasium they are especially tough to play against.

Even though our record was 9–1, I had concerns about this team's ability to compete in the ACC. We had a long way to go before we were capable of holding our own in the conference, and I knew it.

The team wasn't helped by a big scheduling mistake I made. It's our policy at Carolina to get our players as close to home for a game as possible. Even though Serge Zwikker played three years of prep basketball in the Washington, D.C., area, his native land is Holland, so we took an arduous trip over the Christmas holidays to Amsterdam and on into Italy to play the Italian national team. As a result, much-needed practice time was lost, and the trip wore out our players, not to mention the head coach.

We got back home just in time to hop over to Winston-Salem to play Tim

Duncan and a nationally ranked Wake Forest team. They routed us, 81–57. (However, we did win the next two games against Wake that year.) That game stripped us of much of our confidence. To make matters worse, Vince Carter was injured in the game (hip pointer) and we lost him for more than two games. We returned home to play Maryland and built a 22-point lead, only to see it crumble away, and we lost. The loss made national news, and our team was stunned.

"We do that to other teams, they don't do it to us," Antawn Jamison said afterwards.

When we lost at Virginia to go 0–3 in the ACC, they stopped the presses. I told the reporters after the game that I saw some encouraging things in our loss. They weren't listening. North Carolina losing three straight conference games was news, and this was a story that was not going to be ignored. One writer suggested that our program was in shambles and would take years to rebuild. Our players had a team meeting in the locker room at Charlottesville, where they aired their feelings. While the meeting received attention in the press, I think it had little to do with what happened to us the rest of the season, even if it did make good reading. If the meeting was so magical, I don't know why we were 9 down at home the very next game against N.C. State, on the verge of going 0–4 in conference. Even before that game, people looked at our schedule and said we'd be lucky to finish 8–8 in the ACC and get a bid to the NCAA tournament. It looked that way to the coach too. Once again, though, our players refused to quit. Down 9 points to N.C. State with less than two minutes to play, and with N.C. State in possession of the ball, we rallied and won, 59–56. It wasn't pretty, but it was important. Had we gone 0–4 with a team this young, there's no telling which direction our season would have taken.

Still, after losing a tough game at Duke, 80–73, on January 29, 1997, we were 3–5 in the ACC, with away games in the second half of the season against N.C. State, Georgia Tech, Maryland, and Clemson. So 8–8 was looking as though it would be a good conference record. Still, I knew we had a huge challenge in front of us, but I was beginning to be encouraged by what I saw. Our players stuck together and worked hard. Vince Carter not only got healthy, but things began to click for him. Things he had struggled with in his first year and a half were becoming second nature, such as his perimeter defense. All in all, we had improved significantly since the beginning of the season, as I told our team.

As we began to win, I became tougher on the team in practice. Their confidence was back, and my goal now was for them not to get cocky, but to improve and realize the task ahead of us. The next two conference games would serve notice to the rest of the league that we were becoming a different team. We had lost to Florida State by 13 in Tallahassee on January 22, but on February 6 we beat them, 90–62. After losing at Virginia on January 11, we beat them in Chapel Hill on February 8, 81–57. Our third conference game of the season's second half was at N.C. State. They were more than ready. A capacity crowd of 12,400 fans was in rare form, and the noise was deafening. We didn't play one of our best games, but after getting down 11 early in the second half, we battled back an inch at a time, and Ed Cota hit a basket for us with six seconds left to give us a 45–44 lead. Carter then showed how much he had improved defensively when he sprinted from the foul line to the right corner of the court to block N.C. State's last-second shot attempt. That road win gave our team added confidence; the players knew they could win on the road in the ACC without playing their best. The very next game, Georgia Tech had us 16 down in the second half in Atlanta, but we fought back, took the lead on a late Shammond Williams basket, and won, 72–68.

We were rolling. We swept through the second half of the ACC to go 8–0 and finish 11–5 in the conference, after an 0–3 start. We then won the ACC championship by beating Virginia, Wake Forest, and N.C. State in the conference tournament, culminating an eleven-game winning streak. Suddenly, we had twenty-three victories. We came from the back of the pack to the front, and when the smoke cleared, I had coached in 875 basketball victories as North Carolina's head coach. Going into the NCAA tournament, I was just one away from tying Rupp's Kentucky mark of 876.

As champions of the ACC and one of the nation's hottest teams, we were seeded number one in the East. Our first game in the NCAA tournament would be in Joel Coliseum in Winston-Salem against Fairfield. The press came from all over the nation to record the moment, and many of our former players somehow got tickets and were in the stands to watch.

Fairfield played like a team possessed. They led us at halftime in twenty minutes of basketball that was not a fluke, and it took our best offensive half of the season in the second half to win, 82–74. We shot 63 percent from the field in the second half and scored on just about every possession in the game's last fifteen minutes. The Rupp record was tied.

Our next opponent two days later would be Colorado, which had beaten Indiana handily. We won relatively easily, 73–56. During the game, the Rupp record didn't enter my mind, as it never did in games. They were my sanctuary from the hype, a time when I was too caught up in the moment working with my players to think of anything else. Once the Colorado game was over, it was impossible to ignore all the talk and commotion about the record. As the game ended, Serge Zwikker ran onto the court to get the game ball. An official tried to take it from him, but Serge would not relinquish it. I recall going down to congratulate the Colorado coaches and players, and the capacity crowd began to chant my name. That was embarrassing, so I sprinted (if that's what a sixty-six-year-old man with bad knees does) toward our locker room.

I did feel emotional when I got into the tunnel and saw so many of our former players, who'd come from all over the country to be on hand. I was moved by their presence. I'm not going to mention the names of any of the players who were there, because I know I would leave out some, but I can still see their faces, hear their words, feel their hugs. I will never forget it. And sensing at that moment how much the record meant to them, because each of them was such a vital part of it, made me feel better about the whole thing. This was not a story about my breaking Adolph Rupp's record; it was a story about the young men who played on my thirty-six Carolina teams and all the wonderful things they had done. The record is theirs.

I spoke to the team, congratulated them on their victory, told them what we had to do to get ready to play in Syracuse in the East regionals. The players, who had battled back from serious adversity all season, presented me with the game ball that Serge had rescued. I then went down the hall to meet the press. The questions were all about the record. I thanked all of my players over the years. They are all connected, since one class helps recruit future classes. I thanked all my assistant coaches, whom I named, and of course the administration at Carolina for its strong support. I also expressed gratitude for being able to coach my career at the University of North Carolina.

Our team won the East regionals, beat California, a great team, in the Final Sixteen, and advanced to play Louisville for a berth in the Final Four. We jumped on them early and built a 22-point lead, but Louisville came back in the second half to pull within 2. I took a time-out and told our players: "No matter what happens now, you've had a great season." Ademola Okulaja said: "What do you mean by that?" As the players broke the huddle, Ademola called them all together and told them that our season would *not* be ending in the Carrier Dome. The players responded, stepping up their defense and winning going away, 97–74.

We advanced to the Final Four and lost to Arizona, the national champion, to bring an end to a terrific season. Our players, ridiculed in January and berated for being the team that would end Carolina's streak of finishing in the

1961–62 North Carolina Basketball Team
Record: 8–9; ACC: 7–7 (Tied 4th)

Kneeling, left to right: Bryan McSweeney, Charlie Burns, Mike Cooke, Donnie Walsh, Larry Brown, Charlie Shaffer, Peppy Callahan. Standing, left to right: Head Coach Dean Smith, Assistant Coach Ken Rosemond, Richard Vinroot, Art Katz, Jim Donohue, Jim Hudock, Bruce Bowers, Harry Jones, Dieter Krause, Manager Eddie Burke, Trainer John Lacey.

1962–63 North Carolina Basketball Team
Record: 15–6; ACC: 10–4 (3rd)

Front row, left to right: Bill Brown, Mike Cooke, Larry Brown, Yogi Poteet, Peppy Callahan, Bill Taylor. Second row, left to right: Trainer John Lacey, Head Coach Dean Smith, Charlie Burns, Charlie Shaffer, Bryan McSweeney, Ray Respess, Assistant Coach Ken Rosemond, Manager Elliott Murnick. Third row, left to right: Dieter Krause, Richard Vinroot, Billy Cunningham, Art Katz, Bruce Bowers, Terry Ronner, Bill Galantai.

1963–64 North Carolina Basketball Team
Record: 12–12; ACC: 6–8 (5th)

Front row, left to right: Mike Iannarella, Johnny Yokley, Mike Cooke, Ray Hassell, Jim Moore. Second row, left to right: Trainer John Lacey, Terry Ronner, Bill Galantai, Bob Bennett, Billy Cunningham, Art Katz, Bryan McSweeney, Manager Elliott Murnick. Third row, left to right: Head Coach Dean Smith, Ray Respess, Jimmy Smithwick, Charlie Shaffer, Bill Brown, Earl Johnson, Pud Hassell, Billy Harrison, Assistant Coach Ken Rosemond.

1964–65 North Carolina Basketball Team
Record: 15–9; ACC: 10–4 (Tied 2nd)

Front row, left to right: Donnie Moe, Billy Cunningham, Mike Smith. Second row, left to right: Head Coach Dean Smith, Johnny Yokley, Pud Hassell, Bill Brown, Ray Respess, Bob Bennett, Jimmy Smithwick, Assistant Coach Ken Rosemond. Third row, left to right: Trainer John Lacey, Ian Morrison, Mark Mirken, Tom Gauntlett, Bob Lewis, Manager Joe Young-blood.

1965–66 North Carolina Basketball Team
Record: 16–11; ACC: 8–6 (Tied 3rd)

Front row, left to right: Manager Joe Youngblood, Mike Smith, Ray Hassell, Johnny Yokley, Greg Campbell, Manager Bill Cochrane. Second row, left to right: Jimmy Moore, Mark Mirken, Jim Smithwick, Bob Bennett, Dickson Gribble, Head Coach Dean Smith. Third row, left to right: Trainer John Lacey, Assistant Coach Larry Brown, Donnie Moe, Tom Gauntlett, Ralph Fletcher, Jim Frye, Bob Lewis, Larry Miller, Assistant Coach John Lotz.

1966–67 North Carolina Basketball Team
Record: 26–6; ACC: 12–2 (1st)

NCAA Fourth Place   ACC Regular-Season and Tournament Champions   Final National Rank: Three

Kneeling, left to right: Assistant Coach Larry Brown, Greg Campbell, Donnie Moe, Dick Grubar, Bob Lewis, Tom Gauntlett, Larry Miller, Jim Bostick, Gerald Tuttle. Standing, left to right: Assistant Coach John Lotz, Manager Ben Thompson, Jim Frye, Mark Mirken, Rusty Clark, Bill Bunting, Ralph Fletcher, Joe Brown, Trainer John Lacey, Head Coach Dean Smith.

1967–68 North Carolina Basketball Team
Record: 28–4; ACC: 12–2 (1st)

NCAA Second Place   ACC Regular-Season and Tournament Champion   Final National Rank: Four

Front row, left to right: Trainer John Lacey, Head Coach Dean Smith, Jim Delany, Dick Grubar, Larry Miller, Gerald Tuttle, Eddie Fogler, Assistant Coach John Lotz, Assistant Coach Bill Guthridge. Standing, left to right: Manager Randy Forehand, Al Armour, Gra Whitehead, Joe Brown, Rusty Clark, Bill Bunting, Charles Scott, Jim Frye, Ricky Webb, Manager Bob Coleman.

1968–69 North Carolina Basketball Team
Record: 27–5; ACC: 12-2 (1st)

NCAA Fourth Place   ACC Regular-Season and Tournament Champions   Final National Rank: Two

Seated, left to right: Trainer John Lacey, Head Coach Dean Smith, Dick Grubar, Joe Brown, Rusty Clark, Bill Bunting, Gerald Tuttle, Assistant Coach John Lotz, Assistant Coach Bill Guthridge. Standing, left to right: Manager Randy Forehand, Eddie Fogler, Dale Gipple, Ricky Webb, Don Eggleston, Lee Dedmon, Dave Chadwick, Charles Scott, Richard Tuttle, Jim Delany, Manager Bob Coleman.

1969–70 North Carolina Basketball Team
Record: 18–9; ACC: 9–5 (Tied 2nd)

NIT Participant

Seated, left to right: Head Coach Dean Smith, Dale Gipple, Steve Previs, Charles Scott, Eddie Fogler, Jim Delany, Richard Tuttle, Trainer John Lacey. Standing, left to right: Assistant Coach John Lotz, Manager Ben Reid, Kim Huband, Bill Chamberlain, Dave Chadwick, Craig Corson, Lee Dedmon, Don Eggleston, Dennis Wuycik, Bill Chambers, Manager Leroy Upperman, Manager Jon Barrett, Assistant Coach Bill Guthridge.

1970–71 North Carolina Basketball Team
Record: 26–6; ACC: 11–3 (1st)

NIT Champion   ACC Regular-Season Champion   Final National Rank: Thirteen

Seated, left to right: Head Coach Dean Smith, Assistant Coach Bill Guthridge, Dale Gipple, Dave Chadwick, Lee Dedmon, Don Eggleston, Richard Tuttle, Trainer John Lacey, Assistant Coach John Lotz. Standing, left to right: Manager Ben Reid, George Karl, Steve Previs, Kim Huband, Bill Chamberlain, Craig Corson, Donn Johnston, Dennis Wuycik, Bill Chambers, John Austin, John Cox, Manager Jon Barrett, Manager Doug Donald.

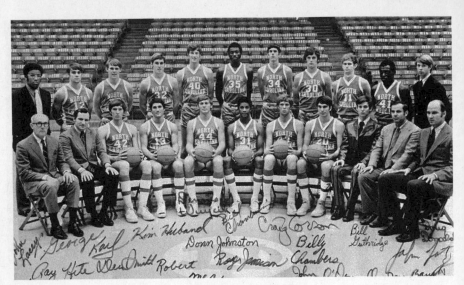

1971–72 North Carolina Basketball Team
Record: 26–5; ACC: 9–3 (1st)

NCAA Third Place   ACC Regular-Season and Tournament Champions   Final National Rank: Two

Seated, left to right: Trainer John Lacey, Head Coach Dean Smith, Kim Huband, Steve Previs, Dennis Wuycik, Bill Chamberlain, Craig Corson, Bill Chambers, Manager Jon Barrett, Assistant Coach Bill Guthridge, Assistant Coach John Lotz. Standing, left to right: Manager Greg Miles, Ray Hite, George Karl, Darrell Elston, Donn Johnston, Robert McAdoo, Bobby Jones, John O'Donnell, John Austin, Roger Jamison, Manager Doug Donald.

1972–73 North Carolina Basketball Team
Record: 25–8; ACC: 8–4 (2nd)

NIT Third Place   Final National Rank: Eleven

Seated, left to right: Head Coach Dean Smith, Trainer John Lacey, Donald Washington, Bobby Jones, George Karl, Donn Johnston, Ed Stahl, Assistant Coach Bill Guthridge, Assistant Coach John Lotz. Standing, left to right: Manager Greg Miles, Brad Hoffman, Ray Harrison, Darrell Elston, Mitch Kupchak, John O'Donnell, Mickey Bell, Ray Hite, Manager Doug Donald.

1973–74 North Carolina Basketball Team
Record: 22–6; ACC: 9–3 (Tied 2nd)

NIT Participant

Final National Rank: Eight

Front row, left to right: Tony Shaver, Manager John Rancke, Manager Greg Miles, Manager Dan Veazey, Dave Hanners.
Second row, left to right: Head Coach Dean Smith, Assistant Coach Bill Guthridge, John O'Donnell, Darrell Elston, Bobby
Jones, Ray Hite, Trainer John Lacey, Assistant Coach Eddie Fogler. Third row, left to right: Brad Hoffman, Ray Harrison,
Bill Chambers, Walter Davis, Tommy LaGarde, Ed Stahl, Geff Crompton, Mitch Kupchak, Bruce Buckley, James Smith,
Mickey Bell, John Kuester.

1974–75 North Carolina Basketball Team
Record: 23–8; ACC: 8–4 (Tied 2nd)

NCAA Final Sixteen

ACC Tournament Champions

Final National Rank: Nine

Seated, left to right: Trainer John Lacey, Head Coach Dean Smith, Donnie Smith, Brad Hoffman, Ed Stahl, Charles Waddell,
Mickey Bell, Dave Hanners, Assistant Coach Eddie Fogler, Assistant Coach Bill Guthridge. Standing, left to right: Manager
Dan Veazey, Phil Ford, John Kuester, Tom Zaliagiris, Walter Davis, Mitch Kupchak, Tommy LaGarde, Bruce Buckley, Eric
Harry, Woody Coley, Bill Chambers, Manager John Rancke.

1975–76 North Carolina Basketball Team
Record: 25–4; ACC: 11–1 (1st)

NCAA Final Thirty-two   ACC Regular-Season Champions   Final National Rank: Six

Seated, left to right: Trainer John Lacey, Head Coach Dean Smith, Phil Ford, John Kuester, Bill Chambers, Mitch Kupchak, Dave Hanners, Keith Valentine, Ged Doughton, Assistant Coach Eddie Fogler, Assistant Coach Bill Guthridge. Standing, left to right: Manager Dan Veazey, Randy Wiel, Tom Zaliagiris, Dudley Bradley, Woody Coley, Tommy LaGarde, Geff Crompton, Bruce Buckley, Eric Harry, Walter Davis, Loren Lutz, Manager Jeff Mason, Manager John Cohen.

1976–77 North Carolina Basketball Team
Record: 28–5; ACC: 9–3 (1st)

NCAA Second Place   ACC Regular-Season and Tournament Champions   Final National Rank: Three

Seated, left to right: Head Coach Dean Smith, Trainer John Lacey, John Kuester, Walter Davis, Tommy LaGarde, Bruce Buckley, Woody Coley, Assistant Coach Eddie Fogler, Assistant Coach Bill Guthridge. Standing, left to right: Manager John Cohen, Dave Colescott, Phil Ford, Randy Wiel, Dudley Bradley, Rich Yonakor, Jeff Wolf, Steve Krafcisin, Mike O'Koren, Tom Zaliagiris, John Virgil, Ged Doughton, Manager Jeff Mason, Manager Rick Duckett.

1977–78 North Carolina Basketball Team
Record: 23–8; ACC: 9–3 (1st)

NCAA Final Thirty-two   ACC Regular-Season Champions   Final National Rank: Ten

Seated, left to right: Trainer Marc Davis, Head Coach Dean Smith, Pete Budko, Jeff Wolf, Tom Zaliagiris, Phil Ford, Geff Crompton, Rich Yonakor, Assistant Coach Eddie Fogler, Assistant Coach Bill Guthridge. Standing, left to right: Manager Jeff Mason, Ged Doughton, Randy Wiel, Al Wood, Mike O'Koren, Dudley Bradley, John Virgil, Mike Pepper, Dave Colescott, Manager Rick Duckett, Manager Kenny Lee.

1978–79 North Carolina Basketball Team
Record: 23–6; ACC: 9–3 (Tied 1st)

NCAA Final Thirty-two   ACC Regular-Season and Tournament Champions   Final National Rank: Three

Seated, left to right: Trainer Marc Davis, Head Coach Dean Smith, Billy Carter, Randy Wiel, Dudley Bradley, Ged Doughton, Dave Colescott, Jimmy Black, Assistant Coach Eddie Fogler, Assistant Coach Bill Guthridge. Standing, left to right: Manager Kenny Lee, Manager Lindsay Reed, Mike Pepper, Al Wood, Mike O'Koren, Rich Yonakor, Jeff Wolf, Pete Budko, Chris Brust, Eric Kenny, John Virgil, Manager Rick Duckett, Assistant Coach Roy Williams.

1979-80 North Carolina Basketball Team
Record: 21-8; ACC: 9-5 (Tied 2nd)

NCAA Final Thirty-two   Final National Rank: 15

Seated, left to right: Trainer Marc Davis, Manager Rick Duckett, Head Coach Dean Smith, Dave Colescott, Mike O'Koren, Jeff Wolf, Rich Yonakor, John Virgil, Assistant Coach Bill Guthridge, Assistant Coach Eddie Fogler, Assistant Coach Roy Williams. Standing, left to right: Manager Kenny Lee, Manager Lindsay Reed, Jim Braddock, Al Wood, Chris Brust, Pete Budko, James Worthy, Eric Kenny, Mike Pepper, Jimmy Black, Manager Joe Stroman, Manager Chuck Duckett.

1980–81 North Carolina Basketball Team
Record: 29–8; ACC: 10–4 (2nd)

NCAA Second Place   ACC Tournament Champions   Final National Rank: Six

Seated, left to right: Trainer Marc Davis, Head Coach Dean Smith, Jimmy Black, Eric Kenny, Al Wood, Pete Budko, Mike Pepper, Jim Braddock, Assistant Coach Bill Guthridge, Assistant Coach Eddie Fogler. Standing, left to right: Manager Joe Stroman, Manager Lindsay Reed, Dean Shaffer, Jeb Barlow, James Worthy, Timo Makkonen, Sam Perkins, Chris Brust, Matt Doherty, Cecil Exum, Assistant Coach Roy Williams, Manager David Daly, Manager Chuck Duckett.

1981–82 North Carolina Basketball Team
Record: 32–2; ACC: 12–2 (Tied 1st)

NCAA Champion   ACC Regular-Season and Tournament Champions   Final National Rank: One

Seated, left to right: Trainer Marc Davis, Assistant Coach Roy Williams, Head Coach Dean Smith, Jim Braddock, Jeb Barlow, Jimmy Black, Chris Brust, Lynwood Robinson, Manager Chuck Duckett, Assistant Coach Eddie Fogler, Assistant Coach Bill Guthridge. Standing, left to right: Manager David Hart, Manager Ralph Meekins, Dean Shaffer, Michael Jordan, James Worthy, John Brownlee, Timo Makkonen, Warren Martin, Sam Perkins, Matt Doherty, Cecil Exum, Buzz Peterson, Manager David Daly.

1982–83 North Carolina Basketball Team
Record: 28–8; ACC: 12–2 (1st)

NCAA Final Eight   ACC Regular-Season Champions   Final National Rank: Eight

Seated, left to right: Trainer Marc Davis, Assistant Coach Roy Williams, Head Coach Dean Smith, Lynwood Robinson, Sam Perkins, Jim Braddock, Matt Doherty, Cecil Exum, Manager Ralph Meekins, Assistant Coach Bill Guthridge, Assistant Coach Eddie Fogler. Standing, left to right: Manager David Hart, Manager Joe Stroman, Steve Hale, Buzz Peterson, John Brownlee, Warren Martin, Timo Makkonen, Brad Daugherty, Michael Jordan, Curtis Hunter, Manager Julie Dalton.

1983–84 North Carolina Basketball Team
Record: 28–3; ACC: 14–0 (1st)

NCAA Final Sixteen   ACC Regular-Season Champions   Final National Rank: One

Seated, left to right: Trainer Marc Davis, Assistant Coach Roy Williams, Head Coach Dean Smith, Kenny Smith, Sam Perkins, Matt Doherty, Cecil Exum, Cliff Morris, Steve Hale, Assistant Coach Eddie Fogler, Assistant Coach Bill Guthridge. Standing, left to right: Manager Dean McCord, Manager Lannie Parrish, Buzz Peterson, Michael Jordan, Joe Wolf, Warren Martin, Brad Daugherty, Timo Makkonen, Dave Popson, Curtis Hunter, Manager Mark Isley, Manager David Hart.

1984–85 North Carolina Basketball Team
Record: 27–9; ACC: 9–5 (Tied 1st)

NCAA Final Eight   ACC Regular-Season Champions   Final National Rank: Seven

Seated, left to right: Assistant Coach Roy Williams, Trainer Marc Davis, Head Coach Dean Smith, Ranzino Smith, Gary Roper, Buzz Peterson, Cliff Morris, James Daye, Assistant Coach Eddie Fogler, Assistant Coach Bill Guthridge, Manager Dean McCord. Standing, left to right: Manager Adam Fleishman, Kenny Smith, Matt Brust, Dave Popson, Warren Martin, Brad Daugherty, Joe Wolf, Curtis Hunter, Steve Hale, Manager Lannie Parrish, Manager Mark Isley.

1985–86 North Carolina Basketball Team
Record: 28–6; ACC: 10–4 (3rd)

NCAA Final Sixteen   Final National Rank: Eight

Seated, left to right: Trainer Marc Davis, Assistant Coach Roy Williams, Head Coach Dean Smith, James Daye, Brad Daugherty, Warren Martin, Steve Hale, Curtis Hunter, Manager Lannie Parrish, Assistant Coach Eddie Fogler, Assistant Coach Bill Guthridge. Standing, left to right: Manager Mike Ellis, Manager Adam Fleishman, Ranzino Smith, Kenny Smith, Kevin Madden, Dave Popson, Joe Wolf, Marty Hensley, Steve Bucknall, Jeff Lebo, Michael Norwood, Manager Mark Isley.

1986–87 North Carolina Basketball Team
Record: 32–4; ACC: 14–0 (1st)

NCAA Final Eight   ACC Regular-Season Champions   Final National Rank: Two

Seated, left to right: Trainer Marc Davis, Head Coach Dean Smith, Assistant Coach Dick Harp, Dave Popson, Kenny Smith, Curtis Hunter, Joe Wolf, Michael Norwood, Assistant Coach Randy Wiel, Assistant Coach Roy Williams, Assistant Coach Bill Guthridge. Standing, left to right: Manager Mike Ellis, Manager Adam Fleishman, Jeff Denny, Steve Bucknall, Pete Chilcutt, J. R. Reid, Marty Hensley, Scott Williams, Kevin Madden, Jeff Lebo, Ranzino Smith, Manager Michael Burch, Manager Jan Baldwin.

1987-88 North Carolina Basketball Team

Record: 27-7; ACC: 11-3 (1st)NCAA Final Eight   ACC Regular-Season Champions   Final National Rank: Seven

Seated, left to right: Trainer Marc Davis, Head Coach Dean Smith, Assistant Coach Dick Harp, Kevin Madden, Jeff Lebo, Ranzino Smith, Steve Bucknall, Marty Hensley, Assistant Coach Randy Wiel, Assistant Coach Roy Williams, Assistant Coach Bill Guthridge. Standing, left to right: Manager Mike Ellis, Manager Justin Kuralt, Rodney Hyatt, Jeff Denny, David May, Pete Chilcutt, Scott Williams, J. R. Reid, Rick Fox, Joe Jenkins, Doug Elstun, King Rice, Manager Michael Burch, Manager Kendria Parsons, Manager Steve Reynolds.

1988–89 North Carolina Basketball Team
Record: 29–8; ACC: 9–5 (Tied 2nd)

NCAA Final Sixteen   ACC Tournament Champions   Final National Rank: Four

Seated, left to right: Trainer Marc Davis, Head Coach Dean Smith, Jim Stewart, Courtney Dupree, Doug Elstun, David May, Steve Bucknall, Jeff Lebo, King Rice, Rodney Hyatt, Assistant Coach Phil Ford, Assistant Coach Bill Guthridge, Assistant Coach Dick Harp. Standing, left to right: Manager Chris Ellis, Manager Justin Kuralt, Coach Randy Wiel, Kevin Madden, Rick Fox, John Greene, Pete Chilcutt, Marty Hensley, Scott Williams, J. R. Reid, Bill Akins, Hubert Davis, Jeff Denny, Strength Coach Harley Dartt, Manager Jerry Hopkins, Manager Steve Reynolds.

1989–90 North Carolina Basketball Team
Record: 21–13; ACC: 8–6 (Tied 3rd)

NCAA Final Sixteen

Seated, left to right: Trainer Marc Davis, Head Coach Dean Smith, Assistant Coach Randy Wiel, Jeff Denny, John Greene, Scott Williams, Kevin Madden, King Rice, Assistant Coach Phil Ford, Assistant Coach Dave Hanners, Assistant Coach Bill Guthridge. Standing, left to right: Manager Greg Baines, Manager Justin Kuralt, Scott Cherry, Henrik Rodl, Rick Fox, Kevin Salvadori, Matt Wenstrom, Pete Chilcutt, George Lynch, Hubert Davis, Kenny Harris, Strength Coach Harley Dartt, Manager Jerry Hopkins, Manager Steve Reynolds.

1990–91 North Carolina Basketball Team
Record: 29–6; ACC: 10–4 (2nd)

NCAA Final Four   ACC Tournament Champions   Final National Rank: Four

Seated, left to right: Trainer Marc Davis, Head Coach Dean Smith, Assistant Coach Randy Wiel, Manager Justin Kuralt, Hubert Davis, Rick Fox, Pete Chilcutt, King Rice, Assistant Coach Phil Ford, Strength Coach Harley Dartt, Assistant Coach Dave Hanners, Assistant Coach Bill Guthridge. Standing, left to right: Manager Jerry Hopkins, Manager Greg Baines, Derrick Phelps, Henrik Rodl, Clifford Rozier, Kevin Salvadori, Matt Wenstrom, Eric Montross, Pat Sullivan, George Lynch, Brian Reese, Scott Cherry, Larry Davis, Manager Maria McIntyre, Manager Sam Rogers.

1991–92 North Carolina Basketball Team
Record: 23–10; ACC: 9–7 (3rd)

NCAA Final Sixteen   Final National Rank: Fourteen

Seated, left to right: Trainer Marc Davis, Head Coach Dean Smith, Strength Coach Harley Dartt, Henrik Rodl, George Lynch, Hubert Davis, Matt Wenstrom, Scott Cherry, Assistant Coach Phil Ford, Assistant Coach Dave Hanners, Assistant Coach Bill Guthridge. Standing, left to right: Manager Greg Baines, Manager Laura Johnson, Assistant Coach Randy Wiel, Thomas Holst, Derrick Phelps, Travis Stephenson, Pat Sullivan, Eric Montross, Kevin Salvadori, Larry Smith, Brian Reese, Donald Williams, Jason Burgess, Manager Sam Rogers, Manager Bobby Dawson, Manager Chuck Lisenbee.

1992–93 North Carolina Basketball Team
Record: 34–4; ACC: 14–2 (1st)

NCAA Champions   ACC Regular-Season Champions   Final National Rank: One

Seated, left to right: Strength Coach Harley Dartt, Trainer Marc Davis, Head Coach Dean Smith, Travis Stephenson, Henrik Rodl, Matt Wenstrom, George Lynch, Scott Cherry, Assistant Coach Phil Ford, Assistant Coach Dave Hanners, Assistant Coach Bill Guthridge. Standing, left to right: Manager Sam Rogers, Manager Bobby Dawson, Manager Laura Johnson, Larry Davis, Derrick Phelps, Pat Sullivan, Ed Geth, Eric Montross, Serge Zwikker, Kevin Salvadori, Brian Reese, Dante Calabria, Donald Williams, Manager Chuck Lisenbee, Manager Eddie Wills, Manager Eran Bloxam.

1993–94 North Carolina Basketball Team
Record: 28–7; ACC: 11–5 (2nd)

NCAA Final Thirty-two   ACC Tournament Champions   Final National Rank: One

Seated, left to right: Manager Bobby Dawson, Strength Coach Ben Cook, Trainer Marc Davis, Head Coach Dean Smith, Brian Reese, Pat Sullivan, Eric Montross, Kevin Salvadori, Derrick Phelps, Manager Chuck Lisenbee, Assistant Coach Phil Ford, Assistant Coach Dave Hanners, Assistant Coach Bill Guthridge. Standing, left to right: Manager Rolf Blizzard, Manager Jim Ervin, Larry Davis, Jeff McInnis, Jerry Stackhouse, Ed Geth, Serge Zwikker, Rasheed Wallace, Larry Smith, Dante Calabria, Pearce Landry, Donald Williams, Manager Bill Bondshu, Manager Eddie Wills, Manager Eran Bloxam.

1994–95 North Carolina Basketball Team
Record: 28–6; ACC: 12–4 (Tied 1st)

NCAA Final Four   ACC Regular-Season Champions   Final National Rank: Three

Seated, left to right: Strength Coach Ben Cook, Trainer Marc Davis, Head Coach Dean Smith, Jeff McInnis, Dante Calabria, Donald Williams, Pat Sullivan, Pearce Landry, Shammond Williams, Assistant Coach Phil Ford, Assistant Coach Dave Hanners, Assistant Coach Bill Guthridge. Standing, left to right: Manager Rolf Blizzard, Manager Chuck Lisenbee, Manager Bill Bondshu, Octavus Barnes, Ryan Sullivan, Chuck McNairy, Ed Geth, Serge Zwikker, Rasheed Wallace, Jerry Stackhouse, Clyde Lynn, David Neal, Manager Jim Ervin, Manager Rob Lancaster, Manager Chris Johnson.

1995–96 North Carolina Basketball Team
Record: 21–11; ACC: 10–6 (3rd)

NCAA Final Thirty-two   Final National Rank: Twenty-four

Seated, left to right: Strength Coach Ben Cook, Trainer Marc Davis, Head Coach Dean Smith, Chris Barnes, Ryan Sullivan, Clyde Lynn, Dante Calabria, David Neal, Shammond Williams, Webb Tyndall, Assistant Coach Phil Ford, Assistant Coach Dave Hanners, Assistant Coach Bill Guthridge. Standing, left to right: Manager Gene Hoffman, Manager Virginia Holt, Manager Jim Ervin, Jeff McInnis, Vince Carter, Ademola Okulaja, Ed Geth, Serge Zwikker, Makhtar Ndiaye, Antawn Jamison, Charlie McNairy, Michael Guzek, Manager Emilly Cole, Manager Chris Stoen, Manager Chris Johnson.

1996–97 North Carolina Basketball Team
Record: 28–7; ACC: 11–5 (Tied 2nd)

NCAA Final Four   ACC Tournament Champion   Final National Rank: Four

Seated, left to right: Strength Coach Ben Cook, Trainer Marc Davis, Head Coach Dean Smith, Shammond Williams, Charlie McNairy, Serge Zwikker, Webb Tyndall, Ryan Sullivan, Assistant Coach Phil Ford, Assistant Coach Dave Hanners, Assistant Coach Bill Guthridge. Standing, left to right: Manager Virginia Holt, Manager Chris Stoen, Manager Emilly Cole, Terrence Newby, Brad Frederick, Vince Carter, Antawn Jamison, Vasco Evtimov, Makhtar Ndiaye, Ademola Okulaja, Michael Brooker, Ed Cota, Manager Jay Blackman, Manager Cori Brown, Manager Amanda Blake.

top three of the ACC, of winning more than twenty games in a season, of playing in the NCAA tournament, held together as a family. They worked, they fought, they made their critics look foolish. They never gave up on themselves.

I don't have a "favorite" Carolina team. If I did, I wouldn't tell anyone. Having a favorite team or a favorite player would be like having a favorite child. Also, I never compared players or teams, nor will I now. I will say, though, that the 1997 team was special for the way it came back, and for what it accomplished in very tough surroundings.

As we prepared to leave Indianapolis after losing in the Final Four, I *was* worn out, however, and I had suspicions this would be my last Carolina team. I had felt that way before, but this time the feelings seemed to run deeper. We'll see, I told myself.

I had it in my contract that after 1986 I could stop coaching at any time and become a consultant to the chancellor or the athletic director at Carolina through the year 2001. My love for coaching was still there. It remained a passion. But those nonbasketball requests were getting to me. I always felt rushed and on deadline to finish something or be somewhere.

What I enjoyed most about coaching were the practices, the relationships with our players, and the games. The bigger the game, the more I enjoyed it. The games I didn't particularly like were the few that we had when we were heavy favorites. I always enjoyed a contest, and walking onto the court for pregame warm-ups not knowing which team would win was thrilling to me. I loved it.

For the last three years or so that I coached, Eddie Fogler, Bill Guthridge, Roy Williams, and I would go to Bill and Barbara Miller's winter house in Florida for our first golf outing after the season. It was usually in April. I would be pretty much exhausted and ready to retire from coaching, but the two Bills, Roy, and Eddie would spend the days down there talking me out of it. They would tell me to relax and try to enjoy the off-season (there was no such thing at Carolina), and the excitement of coaching would return by summertime. These are dear friends who wanted what was best for me. I knew that and respected what they had to say. But at the end of the 1997 season, when our group was gathered in Florida, I wasn't so certain that the drive to coach would return as it always had before. Something felt a little different this time.

Several factors kept coming back to me. Number one, I felt we could have an excellent team in 1998. We had experience returning in Antawn Jamison, Vince Carter, Shammond Williams, Ademola Okulaja, Ed Cota, and Makhtar

Ndiaye. Six of our first seven from the 1997 Final Four team would be back. It wasn't an experienced team on the bench, but those starters had been through the wars and knew how to play. Also, the freshmen coming in— Brendan Haywood, Brian Bersticker, Max Owens, and Orlando Melendez—had good potential.

As for my successor, I certainly hoped it would be someone from the Carolina family. We have men who have demonstrated their ability to coach at the highest level of basketball, college and pro, and it wouldn't make any sense—none at all—to leave the family to find the man to succeed me. Larry Brown, Eddie Fogler, Bill Guthridge, and Roy Williams, all former assistants of mine at Carolina, have all proven themselves over and over again. George Karl certainly has demonstrated his great coaching ability in the NBA, although he was not an assistant at Carolina and doesn't have college coaching experience. No one could argue with the job he's done in the NBA. If someone wanted to look down the line for a younger coach, then certainly Phil Ford should be considered. He is going to be a great head coach for some program in the future.

Still, I left Florida thinking I probably *would* get recharged and be ready to coach again in 1998. But things didn't get much better after that. I *really* didn't have an off-season. I spent time in the summer drawing up plans for the '98 team, and I worked on tweaking our offense and defense. I kept up a busy recruiting pace in July, evaluating the players we planned to recruit in September. I visited recruits' homes and schools. The days seemed to run together, and before I knew it, the fall was upon us.

I talked more about retirement in late September with Bill Guthridge, Eddie, and Roy. Coach Guthridge is great. He tried his best to take as much of the non-basketball-related things off my desk as he possibly could, but there are just some things that I, as the head coach, had to handle. Bill did not want me to step down and encouraged me to take a few more days. He felt I'd be ready to coach by then. Furthermore, he told me that he wouldn't take the job if I did retire. Eddie and Roy said if the job were offered to them, they wouldn't take it. They felt strongly that Bill should be my successor when I stepped down.

As the four of us sat in a room talking about the possibility of my retirement, Roy and Eddie told Bill: "If Coach retires from the bench, you are the man who should take his place." It was the right thing for them to do. What was Bill going to do at that time if he wasn't the head coach? He wasn't going to be assistant to Eddie or Roy, although he has the highest possible respect for both of them. He was *their* coach.

Some of our former assistants, as well as former players who now coach in the NBA or Division 1, came to Chapel Hill on October 3–5, 1997, for our annual coaching get-together. We talked basketball for two days, watched tapes, exchanged ideas. We learned much about basketball in these sessions, as well as had a chance to visit and play a little golf. George Karl, Randy Wiel, Jeff Lebo, and Roy, Bill, and Eddie were all in for this, and Larry Brown had his NBA team in town for training camp.

On October 4 I went to see Dick Baddour, Carolina's athletics director, and told him I was leaning toward retirement. He told me not to rush, but to think it over. I told him to set up a meeting with Chancellor Michael Hooker so I could tell him of my intentions. On Monday, October 6, I was more certain that I would retire. On October 7, I told Chancellor Hooker, who was extremely supportive. He had been a tremendous leader for the university. When he was diagnosed with cancer, we thought he was winning the battle, but he suddenly died in July 1999.

All along, of course, I had been talking this over with my wife, Linnea. Finally I told Linnea early in October that I had to make a decision, that I could not put it off any longer.

Michael Jordan and I had been off playing golf the day before his preseason practice was to begin with the Bulls. As he prepared to leave our parking lot in Chapel Hill to go catch his plane, I said to him: "Confidentially, within the next couple of days I will be announcing my retirement as coach." He said, "If that's what you want, I think it's great. And I'll soon be joining you." I also told John Thompson about my plans. He asked me if I was sick, concerned that I was having heart problems, and as soon as I told him I was healthy, he said, "Fine. I'm with you."

When I told Bill Guthridge that I had absolutely made up my mind to retire, he said, "Oh, no." He said he wouldn't change offices with me. He wanted to keep the one he had, which is much smaller than the head coach's office. There was no way he could do that as head coach, but he wouldn't move out. We had to wait until he took the team to the Alaska Shootout at Thanksgiving to move my things out of the office and put his in there.

I met with our staff—Bill and assistant coaches Phil Ford, Dave Hanners, and Pat Sullivan—to tell them of my decision. Also in that meeting were the great women who work in our office, Linda, Angela, Ruth, and Kay. It was an emotional meeting. "All of you will be moving up one chair," I told the coaches. "I won't be coaching anymore."

The hardest part was late in the afternoon of October 8. The players had just completed their mile run and were told to meet in our locker room. I began telling them of my decision, but I couldn't get through without breaking down. That meeting took some time to complete. The returning players came to see me one by one to sit and talk, after which everything else seemed easy.

I had been very careful to tell our recruits Kris Lang and Jason Capel that while my contract with the university ran through 2001, I wasn't sure I would coach that long. They had verbally committed to Carolina when I thought I would coach them for at least part of their time at Carolina. Still, I told them during recruiting: "If I'm not coaching, I am confident that your coach will be either Bill Guthridge, Eddie Fogler, Roy Williams, Larry Brown, George Karl, or Phil Ford, not necessarily in that order. It has to be one of those." That seemed to satisfy them. I called Lang's family and Capel's family before my retirement news broke to tell them that I would be stepping down as coach. They indicated they would still sign in the November signing period.

The third freshman coming to Carolina in the class with Capel and Lang was Ronald Curry, who was also highly recruited for football. Ronald made a nonbinding verbal commitment to Virginia to play football, which was announced that September on ESPN in the middle of a nationally televised Thursday-night Virginia football game. Ronald visited our campus shortly afterwards, on September 13, 1997, to see our football game against Stanford in Kenan Stadium. That Saturday morning he came to the basketball office with Phil Ford, and we watched some basketball tapes together.

"Have you committed to Virginia?" I asked.

Ronald said he had indicated that he would play football at Virginia. When I asked if he also wanted to play basketball in college, he said he did. "Where do you want to play basketball?" I asked him.

"Here at Carolina," he said.

He subsequently signed a scholarship with Carolina. He started at quarterback on our football team and was a valuable member of Coach Guthridge's basketball team. Along with football coach Mack Brown and Bill G., Phil Ford was instrumental in Ronald's recruitment.

The university held a press conference on October 9, 1997, to announce my retirement from coaching and Bill's appointment as head coach. I just wanted to put out a release, but I was told that wouldn't suffice. I had no idea that ESPN would televise the press conference live. Larry Brown stayed in Chapel Hill for the press conference, even though his team had an exhibition game against the Knicks. Scott Williams, who played in our program and was on Philadelphia's team, also stayed behind. John Thompson came down from Washington, although I tried to convince him to stay and work with his own team. It was great to see them, though. Current and former players were there. I did fine at the press conference until I looked over to one side and saw our players standing there. That was it for me. I couldn't go on.

Some have said that I waited until a week before practice to resign to make sure that Bill Guthridge got the job. That wasn't the case. I would have been dumb to step down in April. I think most coaches are mentally and physically exhausted after the season ends and doubt if they can make it through another year. Coaches take off maybe a day and a half for Christmas, but other than that it's straight through from October 15 until the end of the season. There are no days off. April would be a poor time to make a decision. Bill Guthridge could have been head coach at many places had he wanted to leave Carolina. He was an excellent choice to succeed me.

I had already done the planning for the season. I had made some changes in our secondary break that I was excited about, and had some new things that we wanted to do on offense, which Bill adopted with no changes. Bill also was nice enough to allow me to sit in on some of the planning meetings, which I enjoyed. I tried very hard, though, to stay in the background.

I wasn't sure how I would feel about my decision to retire once the 1998 season began. Did I look back? Yes, but I always arrived at the same conclusion: I made a good decision, and I made it at the right time. I wanted this program to continue to prosper, and it has. Bill and his staff have done a great job with the team. The one mistake I regret is going for a walk around the concourse of our building one afternoon while the team was practicing. I snuck a look at the practice session, and I found I really wanted to go down there and coach and talk to the players. That's the only time that happened. I don't go to practice unless I'm asked to sit with a recruit.

Bill has been great to me. He invites me in to watch tape and attend some staff meetings. I stay away from the games because I don't want to be any kind of distraction. The only games I go to are the ones that aren't on television, and all but one or two of Carolina's games are shown. The hardest thing for me has been not having the same relationships with the players I had coached, especially Shammond, Antawn, Vince, Ademola, Makhtar Ndiaye, and Ed Cota. It would be fun to have those players—as well as the recruits—in the office to sit and talk, but I don't want to do anything to undermine Bill as the head coach. He is the one who should have them in the office talking to them, and he does. Though it's hard, the best thing for me has been to keep my distance. Carolina's players needed to know without question who the head coach was. And the head coach is Bill Guthridge. Period.

Initially, the two toughest things for me about not coaching were not being able to go to practice and almost hiding from players I had coached. I know I wouldn't want a former coach talking to my players if I was head coach.

Okay, there was a third thing: watching Carolina play. It drove me crazy to watch games involving coaches and players I cared so much about. I never got nervous coaching, especially in close games, because I was so busy; a coach has to think ahead. I would always wonder how fans could be so nervous watching a basketball game. Believe me, I know now. I watched the games alone because I was prone to yell out if I saw a player not carry out his assignment, or if we got a bad officiating call. I never dreamed that watching a game could be so hard. I am the team's biggest fan now.

Inexplicably, things haven't slowed down all that much since I gave up coaching. While I'm learning to say no to most requests—many of them worthwhile—the day is still full. It still looks as if I'm under siege in my office, things are stacked so high. But I keep chipping away, trying to gain on it a little each day. When I become frustrated by the mountain of things to do, I try to recall one of our Thoughts of the Day: "How do you remove a mountain? One pebble at a time."

ESPN, on its ESPY awards show, gave me its award for courage. I certainly appreciated the honor, but initially turned it down because I hadn't done anything courageous. They told me it was because of our determination to improve race relations with the work we did with our Carolina basketball team, including the recruitment of Charles Scott, and other desegregation efforts in Chapel Hill, many of which were led by our pastor, Bob Seymour, and fellow members of the Binkley Church. The ESPN award is named in memory of Arthur Ashe, whom I admired greatly. When I told the people at ESPN that I didn't deserve an award for just doing what was right, they told me that Arthur's widow, Jeanne, wanted me to have it, so I went to New York to receive it. I was extremely surprised to see a good representation of my former players waiting for me onstage when Senator Bill Bradley presented the award. I had prepared a two-minute acceptance speech. However, upon seeing the players and looking at a completely filled Radio City Music Hall, I forgot what I intended to say.

I worked the 1998 NCAA men's basketball tournament for CBS television. I was in the studio with Greg Gumbel and Clark Kellogg. It was a good experience, and I was supposed to repeat it in 1999, but in early March I returned the contract unsigned since I needed to work on this book and meet the publishing deadline for the manuscript. All the CBS people were cordial and did all they could for this rookie. Greg and Clark were great company.

I had one of the most interesting, as well as intimidating, experiences of my life in June 1998. Linnea and I were invited to a dinner at the White House in honor of South Korean president Kim Dae Jung. Quite honestly, I didn't know why I was there. I thought a longtime friend, Erskine Bowles, President Clinton's chief of staff, had something to do with it, but apparently he did not. Linnea and I were given the Queen's Bedroom, just across from the Lincoln Bedroom and on the President's floor. After arriving in the afternoon, we were given passes allowing us permission to move around the White House, which we did. On the way to the cocktail party we bumped into President Clinton outside our bedroom, and I asked him if Erskine was going to be there, and he said he wasn't sure, but would make a call to tell him we were there. Now, I have been lucky enough to stand on the first tee getting set to play a round of golf with Jack Nicklaus, but this White House occasion made me much more nervous.

"Stay close by," I told Linnea, "because I don't know anybody here."

I was so relieved to walk into the room to see one of our former players, Bill Harrison, now the CEO of Chase Manhattan, there with his wife, Anne. Bill and Erskine were close friends in prep school and college.

I believe I might have been invited because President Kim Dae Jung's son, who was there, was a fan of Carolina basketball. I autographed some things for him after the dinner. Erskine and Crandall Bowles, Bill and Anne Harrison, Linnea and I decided to go up to the sitting-room area located between our room and the President's area to visit following dinner. President Clinton walked in, dressed in a sweatshirt, and spent some time with us. He is a charming man, very easy to talk to, and he put me at ease. He excused himself so he could make a telephone call to Chelsea, who was in final exams at Stanford.

The next morning it was raining lightly outside as we were having coffee outside our bedroom. President Clinton came to say good-bye on his way to play golf with Senator Chris Dodd of Connecticut. He said, "You are welcome to join us. We are only playing nine holes at the Army-Navy course." It was tempting, but we had our plans to get back to Chapel Hill, so I declined with thanks. I watched the President leave for the golf course, and it took a caravan of about ten to twelve cars. What began as an intimidating experience ended up being a twenty-four-hour highlight tape for Linnea and me.

In early September I was devastated by the violent death of one of my best friends and golfing partners, Buck Adams. Buck was the first golf professional at the Country Club of North Carolina in Pinehurst and was retired from there after a highly successful career. He played for a time on the PGA Tour and later on the Senior Tour. He was not only a golfing partner, he was my golf teacher, my golf mentor. As soon as our basketball season was over each spring, I would make the hour drive from Chapel Hill to Pinehurst for a lesson from Buck. I always left his sessions believing that I understood the secrets of the golf swing, only to find later that some other hitch would crop up. Buck was a superb teacher, and he always gave me great confidence. For years I had trouble with my chipping game and often would skull or "chili-dip" the short shots. He worked with me so much that he even started to chili-dip himself once in a while. Buck's heart was in the right place: He too loved Carolina basketball.

Buck and I played together as often as we could. In August 1998 the two of us, plus friends Tommy Kearns, the starting point guard on UNC's 1957 national champions, and Brokie Lineweaver, a Carolina alumnus, took a golf vacation to California. We played Cypress, Pebble Beach, Spanish Bay, and Carmel Valley Ranch. Buck and I stayed at the Lodge at Pebble Beach on this trip and spent an inordinate amount of time just talking and visiting. He was a remarkable man, genuine and generous, warm and considerate.

Ten days after this golf outing, Buck was shot and killed in his home. It was tragic and heartbreaking, a truly traumatic loss. I was one of several speakers at his funeral, and it was so hard for me to get through it. Buck had many friends, not only in North Carolina but across the country. I lost a dear friend, and he is often on my mind.

I keep a small office in the Smith Center, and come to work just about every day. It's Coach Guthridge's basketball program, and I make sure I stay far in the background unless I'm asked to help in some way. I'm available to meet recruits when they visit our campus. Sometimes I'm asked to meet recruits visiting for other sports. I remember meeting track world record holder Marion Jones as a high school prospect from California. She was a member of our women's NCAA championship basketball team in 1994. Of course, I have many wonderful things to tell recruits about the University of North Carolina and our college town of Chapel Hill.

I was the luckiest coach in the world for being able to do my job at the University of North Carolina. I was head coach for thirty-six years. That's a long time to be in any job, especially one as competitive and as public as head basketball coach at North Carolina. I never dreamed I would coach that long when I began in the profession. Let me say, too, that being a head coach today is easier than it was when I began. That's because the NCAA wisely passed rules restricting the time coaches can be gone recruiting, and coaches can't scout opponents in person. You get some time at home now. When I began, you could recruit as often as you wished. I used to grab a plane after practice, fly to see a prospect play or to scout an opponent, and then fly back home that night after the game. I was gone too much of the time. All coaches were at that time. It was the nature of our game. If you wanted to be good, you had to do it.

I'm still not in the business of blueprinting my life. It'll be interesting to see which path I follow after my work is done here at Carolina.

Afterword

Much has happened—some good and some sad—since the hardcover edition of this book was published in the fall of 1999. I was surprised and grateful to receive so many letters, and many of them mentioned chapters 7 and 11 in particular. Chapter 7 dealt with our method of teaching Carolina basketball, which, judging from the letters, could also apply to business team building. Chapter 11 dealt with my theological position as to what I believe.

My successor as Carolina's head coach, Bill Guthridge, retired after three seasons. Roy Williams seriously considered the job but decided to stay at Kansas. Matt Doherty became Carolina's head coach in July 2000. Three outstanding assistant coaches with deep Carolina loyalties lost their jobs in the transition. Two of my dearest friends, Dick Harp and John Lotz, both of whom are spoken of often and warmly in the book, died within the space of twelve months. Al McGuire, a good friend and the former sensational coach at Marquette, who is also mentioned frequently, died of a blood disorder on January 26, 2001.

One of my daughters, Kristen, finished all the work for a degree in sociology at Carolina. She chose to go a fifth year in order to earn a degree in elementary education and is now student teaching. Kelly is a junior at the University of Pennsylvania, where she is in a premed program, majoring in the biological basis of behavior, with a minor in Spanish. Each seems committed to a life of helping others, which pleases their parents. They've done well academically at two great universities.

My oldest grandchild, Drew Kepley, matriculated at Carolina in August 2001. Preceding Drew at Carolina were my two nieces, Sarah and Elizabeth, in addition to my three older children, Sharon, Sandy, and Scott. My sixth grandchild, Samuel Combs, was born March 28, 2001, to Sandy and her husband, Steve Combs.

One of our former players, Vince Carter, created a stir among NBA players when he returned to Chapel Hill to receive his diploma on the day that his team, Toronto, was going to play against Philadelphia in the seventh and deciding game of their 2001 NBA playoff series. I was happy for two of my former players, Larry Brown and George Karl, when the teams they coach (Philadelphia and Milwaukee, respectively) met in the NBA Eastern Conference finals in 2001. Two of our former Carolina players, George Lynch (Philadelphia) and Scott Williams (Milwaukee), were in the starting lineups for their respective teams.

My contract with Carolina expired at the end of June 2001. Dick Baddour, the athletics director, said he hoped I would remain associated with the university as a consultant and asked what I wanted in the way of a new contract. I suggested that I make the same salary I earned when former chancellor William Aycock hired me to become UNC's head coach in 1961: $9,200 annually. I am also provided with a small office in the Smith Center and a secretary.

While I'm no longer coaching, I seem to be just about as busy as ever. I still live in the same house I built in 1975 on six acres outside of Chapel Hill. I'm ten minutes from the office but pass farmland populated with cows and horses on the drive into town. I go to the office each day when I'm in Chapel Hill, although I do have the freedom to leave when I choose. The best thing about no longer coaching is that I don't have a list of prospects to call each night, so my evenings are relatively free. I served on a so-called blue-ribbon NCAA committee that studied basketball-related issues, do some speaking on campus and at basketball clinics in the United States (and did one in Europe), assist the university in fund-raising, stay in contact with many of my former players, and never seem to catch up with the mail and telephone calls.

Still, the most enjoyable time for me is during basketball season. I visited with Bill Guthridge almost daily for three seasons, and this past season I met with Matt Doherty weekly to talk about our basketball team. I have always enjoyed the offensive and defensive strategies in our game. Of course, the mental game is equally important.

I also play a little golf. Even though I hit more practice balls than I ever did, I haven't improved. I am on the Presidents Council, a group that is making plans for the return of the U.S. Open golf tournament to Pinehurst No. 2 in 2005. That is certainly enjoyable, since Pinehurst president Pat Corso and the other council members are great company, and Pinehurst No. 2 is one of my favorite courses.

I was on the steering committee that worked against legalizing the lottery in North Carolina. A lottery often turns out to be an additional tax on poor people and creates many social ills that cause even more poverty. The record seems to indicate that poor people are most often enticed to spend money in hopes of hitting the jackpot. It's been said that a person has a better chance of being hit by lightning than he or she does of winning the lottery. I took a role in the campaign to declare a moratorium on the death penalty in North Carolina. I am on the boards of the Thurgood Marshall Legal Defense Fund and the Naismith Basketball Hall of Fame, and Linnea and I are on the board of the National Childhood Cancer Foundation.

My schedule has kept me from doing some things that I would have liked to have done, such as accepting Bill Bradley's invitation to help him kick off his campaign for president of the United States in Iowa.

This might surprise some of you, as it did me, but in the spring of 2001 I flirted with the idea of coaching again, this time in the NBA. One of the teams called to find out if I would be interested in going back to the bench. The flirtation lasted only a couple of days. Although I had received several offers to coach NBA teams from 1970 through 1996, the idea of coaching in the pros now was somewhat interesting to me because of the rules changes that became effective with the 2001–02 NBA season. The new rules allow for more defensive strategy, which also affects offensive thinking. They also give the have-nots a better chance to compete against teams with more talent. Furthermore, I always though it would be fun to coach in a best-of-five or best-of-seven playoff series. It would be interesting and challenging to make adjustments from game to game in the playoffs. After all, I never said I was tired of coaching. It was the peripheral things that go with coaching college basketball that influenced me to get out. Do I miss it? If you're talking about the aspects of pure coaching, then the answer is yes. I miss the preparation, the teaching, being on the floor for practice, and the rush of competing in big games. I don't miss the many other duties, such as making speeches, going to meetings, and traveling, plus the telephone calls and recruiting that are very much a part of coaching at a school such as North Carolina. For those reasons, I know I made the right decision to retire as North Carolina's basketball coach in 1997.

After three years as Carolina's head coach, Bill Guthridge experienced firsthand how I felt. After the 1999–2000 season, he and I discussed his situation as Carolina's head coach. He had reached age sixty-two, and some people were using it against him in recruiting, just as they did to me. Those who believe in negative recruiting pull it off like this: "Why would you think of going to North Carolina to play for Coach Guthridge? More than likely he will retire before you finish your college eligibility. Then you would be forced to play for a coach who didn't recruit you."

Bill and Leesie took a trip to Europe during the last two weeks of May 2000, before the start of Carolina's summer basketball camp. He thought the trip might rejuvenate him. He hoped he would return rested and excited about coaching. But soon after he got back, he came into my office and said, "I've hit the wall. Now I know how you felt when you said you were tired and didn't feel like you should continue as head coach. I feel the same way."

Many observers of Carolina basketball felt the best and most logical candidates to succeed Bill as Carolina's head coach would be former staff members Roy Williams and Eddie Fogler. Roy had amassed an amazing record in twelve years as head coach at Kansas, while Eddie had enjoyed a remarkable head coaching career at three schools: Wichita State, Vanderbilt, and South Carolina. His teams won Southeastern Conference championships at Vanderbilt and South Carolina even though he never had a player who was a first-round NBA draft pick.

Roy's background at Carolina as a ten-year assistant coach is chronicled earlier in this book. He had long been linked with the Carolina job. Countless newspaper stories had long speculated that he would succeed me as Carolina's head coach. When that job went to Bill, numerous other newspaper stories later appeared—both in Kansas and in North Carolina—predicting that Roy would succeed Bill. Such speculation seemed to gain momentum each winter because Roy and Wanda usually made a trip to Chapel Hill to see a Carolina game. People just wouldn't accept Roy's candid explanation that he was in town to see his son, Scott, play for Carolina, and later to see his daughter, Kimberly, perform on Carolina's dance team.

My old college roommate and teammate at Kansas, Charlie Hoag, had invited me to Topeka in mid-June 2000 to participate in a golfing event sponsored by the Kansas athletics department. By then, Bill had convinced me that he wanted to retire from coaching. Roy and I spent some time talking about the Carolina job while I was there.

The official announcement of Bill's retirement came on June 30. Along with it came speculation, not only in North Carolina and Kansas press reports but nationally, that Williams would leave Kansas to succeed Bill at North Carolina. I received an interesting telephone call upon Bill's retirement. It was from one of my former players, Matt Doherty, then the head coach at Notre Dame, who asked if he should pursue the Kansas job if Roy resigned from there to come to Carolina. I told him that if the Kansas job opened and he were offered the position, it would be difficult choosing the KU situation over his Notre Dame program.

Basketball, even in North Carolina, is usually not a hot topic in the dog days of summer. The news about Bill's retirement, the speculation about Roy, and other reporting on the subject put the story on the front pages of North Carolina newspapers. Many writers, talk show hosts, and fans thought they had it figured out. Were they ever in for a surprise!

Athletics director Dick Baddour indicated to me that he hoped to hire a person from our Carolina coaching tree to become UNC's head coach. However, he had gambled—when Mack Brown left as Carolina's head football coach to go to Texas—by naming Carl Torbush, Brown's defensive coordinator, to be head coach. That had not worked out as well as Baddour had hoped. So, he told me he wanted the new basketball coach to come from the head coaching ranks. Although I knew we also had experienced and successful head coaches in addition to Roy and Eddie, I was disappointed because this edict would eliminate Phil Ford as a candidate for the Carolina job. I knew without any reservations that Phil was capable and ready to coach at this level. I had hoped that he would get a fair hearing on his candidacy if it didn't work out with the more experienced head coaches.

With Bill Guthridge and me acting as consultants, Baddour called Kansas and South Carolina for permission to interview Williams and Fogler. Eddie shared with Dick something that he had told me earlier: He did not intend to remain in coaching beyond age fifty; therefore, he would not be a candidate for the Carolina job. But Eddie told Dick that he would help him recruit Williams. Eddie, who had been on my coaching staff for fifteen years, had helped train Roy when he joined us from high school coaching.

While Dick was contacting Kansas and South Carolina, he asked me to make two telephone calls to professional teams. One was to Pat Croce, the president of the Philadelphia 76ers, for permission to interview Larry Brown, Philadelphia's head coach. The other was to U.S. senator Herb Kohl of Wisconsin, owner of the Milwaukee Bucks, for the right to interview his head coach, George Karl. Croce granted us permission to interview Larry. However, Senator Kohl would not allow us to interview George for the Carolina job. He told me George was bound by contract to the Bucks. He did say we could talk to George, but not about the UNC job. I laughed, telling Senator Kohl that we didn't need permission just to talk to George. Not getting the opportunity to interview George was disappointing to him and us. George was the only candidate of former players not to have collegiate coaching experience, but that was of little concern. He is one of the best basketball coaches in the world, winning in the Continental Basketball Association, the European League at Madrid, and in the NBA.

Meanwhile, Dick had expanded his list to include talented coaches and former Carolina players Randy Wiel, Buzz Peterson, Jeff Lebo, and Matt Doherty. Jeff had served as Eddie Fogler's assistant at Vanderbilt and South Carolina before being named head coach at Tennessee Tech, where he would be voted Coach of the Year in the Ohio Valley Conference in 2000–01. Matt was assistant to Roy at Kansas for seven years before going to Notre Dame and taking the Irish to the NIT finals in his first year in South Bend. Buzz had done a fantastic job at Appalachian State, taking that Southern Conference team to the NCAA tournament. He went from there to Tulsa as head coach for the 2000–01 season, and his team won the NIT championship. Shortly afterward, he accepted an offer to become head coach at the University of Tennessee. Randy, who rebuilt programs at UNC–Asheville and Middle Tennessee State University, had been offered other mid-Division 1 jobs but elected to stay at Middle Tennessee State.

It was against that backdrop that Roy finished a round of golf with his regular foursome in Lawrence. It was Saturday, July 1, 2000. They hugged on the eighteenth green and Roy said, "The next time I come back here to play, I will be here as a visitor." He and Wanda left Lawrence the next day to travel to their vacation home on the South Carolina coast before coming to Chapel Hill for the interview. In what turned out to be an important aside, Roy promised Kansas chancellor Robert Hemenway that he would not make a final decision on his coaching future until he returned to Lawrence and talked to him and Bob Frederick, who was then the athletics director at Kansas.

The next few days were hectic. Roy came to Chapel Hill for an official interview on July 3. Bill Guthridge was vacationing at the beach and would be available by telephone. He called Roy twice during the two-day visit to Chapel Hill. That evening, Linnea and I, Roy and Wanda, and Dick and his wife, Linda, had dinner together. Afterward, Roy and I sat in Bill's office and talked from nine o'clock until almost midnight about the Carolina job. We covered all aspects of it. I certainly recruited Roy as hard and fairly as I could. Of course, I did think Carolina was the best job for him and he was the best to carry on the Carolina basketball program for the next twenty years. For instance, I told him that during his tenure as Kansas head coach, he had recruited three of his best players from Iowa. With Steve Alford now head coach at Iowa and Larry Eustachy building a strong program at Iowa State, it would be difficult to recruit there again. Roy seemed excited. Everything seemed to be falling into place for him to come to Carolina as head coach.

The morning of July 4, Roy and I played nine holes of golf at our new University Finley course, designed by Tom Fazio. John Inman, our men's golf coach and former NCAA champion, played with us, as did Johnny Cake, the golf pro at Finley. They must have been recruiting hard, too, because Roy was the medalist with a score of 37.

Roy and Dick met in Dick Baddour's office on July 4 after Roy visited by phone with incoming chancellor James Moeser. Chancellor Moeser was the dean of fine arts at Kansas from 1975 through 1986. He became Carolina's chancellor on August 1, 2000, after serving in the same capacity at the University of Nebraska for four years. His wife, Dr. Susan Moeser, is a KU graduate. I have known her father, Glee Smith, since 1984, when we both received KU's most prestigious award, the Distinguished Alumnus Award.

Roy's meeting with Dick was informal. At dinner the night before, Dick had asked Roy if he could do anything to enhance his visit. "I sure would like some North Carolina barbecue for lunch tomorrow," Roy replied. The next morning, when Dick set out to fulfill Roy's request, he found the leading barbecue restaurants in the Chapel Hill area closed for Independence Day. While Roy and I were playing golf, Dick dispatched two members of the athletics department to Goldsboro, about a ninety-minute drive one way, to purchase barbecue for lunch. Roy was embarrassed that Dick had gone to such trouble to satisfy his menu request. It was a small way for Dick to show Roy how much we wanted him to come to Chapel Hill as coach.

Baddour assured Roy that he was Carolina's choice for head coach. Bill Miller, our good friend as well as the financial adviser for Bill, Roy, Eddie Fogler, and me, busied himself with writing Roy's Carolina contract. There were no snags. No unreasonable demands were made by either side. Roy shouldn't have to take a pay cut to come to Chapel Hill from Kansas, and he wouldn't have. All agreed with that, although it was far from Roy's top priority. He wasn't worried about the money. Although Roy never said for certain that he was coming, I think Dick, Bill Guthridge, and I, along with Bill Miller, felt sure that he would take the job at North Carolina.

Roy and Wanda returned to the beach late on July 4. Roy flew to Lawrence the evening of July 5, a Wednesday. The Durham *Herald-Sun* ran a huge front-page headline and story on July 5, which Roy probably saw, stating that Roy would be Carolina's new coach. The next morning, Roy met with Chancellor Hemenway and Bob Frederick. They knew what a great coach they had. Obviously, they didn't want to lose him to North Carolina. They did a good job of communicating that message.

After the meeting, Roy—his heart being tugged in two directions—went for a walk on the Kansas campus. There were signs urging him to remain a Jayhawk. His secretary printed out thousands of e-mail messages from Kansas fans urging him to stay with the program. She made sure Roy saw them.

During his tenure as head coach of Kansas, Roy expended great effort to build the same kind of basketball family there that he had left at North Carolina. The interest in his players remained strong after they graduated and went on to their professional lives. He indeed had built a special program at Kansas, one that meant more to him than many people in North Carolina could imagine. "The people in North Carolina don't understand what I have in Kansas," Roy said, "and the people in Kansas don't understand what I would have in North Carolina." Many things affected his decision making during these days. First, he was extremely loyal to his Kansas players, as he should have been. Two, one of his lettermen, John Gurley, brought his young son over to see Roy and said, "Here he is, Coach. I hope you're here to coach him." Some of Roy's NBA players also came by to urge him to remain at Kansas. KU mounted an impressive campaign to keep its coach. All of this was taking place on the morning and early afternoon of July 6.

Still, we expected Roy to make his announcement that he was coming to North Carolina. I had told him that I was going to play golf with a friend that afternoon in Durham. Although I never before had taken a cell phone to the golf course, I did that day because I expected a call from Roy. Our golf round concluded just before six. The phone had not rung. "I'm getting nervous that something has happened to convince him to stay in Kansas," my playing partner said.

Shortly after leaving the golf course, the phone rang in my car. It was Roy, who was very emotional. He told me he was going to remain at Kansas. I'm not going to kid you: Some in our basketball family—Bill, Eddie, and others—were angry with Roy for turning down the job. Roy told me and others that he was afraid he had let me down. That's the last thing I wanted him to feel. I had never asked him to take the Carolina job. Certainly, he knew that I wanted him to coach at Carolina, but it was his decision to make. I had told him that from the very beginning. There was no way I was going to put pressure on him. You want your friends to do what they want to do. After much soul-searching, Roy felt that staying at Kansas was best for him.

I was disappointed—and surprised—that Roy wouldn't be North Carolina's coach, but I also understood. He and I remain close friends. We continue to talk by phone frequently and play golf together several times in the off-season. He is a great coach and a special friend.

Did North Carolina make a mistake in its recruitment of Williams? I don't think so. In hindsight, maybe UNC could have held a dual news conference announcing Bill's retirement and Roy's hiring at the same time. That would have killed the speculation about Roy before it had a chance to start. Also, we could have insisted that Roy give us a yes or no answer before returning to Lawrence. That's second-guessing, though. Kansas is Roy's program. He will continue to do well there.

With the search for a new coach back in full swing, Baddour immediately called Notre Dame and received permission to talk to Matt Doherty. He also asked for and received permission to talk to Randy Wiel and Jeff Lebo.

Matt came to North Carolina for his interview on Saturday, July 8. He left without being offered the job, but he certainly made a favorable impression on Dick in person and by phone with Chancellor Moeser. Bill and I also had separate visits with Matt. I know Matt well, but still I quizzed him about basketball and what he intended to do with the program if offered the job. I was also very impressed with him.

At this point, I told Dick that Larry Brown was my first choice. He was highly qualified. His 1988 Kansas team won the national championship. He also took Kansas to the Final Four in 1986 and coached UCLA to the NCAA Finals in 1980. That was three trips to the Final Four and one national championship in only eight years of college coaching.

Larry had also been my assistant for two years after playing for me my first two years as head coach. His magnificent record as an NBA coach could help in recruiting. I knew that the basketball coaches at the other ACC schools would be unhappy to learn that Carolina had hired Larry Brown. As one of the top coaches in the world, Larry's salary at Philadelphia was in excess of $5 million a year. The money differential between coaching the 76ers and coaching Carolina is huge. But Larry is the only one who could make a judgment on that.

Dick called Larry to set up a visit with him and his wife in Malibu, where

Larry has a summer home. Dick and Larry had met only briefly on two occasions over the years, so he and our excellent faculty rep, Dr. Jack Evans, took a private plane to Los Angeles on July 9 to meet with him. That night, I received a phone call from Dick, whose plane, on its return flight, had landed in Oklahoma for refueling. He and Jack were very impressed with Larry. Dick said he had asked Larry a couple of tough questions, but Larry handled the situation beautifully. We said we would talk the next morning in his office. He scheduled our meeting for eleven o'clock on Monday, July 10.

Just before Dick and I met, I called Larry to see if he was still interested in returning to Chapel Hill to be our head coach. I was surprised when he told me that Dick had posed some questions that he thought amounted to reasons for him *not* to take the job. He told me he was removing his name from consideration and to convey that to Dick. I told him I was certain Dick thought he would do a fabulous job. Larry said he appreciated my wanting him to take the job, but he had made up his mind.

In looking back, I'm certain Dick believed Larry could do a great job at Carolina, but in interviewing him, he wanted Larry to *want* the job. Larry has always been recruited in a big way for all his jobs, and deservedly so. So this was an unusual situation for Larry.

With experienced coaches George Karl, Larry, Roy, and Eddie out of contention, I made a call to Rick Majerus, the outstanding head coach at the University of Utah, to determine if he had any interest in the Carolina job. I think Rick was interested, but it would have taken him a day or two to get things in place before he could talk seriously as well as receive permission from his athletics director to talk.

I passed Rick's name along, but Dick had the search on a fast track by then. He and Chancellor Moeser seemed to have their eyes trained on Notre Dame, where Matt Doherty had been head coach for one year. Matt was a member of our 1982 NCAA championship team and graduated in 1984. After a short career on Wall Street, he coached as an assistant at Davidson College for two years and served as one of Roy's Kansas assistants for seven years. He went from Roy's staff to head coach at Notre Dame, where his team posted a 22–15 record in 1999–2000 with some great wins in the Big East. His team made it all the way to the NIT championship game before losing to Wake Forest.

Dick received a call from Matt on July 10, indicating that Notre Dame was making counteroffers, and he hoped Dick's decision would soon be forthcoming. It was. Dick and Chancellor Moeser decided that Matt was the best person to lead Carolina basketball. As consultants, Bill and I concurred.

The official announcement came at a press conference in Chapel Hill on July 11. I made the remark at the press conference that the day was both a celebration and one for grieving. The celebration was for Matt, our charismatic new head coach. The grieving was for our three tremendous assistant coaches who had worked for Bill and me. They were not retained. I was deeply saddened with that decision.

I have no quarrel at all with a head coach being allowed to name his assistant coaches. The importance of that is understood by everyone who has ever been a head coach. Also, Matt would have left his handpicked Notre Dame assistants without a job had he kept our Carolina staff intact. Nevertheless, the biggest disappointment in the coaching change was that our assistant coaches were suddenly out of coaching. A friend of Carolina basketball looked it up and learned that those three men—Phil Ford, Dave Hanners, and Pat Sullivan—together had played and/or coached in nineteen NCAA Final Fours for North Carolina. That is truly amazing. Each of them played major roles in Carolina's basketball success, that's for certain. Plus, they were well liked and highly respected both by the players and the university community. It was a very emotional time. As you would surmise, those three have remained extremely loyal to the program under Matt's leadership.

Phil has become associate vice president of Carolina's Educational Foundation and is also doing some work as an analyst on televised college basketball games. Last fall, Matt was recruiting Sean May, the six-foot-nine son of former Indiana All-America basketball player Scott May. Phil and Scott were teammates on our gold medal–winning 1976 Olympic basketball team, which trained for six weeks at Chapel Hill before going to Montreal. When Sean and his dad visited Chapel Hill on recruiting trips, Matt wisely asked Phil to help in Sean's recruitment. As employees of UNC, Phil and I are permitted to visit with prospects when they visit our campus.

Larry Brown hired Dave Hanners as an assistant coach and lead scout for the Philadelphia 76ers. Pat Sullivan, after spending a year scouting for Carolina's Mitch Kupchak, the general manager of the Los Angeles Lakers, and for our good friend Kevin O'Connor, general manager of the Utah Jazz, chose to return to college coaching. He is assisting his good friend Ann Hancock with the women's program at UNC–Wilmington.

I feel thoroughly confident in saying that Phil is going to get his chance to be a Division 1 head coach. He is a brilliant coach, one of the brightest I've been around. He came very close to getting a head job—a good one—in the spring of 2001.

As head coach of our Carolina junior varsity team, which consisted of nonscholarship players, Phil's teams consistently defeated prep schools and community colleges that had players who were on their way to becoming Division 1 scholarship basketball players. The list of men who coached our jayvee or freshman teams is impressive: Larry Brown, Bill Guthridge, Eddie Fogler, Roy Williams, Randy Wiel, Phil Ford, and Dave Hanners. I can't think of a better group of basketball coaches.

Matt's first season at Carolina resulted in a sparkling record of 26–7, co-champions of the ACC regular season. His team was voted number one in the nation by the Associated Press in a mid-February poll, and finished the season ranked in the AP Top Ten. Carolina was a number two seed in the NCAA tournament. Matt was a bright student in school and on the court. He is a tireless worker, energetic, and loves to teach and coach. He is an excellent speaker, which helps in recruiting and on his television show. I'm confident Carolina's program is in excellent hands. He was voted National Coach of the Year by the Associated Press in his first year as Carolina's coach.

Matt said on several occasions that Coach Guthridge left him an excellent and veteran team, which was certainly true. He did, however, miss Ed Cota at point guard. None of us would have expected less from Bill. Even though Bill also inherited a good team, it still was not easy for him to step in as head coach of a program that had won so many games over a long period of time. Expectations are high for Carolina basketball and often unrealistic. Bill handled those pressures well. It didn't surprise me. I knew for many years that Bill had what it took to be an excellent head coach. Two Final Fours in three years would enhance most résumés.

Bill faced a big challenge in the 1998–99 season. He lost Antawn Jamison and Vince Carter to the NBA after their junior seasons. In addition, Shammond Williams and Makhtar Ndiaye, both starters on the 1998 team that won the ACC championship, advanced to the Final Four, and finished number one in the nation in the final AP college basketball poll of that season, graduated. We often talk about role models in athletics. Well, while it's true that some athletes don't shoulder that responsibility very well, one would be hard-pressed to find three who set better examples for youth than Antawn, Vince, and Shammond.

Shammond, a six-foot-two guard, didn't receive a single Division 1 scholarship offer when, as a good student, he graduated from Southside High School in Greenville, South Carolina. Even though Clemson University and Furman University are located within thirty minutes of his home, neither recruited him. Only Presbyterian College, a small Division 2 school in Clinton, South Carolina, showed great interest in him as a student-athlete.

Shammond, who had a stubborn streak plus a heart filled with determination, wanted a Division 1 scholarship. He felt he could play college basketball at the highest level, and he was prepared to do whatever it took to prove it. It had been his dream for many years. He worked on his game for hours and hours at a time. People talk about "gym rats." The mold was cast in Shammond's image. Shammond decided to attend preparatory school at Fork Union Military Academy in Virginia for a year after his graduation from high school in order to be "discovered" as a Division 1 basketball prospect. He continued his good work academically and was selected Best Drilled Cadet in competition with 650 other students. It's the highest military award given by Fork Union.

Eddie Fogler, the head coach at South Carolina, saw him in a summer league in Charlotte before Shammond left for Fork Union. Eddie was impressed by his quickness and leadership. In early September, Bill Guthridge received a call from a respected AAU coach who thought we should check out Shammond, since we were looking for a guard. Coach Guthridge saw that Shammond had defensive quickness plus the ability to make outside shots. Three days later, Bill and I went to see him practice at Fork Union and thought we should recruit him. After practice I talked to the highly respected coach at Fork Union, Fletcher Arritt, who had only great things to say about Shammond. We then talked to Shammond and offered him a scholarship that night. He signed with us in the early signing period in November after visiting Chapel Hill.

After playing sparingly as a freshman on our 1995 Final Four team, Shammond then became an important starter for us for the next three years. He loved to have the crucial shot and would come through in the clutch. He played on Carolina teams that went to three NCAA Final Fours and won two ACC championships.

This young man, who couldn't beg a Division 1 scholarship while playing on a high school championship team, was a second-round NBA draft pick and now is a highly paid, extremely valuable player for Seattle in the NBA. Incidentally, his extraordinary mother, Pam, is an aunt of Kevin Garnett, an NBA all-star.

Young people with raw talent who need time to develop it, and who at first don't succeed, could learn much by studying the career of Shammond Williams. He was a special player in our program as well as a terrific young man.

As a person, the same can be said about Vince Carter. But unlike Shammond, Vince came to Carolina as a highly recruited McDonald's All-American. Before choosing Carolina, he had narrowed his choice of colleges to Florida State, Florida, Duke, and Kentucky. Sometimes prospects who earn such accolades as a high school player come to college basketball spoiled and thinking they know it all. Vince was a gifted athlete when he came to Chapel Hill but knew he still needed work and experience before he could advance to the NBA. To his credit, he listened, worked hard, and improved every area of his play dramatically, except for his leaping ability. There was no need to improve that, since he was one of the best jumpers in the history of college basketball. He was a well-rounded star player when he left Carolina.

Now an NBA all-star with Toronto, Vince made news off the court in May 2001. He showed up in Chapel Hill on Mother's Day morning to receive his Carolina diploma during commencement exercises. As I said, Vince left Carolina basketball after his junior season to enter the NBA draft. It proved to be a wise financial decision, and it certainly didn't hurt him academically, either. He continued to pursue his college degree while playing professional basketball, as he had promised his mother.

I understand why he was proud of his achievement and wanted to be in Chapel Hill to receive his diploma. His presence on the Carolina stage that Sunday morning, all decked out in a Carolina blue cap and gown, created a mini-controversy because Toronto was scheduled to play Philadelphia late that afternoon in the seventh game of their Eastern Conference playoffs.

Because I knew he would put himself under great media pressure in Game 7 if he showed up in Chapel Hill on the day of the game, I left Vince a message on his cell phone Saturday afternoon, basically saying that his goal all along had been to earn his degree, which he had done. Everyone would understand if he chose to be with his team instead of in Chapel Hill. After all, being there that morning to receive his diploma was symbolic. He already was a Carolina graduate.

However, the symbolism was important to Vince and his mom. After receiving his diploma and briefly celebrating with former Carolina teammates Brendan Haywood, Michael Brooker, and Max Owens, who were also graduating, Vince boarded a private jet provided by the Raptors and traveled to Philadelphia for that afternoon's game. I'm sure being in Chapel Hill on Sunday morning had no adverse effect on Vince's individual performance. I thought he played well. And after all, NBA players don't sit in their hotel rooms on the morning of a game staring at four walls.

A small number of NBA players and a few commentators criticized Vince for his decision to go to Chapel Hill. One called him selfish, which was absurd. On the other hand, scores and scores of respected sports columnists, along with many editorial page writers, saw the good in what Vince did and praised him for it. Certainly, Vince demonstrated a well-grounded sense of values by wanting to be at his school to get his diploma. He sent an inspiring message to young basketball fans all across America. Here is an NBA all-star who values his education as much as he does his ability to play basketball. I wrote to Vince and his mom to apologize for even suggesting that he could miss the Carolina ceremony. What he did was a tremendous affirmation of the value of education.

Though still a young man, Vince had a sensational three-year career at Carolina. He made All-America and played in two Final Fours and on two ACC championship teams. His three Carolina teams averaged twenty-eight wins a season. He was also a member of the 2000 U.S. Olympic gold-medal team and is now considered one of the NBA's superstars. And he is a graduate of the University of North Carolina. His Carolina jersey, number 15, is honored and hangs in the Smith Center rafters.

I like his style.

The same is true of Antawn Jamison. He came to Carolina from Providence High School in Charlotte in the same class with Vince and Ademola Okulaja. In recruiting Antawn, we thought he had size, good hands, great quickness, and speed in addition to coming from a great home environment. Still, of those three incoming freshmen, his basketball skills (shooting, dribbling, passing, etc.) were behind the other two. It was a pleasant surprise to see his quick development of those skills, which continue to improve each year in the NBA. He, too, left Carolina basketball after his junior season.

There was never any doubt about Antawn earning his degree. After his outstanding freshman season, we thought there would be the possibility that Antawn would leave school a year early for the NBA. Therefore, he went to both sessions of summer school for each of the next two summers. Earning his degree was important to him personally and also to his parents. Not only was Antawn National Player of the Year as a junior, he was at the same time a fierce competitor and a sportsman. He played the game with a smile on his face. He was always polite and considerate of his coaches and teammates, and also of fans and the media. His jersey, number 32, is retired in the rafters of the Smith Center. Antawn received his diploma in December 2000 ceremonies in Chapel Hill, at the same time that Jerry Stackhouse received his. Think about the positive impression that picture had on young people across

America: Antawn, an NBA star with the Golden State Warriors, and Jerry, a star with the Detroit Pistons, in Chapel Hill during basketball season, dressed in cap and gown, receiving their Carolina diplomas. Jerry had the toughest challenge, since he left school after his sophomore year.

So, Coach Guthridge, with this talent missing, did face a tough task in the 1998–99 season. The good news is that he returned one of our best leaders, Ademola Okulaja, whom we recruited from Germany after receiving a tip from one of our former players, Henrik Rodl. Coach Guthridge and I have thanked Henrik on countless occasions for recommending Ademola to us. Playing with a young and inexperienced team, Carolina won twenty-four games and qualified for the NCAA tournament in 1999.

Expectations were high for the 1999–2000 season, mainly because Bill had an experienced team returning. Ed Cota, an excellent point guard and an All-ACC player, and center Brendan Haywood were talented and experienced players. Jason Capel, a sophomore, was also back. Jason's father is a highly respected coach, and Jason plays the game with savvy and skill. He gave Bill an unselfish player who was well schooled in all areas of the game.

However, some unfortunate things happened that hampered the team's early development. Kris Lang, six-eleven, who was counted on to be an inside presence along with Haywood, became ill in September with a serious illness that hospitalized him. He lost weight and fitness after he had worked hard in the summer to improve his strength, conditioning, and basketball skills. The illness put Kris back to ground zero. He worked overtime when he returned in an effort to regain his edge and came down with shin splints, which bothered him off and on for the entire season. Bill was also counting on Brian Bersticker, a fine six-foot-eleven player, to play a significant role on the team. Brian broke a bone in his foot during the summer, which hampered his conditioning. Then he broke the foot again in December while the team was playing in Charlotte. He missed the rest of the season.

Even with these players out, and playing against one of the toughest schedules in the history of college basketball, Bill and his staff held the team together through the tough times. Carolina played twelve nonconference games that season against teams that went to the NCAA tournament. It finished the regular season with a record of 18–14. The critics had a field day. But the team wasn't finished. Seeded eighth in the NCAA tournament, UNC got hot at the right time. It beat an athletic Missouri team in the tournament's first round. Then Carolina got everybody's attention by beating Stanford, a number one seed, in round two. Continuing its excellent play, UNC beat fourth-seeded Tennessee and then third-seeded Tulsa to advance to the Final

Four. Carolina lost in the semifinals to Florida, which earlier had eliminated Duke. Carolina finished the season with a record of 22–15.

One of the excellent players on Bill's last team was freshman Joseph Forte. As a sophomore, Forte continued his good play for Coach Doherty and made first-team AP All-America. After the 2000–01 season, I was asked by Joseph's mother, Wanda Hightower, and also by Matt to help Joseph ascertain his position in the NBA draft, in the event he decided to leave college basketball two years early. I made a couple of calls to NBA friends, who told me that if Forte entered the draft, he most likely would be picked somewhere between numbers thirteen and twenty in the first round. Armed with this information, Matt and I met with Joseph and his mother. I told them I thought it would be wise if Joseph returned to Carolina for his junior season. It was my opinion that he would improve as a player and at the same time significantly improve his 2002 draft position, which would have meant substantially more money for him. More important, it would have been far easier for him to earn his degree if he finished his junior year before going pro. Matt told us that he had plans to use Forte at point guard at times during the 2001–02 season, which would have enhanced his draft position. In this meeting, however, it became clear to Matt and me that Joseph had made up his mind that he was going to enter the draft if he could be certain that he would go in the first round. Because Joseph and his mother obviously had made the decision for him to enter the 2001 NBA draft before getting complete information from us, I didn't see the need to pursue the matter any further, because I knew Joseph would go in the first round. He did, as the twenty-first player picked. He signed with the Boston Celtics. His Carolina teammate, Brendan Haywood, the leading shot-blocker in Carolina history, was the twentieth player taken in the first round. He signed with Orlando but is now with Washington.

Some people who love college basketball are wringing their hands because we're losing some college players—and now a few high school players—to the NBA. I think college basketball is going to come out of this just fine. We can't blame these young people for taking advantage of professional basketball contracts that will secure their financial future as well as fulfilling their dreams. Athletes in other sports do it often with very little fanfare. It would suit me if every NCAA basketball player were eligible for the draft. If he was taken high and was guaranteed a no-cut contract, then he could either start his career in professional basketball or stay in school.

There are many examples of athletes in other sports turning professional at an early age with very little media attention. For instance, Tracy Austin won the U.S. Women's Open tennis tournament as a pro when she was just sixteen. It is difficult to tell any high school graduate that he or she can't sign a professional baseball contract, or act in a movie, play in a band, enlist in the armed services, or simply secure a job that we hope will be a vocation in which he or she has interest and aptitude.

Remember, there are only twenty-nine first-round NBA draft picks each year with guaranteed contracts. There will be plenty of talent available to keep college basketball exciting to the fans.

So, while I don't think we need to be greatly alarmed because a few college underclassmen and some high school graduates put their names up for the NBA draft, there are other issues facing Division 1 basketball that are both serious and threatening to the well-being of the sport.

These problems were the catalyst for the formation of a blue-ribbon NCAA committee in 1998, of which I was a member. After several meetings in Chicago, which cost more than $300,000 in expenses to stage, we issued a report in July 1999. In summary, we accomplished very little. In fact, we left the tough questions unanswered.

The committee was comprised of twenty-nine members, which was too large and cumbersome. Only thirteen of those twenty-nine were in positions of power to bring about change—five presidents and eight directors of different-sized athletics programs. I wished that those thirteen could have voted on the issues before us after listening to arguments for change. I was pleased that C. M. Newton and Terry Holland were on the committee. They had each experienced college basketball as an athlete, as a head coach at the top level, and as an athletics director. Nevertheless, while the three of us agreed on many important issues, committee members who had little experience in Division 1 men's basketball consistently defeated our proposals for change.

The committee listed problems facing Division 1 men's basketball. These received the most extensive review:

1. The welfare of the basketball student-athlete.
2. Low graduation rates and high attrition (transfers to other schools) of Division 1 men's basketball players.
3. The environment that currently exists in the summer basketball recruiting process.

C.M., Terry, and I believe that if the committee had recommended three simple reforms, and the presidents in charge of the NCAA had adopted them, they would have solved the most serious problems now plaguing Division 1 men's basketball.

These are the reforms we wanted and suggested, without gaining committee approval:

1. A $2,000 annual stipend to cover the full cost of attendance for Division 1 men and women basketball players on full scholarship, as well as Division 1-A scholarship football players. From the late 1940s until the 1972–73 school year, a full scholarship included fifteen dollars a month for "laundry and incidentals." However, the NCAA convention of January 1972, which later became known as the "Cost Containment Convention," whacked away at athletics department expenses. Many worthy programs fell by the wayside thanks to this convention's work, including the fifteen dollars a month for incidentals as well as school-bought travel blazers for football and basketball players to wear on road trips. Of course, these measures hurt the athletes from poor families the most. They couldn't call home for spending money and money for a sports coat.

Most economists would agree that $15 a month in the late forties, or even in 1972, would amount to about $2,000 a year in today's economy. Furthermore, many nonathletic scholarships today provide the full cost of attendance. Sometimes, that even includes transportation costs from home to campus, which, of course, is not allowed by the NCAA. You would be surprised how many poor athletes can't afford to go out for a pizza and a movie with their classmates. It's difficult for them to feel a part of the student body when they face such financial limitations.

The $2,000-a-year stipend for Division 1 men and women basketball players could come from the $6.2 billion that CBS is going to pay over the next eleven years to televise the NCAA Division 1 men's basketball tournament. An argument could be made that this stipend should be based on need. If so, only the very wealthy should be excluded.

The checks for the athletes should come directly from the NCAA. Division 1-A football players should receive money from the NCAA only if a Division 1-A playoff is started. Otherwise, money for the football players should come from proceeds generated by the twenty-six Division 1-A football bowl games.

The stipend would certainly address in a meaningful way the number one problem area cited by our committee: the welfare of the basketball student-athlete.

2. A year-in-residence. Each new basketball student-athlete—high school graduates coming as freshmen, or transfers from another four-year college, or junior college transfers—would be required to be a full-time student for one academic year before earning the privilege of playing varsity basketball. This proposal is not as radical as it might appear on the surface when one considers that most Division 1 football programs already practice a form of it by "redshirting" 90-plus percent of their freshmen. Also, a transfer from a four-year college now must spend a year-in-residence before competing on the varsity.

If this rule were passed, it would help solve the three main problem areas cited by our committee. The university would send forth a clear message to the athletes that they are students first and foremost. The year-in-residence would also provide new students a fair chance to build a solid academic foundation during their first year on campus without having to worry about the extensive demands of playing varsity basketball. They wouldn't have to miss classes to go on road trips, spend time in team meetings, or spend the extra practice time required of a freshman playing on the varsity. Also, they would have the Thanksgiving, Christmas, and spring vacations that other students enjoy but aren't usually available to varsity basketball players. Without the demands of participating in varsity basketball, the first-year athlete would stand a better chance of adjusting to being away from home for the first time and would be encouraged to make friends with students who are not athletes.

Assuming they would be on freshman teams, the new athletes would become friends with nonscholarship players. After all, the NCAA maintains that its core mission is "maintaining intercollegiate athletics as an integral part of the education program and the athlete as an integral part of the student body."

Not only would a year-in-residence be in the best interests of the basketball student-athlete, it would also help solve the low graduation rates and high attrition cited by our committee. Some freshmen end up transferring if they were disenchanted with the playing time they received their first year. However, if that decision were faced after their sophomore year, when they felt more a part of the student body and had made many friends on campus, it would be more difficult for them to decide to transfer.

A year-in-residence without the demands of varsity basketball would unquestionably help the freshmen academically, while the transfer student would receive an additional year of college education with its academic benefits. One large conference has a graduation rate of 17 percent for junior college basketball players who transfer to their four-year schools. That is even below the often criticized graduation rate for those entering and playing as freshmen.

Making freshmen and transfers spend a year-in-residence before competing in varsity basketball competition would also alleviate many of the problems that exist today with summer recruiting. Unfortunately, basketball
recruiting has become the third "big-time" sport as far as interest is concerned in basketball-crazed areas such as the ACC and elsewhere. It is amazing how much attention, time, and space the media devote to summer
recruiting. In my opinion, if the fans and the media had to wait a year before
seeing the freshman phenom or junior college star play on the varsity, the interest in summer recruiting would be cut in half. That's a worthy goal.

I brought to the committee's attention that a rule in effect now for college
basketball players could help with the summer recruiting problems if it were
also in place for high school players. College basketball players can't play
organized basketball out of season except in NCAA-approved leagues located no more than one hundred miles from either the player's home or his
school. However, a high school prospect is allowed to play in several states
and for several different teams during the summer between his junior and senior high school seasons. This play takes place on weekends in spring and
fall, and is constant in the summer. These young players are recruited and
then given expenses to fly around the country to play against other top high
school prospects. It's a system that invites corruption.

The NCAA now has a rule in effect requiring high school students to take
certain courses before they can receive a Division 1 basketball scholarship.
If it would also decree that high school juniors and seniors interested in
playing Division 1 basketball could not play in organized basketball games
more than one hundred miles from their home or school, it would be a valuable tool for needed reform. In fact, such a rule, coupled with a year-in-
residence, would, in my opinion, alleviate most of the problems that come
from summer basketball.

A year-in-residence is not a novel idea. For more than forty years it was
required of all students before they could participate in any sport in varsity
competition at the Division 1 level. The exception to this rule was during
World War II and the Korean War, and to date, I haven't met one athlete who
experienced this rule who hasn't said it was best for him. At the several
schools whose statistics I've checked, graduation rates for athletes were
higher then than they are now. As we stated earlier in the book, the abolition
of freshman ineligibility came about as a way to save money on scholarships. We have now reached the point where we can't afford *not* to return to
a year-in-residence if we truly have the best academic interests of the
student-athlete at heart.

3. Allow each college or university to set its own admission requirements for athletes. Three provisions must be passed in order to make this work. First, there must be a year-in-residence for each new student on campus before he can participate in varsity basketball competition. Second, the NCAA should continue to prescribe the academic curriculum for any high school student who hopes to qualify for an athletic scholarship to a Division 1 school. This rule helps high school students be more prepared for college whether or not the individual qualifies for financial aid. Third, the NCAA should tell each Division 1 school that the lowest 1 percent of freshman admissions (based on each school's admission criteria) cannot be recruited athletes. I believe it is correct that all Division 1 schools give a break to an outstanding athlete. The Ivy League, the ACC, the Big Ten, the Pac-10, and others do this in the belief that the athlete could help the university if his high school record indicates he could graduate.

I am tired of coaches and others who say that a young man is better off being in college even if he doesn't earn a degree. Perhaps he would be better off in the Marine Corps. He would certainly be more disciplined to do college work, or hold a job, after experiencing the Marines. The principal point is that when we claim to be helping young men by recruiting them to college, even when we know they have no reasonable chance to graduate, we are helping them only because they can help us win games. With the 1 percent rule, we would help a small group of students who couldn't help us athletically. Still, we would give them a chance for a college education.

In order for the recruited athlete to remain eligible, he must make normal progress toward a degree. Normal academic progress should be determined by each individual university, which should use current standards as the barometer to define "normal progress."

The NCAA admission standards requiring a certain score on the SAT, a certain grade average in core courses, and other requirements are not working. We all know that. I have been around college basketball a long, long time, and I can't recall a single incident involving a great player who wanted to play college basketball who wasn't admitted somewhere. Obviously, this means the NCAA standards are being circumvented, and easily so. A great player is going to find a college somewhere that will take him, regardless of his test scores and high school grades. The past proves that. We would be much better off letting each college and university set its own academic standards for admission. This could also improve the graduation rate for football and basketball players, because each college and university knows best what academic standards a prospective student must meet to have a decent chance to graduate from that institution. Also, when one considers that the most recent NCAA graduation report indicated that 48 percent of Division 1 football players and 34 percent of men's basketball players graduated, the need for change is obvious.

The Knight Commission on Intercollegiate Athletics, formed in 1989 with the stated purpose to study and propose a reform agenda for college sports, issued its final report in the summer of 2001 after spending even more money than our NCAA committee. Its first report, issued in 1991, did help put the presidents and chancellors of NCAA colleges and universities in charge of their athletic departments. We have since learned that the presidents have neither the time nor the experience to do this particular job. Instead, they lean heavily on conference commissioners, who control the distribution of Division 1-A football bowl revenues.

In its final report, the Knight Commission deplored the low graduation rate of Division 1 football and basketball players and recommended a coalition of presidents lead a campaign toward academic reform, which included a de-escalation of high salaries for coaches, a reduction in the "arms race" to build and expand athletic facilities on campus, and less commercialism in college athletics. One commission member said, "It appears we are trying to put the genie back in the bottle." If he's saying the genie won't fit back in the bottle, I would agree with him.

College presidents and chancellors are in charge of their *entire* university. But they must also be a fund-raiser and listen to faculty, students, and alumni who contribute. Back in the 1940s, the University of Chicago was a Big Ten football power. However, Dr. Hutchens, the university president, didn't like the way football fit into his school's overall mission, so he disbanded it. I can't imagine any leader of a Division 1-A school making a unilateral decision such as that today. Our culture demands that universities compete and do well.

Claiming it supports academic reform, it's interesting that the Knight Commission gave only casual consideration to a year-in-residence proposal: "While the arguments in favor of freshmen ineligibility are compelling in many respects, it is also true that such a policy would preclude many athletes who are fully capable of succeeding academically and competing at a high level their freshman year from doing so." So, the commission's newly stated goal of academic reform was overruled by money, pure and simple. It is saying, in effect, that an athlete on scholarship should "earn his keep." That's unfortunate. It's true that a very few freshman athletes could handle academics and varsity athletics well. It's equally true that a few freshmen could handle junior and senior chemistry courses. But the university says they can't enroll in those classes as freshmen.

The Knight group also mentions a goal of de-escalation of coaches' salaries as well as declaring "arms control" in the construction of expensive new on-campus athletic facilities. To begin with, I know many good coaches who would take much less than today's going rate for the privilege of coaching college basketball. The presidents can, and ought to, determine how much the coach makes from the school, from a shoe contract, and from doing radio and television shows. Also, the presidents could refuse to approve new athletic facilities for their campus, but they won't. How could the NCAA pass a rule that would limit how much a coach is paid, or regulate the construction of athletic facilities? It couldn't. We have precedents here. For instance, the NCAA paid millions to settle a lawsuit brought by "part-time" basketball coaches who had been limited, by an NCAA rule, to making $20,000 a year. As head coach at North Carolina, I was underpaid my first twenty-four years (compared to faculty) and vastly overpaid my last thirteen years. I never discussed my salary with university officials, nor did I ever ask for a raise.

In an example of naïveté, the Knight Commission called for the NBA and the NFL to develop and finance their own minor leagues. Do you think the NBA and/or the NFL is going to listen to the Knight Commission? Hardly. Furthermore, every high school basketball player would rather play at a Division 1 school and take college classes in hopes of hearing Dick Vitale refer to them on ESPN as a "diaper dandy." So, unless the new NBA developmental league stumbles into a lucrative television contract, which is highly unlikely, it won't serve as a suitable place for those young men who don't wish to pursue a degree.

The Knight Commission laments what it calls the "burgeoning commercialization of college sports." Make no mistake: when the commission refers to "college sports," it is really talking about Division 1 football and basketball. Well, the "burgeoning commercialization" was born on the very same day that college presidents, athletics directors, and conference commissioners invited television on campus to show our games in exchange for a huge amount of money. It should not be surprising that the money comes with some strings attached. After all, beginning in 2002, CBS will pay the NCAA $6.2 billion over eleven years for rights to telecast the NCAA men's basketball tournament.

The positive side of having television a part of the mix is that it has afforded our faculty, students, alumni, and general fans a chance to see Carolina basketball games that were played in the United States and other countries. Television also helps our school rank among the collegiate lead-ers in athletic paraphernalia sold, and those profits go to the university's nonathletic scholarship fund.

Believe me, we are going to have commercialization if we are to raise the money it takes to fund all of the sports that college athletics departments try to maintain. It is not as if the athletics departments are raking in this money for their own benefit. It is spent on the student-athletes so they can offer wrestling, tennis, golf, crew, soccer, lacrosse, and other non-revenue-producing sports. The athletics department budget at North Carolina, which fields fourteen varsity sports for women and fourteen for men, was $34 mil-lion for the 2001–02 school year. In order to make ends meet, it takes foot-ball and basketball gate receipts, and television money generated by those two sports, plus alumni donations that provide the donor the right to pur-chase football and basketball season tickets. And it's a struggle even then. Many leading Division 1 schools are being forced to drop non-revenue-producing sports because they can't afford to pay for them.

So, yes, Division 1 football and basketball are commercialized. They will continue to be as long as our games are televised and as long as those two sports are asked to support most of the budgets of the nonrevenue sports.

I am disappointed that the Knight Commission, after years of meetings and the expenditure of much money, apparently feels the solution to the problems afflicting Division 1 football and men's basketball would be to adopt Division 3 guidelines. It's true, salaries for coaches in Division 3 are not a matter of concern. Nor are Division 3 football and basketball pro-grams heavily commercialized. I don't know of any Division 3 programs that spend lavish amounts on athletic facilities. And the graduation rates for football and basketball players at Division 3 certainly are better than at Division 1.

To be sure, I have the highest respect for Division 3 athletics. The cam-puses that compete at that level, as well as the athletes who participate, are well served. But this is the twenty-first century, and Division 1 football and basketball will not return to that landscape and haven't been there since World War II. Talking about an "arms race," it's my opinion that college ath-letics in general would be better served if we quit spending hundreds of thousands of dollars on studies suggesting that Camelot would be revisited if only we returned to yesteryear. Instead, let's take what we have now in Di-vision 1 football and basketball and improve it.

Billy Armfield, a friend and member of the Carolina board of trustees, re-cently wondered if the Division 1 basketball player of today is as disciplined and committed as the one of twenty years ago. It's true that the recruited athlete today is spoiled by the recruiting process and unrealistic expectations. The athletes of today are much more aware of the world in which we live than were athletes of twenty or thirty years ago. This could be attributed to movies, television, the Internet, books, and newspapers, among other things. Still, human nature hasn't changed in my many years of coaching basketball. The athletes continued to respond to fair descipline and appreciated it later. They were also aware that their coach had the power to determine how much playing time each would receive in the games.

Because we do have negatives that afflict Division 1 football and basketball, we dwell on the problems (which we should) but often overlook the benefits that these programs have on the athletes who participate. While it might sound corny to some, the Division 1 athletes are learning values such as sacrifice, unselfishness, discipline, responsibility, and, yes, courage. To be a part of a team in any NCAA division is a learning experience for which we become more grateful as the years pass. I have had former junior varsity basketball players at Carolina, who never made the varsity, tell me that playing on the jayvee team was the highlight of their college experience.

Bill Bradley, who played high school basketball in Crystal City, Missouri, then at Princeton University, and professionally in Italy and for the NBA New York Knicks, wrote of what playing the game meant to him. In his book *Values of the Game,* Bill put it eloquently: "After all the years, the game is still full of joy and the lessons learned from it stay with you. Even though the game has changed, the old values still flow through it."

Yes, we can improve on what we have now in Division 1 basketball, and we should. At the same time, the lessons and values the game provides are well worth protecting and enhancing.

Sadly, I've experienced some deep personal losses since this book was first published. Dick Harp, who was assistant coach at Kansas when I played there, and later became KU's head coach with Wilt Chamberlain as one of his players, died on May 22, 2000. Dick came to Chapel Hill to serve as an assistant on my staff after retiring as vice president of the Fellowship of Christian Athletes. He was a tremendous help to all of us. John Lotz, one of my early Carolina assistants and a man who played a valuable role in the success that UNC basketball has enjoyed, died on May 5, 2001.

Dick died after a lengthy illness. Most of the members of our 1952 Kansas national championship team were in Lawrence for Coach Harp's memorial service. Jerry Waugh, KU's basketball captain in 1951 and later

Dick's assistant coach, spoke on behalf of the players. All who knew Dick respected him as a great man and cared deeply for him.

He is given much attention earlier in this book. He was a special friend and mentor. I learned so much from him, and not only about basketball. Dick's death, while certainly sad, was not a huge shock. His health had been in decline for a couple of years.

It was a different story for John Lotz. John became ill late in the fall of 2000. He seemed to take a significant turn for the better and appeared to be on his way to recovery when he suffered a relapse in April 2001. He died early in May at age sixty-four.

I wrote earlier in the book about John's coaching skills and his abilities as a recruiter. Suffice it to say he was invaluable in helping us build the Carolina basketball program.

But as good as he was at it, basketball was only a small part of John's life. His major goal was to help people, especially the underdogs in our society. He was their champion, whether it involved visiting prisons to speak to inmates, or leading campaigns to feed the hungry. He was immensely popular with Carolina's student-athletes. His door was always open for them to come and talk. They knew it, and visited with him often.

"I ate a lot of meals at the Lotz house," said former Carolina football quarterback star Mark Maye, "and got some mighty good advice each time I went there."

There's just no telling how many late-night telephone calls John received from people needing his help. To my knowledge, he never turned anyone away. He also had the skill to hold an audience spellbound with his oratory. John's faith and family were the centerpieces of his life. He was legendary for handing out inspirational audio tapes, books, and newspaper clippings to his many friends and acquaintances.

If you could put a price tag on the goodwill he generated on behalf of the University of North Carolina, it would be in the millions of dollars. His files were filled with letters from people thanking him for making a difference in their lives.

His memorial service at University Baptist Church in Chapel Hill drew an overflow crowd. People came from near and far to show their love and pay their respects. As you might suspect, the Carolina basketball family was well represented. John's wife, Vicki, and daughters Corrie and Laci have many wonderful memories of him that will comfort them forever.

One of our former All-America basketball players at Carolina, Al Wood, was one of the speakers at John's memorial service. "Some people like to put a foot in your back when you're down and grind away," Al said. "Not so with John. His style was to lean over to those in need and extend a helping hand."

That indeed was John's way of living—in the service of others. He and I were such close friends that he really was like the brother I never had.

John Lotz and Dick Harp were major influences on me as well as extraordinary friends. I am extremely lucky to have had them in my life for so many years.

Finally, let me take this opportunity to thank the unbelievable number of people who have told me in one way or another how much they enjoyed this book, and that some part of it meant something special. I have received letters and telephone calls from all over the world, including many from people whom I have respected for many years. I wish I felt comfortable enough to name a few who have responded. But I wouldn't dare, knowing that I would leave out the names of many.

At my retirement news conference on ESPN, the late Michael Hooker, who was our enthusiastic and talented chancellor at the time, made the comment that I had done more for my university than anyone he had ever known in higher education. I didn't deserve such an accolade, but considering my love for the University of North Carolina, it certainly means a lot to me.

In retrospect, the writing of this book gave me a chance to relive many wonderful and happy moments. Some sad ones, too.

That's life, taking the good with the bad. While not every moment can be a happy one, I'm extremely fortunate and grateful for having so much good in my life, much of it provided by the young men who played for me at the University of North Carolina. I hope they know how I feel about them. I believe they do.

Appendix

University of North Carolina
Lettermen Under Coach Dean Smith

CLASS OF 1962

Peppy Callahan
Degree: B.A., Mathematics Education
Graduate Work: M.A.T., Mathematics Education, 1964
Present Position: Colonel, U.S. Air Force (Retired), Melbourne, Florida

Hugh Donohue
Degree: B.A., History and Education
Present Position: Women's Basketball Coach, Purchase College, SUNY, Purchase,
  New York

Jim Hudock
Degree: B.S., Industrial Relations
Graduate Work: D.D.S., 1968
Present Position: Retired Dentist, Kinston, North Carolina

Harry Jones
Degree: B.A., Philosophy
Graduate Work: M.A., Philosophy, 1963
Present Position: Teacher, Lansing, North Carolina

* Has played professional basketball in the NBA or the ABA.
† Has played professional basketball in Europe, Australia, South America, with Athletes in Action, or
in the Continental Basketball Association.
Degree was earned at another university.

Donnie Walsh
Degree: B.A., Political Science
Graduate Work: J.D., 1965
Present Position: President, Indiana Pacers, NBA

CLASS OF 1963

*Larry Brown
Degree: B.A., History
Present Position: Head Coach, Philadelphia 76ers, NBA

Charles Burns
Degree: B.A., Sociology
Present Position: Sales Representative, Levi Strauss, Lexington, Kentucky

Dieter Krause
Degree: B.A., Recreation Administration
Present Position: Lieutenant Colonel, U.S. Army (Retired), Colonial Heights, Virginia

Yogi Poteet
Degree: B.A., Sociology
Graduate Work: M.A.T., Sociology, 1965
Present Position: School Dean, U.S. Army, Logistics Management College, Fort Lee, Virginia

Richard Vinroot
Degree: B.S., Business Administration
Graduate Work: J.D., 1966
Present Position: Attorney, Former Mayor, Charlotte, North Carolina

Manager:

Eddie Burke
Degree: B.S., Industrial Relations
Present Position: Partner, IBM Marketing Agency, Eastern Technology Associates, Wilmington, North Carolina

CLASS OF 1964

Bruce Bowers
Degree: B.A., History
Graduate Work: Financial Services, 1983
Present Position: Senior Trust Officer, Whittum & Leahy, Quincy, Massachusetts

Mike Cooke
Degree: B.A., English
Present Position: Partner, Apparel Brokers, Myrtle Beach, South Carolina

Art Katz
Degree: B.A., Education
Graduate Work: M.A.T., Education, 1967
Present Position: High School Teacher and Health Specialist, Wayne, New Jersey

Bryan McSweeney
Degree: B.A., Political Science
Graduate Work: M.B.A., Finance, 1975
Present Position: Financial Planner, Citicorp Investment Services, San Jose, California

Charles Shaffer
Degree: B.A., History
Graduate Work: J.D., 1967
Present Position: Attorney, Atlanta, Georgia

Manager:

Elliott Murnick
Degree: B.A., Political Science
Present Position: Sports Promotion, Raleigh, North Carolina

CLASS OF 1965

Bill Brown
Degree: B.A., History
Graduate Work: J.D., 1968
Present Position: Attorney, Atlanta, Georgia

*Billy Cunningham
Degree: B.A., History
Present Position: President, Cunningham Corporation, Philadelphia, Pennsylvania

Bill Galantai
Degree: B.A., History
Graduate Work: M.A., Education, 1972; Ph.D., Education, 1976
Present Position: New York City Schools, Baldwin Harbor, New York

Pud Hassell
Degree: B.A., History
Graduate Work: J.D., 1968
Present Position: Attorney, Raleigh, North Carolina

Ray Respess
Degree: B.S., Industrial Relations
Present Position: Business Manager, Caswell Training Center, Kinston, North Carolina

Terry Ronner
Degree: B.S., Business Administration
Present Position: Business Broker, Wilmington, North Carolina

Mike Smith
Degree: B.S., Mathematics
Present Position: Retired Manager, Indiana Bell, Indianapolis, Indiana

CLASS OF 1966

Bob Bennett
Degree: B.A., Political Science
Graduate Work: J.D., 1969
Present Position: Attorney, Los Angeles, California

Bill Harrison
Degree: B.A., Economics
Graduate Work: M.B.A., Business Administration, 1967; Harvard Business School, SMP
    Program, 1979
Present Position: Chairman, Chase Manhattan Corp., New York, New York

Ray Hassell
Degree: B.A., History
Present Position: Financial Consultant, Myrtle Beach, South Carolina

Mike Conte (formerly Iannarella)
Degree: B.A., English
Graduate Work: M.A., English, 1967
Present Position: Numismatist, Sharon Hill, Pennsylvania

Earl Johnson
Degree: B.S., Political Science
Graduate Work: D.D.S., 1970
Present Position: Retired Dentist, Raleigh, North Carolina

Jim Moore
Degree: B.A., Psychology
Graduate Work: Psychology, 1967
Present Position: Independent Insurance Agency Owner, Wilmington, North Carolina

Jim Smithwick
Degree: B.S., Chemistry
Graduate Work: M.D., 1970
Present Position: Pediatrician, Laurinburg, North Carolina

John Yokley
Degree: B.S., Industrial Relations
Present Position: Vice President, Universal Furniture Industries, Inc., High Point, North
    Carolina

Manager:

Joe Youngblood
Degree: B.A., Political Science
Present Position: Fletcher Chevrolet-BMW, Fletcher, North Carolina

CLASS OF 1967

Tom Gauntlett
Degree: B.A., Political Science
Graduate Work: Law School, one year
Present Position: Chief Executive Officer, Payne Precision Color, Dallas, Pennsylvania

*Bob Lewis
Degree: B.A., Recreation Administration
Present Position: John F. Kennedy Center for the Performing Arts, Washington, D.C.

Mark Mirken
Degree: B.A., Political Science
Graduate Work: J.D., 1970
Present Position: Attorney, KSL Media, New York, New York

Donnie Moe
Degree: B.S., Business Administration
Graduate Work: M.B.A., Business Administration, 1973
Present Position: Vice President/General Manager, Martin-Marietta Aggregates,
   Greensboro, North Carolina

#Ian Morrison
Degree: B.S., Education
Graduate Work: M.S.W., 1974
Present Position: Teacher and Coach, Church Hill, Tennessee

Managers:

Bill Cochrane
Degree: B.A., Education
Graduate Work: M.A., Education, 1968
Present Position: High School Teacher and Basketball Coach, Virginia Beach, Virginia

Fred Emmerson
Degree: B.S., English
Graduate Work: Law, 1972
Present Position: Attorney, Chapel Hill, North Carolina

Ben Thompson
Degree: B.A., English
Graduate Work: D.D.S., 1971; M.S., Prosthodontics, 1973
Present Position: Dentist, Winston-Salem, North Carolina

CLASS OF 1968

Greg Campbell
Degree: B.S., Business Administration
Graduate Work: M.H.A., 1997
Present Position: Vice President for Finance and Chief Financial Officer, Rex Health Care, Raleigh, North Carolina

Ralph Fletcher
Degree: B.S., Business Administration
Graduate Work: M.B.A., Business Administration, 1969; Advanced Management Program, 1983
Present Position: Retired Managing Director, Salomon Brothers, New York, New York

Jim Frye
Degree: B.A., Psychology
Graduate Work: M.A., Education, 1981; Law School, one year; Administration Degree, 1991
Present Position: Dean of Students, Carl Sandburg High School, Orland Park, Illinois

Dickson Gribble, Jr.
Degree: B.A., Chemistry
Graduate Work: M.B.A., Business Administration, 1978
Present Position: Colonel, U.S. Army (Retired); Program Manager, BTG, Inc., Columbia, Maryland

*Larry Miller
Degree: B.S., Business Administration
Present Position: Real Estate, Virginia Beach, Virginia

CLASS OF 1969

#Jim Bostick
Degree: A.L., B.A., Engineering
Graduate Work: M.S., Biomedical Engineering, 1981
Present Position: Manager, VCU, Mid-Range Computer Systems, Richmond, Virginia

Joe Brown
Degree: B.S., Business Administration
Present Position: Banker, BB&T, Winston-Salem, North Carolina

*Bill Bunting
Degree: B.A., Education
Present Position: Housing Production Officer, North Carolina Housing Finance Agency, Raleigh, North Carolina

Franklin "Rusty" Clark
Degree: B.A., Zoology
Graduate Work: M.D., 1973
Present Position: Retired Trauma Surgeon, Fayetteville, North Carolina

*Dick Grubar
Degree: B.S., Business Administration
Present Position: President, Weaver Properties; City Councilman, Greensboro, North
  Carolina

Gerald Tuttle
Degree: B.S., Physical Education
Present Position: Chief Executive Officer, Classic Leather, Inc., Hickory, North Carolina

Managers:

Robert Coleman
Degree: B.A., Recreation Administration
Graduate Work: M.S., Recreation Administration, 1974
Present Position: Owner/Distributor, Thomas Built Buses, Columbia, South Carolina

Randy Forehand
Degree: B.A., Zoology
Graduate Work: M.D., 1974
Present Position: Physician, Allergy/Pulmonary Clinic, Richlands, Virginia

CLASS OF 1970

Jim Delany
Degree: B.A., Political Science
Graduate Work: J.D., 1973
Present Position: Commissioner, Big Ten Conference, Park Ridge, Illinois

Eddie Fogler
Degree: B.A., Mathematics
Graduate Work: M.A.T., Education, 1972
Present Position: Head Basketball Coach, University of South Carolina, Columbia, South
  Carolina

*Charles Scott
Degree: B.A., History
Present Position: President, CTS Enterprises, Telemarketing, Atlanta, Georgia

Ricky Webb
Degree: B.A., Chemistry
Graduate Work: D.D.S., 1973; Specialization Certificate in Periodontics, 1975
Present Position: Periodontist/Real Estate Developer, Greenville, North Carolina

Gra Whitehead
Degree: B.S., Business Administration
Present Position: President, Grasunan Farm, Agribusiness, Scotland Neck, North
  Carolina

Manager:

Leroy Upperman
Degree: B.A., History
Graduate Work: J.D., 1973
Deceased

CLASS OF 1971

†Dave Chadwick
Degree: B.A., RTVMP
Graduate Work: Ed.S., 1976; D.Min., 1980
Present Position: Senior Pastor, Forest Hill Presbyterian Church, Charlotte, North
  Carolina

*Lee Dedmon
Degree: B.A., Recreation Administration
Graduate Work: M.A., Education, 1976
Present Position: Principal, East Gaston High School, Mt. Holly, North Carolina

Don Eggleston
Degree: B.A., Political Science
Graduate Work: J.D., 1974
Present Position: Attorney, Greensboro, North Carolina

Dale Gipple
Degree: B.A., Political Science
Present Position: Sales Representative, Nike Shoe Company, Raleigh, North Carolina

Richard Tuttle
Degree: B.A., Recreation Administration
Present Position: Assistant Recreation Director, Parks and Recreation, Gastonia, North
  Carolina

Manager:

Ben Reid
Degree: B.A., History
Graduate Work: J.D., 1974
Present Position: Attorney, Miami, Florida

CLASS OF 1972

*Bill Chamberlain
Degree: B.A., General Studies
Present Position: Teacher and Head Basketball Coach, Laurinburg High School,
  Laurinburg, North Carolina

Billy Chambers
Degree: B.S., Chemistry
Graduate Work: D.D.S., 1976; M.S., 1979
Present Position: Pediatric Dental Specialist, Asheville, North Carolina

†Craig Corson
Degree: B.A., Psychology
Graduate Work: M.B.A., Business Administration—Finance, 1983; Ph.D., Psychology,
    1995
Present Position: High School Math Teacher, Contoocook, New Hampshire

Mike Earey
Degree: B.S., Business Administration
Present Position: Senior Vice President, Central Carolina Bank, Wilmington, North
    Carolina

†Kim Huband
Degree: B.A., English
Graduate Work: M.S., Recreation Administration, 1976
Present Position: Parks and Recreation Planner, Department of Natural Resources and
    Community Development, Raleigh, North Carolina

*Steve Previs
Degree: B.A., RTVMP
Present Position: Trader, Jeffries International Ltd., London, England

*Dennis Wuycik
Degree: B.A., Economics
Present Position: Publisher/Director/Broker, DMW Enterprises, Chapel Hill, North
    Carolina

Manager:

Jon Barrett
Degree: B.A., Political Science
Graduate Work: J.D., 1978
Present Position: Attorney, Charlotte, North Carolina

CLASS OF 1973

John Austin
Degree: B.S., Industrial Relations
Deceased

John Cox
Degree: B.A., Psychology
Graduate Work: M.Ed., Education, 1975
Present Position: Teacher and Businessman, Durham, North Carolina

†Donn Johnston
Degree: B.A., Political Science
Graduate Work: J.D., 1980
Present Position: Employee Benefit Consultant, Ivyland, Pennsylvania

*George Karl
Degree: B.S., Political Science
Present Position: Head Coach, Milwaukee Bucks, NBA

*†Robert McAdoo
Degree: B.S., Sociology
Present Position: Assistant Coach, Miami Heat, NBA

Manager:

Doug Donald
Degree: B.S., Industrial Relations; B.A., Political Science
Present Position: Longley Supply Company, Wilmington, North Carolina

CLASS OF 1974

*Darrell Elston
Degree: B.A., History
Graduate Work: Accounting, 1982
Present Position: Materials Management, GM/Delco, Inc., Kokomo, Indiana

Ray Hite
Degree: B.S., Education
Graduate Work: M.Ed., Education, 1975
Present Position: Vice President, Commercial Leasing, Carey Winston Realtors, Chevy
    Chase, Maryland

*Bobby Jones
Degree: B.A., Psychology
Present Position: Director of Development, Athletic Director and Basketball Coach,
    Charlotte Christian School, Charlotte, North Carolina

†John O'Donnell
Degree: B.A., Psychology and Political Science
Graduate Work: M.D., 1980
Present Position: Orthopedic Surgeon, Baltimore, Maryland

Manager:

Greg Miles
Degree: B.A., Political Science
Deceased

CLASS OF 1975

Mickey Bell
Degree: B.S., Business Administration
Present Position: Retired President, Converse Inc., North Reading, Massachusetts

Ray Harrison
Degree: B.A., Recreation Administration
Present Position: Retired, Burlington, North Carolina

†Brad Hoffman
Degree: B.S., Business Administration
Present Position: Vice President, Contract Sales, Classic Leather/St. Timothy Chair
     Company, Hickory, North Carolina

†Ed Stahl
Degree: B.S., Business Administration
Present Position: Owner/President, Shot Doctor Basketball USA, Raleigh, North Carolina

Charles Waddell
Degree: B.S., Industrial Relations
Graduate Work: M.B.A., 1984
Present Position: Assistant Director of Business Operations, Carolina Panthers, Charlotte,
     North Carolina

*†Donald Washington
Degree: B.A., Studio Art
Present Position: President, The Washington Corporation, Upper Marlboro, Maryland

Manager:

John Rancke
Degree: B.A., Recreation Administration
Present Position: Assistant Director, Lumberton Parks and Recreation, Lumberton, North
     Carolina

CLASS OF 1976

†Bill Chambers
Degree: B.A., Psychology
Graduate Work: Education, 1983
Present Position: Head Basketball Coach, Greensboro College, Greensboro, North
     Carolina

Dave Hanners
Degree: B.A., Education
Graduate Work: M.A.T., English, 1978
Present Position: Assistant Basketball Coach, University of North Carolina, Chapel Hill,
     North Carolina

*Mitch Kupchak
Degree: B.A., Political Science and Psychology
Graduate Work: M.B.A., 1987
Present Position: General Manager, Los Angeles Lakers, NBA

Tony Shaver
Degree: B.S., Business Administration
Graduate Work: M.A.T., Social Studies, 1981
Present Position: Assistant Athletic Director and Head Basketball Coach, Hampden-Sydney College, Hampden-Sydney, Virginia

Manager:

Dan Veazey
Degree: B.A., History
Graduate Work: M.D., 1981
Present Position: Physician, Hendersonville, North Carolina

CLASS OF 1977

†Bruce Buckley
Degree: B.A., Mathematics
Graduate Work: J.D., 1981
Present Position: Attorney, Charlotte, North Carolina

Woody Coley
Degree: B.A., Economics
Present Position: Real Estate Developer, Trammell Crow Company, Orlando, Florida

*Walter Davis
Degree: B.A., Recreation Administration
Present Position: Radio and TV Analyst, Denver, Colorado

#Eric Harry
Degree: A.S., Computer Science
Present Position: Software Consultant, Durham, North Carolina

*John Kuester
Degree: B.A., Education
Present Position: Assistant Coach, Philadelphia 76ers, NBA

*†Tommy LaGarde
Degree: B.A., Economics
Present Position: Investments; Commissioner, National Inline Basketball League, New York, New York

#James Smith
Degree: B.A., Humanities
Graduate Work: M.A., Education, 1979
Deceased

CLASS OF 1978

*†Geff Crompton
Degree: B.A., Recreation Administration
Present Position: Test Department, Talla-Com Industries, Tallahassee, Florida

*Phil Ford
Degree: B.A., Business Administration
Present Position: Assistant Basketball Coach, University of North Carolina, Chapel Hill,
    North Carolina

†Tom Zaliagiris
Degree: B.A., Education
Present Position: President, Taylor-King Furniture, Inc., Taylorsville, North Carolina

Managers:

John Cohen
Degree: B.A., History
Present Position: President and Co–Chief Executive Officer, Carlyle and Company
    Jewelers, Greensboro, North Carolina

Jeff Mason
Degree: B.A., Journalism
Graduate Work: J.D., 1983
Present Position: Attorney, Chapel Hill, North Carolina

CLASS OF 1979

*†Dudley Bradley
Degree: B.A., Sociology and Recreation Administration
Present Position: Head Basketball Coach, Brevard College, Brevard, North Carolina

Ged Doughton
Degree: B.A., Political Science
Present Position: Financial Consultant, Carroll Financial Associates, Charlotte, North
    Carolina

#Loren Lutz
Degree: B.A., Physical Education
Graduate Work: M.S., Computer Sciences, 1997
Present Position: Graduate School, Colorado Springs, Colorado

#Keith Valentine
Degree: B.A., Recreation Administration
Present Position: Computer Operator, Heilig-Meyers, Richmond, Virginia

†Randy Wiel
Degree: B.A., Education
Graduate Work: M.S., Education, 1987
Present Position: Head Basketball Coach, Middle Tennessee State University,
    Murfreesboro, Tennessee

Manager:

Rick Duckett
Degree: B.A., Education
Graduate Work: M.S., Education, 1980
Present Position: Head Basketball Coach, Winston-Salem State University, Winston-
    Salem, North Carolina

CLASS OF 1980

Dave Colescott
Degree: B.A., Education
Present Position: Director of Business Development and National Accounts, Hanes
    Hosiery, California

†#Steve Krafcisin
Degree: B.S., Recreation Administration
Graduate Work: M.E., Physical Education, 1982
Present Position: Assistant Basketball Coach, Iowa State University, Ames, Iowa

*Mike O'Koren
Degree: B.A., Recreation Administration
Present Position: Assistant Coach, New Jersey Nets, NBA

†John Virgil
Degree: B.A., Recreation Administration
Present Position: Sales, L'Eggs Products, Norcross, Georgia

†Jeff Wolf
Degree: B.A., Political Science
Present Position: Head Basketball Coach, Kohler High School, Kohler, Wisconsin

*†Rich Yonakor
Degree: B.A., Recreation Administration
Present Position: Computer Programmer, Nashville, Tennessee

Manager:

Kenny Lee
Degree: B.S., Business Administration
Present Position: City Executive, BB&T, Chadbourn, North Carolina

CLASS OF 1981

†Pete Budko
Degree: B.A., Physics
Present Position: Director Real Estate Capital Markets, First Union, Charlotte, North Carolina

Eric Kenny
Degree: B.A., Chemistry
Graduate Work: M.D., 1985
Present Position: Rheumatologist, Lynchburg, Virginia

†Mike Pepper
Degree: B.S., Industrial Relations
Present Position: Vice President, CB Commercial Real Estate Group, Inc., McLean, Virginia

*†Al Wood
Degree: B.A., Recreation Administration
Present Position: Evangelist, Break Free Outreach Ministry, Monroe, North Carolina

Manager:

Lindsay Reed
Degree: B.S., Industrial Relations
Graduate Work: M.Div., one year; M.Ed., Elementary Education, 1991
Present Position: Teacher, East Petersburg Elementary School, Elizabethtown, Pennsylvania

CLASS OF 1982

†Jeb Barlow
Degree: B.S., Business Administration
Present Position: Sales, Standard Oxygen Service, Little Rock, Arkansas

Jimmy Black
Degree: B.A., RTVMP
Present Position: Investment Broker, Morgan-Keegan, Durham, North Carolina

†Chris Brust
Degree: B.A., Recreation Administration
Present Position: Business Manager, Toyota New Bern, New Bern, North Carolina

Managers:

David Daly
Degree: B.A., RTVMP
Present Position: Television Producer, Charlotte, North Carolina

Chuck Duckett
Degree: B.A., History and Political Science
Present Position: Partner, Battle and Associates, Winston-Salem, North Carolina

CLASS OF 1983

†Jim Braddock
Degree: B.A., Psychology
Present Position: Teacher and Coach, Hammond Academy, Columbia, South Carolina

*James Worthy
Degree: B.A., Recreation Administration
Present Position: CBS-TV Sports Basketball Analyst and President, Big Game James, Inc., Los Angeles, California

Managers:

Julie Dalton Loos
Degree: B.A., Journalism and Psychology
Present Position: Creative Memories Consultant, Ballwin, Missouri

Ralph Meekins
Degree: B.A., Psychology and Physical Education
Graduate Work: J.D., 1986
Present Position: Attorney, Shelby, North Carolina

Joe Stroman
Degree: B.A., Physical Education
Present Position: Owner, Window Cleaning Unlimited, and Firefighter, Gastonia, North Carolina

CLASS OF 1984

Matt Doherty
Degree: B.S., Business Administration
Present Position: Head Basketball Coach, University of Notre Dame, South Bend, Indiana

†Cecil Exum
Degree: B.A., Recreation Administration
Present Position: Director, Junior Basketball, Victoria, Australia

Timo Makkonen
Degree: B.S., Business Administration
Graduate Work: M.B.A., 1986
Present Position: Vice President and Chief Financial Officer, Cornerstone Company, Chicago, Illinois

*Sam Perkins
Degree: B.A., RTVMP
Present Position: Professional Basketball Player, Indiana Pacers, NBA

Managers:

David Hart
Degree: B.A., Economics; B.S., Business Administration
Present Position: Owner, AAA Blind Factory, Hendersonville, North Carolina

Holly Jones
Degree: B.A., Public Policy Analysis
Graduate Work: M.Div., 1987; M.P.H., 1993
Present Position: Executive Director, YWCA, Asheville, North Carolina

CLASS OF 1985

*Michael Jordan
Degree: B.S., Geography
Present Position: CEO, Michael Jordan Enterprises, and CEO and Co-Founder, Michael Jordan Foundation, Chicago, Illinois

Cliff Morris
Degree: B.S., Biology
Graduate Work: M.D., 1989
Present Position: Cardiovascular Surgeon, Chester, Virginia

†Buzz Peterson
Degree: B.S., Geography
Present Position: Head Basketball Coach, Appalachian State University, Boone, North Carolina

#Lynwood Robinson
Degree: B.S., Communications
Graduate Work: Film Directing, 1994
Present Position: Film Director, Toronto, Canada

Gary Roper
Degree: B.A., Chemistry
Graduate Work: M.D., 1989
Present Position: Physician, Internal Medicine, Andrews, North Carolina

#Dean Shaffer
Degree: B.S., Social Sciences
Present Position: Sales Representative, Kenan Transport, Tampa, Florida

Managers:

Dean McCord
Degree: B.A., Chemistry
Graduate Work: Ph.D., Molecular and Cellular Pathology, 1992; J.D., 1995
Present Position: Attorney, Smith Anderson, Raleigh, North Carolina

Jane Snead Simms
Degree: B.S., Mathematical Sciences
Present Position: Software Design Manager, Bell Northern Research, Research Triangle
  Park, North Carolina

CLASS OF 1986

†#John Brownlee
Degree: B.A., Psychology
Present Position: Owner, JFB Realty, Dallas, Texas

*Brad Daugherty
Degree: B.A., RTVMP
Present Position: TV Analyst, CBS, Ray-Com, Atlanta, Georgia

James Daye
Degree: B.A., Education and English
Present Position: Coach and Teacher, Buffalo, New York

†Steve Hale
Degree: B.A., Biology
Graduate Work: M.D., 1991
Present Position: Pediatrician, Essex Pediatrics, Essex Junction, Vermont

*†Warren Martin
Degree: B.A., History and Geography
Graduate Work: Teacher Certification, Education, 1988
Present Position: Teacher and Basketball Coach, McDougle Middle School, Chapel Hill,
  North Carolina

Managers:

Mark Isley
Degree: B.A., Education
Present Position: Teacher and Head Basketball Coach, Southern Alamance High School,
  Graham, North Carolina

Lannie Parrish
Degree: B.A., Economics
Present Position: Consultant, Raleigh, North Carolina

CLASS OF 1987

†Curtis Hunter
Degree: B.A., African Studies
Present Position: Head Basketball Coach, North Carolina A&T, Greensboro, North
    Carolina

Michael Norwood
Degree: B.A., Economics
Present Position: Financial Consultant, Wheat First Butcher Singer, New Bern, North
    Carolina

*†Dave Popson
Degree: B.A., Geography
Present Position: Correctional Activities Specialist, Hunnlocks Creek, Pennsylvania

*Kenny Smith
Degree: B.A., Industrial Relations
Present Position: NBA Television Analyst, Turner Sports, Atlanta, Georgia

*Joe Wolf
Degree: B.A., Industrial Relations
Present Position: Professional Basketball Player, NBA (Free Agent)

Managers:

Jan Baldwin Webster
Degree: B.A., Mathematics and Education
Graduate Work: M.A., Educational Administration Supervision, 1990
Present Position: Assistant Principal/Athletic Director, Rugby Middle School,
    Hendersonville, North Carolina

Adam Fleishman
Degree: B.S., Business Administration
Graduate Work: M.B.A., 1991
Present Position: Financial Consultant, Smith Barney, Chicago, Illinois

CLASS OF 1988

Joe Jenkins
Degree: B.A., Biology
Graduate Work: M.D., 1998
Present Position: General Surgery Resident, University of North Carolina Hospitals,
    Chapel Hill, North Carolina

†Ranzino Smith
Degree: B.A., Afro-American Studies
Present Position: Research Assistant, State Bureau of Investigation, Raleigh, North
  Carolina

Managers:

Mike Ellis
Degree: B.A., Education
Graduate Work: M.A., Educational Administration, 1990
Present Position: Assistant Basketball Coach, Virginia Commonwealth University,
  Richmond, Virginia

Kendria Parsons Sweet
Degree: B.A., International Studies
Graduate Work: M.A., Sports Administration, 1994
Present Position: Account Executive, Laquire-George-Andrews, Charlotte, North
  Carolina

CLASS OF 1989

*†Steve Bucknall
Degree: B.A., RTVMP
Present Position: Professional Basketball Player, London, England

*Jeff Lebo
Degree: B.S., Business Administration
Present Position: Head Basketball Coach, Tennessee Tech, Cookeville, Tennessee

David May
Degree: B.S., Chemistry
Graduate Work: M.D., 1993
Present Position: Gastroenterologist, Gastroenterology Association, Asheville,
  North Carolina

Manager:

Michael Burch
Degree: B.A., Economics and Industrial Relations
Graduate Work: Master's Degree Program, Sports Management, 1991
Present Position: Manager, Events Services, Houston Rockets, NBA

CLASS OF 1990

Jeff Denny
Degree: B.A., Industrial Relations
Present Position: Investment Counselor, BB&T, Chapel Hill, North Carolina

John Greene
Degree: B.A., Industrial Relations
Present Position: Sales Manager, Tenneco Building Products, Denver, Colorado

Marty Hensley
Degree: B.A., Industrial Relations
Present Position: Investment Counselor, BB&T, Raleigh, North Carolina

#Rodney Hyatt
Degree: B.A., History
Present Position: Coach and Teacher, Wadesboro Middle School, Wadesboro, North Carolina

†Kevin Madden
Degree: B.A., Geography
Present Position: Teacher and Coach, Staunton, Virginia

*J. R. Reid
Degree: B.A., RTVMP
Present Position: Professional Basketball Player, Los Angeles Lakers, NBA (Free Agent)

*Scott Williams
Degree: B.A., RTVMP
Present Position: Professional Basketball Player, Milwaukee Bucks, NBA

Manager:

Steve Reynolds
Degree: B.A., Education
Present Position: Head Basketball Coach and Teacher, Central Davidson High School, Lexington, North Carolina

CLASS OF 1991

*†Pete Chilcutt
Degree: B.A., Industrial Relations and Psychology
Present Position: Professional Basketball Player, Vancouver Grizzlies, NBA (Free Agent)

#Doug Elstun
Degree: B.A., Economics
Present Position: Investment Adviser, William Larmer and Associates, Kansas City, Missouri

*Rick Fox
Degree: B.A., RTVMP
Present Position: Professional Basketball Player, Los Angeles Lakers, NBA; Actor

†King Rice
Degree: B.A., RTVMP
Present Position: Assistant Basketball Coach, Providence College, Providence, Rhode
  Island

Managers:

Chris Ellis
Degree: B.A., Physical Education
Present Position: Local Sales Manager, Open Plan Systems, Raleigh, North Carolina

Jerry Hopkins
Degree: B.S., Pharmacy
Present Position: Pharmacist, Revco Drug, Charlotte, North Carolina

Justin Kuralt
Degree: B.A., Geography
Present Position: Health Care Representative, Pfizer Inc., Hickory, North Carolina

Maria McIntyre
Degree: B.S., Business Administration
Graduate Work: J.D., 1996
Present Position: Lawyer, Nashville, Tennessee

CLASS OF 1992

Jason Burgess
Degree: B.S., Biology
Graduate Work: M.D., 1996
Present Position: Resident, General Surgery, New Hanover Regional Medical Center,
  Wilmington, North Carolina

*Hubert Davis
Degree: B.S., Administrative Criminal Justice
Present Position: Professional Basketball Player, Dallas Mavericks, NBA

Manager:

Greg Baines
Degree: B.S., Business Administration
Graduate Work: Master's of Accounting, 1992
Present Position: Accountant, G.B. Baines Associates, Laurinburg, North Carolina

CLASS OF 1993

†Scott Cherry
Degree: B.S., Business Administration
Present Position: Assistant Basketball Coach, George Mason University, Fairfax,
  Virginia

*George Lynch
Degree: B.A., African Studies
Present Position: Professional Basketball Player, Philadelphia 76ers, NBA

†Henrik Rödl
Degree: B.S., Biology
Present Position: Professional Basketball Player, Berlin, Germany

Travis Stephenson
Degree: B.A., Political Science
Present Position: Sales, Stay Clean, Angier, North Carolina

*†Matt Wenstrom
Degree: B.A., Political Science
Present Position: Banking Center Manager, Bank of America, Houston, Texas

Managers:

Laura Johnson
Degree: B.A., Speech Communications
Present Position: Assistant Athletic Director, University of North Carolina at Asheville, Asheville, North Carolina

Sam Rogers
Degree: B.A., History and Geography
Graduate Work: Teacher's Certification, 1995; Officer's Candidate School, 1997
Present Position: Officer, U.S. Army, California

CLASS OF 1994

*#†Kenny Harris
Degree: B.S., Business Administration
Present Position: Professional Basketball Player, Yakima Sun Kings, CBA

*Eric Montross
Degree: B.A., Speech
Present Position: Professional Basketball Player, Detroit Pistons, NBA

†*Derrick Phelps
Degree: B.A., African Studies
Present Position: Professional Basketball Player, Bonn, Germany

†Brian Reese
Degree: B.A., African Studies
Present Position: Professional Basketball Player, Seoul, Korea

*#Clifford Rozier
Degree: B.A., Pan-African Studies
Present Position: Professional Basketball Player (Free Agent)

†*Kevin Salvadori
Degree: B.A., Psychology
Present Position: Professional Basketball Player (Free Agent)

Larry Smith
Degree: B.A., Economics
Present Position: Sales Representative, Unisource, Jessup, Maryland

Managers:

Eran Bloxam
Degree: B.S., Business Administration
Graduate Work: Master's of Accounting, 1994
Present Position: Accounting Manager, Quintiles Trans National Corp., Raleigh, North
  Carolina

Bobby Dawson
Degree: B.A., Physical Education
Graduate Work: Sports Administration, 1995
Present Position: Assistant, UNC Ticket Office, Chapel Hill, North Carolina

Eddie Wills
Degree: B.A., Economics
Present Position: Assistant Basketball Coach, Ferrum College, Ferrum, Virginia

CLASS OF 1995

Pearce Landry
Degree: B.S., Biology
Present Position: Associate, First Union-Capital Partners, Charlotte, North Carolina

Pat Sullivan
Degree: B.A., Communications
Present Position: Assistant Men's Basketball Coach, University of North Carolina, Chapel
  Hill, North Carolina

†Donald Williams
Degree: B.A., African Studies
Present Position: Professional Basketball Player, Philippines

Managers:

Rolf Blizzard
Degree: B.S., Business Administration
Graduate Work: M.P.A., 1997
Present Position: Legislative Assistant, North Carolina Senate, Raleigh, North
  Carolina

Bill Bondshu
Degree: B.A., Political Science and English
Present Position: Legislative Assistant, House of Representatives, Washington, D.C.

Robert Lancaster
Degree: B.A., Physical Education
Graduate Work: Counseling, 1997
Present Position: Counselor/Recruiter, Carteret Community College, Morehead City,
    North Carolina

Chuck Lisenbee
Degree: B.A., Biology and African-American Studies
Graduate Work: Basic Law Enforcement Training, 1995
Present Position: Special Agent, U.S. Department of State, New York, New York

CLASS OF 1996

*†Dante Calabria
Degree: B.A., Business Administration
Present Position: Professional Basketball Player, Paugres, France

†Ed Geth
Degree: B.A., Communications
Present Position: Ticket Office Assistant, University of North Carolina, Chapel Hill,
    North Carolina

Clyde Lynn
Degree: B.A., Sociology
Present Position: Assistant Basketball Coach, St. Mary's College, St. Mary's City, Maryland

David Neal
Degree: B.A., Physical Education
Graduate Work: Teacher's Certification, 1998
Present Position: Head Basketball Coach, Louisburg High School, Louisburg, North
    Carolina

Managers:

Jim Ervin
Degree: B.A., Journalism and Mass Communications
Graduate Work: M.A., Sports Administration, 1998
Present Position: Assistant Marketing Director, University of North Carolina, Chapel Hill,
    North Carolina

Chris Johnson
Degree: B.A., Honors American History
Graduate Work: Associate Degree, Mortuary Sciences, 1997
Present Position: Graduate Student, University of South Carolina, Columbia, S.C.;
    Director, Leevy's Funeral Home, Columbia, South Carolina

CLASS OF 1997

†#Larry Davis
Degree: B.A., Media Arts/Communications
Present Position: Professional Basketball Player, Cádiz, Spain

*†Jeff McInnis
Degree: B.A., African-American Studies
Present Position: Professional Basketball Player, Orlando Magic, NBA

Charlie McNairy
Degree: B.A., History
Present Position: President, Away Communications, Raleigh, North Carolina

*Jerry Stackhouse
Degree: B.A., African Studies
Present Position: Professional Basketball Player, Detroit Pistons, NBA

Webb Tyndall
Degree: B.S., Health Policy and Administration
Present Position: Vice President, Away Communications, Raleigh, North Carolina

*Rasheed Wallace
Degree: B.A., Philosophy
Present Position: Professional Basketball Player, Portland Trailblazers, NBA

*†Serge Zwikker
Degree: B.A., Communications
Present Position: Professional Basketball Player, Lugo, Spain

Managers:

Emilly Cole
Degree: B.A., Psychology
Present Position: Studying in Italy

Gene Hoffman
Degree: B.A., Communications
Present Position: Director of Business Development, Pretty Good Privacy Inc., San
  Mateo, California

Virginia Holt
Degree: B.A., Journalism
Present Position: Assistant Account Executive, Focused Communications, Charlotte,
  North Carolina

CLASS OF 1998

*†Makhtar Ndiaye
Degree: B.A., International Studies
Present Position: Professional Basketball Player, Vancouver Grizzlies, NBA (Free Agent)

*†Shammond Williams
Degree: B.A., Industrial Relations
Present Position: Professional Basketball Player, Seattle Supersonics, NBA

Managers:

Amanda Baker
Degree: B.A., Journalism and Mass Communications
Present Position: Administrative Assistant, Square One Marketing, Raleigh, North Carolina

Heidi Bartel
Degree: B.A., Communications
Present Position: Marketing Administrative Manager, Chicago, Illinois

Natalie Batten
Degree: B.A., Political Science and Communications Studies
Present Position: Analyst, Andersen Consulting, Raleigh, North Carolina

Matt Grice
Degree: B.A., Economics
Graduate Work: Master of Accounting, 2000
Present Position: Graduate Student

CLASS OF 1999

*Vince Carter
Degree: B.A., Communications
Present Position: Professional Basketball Player, Toronto Raptors, NBA

Brad Frederick
Degree: B.A., Political Science/History
Present Position: Assistant Basketball Coach, Vanderbilt University, Nashville, Tennessee

*Antawn Jamison
Degree: B.A., African Studies
Present Position: Professional Basketball Player, Golden State Warriors, NBA

Ademola Okulaja
Degree: B.A., International Studies
Present Position: Professional Basketball Player, Berlin Germany

Scott Williams
Degree: B.A., Business Administration
Present Position: First Union Bank, Charlotte, North Carolina

Managers:

Cori Brown
Degree: B.A., African Studies
Present Position: Sports Management, Los Angeles, California

Blake Fromen
Degree: B.A., Journalism and Mass Communications
Present Position: Sports Marketing, Breckenridge, Colorado

Christopher Stoen
Degree: Exercise and Sports Science
Present Position: Event Management, Red Bank, New Jersey

UNDERGRADUATES WHO PLAYED FOR DEAN SMITH

Michael Brooker, Class of 2001
Ed Cota, Class of 2000
Vasco Evtimov, Class of 2001
Terrence Newby, Class of 2000
Ryan Sullivan, Class of 2000

LETTER WINNERS UNDER DEAN SMITH

An Academic Summary of the Letter Winners Since 1962

Total number of letter winners since 1962:   245
Letter winners who have graduated as of September 1, 1999:   237
Number who have done graduate work: 93

An Athletic Summary of the Letter Winners

Letter winners who have played basketball in the NBA or ABA: 57
Letter winners who have played basketball overseas, in the CBA or GBA: 54

Present Occupations of the 245 Letter Winners

Businessmen: 117
Coaches and Teachers: 39
Professional Athletics: 36
     Players (NBA):   18
     Player (CBA):   1
     Coaches (NBA):   5

      Players (Overseas): 8

      Administrators/Personnel (NBA): 4

      Administrators (NFL): 1

Attorneys: 15

Physicians: 11

Students currently in graduate or professional school: 1

Dentists: 3

Officers in the Armed Forces: 2

Recreation Departments: 3

Pastors: 2

Law Enforcement Officer: 1

Numismatist: 1

Pharmacist: 1

Retired: 8

Deceased: 4

The 246 letter winners currently reside in 30 states, the District of Columbia, and 10 foreign countries.

Index

ABOUT THE TYPE

This book was set in Times Roman, designed by Stanley
Morison specifically for *The Times* of London. The typeface was introduced in the newspaper in 1932. Times
Roman has had its greatest success in the United States as a
book and commercial typeface, rather than one used in
newspapers.